D0946901

PEASANT SOCIETY IN KOṄKU

PEASANT SOCIETY IN KOṄKU

A Study of Right and Left Subcastes
in
South India

BRENDA E. F. BECK

UNIVERSITY OF BRITISH COLUMBIA PRESS
VANCOUVER

Peasant Society in Koṅku
A Study of Right and Left Subcastes in South India

Printed in the United States of America

To my grandmother, Sophia Lyon Fahs, whose life and work
have greatly influenced my thinking

CONTENTS

LIST OF ILLUSTRATIONS

Figure   *Page*

Plates

Page

LIST OF TABLES

PREFACE

The main concern of this book is to study how the social and territorial organization of various castes in a particular area of South India are inter-related. However, while I was in the process of researching, writing, and revising the work that follows, my theme went through several stages before it took this final form. In short, as the work progressed, the basic ideas underlying it developed and changed. Thus, before the principal theme is elaborated on in any detail, a few comments are appropriate on how it evolved.

My interest in comparing the traditional organization of a number of castes within a given region in India dates back to about 1964, when I wrote a library thesis comparing the wedding ceremonies of different castes of the old CōRa NāTu area of Madras State.[1] This area is roughly equivalent to the modern Districts of South Arcot and Tanjavur, and the eastern part of Tiruchirappalli. In my thesis I concluded that the details of the nuptial rituals performed by the many communities in this region varied systematically with their position in the over-all caste hierarchy.[2] In other words, an ordered set of ritual or symbolic substitutions could be found as one moved gradually down the local social ladder.[3]

As a result of this finding, I decided to explore another aspect of the same problem in a doctoral dissertation, this time basing my findings on actual fieldwork. I had already become interested in both social organiza-tion and ritual; so I sought a detailed problem for comparative study that would involve aspects of both. I was intrigued by the sketchy discussion of the lineage or clan cult in Louis Dumont's study of the Kallar and de-cided to focus my inquiries on this topic.[4] At his suggestion, I determined to do fieldwork in the Koṅku region, which includes modern Coimbatore District, plus a part of southern Salem.

When I arrived in India, therefore, I was prepared to carry out a de-tailed comparative study of clan temples and clan ceremonies in different caste or subcaste groups. I assumed that this could best be done from the vantage point of a village. Thus, I soon set out to find such a research base

[1]The name of Madras State was officially changed in 1968 to "Tamilnadu."

[2]My data were drawn almost entirely from Edgar Thurston, *Castes and Tribes of Southern India*, 7 vols. (Madras: Government Press, 1909). The thesis, entitled "The Examination of Marriage Ritual Among Selected Groups in South India," is in the Bodleian Library, Oxford University.

[3]The hierarchical order of castes I used was based on an attempted ranking by W. Francis, in 1901. See Dominion of India, *Census of India, 1901*, Vol. XII, *Madras, Part I, Report* (Madras: Government Press, 1901).

[4]Louis Dumont, *Une Sous-Caste de l'Inde du Sud* (Paris: Mouton, 1957), especially pp. 317–79.

in the center of the Koṅku area.[5] Once settled in a village, however, I quickly discovered that clans were only a minor part of local social organization and that to do a meaningful study I needed to broaden my base of inquiry. This seemed easy enough, and soon I had collected extensive information on various related topics. Much to my dismay, though, when I tried to find some tentative pattern in this data after about eight months of work, I discovered that there was nothing like the neat set of substitutions as one moved down the caste hierarchy that I had found in my earlier library research on ritual.

Nonetheless, I persisted with the collection of data, hoping that at some point it would form a coherent pattern. Finally, one day while I was questioning an elderly and respected drum-player at an important local temple, I found the clue I had hoped for. At last I had something that I thought might enable me to fit together the fragments of information I had collected.[6] He told me that during the annual festival for the local goddess, Māriyamman̠, an important distinction was once made between "right" and "left" subcastes.[7] Each subcaste classified as "right" had some essential ceremony to perform as part of the ritual at her temple, while no "left" subcaste was similarly employed. Long ago, women of the "left" subcaste category were not allowed past a certain leaf-decorated arch (tōraNam) which was constructed at some distance from the temple entrance during the festival period. My informant the drum-player, now an old man, remembered this prohibition having been relaxed while he was still a child, some fifty or sixty years ago. However, although such restrictions no longer apply, the archway is still constructed each year as part of the ceremonial activity.

Previously I had read about this traditional left-right division of castes in some of the early English and French works on South India, but I had thought of it as pertaining only to earlier periods. It had never occurred to me (nor, apparently, to other ethnographers) to investigate the matter in the field. I quickly made further inquiries, searching among other long-time residents of the area for other informants. I soon found that older men, drawn from the middling to low-ranking castes, were the only people still to recall something of the social significance of the terms "right" and "left," so prominently used in documents I had seen which dated from earlier centuries.

---

[5]See Appendix A for details.

[6]Informant no. 1. See Appendix B for a complete list of my informants who are cited in the text; their names, subcastes, and place of residence are given.

[7]The Tamil terms for "right" and "left" are *valaṅkai* and *iTaṅkai* respectively. These words have been translated as "right-hand" and "left-hand" by earlier scholars. But, since there is no clear distinction made between hand, arm, and side of the body in the Dravidian languages, I have chosen to use the words "right" and "left" without qualification, thus preserving this important ambiguity.

These initial inquiries into the matter of right and left affiliation finally centered on six men, each of whom provided a list of the members of the two divisions from memory.[8] Questioned independently, these men suggested a fairly consistent sorting of local subcastes into two opposed groups. Some confusion did arise, though, from their efforts to label the groups as "left" and as "right." Four of the six (Informants nos. 1, 2, 3, and 5) were ready to label the group that contained the artisans, most merchants, and the leatherworkers as "left." But the two others, both of whom belonged to this half of the social order themselves, wished to label it as "right." In this way it became clear that "left" was a less flattering term than "right." Even though all my informants agreed on the approximate membership of the two groups, there was clearly some competition for the label with greater prestige.

From the confident demeanor of the four informants who claimed that the artisans and their associates were "left" and the hesitancy of those who claimed these groups were "right," it seemed that the former had provided me with the socially accepted interpretation in this naming dispute. There was no need to confirm the matter, however, in order to collect data on the contrasting customs and traditions of these two distinct groups of subcastes. Later, when I returned from the field, I checked my lists of division membership with those given in various early descriptions of the Madras region. These historical commentators confirmed my earlier identification of the "left" as the division composed of the artisans, the leatherworkers, and their various associates.[9]

I was further puzzled by the fact that two communities, the Aiyar Brahmans and the KaruNĭkar PiLLai, were generally omitted from the divisional membership lists that informants supplied. Informant no. 1 had suggested that the PiLLai, at least, belonged to the right; but according to my data on social customs, this group more closely resembled the high-ranking communities of the left. After a careful consideration of the matter, I decided to follow historical sources (and the advice of the majority of my informants) and place both the Brahmans and the PiLLai above the

[8]Informants nos. 1, 2, 3, 4, 5, and 6. In an article I wrote, I stated that there were five informants, but in looking over my fieldnotes, I have since been reminded that there was a sixth. Brenda E. F. Beck, "The Right-Left Division of South Indian Society," *The Journal of Asian Studies* 29, no. 4 (1970): 781.

[9]See, for example, the following works: Presidency of Madras, *Manual of Administration of the Madras Presidency,* 3 vols. (Madras: Government Press, 1893), 1:69–70 and 3:1036–37; Thurston, *Castes and Tribes,* 1:213, 2:121, 4:295, 330, and 6:91, 360–61; L. K. Ananthakrishna Iyer, *The Mysore Tribes and Castes,* 4 vols. (Mysore: Mysore University, 1928–36), 4:467; Francis Hamilton Buchanan, *A Journey from Madras Through the Countries of Mysore, Canara, and Malabar,* 3 vols. (London: T. Cadell and W. Davies, 1807), 1:53, 77–80; J. A. Dubois, *Hindu Manners, Customs and Ceremonies* (Oxford: Clarendon Press, 1906), p. 154, and Manuscript D, no. 2751, Mackenzie Manuscript Collection, Madras University Library, Madras.

social split, making them, in a sense, neutral.[10] As the Tamil terms for the division seem to refer to the sides of a social body, so these two communities can be considered as forming a "head" for that social order. Although this imagery is not explicit in classical works on caste, it does seem appropriate in the light of several well-known myths about the origin of the right-left division.[11]

Once this picture concerning which subcastes traditionally belonged to which division was clearly established, I set out to re-examine my collected data in this new framework. Now a very clear pattern of right-left contrasts began to emerge. Each topic I considered, whether it was descent-group organization or the details of food exchange, appeared to make new sense when I divided the subcastes into these two over-arching categories. It also became clear, very early in this analysis, that the right-left split was not, in itself, enough to explain all the variations in custom I had observed. My initial variable, a subcaste's general rank in the social hierarchy, remained important. Each example that I studied made it increasingly clear that the high-ranking communities of the two divisions provided more of a contrast in their social organization than did similarly opposed groups of low status.

At about the same time that this right-left division became significant in interpreting my existing data, a corresponding evolution in the basic unit of my observations took place. Because of the earlier stress laid on "villages" and on small-scale studies of individual settlements in my research training, I initially chose to limit my inquiries to a very small area. Towards the end of my stay in Koṅku, however, I began to take a more serious interest in what my informants were telling me about caste and subcaste organization at higher levels. I noticed that they referred frequently to the revenue village, to the administrative territory, and to the region as a whole. These were their units of analysis, and I came to appreciate them only gradually. Step by step, I became forced to admit that my local friends did not view their world in terms of anthropological topics. They spoke, rather, of a hierarchy of social territories, and often spontaneously discussed local traditions and experiences in terms of what seemed to me a novel framework. For them, the units which made up the local hierarchy formed a series of real conceptual levels. Nonetheless, despite this education I received in the field, I persisted in using traditional an-

---

[10]Burton Stein, "Brahman and Peasant in Early South Indian History," *The Adyar Library Bulletin* 31-2 (1967–68): 254, and N. S. Reddy, "Community Conflict Among the Depressed Castes of Andhra," *Man in India* 30, no. 4 (1950): 5, 12.

[11]Thurston, *Castes and Tribes,* 1:187–90, 3:117, 325–31, and 4:316; Gustav Oppert, *On the Original Inhabitants of Bharatavarsa or India* (Westminster: A. Constable and Co., 1893), p. 59; A. M. Hocart, *Caste: A Comparative Study* (London: Methuen, 1950), pp. 63–67, and Republic of India, *Census of India, 1961,* Vol. IX, *Madras,* Part VI, *Village Survey Monographs,* no. 3, Arkasanahalli (Madras: Government Press, 1964), p. 10.

thropological categories in writing up my observations for the first time. As a result of this experience, and because of the discomfort I had felt in forcing my data into a "foreign" mold, I finally recognized the wisdom of utilizing my informants' own units as a basic organizational principle in my account of Koṅku customs and ideas. I have completely rewritten my earlier work, therefore, in an attempt to highlight these several tiers of regional organization in this book.

Because the main theme of this work is concerned with territorial organization, it has been necessary to include details that make an adequate concealment of the location of the study impossible. Although I could have used a pseudonym for ŌlappāLaiyam, I believe that it would have been quite contrary to the interests of the local populace to misname towns, temples, or other major landmarks that I discuss. Without such an effort at concealing well-known places, however, any fictitious name invented for the settlement of ŌlappāLaiyam itself seemed a superficial solution. Instead of following established custom in this matter, I have preferred to rely entirely on personal judgment in the selection and wording of the information presented. Uppermost in my mind has always been a concern to include only information that would not offend the many people who assisted me and that would not jeopardize their well-being. In practice, I found that I had to omit very little material for these reasons, and what I did leave out seemed to be of minimal importance to my main theme. I am very grateful to the residents of ŌlappāLaiyam for providing me with a key to understanding much that is fine and traditional in the organization of their region as a whole. I hope that they will forgive any errors or oversights on my part, and that they will be able to remember with pride their contribution to this work.

Brenda E. F. Beck

ACKNOWLEDGEMENTS

During my twenty-three months of research in India, my work was supported jointly by the National Science Foundation of America and by the American Institute of Indian Studies. While I was writing up the results of my study, I received further grants from the Committee on Southern Asian Studies of the University of Chicago, the Faculty Research Fund of the University of British Columbia, and the Social Science Research Council of Canada. The aid of all these institutions is very much appreciated.

This book has been published with the help of a grant from the Social Science Research Council of Canada, using funds provided by the Canada Council.

Hundreds of people, both in India and in the West, have helped me at various stages of this study's development. I cannot begin to name, individually, all of those who assisted me. But it is my hope that each will somehow share in the joy of completion without feeling obliged to share my responsibility for specific statements. A list of major informants is given in Appendix B of this book. In addition, however, I would like to single out a few people for very special thanks. My two dissertation supervisors at Oxford, Rodney Needham and R. K. Jain, have provided invaluable advice and assistance from the beginning of this undertaking. Louis Dumont, my long-time mentor in Paris, has taken considerable interest in this work and has been most helpful. McKim Marriott of the University of Chicago was of great assistance in guiding the work through a lengthy revision, and David J. Elkins of the University of British Columbia made many useful suggestions at all stages of its development. The study also owes a great deal to the patience, support, and enthusiasm of my companion and cook, K. Pāppammāl and to her son, my invaluable assistant K. Cuntaram.

B.E.F.B.

INTRODUCTION

Two broad questions dominate this book. The first one is, what are the various spatial components or nesting tiers of social organization that exist in a traditional region of South India? And the second, how do the internal structures of the several castes in such an area differ in terms of how they function in and relate to these culturally defined units? The chapters that follow provide a case study of Koṅku, one of five traditional regions in Tamilnadu (Madras State).[1] Each chapter has been organized around one of five social and territorial units which local residents use to describe and discuss social organization among themselves. Each one of these units (the region, the administrative territory, the revenue village, the hamlet, and the household) can be contrasted with others of the same magnitude. At the same time, each one can be subsumed under some single, over-arching unit on a higher plane. Indeed, the whole is like a set of Chinese boxes.

Given the over-all plan just described, it will be helpful first to clarify the meaning of certain critical local terms that will be used repeatedly throughout this book. Madras State contains five traditional *NāTu,* or political regions, of which Koṅku is one. Within Koṅku, there are twenty-four primary subdivisions, also referred to as *nāTu.*[2] A NāTu is a very large area which is culturally and historically distinct, while a nāTu is primarily a convenient administrative and ceremonial unit. The latter is the level at which petty chiefs operated in previous centuries, and the area within which subcaste groups are accorded individual identity in ritual and legal matters. Within each nāTu are revenue villages called *kirāmam.*[3] The revenue village, in contrast to the nāTu, is most important as an economic unit. It is the level at which land is assessed and at which tax relief is granted in times of great hardship. It is the territory whose residents used to share a corporate responsibility for revenue payment and in which the supervision of tax collection still rests with a *MaNiyārar,* or village munsif.[4] The kirāmam is also the area frequently identified with a local

---

[1]See chapter 1, pp. 19–24 for details on the location of the Koṅku region.

[2]In some cases, the same Tamil word is used to refer both to a unit and to a subdivision of that unit. To distinguish between the two meanings throughout this study, such a word is capitalized when the larger unit is meant, while a lower-case letter is used when the smaller unit is intended. Thus *NāTu* is used for reference to a large area or cultural region, and *nāTu* (political territory) is used for the subdivisions of such a unit.

[3]The modern panchayat area roughly corresponds to the traditional kirāmam in size and function.

[4]The munsif, of course, does not actually collect the tax. He has an assistant, or *talaiyēri,* to run errands for him and an accountant, a *KarNam* or KaNakku PiLLai, to keep the land records.

1

goddess for whom an important annual festival is performed.

Below the kirāmam level are individual hamlets, or *Ūr,* and within these, particular settlements called *ūr.*[5] A hamlet, or grouping of settlements, constitutes a viable cooperating unit in the management of day-to-day affairs, while an ūr is simply a residential site and may contain only a few houses. A hamlet or Ūr area will generally include an untouchable settlement and also the houses of any other persons in the immediate area who provide labor for local landowners. Hamlet areas, furthermore, celebrate annual festivals. In Koṅku the enactment of such an annual ceremony always symbolizes, among other things, the interdependence and hierarchical relations of the people who perform it.[6] In contrast, the residential site does not constitute a viable social grouping, and hence regular, yearly ceremonies are not found associated with it. However, the reader should not be misled by the terminology used here, as a large settlement may constitute a hamlet in itself.

Finally, within each settlement are the *kuTumpam,* or individual household units. These are the groups that eat food from the same cooking hearth. According to local usage, people who utilize the same living site, but who do not share food, constitute two separate kuTumpam units. KuTumpam units can vary greatly in size. Ideally, a unit will contain at least one married couple, but because of deaths, incompatibility, and various economic hardships, this is not always the case. A kuTumpam may be as large as a large joint family, or as small as a solitary mother and child.

The same kind of multilevel organization observed in the foregoing description is also present when *Jāti,* or caste units, are considered. In this work, five such levels will be discussed in some detail: the caste, the subcaste, the clan, the lineage, and the family. The broadest of these groupings, the Jāti, are generally identified by specific names which serve to characterize the occupation or social status of their members. Examples would be the KavuNTars (agriculturalists), the CeTTiyār (merchants), and the Paṟaiyar (drummers). Other Jāti names such as "PiLLai," "Nāyakkar," and "VēTar" have little occupational significance, but they still give the listener a good idea of their members' social standing. Since many of these terms are vague, Jāti names are sometimes modified by occupational indicators. "KaNakku PiLLai," for example, is the descriptive label used for village accountants. Even with this addition, the term "PiLLai" in Koṅku remains essentially a caste name.

Subcastes or *jāti,* by contrast, are divisions of these broad occupational

---

[5]*Ūr* ("hamlet") is capitalized to distinguish it from *ūr* ("settlement"). See p. 1, n. 2.)

[6]This is clear from the different ritual responsibilities assigned to the participants, and from a status hierarchy implied by the order in which the *piracātam,* or offerings dedicated to the deity and blessed by it, are distributed.

and social groupings that have a ritually specific identity.[7] This is the level at which uniform rules supposedly apply to group members.[8] Here, dietary restrictions and variations in the minutiae of life-cycle ceremonies are, in principle, uniform. (In the past this uniformity even applied to certain facets of house construction and personal dress.) The subcaste is thus a ritual peer group, and it is the unit within which members are expected to find marriage partners. To take the PiLLai example again, the KaruNīkar are a subcaste or jāti within the larger PiLLai caste category. Hence subcastes are primarily kin groupings and only secondarily occupational categories.

Within these subcaste groupings are individual descent units or clans which trace their ancestry through the male or the female line, or through both.[9] Such units are always exogamous in principle, although, as with the rule of subcaste endogamy, there are always some exceptions in practice.[10] The minimal feature of these units is that members of the group share an inherited name and are enjoined not to marry anyone else who has inherited the same name.[11] Furthermore, clan names usually have some ritual significance. Either they refer to some mythical ancestor of great repute, or they suggest an association with some vegetable or animal object. In cases where this animal or vegetable content is recognizable, a tradition of avoiding eating or killing the species named is generally present for members as well.[12]

Finally, within the clan are lineages, and within each lineage are families. Unlike clans, lineages represent groupings in which each member has a knowledge of his own unilineal genealogical connection with other members, although it is not necessary for anyone to know all the connections

---

[7]*Jāti* ("caste") is capitalized to distinguish it from *jāti* ("subcaste"). (See p. 1, n. 2.)

[8]The rules are not always successfully enforced, but this is the level at which there should be uniformity in ritualized, public matters.

[9]I know of only one subcaste in all of South India in which descent units are reported to be entirely absent. Even in this case, however, the findings would seem to represent a recent and quite possibly transitional phenomenon. See Louis Dumont, "Distribution of Some Maravar Sub-castes," in Bala Ratnam, ed., *Anthropology on the March* (Madras: The Book Centre, 1963), p. 305. Possibly there are some further examples among the lower-ranking castes of North Arcot. (Joan Mencher Southworth, personal communication.)

In some South Indian communities (the Todas, for example), both matrilineal and patrilineal descent groupings are recognized. In the Koṅku region, I found only the patrilineal type.

[10]Dumont, "Distribution of Some Maravar Sub-castes," p. 302. Here Dumont refers to a community of Ambanattu (AmpanāTu, perhaps) Maravar who live in an area isolated from others belonging to their group. Again, the situation may be transitional. I am not aware of any exceptions in my own field material.

[11]Thus, in a subcaste with matrilineal units, a man will avoid women who bear his mother's clan name in his search for a wife; only his sisters will be able to pass that name on to succeeding generations.

[12]Many clan names nowadays are just names, their original meaning being difficult or even impossible to decipher. Whenever an interpretation did seem possible, an ancestral or totemic association was repeatedly evident.

of each to the whole. A lineage is generally limited to a depth of about four generations. Its members usually live near one another, and, except in cases of intense factionalism, they cooperate in the celebration of life-cycle ceremonies, such as weddings and funerals. They also share in pollution during the three-day funeral period which follows the death of any adult member, and they are subject to certain ritual restrictions at this time.[13] Lineages, of course, occasionally split into two.[14] When they do, death pollution is restricted to members of the subdivision. Relations with the other half of the group gradually drop off until only the name, characterizing common clanship, is left. Individual families within each lineage are directed by the eldest capable resident male. A family is the largest unit having joint property rights. The family, according to this definition, may include several cooking units or kuTumpams, but ideally the membership of hearth and property-holding groups is identical.

Resembling the correspondence between household and family, is the relation between caste organization and the structure of the region as a whole. Subcastes are often associated with subregional or nāTu territories, and clans are often linked to a kirāmam area. The main difficulty in discussing the degree of match between these territorial units and the social groupings just outlined is that this relation does not hold equally well for all subcastes. As outlined in the Preface, subcastes in Koṅku tend to be grouped into two over-arching blocs known as the "right" and the "left"; and the connection just described is far more applicable to those belonging to the former division than it is to those of the latter.

Table 1 provides a key to the names of the subcastes resident in the area discussed, along with their general divisional classification. Where a caste is mentioned as a member of both blocs, a split at the subcaste level is evident. Some merchants, barbers, and washermen are thus classified as right, while others, who serve members of the opposed bloc, are classified

---

[13]In the Indian view, pollution can best be thought of as a state in which man's control over basic life processes is lost. Death, as the ultimate form of such a loss, is a highly polluting condition. Furthermore, death pollution is contaminating. When a man dies, his condition is shared, with reduced intensity, by all members of his lineage, regardless of whether they all attend his funeral rites. People who are polluted are subject to various degrees of restriction on their activities, including prohibitions on temple entry and on approaching other symbols of divinity. This management also involves prohibitions on touching food or other substances (such as cloth) that are likely to be used later by others who are not equally contaminated. Certain basic substances, notably water, fire, oil of sesamum, tumeric, and the five products of the cow, counteract pollution and help to reduce it when they are applied in ritually prescribed ways. These substances have a special power which informants could not explain, but which is probably derived from their basic propensity to serve as mediators between cosmic and human realms of activity. Somehow, these substances take over control of any immediate disorder, leaving the victim free to regroup his forces and to prepare for future challenges.

[14]Clans may also split, but this is a very unusual occurrence, and I have come across only historical and semi-mythological descriptions of such an event. Terms for clan and lineage groupings vary by caste. They are discussed in more detail in chapter 2.

TABLE 1
SUBCASTES OF THE KOṄKU REGION
(by their relative rank at a Brahman feast and their divisional affiliation)

Seating Order	Left Division	Neutral	Right Division
A		(1) Aiyar *Brahman* priest and scholar	
B	(3) CōLi *Ācāri* artisan (4) KōmuTTi *CeTTiyār* merchant (6) Koṅku *Ācāri* artisan (7) Kaikkōlar *Mutaliyār* weaver, warrior, and merchant	(2) KaruNīkar *PiLLai* accountant and scribe	(5) Koṅku *KavuNTar* farmer (8) OkaccāNTi *PaNTāram* cook, local priest (9) Koṅku *UTaiyār* potter and builder
C	(11) VaTuka *Nāyakkar*[1] well-digger and earth-remover		(10) Maramēri *NāTār* palmyra-palm climber
D	(13) VaTuka *VaNNār* washerman (15) PāNTiya *Nāvitar* barber		(12) Koṅku *VaNNār* washerman (14) Koṅku *Nāvitar* barber
E	(17) KūTai *Kuravar* basket-maker (18) Moracu *Mātāri* leatherworker and laborer		(16) Koṅku *Paraiyar* drummer

NOTES: The subcastes listed in the table include only those resident in Kannapuram kirāmam in 1965. Other groups discussed in this work, such as the VēTTuvar KavuNTars, and the VēTar, do not appear in the table, as they do not have a clearly determined rank at Brahman feasts held in this area.

Subcaste names precede the caste names, which appear in italics. The traditional occupation associated with each group is given below its name. The alphabetical divisions indicate the order in which groups of subcastes are seated at a Brahman feast; those whose names appear near the top of the table are served first. Brahmans do not make a rank distinction between the subcastes whose names are aligned horizontally in the table. The internal rank orders within each alphabetical division are derived from other kinds of ranking criteria, which are discussed in chapter 4. The number in front of each caste corresponds to a code list introduced on p. 159. These numbers are used as a type of shorthand on many of the scalograms in chapter 4.

The subcaste name "VaTuka" was given as "VaTukku," and the name "KaruNīkar" as "KaruNīkal" in my article, "The Right-Left Division of South Indian Society," *The Journal of Asian Studies* 29, no. 4 (1970): 779–98. Furthermore, in this work a final *r* rather than a final *n* has been used for all Tamil caste names, as the former ending suggests maximal respect. The one exception is the Brahman community, whose name is so familiar in the West that I have adopted a standard English spelling for it. I have been informed and corrected on these details by Informant no. 20.

as left. In addition to the right-left classification of subcastes in the Koṅku area, Table 1 provides information on the relative rank of these groups as expressed by their seating order at a Brahman feast.[15]

Caste rank is closely related to the variations in social customs which are discussed later. In addition, the issue of rank and the social judgments that determine it form part of the larger Hindu world-view, some important features of which are outlined briefly here. Although the concept of society about to be described is drawn from classical Hindu sources and is clearly more of a theoretical framework than a practical guide, it is important as a key to Hindu ideas of rank. According to early texts, there are four *varna,* estates or social classes, those of priest-scholar (Brahman), warrior-king (Kshatriya), farmer-merchant (Vaishya), and laborer-serf (Shudra).[16] The four classes are listed in the texts, as they are here, in descending order, according to their social position. These early writings also provide a certain amount of explanation for the rank order they employ. According to them, the Brahman is the only one who may perform sacrifices for the gods. The king, who ranks second, has control over people and territory, while the peasant or merchant, who is third, has control over animals or material things. The laborer or serf, on the other hand, controls nothing and is the mere subject of others.

From this sketch of the classes and their social position it becomes clear that some notion of power or control lies behind classical Indian ideas about rank. The surprising feature of this theory of hierarchy is the penultimate position accorded the Brahman priest. This position must be understood, I think, in terms of the Hindu concept of power. In the classical Indian view, the Brahman has an influence on cosmic events that is greater than anything a king can claim, because of his ability to communicate with the gods. Such communication is viewed as a type of power to intervene in and influence divine affairs. This control over universal forces (which are often represented as a pantheon) that the Brahman can wield stems directly from his state of ritual purity. A Brahman initially inherits this state of purity from his parents and can then maintain it by the exercise of great ritual care in everyday matters.

---

[15]Details describing how the right-left affiliation of each group was obtained have already been given in the Preface, pp. xiv–xvi.

The order of precedence in Table 1 is referred to repeatedly in the text, when such adjectives as "leading," "high-ranking," "low-ranking," or "low-status" are used in connection with particular groups. But a group's rank as a guest at a Brahman feast is not the only criterion that an observer could employ for establishing its social position. A number of others are discussed in chapter 4. For the sake of providing a common point of reference, however, the Brahman feast has been taken as the standard throughout this work.

[16]The idea of *varna,* or class, can be traced back in early texts at least as far as the late Vedic period. A. L. Basham, *The Wonder That Was India* (New York: Grove Press, 1954), p. 35.

The Indian concept of purity has repeatedly eluded definition, but it can be said to be essentially a physiological state obtained by the strict management of bodily processes, and bodily wastes. Thus purity is vitally linked to self-control and to a need for an agreed-upon division of labor. Some groups must take upon themselves the task of removing impurity so that others can heighten their own state of purity in order to intercede with the gods on behalf of all. Hence, for the Hindu, the notion of purity is linked to the ultimate kind of power that human beings can achieve, control over the elements of the universe through control of one's intimate physiological processes. Brahmans are born purer than other mortals and hence they logically rank first in any competition to influence the gods. Others of lower birth, however, can also obtain these special powers through following the path of renunciation, selfless devotion, and self-control.

Next in the hierarchy of powers, from this classical Hindu perspective, is power over other mortals, the control wielded by kings. This power is ultimately that of physical force, and is accordingly also associated with the profession of the warrior. Third in the rank order comes material power, the control which peasants exercise over animals or that merchants have over goods. And finally, of course, is the state of total powerlessness where a person lacks control both over his own body and over other persons or external things. This is why, it would seem, that low status in India is so often associated with intemperate behavior such as a readiness to show anger and with sexual passion, poor judgment, and a lack of personal cleanliness. Of course, it is also associated with lack of political influence or of monetary wealth.

In this world-view, all three kinds of power are ultimately interconnected. A king wields political power over farmers and merchants, and because the latter control animals and material goods, he will have indirect power over these resources as well. In turn, because of their ability to intercede with the cosmic forces, Brahman priests are believed to exercise a measure of control over all earthly forms of life, kings, farmers, and serfs alike. Such a logic can be pushed even further. Any person who practices sufficient self-discipline may be said to exercise a certain diffuse power over his fellow human beings. In this sense, every individual is linked to forces of cosmic scope and can potentially direct them. This was the world-view which Gandhi stressed, and which won him such an immense political following. I have also come to understand it as the rationale behind the dynamics of the right- and left-caste organization described in this book. The conceptualization of the social order in terms of a single head and a bifurcate body is an outgrowth of the fundamental Hindu idea of power just outlined. The bifurcate body serves as a metaphorical expression of how rivalries for status develop in an actual social setting, given this concept of a social hierarchy based on different types of power.

The head in this scheme is represented by the Brahman caste. Both in theory and in practice, members of the Brahman community are generally given precedence in ritual matters. Once this group is granted first place, however, difficulties about the ranking of inferior groups immediately emerge. Typically, a land-owning agricultural community is dominant in terms of local political power and controls much of the day-to-day labor and production activity. The members of this group claim status on account of their kinglike position and back up their assertions by demonstrating their local, territorial hegemony. Groups that are dependent on this dominant agricultural community for employment will support the claims of their patrons and ally themselves with them. On the other hand, subcastes that are less immediately dependent on land and on agricultural production for a livelihood do not accept the landowners' claims. Instead, they point to the inferior ritual position of the farmer, who takes life from creatures in the soil with his plow. These subcastes try to acquire material wealth as a means of becoming relatively independent economically of the local landowners. This they attempt to combine with an emphasis on ritual purity and self-control. In terms of the traditional hierarchy, they then claim that material and ritual power add up to some total prestige quotient which is greater than that of a group wielding political and territorial control alone. In the Indian view, material wealth is one kind of power, as we have seen; but only in combination with ritual self-discipline can it become superior to royal or kingly status. By itself, the latter outranks status measured in material or financial terms.[17]

Such rivalry leads to the development of a bifurcate prestige structure in which some groups focus their efforts on the control of territory and of other men, while others are more concerned with the acquisition of material wealth and with a self-acclaimed ritual superiority. These two paths to prestige are very difficult to combine in the Indian setting. Traditionally, land could be acquired only through inheritance or by conquest; hence groups which did not already hold territorial control were excluded from access to it. It is important to recognize that the introduction of British law, in which land was defined as a commodity that could be bought and sold, opened up the route to this kind of power to previously landless but materially wealthy groups. The residents of the Koṅku area, however, have been slow in making use of the new rules. Patterns of land ownership, by subcaste, have not yet changed greatly from those that existed in pre-

---

[17]Den Ouden has also pointed to this phenomenon of rank indeterminacy where wealth and claims to ritual purity are staked against local territorial control. See his case study: J. H. B. Den Ouden, "The Komutti Chettiyar: Position and Change of a Merchant Caste in a South-Indian Village," *Tropical Man* 2 (1969): 45–59.

British days. Therefore, access to material wealth has remained relatively independent of access to land and to the political power accompanying it. Instead, it has been combined with a stress on ritual purity achieved by the observance of elaborate dietary and interaction restrictions, particularly in the case of a few high-ranking professional and merchant communities.

By contrast, members of the local KavuNTar or farming community in Koṅku spend much time interacting with those whose labor they oversee. It is by their very involvement in local affairs, and by their willingness to perform technically polluting tasks such as plowing, that the KavuNTars succeed in maintaining their position of dominance. Instead of emphasizing withdrawal, they attempt to participate in, and hence to control, as much local activity as possible. Such an approach to power does not mix well with a concern for restricting interaction and types of work activity, the strategy that forms an important component of their rivals' claims to prestige.

In Koṅku there is only one group that successfully combines these two approaches to status, the territorial-political and the material-ritualistic. This is the PiLLai community.[18] As local accountants, members of this group are in a unique position. They keep the land records and thus are in a position to exercise considerable influence in determining the outcome of various rivalries within the KavuNTar community. They also enjoy titles to considerable amounts of tax-free land in compensation for their official work. The PiLLai themselves prefer to remain aloof from the specific tasks of agricultural production, refusing, for example, to plow.[19] Instead, they always hire agricultural labor or invite tenants to work their land. (The latter is more common.) Furthermore, they are vegetarians, and they follow Brahman custom in a number of other ritual matters. This combination of land-linked political power and ritual care serves to place the PiLLai community above the KavuNTars. They are viewed as being almost equal in rank to the Brahmans and hence as part of the "head" or neutral area of the social body, which stands above the rival prestige ladders just described.

There are, however, a few caste communities which have membersubcastes in both halves or divisions of this social order. In the case of the service castes, the reasoning behind this split is straightforward. Each social division is a unit that cooperates in many ritual matters. The service groups, in particular the barbers and the washermen, are therefore divided accordingly. One subcaste will serve the right bloc, and a second the left.

---

[18]In some parts of Koṅku the Mutaliyār group, rather than the PiLLai, are probably considered to rank second, after the Brahmans.
[19]The Brahmans who have rights to small amounts of temple land manage their holdings in a similar fashion.

Since the members of the left bloc do not cooperate so extensively as those of the right, however, their sense of unity is not as strong. Each left service group does not necessarily serve all the communities in its division; instead, arrangements are often made on a subcaste-to-subcaste basis. As a result, several subdivisions of left service groups can often be involved.

In the case of merchants (CeTTiyār) on the other hand, divisional alignment of the various subcastes seem to stem from practical, political and economic concerns. These merchant groups are rivals and it is not surprising, therefore, that when two groups are present they tend to ally themselves with opposite blocs. In addition, however, there may be a certain practical rationale behind this split in divisional affiliation. One group, the Koṅku CeTTiyār, claims to have a special tie to the KavuNTar community. Members of this subcaste say that they originally broke off from the former as brothers who took to marketing the agricultural produce which their other siblings had grown.[20] They claim to have been allied with the KavuNTar community ever since. The KōmuTTi CeTTiyār, by contrast, have no special tie to a landed group. They are independent merchants who generally own large stores and sell a particular line of goods. Unlike the Koṅku CeTTiyār, the KōmuTTi are not so much brokers as business managers, and they have come to be identified as members of the left bloc.[21]

As well as the difference in the prestige criteria used by the left and right divisions, there is a contrast in the life-styles exhibited by members of the two blocs. This can be illustrated by a few sketches of everyday life. Well-to-do KavuNTars of the right bloc, for example, live in fine, manor-style dwellings with much open courtyard space and many storerooms. There is always activity in these homes. People who work for the family come and go constantly. Some employees are engaged in household tasks such as cooking and sweeping, while others bring messages from the fields or stand waiting for a noonday meal. Both men and women of the family direct this activity, and members of both sexes go to the fields in shifts to oversee family-run operations there. KavuNTar men will touch a plow with pride, and even the wealthiest KavuNTar women will help with sowing, weeding, and transplanting. KavuNTars love to direct and manage activity and will participate in any or all aspects of the work at hand in order to set an example. KavuNTar men are expansive in their bodily

---

[20]This story contrasts with that recorded in an old manuscript found in the area and discussed in chapter 1, pp. 36–37. There, the Koṅku CeTTiyār escape from the persecution of some distant king, flee to Koṅku, request KavuNTar protection, and eventually form a political alliance with this group.

[21]The Koṅku CeTTiyār are not listed in Table 1 because no member of this community was resident in the local area where my ranking data were collected. They will be referred to, however, at various points throughout the book, as they are an important group in the region as a whole.

movements. People say they can recognize a KavuNTar by the swagger in his walk and by his easy show of anger. Members of this community are famous for resolving differences in open fights. The houses of this group are always open to visitors. A well-dressed stranger will readily be invited into the inner rooms and treated like an honored guest.

The Brahmans in the rural areas form a striking contrast with the KavuNTar group just described. Although it is officially non-aligned or neutral, I consider this community to provide a "model" for left-bloc behavior. The attitudes of these priestly families are widely emulated by other groups that are recognized members of the left division. Hence they are important to this bloc in the same way that KavuNTars, as major pace-setters, are to the right.

In the rural areas of Koṅku, the Brahmans are nearly all Sivite, and they form a small and relatively poor group. I encountered very few who did not make a living through their ritual services; yet they receive barely enough from their work as priests to feed, clothe, and educate their offspring. Members of this community are not isolated in special Brahman settlements; instead they live in modest houses which are sometimes right in the midst of the KavuNTar community. However, they clearly set themselves off from others socially by not allowing members of other castes to enter their homes. Employees are kept to a minimum, and when summoned they are allowed to enter the courtyard at most. Brahman women do all the cooking and much of the family cleaning and washing themselves. They rarely leave the house except to go to the temple or to visit relatives. When an adult male Brahman enters a non-Brahman house to perform some ceremony, he walks quickly and directly to the spot indicated, looking downward and holding his limbs to his body as if to minimize the contact as much as possible. He will leave abruptly as soon as his part in the ceremony is completed and bathe before re-entering his own home. In performing temple ceremonies, a Brahman priest will join his relatives in a back corner whenever he is not directly occupied. He will not mingle with the crowds. Members of this community are also particular about informal visits to the homes of other castes; for example, they generally refuse to sit down and they usually agree to stay only a few minutes. They will never eat in the house of a member of another caste and only accept raw food stuffs that they will later cook themselves.

The Brahmans are a proud group, just as the KavuNTars are, but the expression of this self-esteem takes a contrasting form. Instead of a swagger and an eagerness to dominate, the Brahman exhibits an aloofness of manner and extreme touchiness in matters requiring interaction. Members of this group are not interested in managing the activities of others. Any business with non-Brahmans is conducted with brevity on an exterior porch near the doorstep of the house. Strangers are not invited inside.

Furthermore, Brahmans throttle their tempers, and are circumspect in bodily movement. I have never seen a Brahman in the area strike another man in anger, but such incidents are commonplace in the KavuNTar community.

Just as the other primarily agricultural caste of the right (the NāTār) tends to imitate KavuNTar mannerisms, so do the higher-ranking and more independent castes of the left imitate Brahman behavior. The KōmuTTi CeTTiyār and the CōLi Ācāri, for example, emulate Brahmans by refusing cooked food from members of all other subcastes, by being very selective in their choice of friends, and by displaying an air of aloofness when others wish their services. These groups are also very particular about their marriage connections, always insisting on closely related women who fall precisely into the correct terminological category.[22] Both curry favor with Brahman families, and I have often observed women of these two subcastes visiting the homes of members of the Brahman community.

As one moves down the social hierarchy in either division this pattern of behavioral resemblances becomes less marked. Instead, more emphasis is placed on ritual or symbolic equivalence between member-groups and division leaders or models. The service subcastes of the right division, for example, do not have an opportunity to manage the affairs of others, and they lack the social importance that would allow them to walk with a swagger. These people compensate for such practical differences between themselves and their bloc superiors by insisting on the fact that their household ceremonies are exactly or nearly the same as those performed by right-division groups with more prestige. Less independent still are the untouchables, the lowest-ranking communities of all. Interestingly enough, it is these communities that make the strongest claims for a special ritual connection with those higher-ranking groups with which they share a common block identity.

After this brief introduction to the over-all contrast in the life-styles of the members of the two divisions, it is now appropriate to take up a few of the major differences in the social organization of the two opposed blocs. In terms of a hierarchy of internal subcaste authority, for example, there is a clear difference between the primarily secular criteria employed by members of the right and the stress placed on sacred leadership by subcastes of the left. For members of the right, leadership positions are inherited, passed down from father to son; and the definitions of office refer primarily to political and territorial criteria. In the organization of left-division groups, by contrast, there are fewer rungs in the hierarchy of internal, subcaste authority. Here the stress is on the leadership of the most

---

[22] A KavuNTar, by contrast, will readily marry a woman of means, even though her genealogical relationship to him may be unknown or may place her, technically, in the "wrong" terminological category.

learned of the group's many members. Most positions of respect in this superstructure are not linked to territorial subdivisions or kinship at all. Instead, leaders tend to be selected by general acclamation, praise being given for outstanding religiosity. The highest levels of the left-division organization generally bypass local boundaries entirely and are centered on all-South Indian pilgrimage sites. At this level, the headmen are usually *canyācis* ("world-renouncers") whose life-style stresses celebacy and dependence on the alms of devotees.[23]

Another form of contrast is provided by the kinship terms used by the two divisions. These vary in some important details. The terms of the right subcastes distinguish clan lines and are well suited for fostering the development of politically and economically motivated marriage alliances. The left subcastes, on the other hand, classify their grandparents by sex alone, without differentiating between descent lines. The right communities all state a preference for marriage with the matrilateral cousin, while a few high-ranking left-division groups indicate the choice of a patrilateral cousin instead. From these differences it follows that the relation between descent lines is stressed by the first group of subcastes, while the tight-knit unity of marriage circles is emphasized by the second.

The right subcastes make no distinction between the terms for mother's brother and father's sister's husband, nor between the terms for matrilateral and patrilateral cousins.[24] The left subcastes, by contrast, use slightly inferior terms for matrilateral uncles and cousins, while they reserve slightly superior terms for their patrilateral equivalents. This tendency to distinguish between wife-givers and wife-takers on the part of left-division groups is associated with their special emphasis on dowry and their determination that the receiver of the bride be a superior. This does not contradict their patrilateral cross-cousin marriage preference when it exists, however; for the superior-inferior distinction is easily reversed in succeeding generations. This is so because among the left subcastes clan lines are weak. The hierarchy of individual givers and takers rather than that of whole descent groups is considered of prime importance.

The over-all hierarchy of clan rights in local territories is a persistent theme in the ceremonies performed by right-division castes. This hierarchy is not expressed in the kin terminology, however, since any rank order linked to kin relationships would quickly become confused by the complex web of clan intermarriages. Instead, it is expressed on ceremonial occasions, where rank orders change more slowly, in response to long-

---

[23]The VēTTuvar KavuNTars, discussed briefly in chapter 2, n. 17, are probably an exception to most of these generalizations concerning the political and religious organization of left-division groups. The information I collected in the field was insufficient to enable me to do more than point out this interesting difference.

[24]They can be distinguished genealogically, of course, but not as kin categories.

term alterations in relative descent-group power or prestige.

A further element of contrast is provided by the deities worshipped by the subcastes of the two divisions. The right communities owe their first allegiance to territorially based divinities who protect well-defined local areas. They are also devoted to the guardian figures of specific subcaste and clan groups. The left communities, by contrast, worship gods and goddesses whose names are familiar in literary works, and who are not strongly associated with any particular territory or social group. This pattern of worship is in keeping with the stress they place on the value of scholarship and of the knowledge of classical texts. Their favorite deities tend to have generalized concerns—to be linked to such universal experiences as birth and death and to the relief of human suffering. It will be seen later that all devotees are treated as equals at left-caste festivals. No formalized ranking can be observed on such occasions. At right-caste festivals, on the other hand, the hierarchical relationship among participants is emphasized in the ceremonies that are performed.

In the past, visible signs of right-left membership in Koṅku were displayed by the women of the two divisions. Females of the higher-ranking subcastes of the right division, for example, bared their right shoulder, throwing the end of their sari over the left. Women belonging to subcastes of similar rank in the opposite group bared their left shoulder, throwing the sari over the right. This distinction is still observed by some of the older women of the area today. Furthermore, the pendant of a woman's wedding necklace was hung in a particular way for one group, but it was inverted or hung "upside-down" for the other. There were also certain ritual restrictions on the women of each division, but apparently no parallel rules were in existence for men. Thus, left women could not enter the temple area of a right deity during its festival, nor could they allow their husbands sexual intimacy if they were employed as soldiers by leaders of the opposite bloc.[25]

All of the contrasts summarized here between right and left subcastes serve to introduce the reader to an over-all pattern. The details of these contrasts and the many exceptions to them will form the subject matter of the following chapters. The defect of this summary is that it has not been connected to a second primary variable: the general standing of a subcaste in the social hierarchy of the region. In short, the highest-ranking groups of the two divisions provide a marked contrast. The generalizations made here refer largely to them. As one moves down the social ladder, however, the customs of subcastes in the two blocs become more and more alike. Among these groups there is evidence of a "compromise" between the

---

[25]This particular detail was gleaned from the comments of historical observers. My own informants did not mention it. See Thurston, *Castes and Tribes,* 6:15.

differences displayed by social superiors.[26] Between untouchable groups in the two divisions, therefore, the contrasts are fewer than those exhibited by high-ranking groups. Finally, because most low-status subcastes of both divisions work as field laborers under the direction of high-ranking members of the right, the right-division pattern exercises more influence on the customs of these subcastes than might otherwise be expected.

The main feature of social organization underlying much of the argument in the following chapters is the presence of a dominant caste. This term has often been used loosely with extraneous details assimilated to essential ones in the attempt to define it. "Dominant caste," in my usage, refers to the subcaste community that controls a majority of the local labor force in a given area. This control refers to rights of access to primary resources and the power to allocate those tasks that entitle a man to a share in these resources. Rights to land are perhaps the best and most direct measure of this in an agricultural economy, although rights to mineral resources, and to communication routes, etc., can also be important.[27] According to this definition, a subcaste that is dominant in a small area may be overshadowed by some other group in the context of a larger region. Thus, one cannot speak of dominance per se, but must refer to the specific area controlled.[28]

This definition of dominant caste, I believe, is more accurate than a usage that includes some measure of the size of the group in question. It is quite common in South India to find a very large community of untouchables resident in an area. They may be more numerous than any other single group, and yet they could never be called dominant in an economic or a political sense. Similarly, there are areas of Tanjore and of Kerala where the total Brahman population relative to other castes is very small and yet where this community wields a quite considerable proportion of the economic and political power. Size in itself, therefore, is not a fundamental factor in determining a group's dominance.

The percentage of the total land acreage owned by a particular group, is not the variable that directly measures the degree of influence and control over local populace that the group enjoys. One family can own thousands of acres (or could until the enactment of land-ceiling legislation), but because it cannot cultivate that land itself, it must lease it out to ten-

[26]For an attempt to summarize these differences in graph form, see Brenda E. F. Beck, "The Right-Left Division of South Indian Society," *The Journal of Asian Studies* 29, no. 4 (1970): 779–98.

[27]In an excellent article on this question, Walter Neale presents essentially the same view as the one stated here. Walter C. Neale, "Land is to Rule," in Robert Eric Frykenberg, ed., *Land Control and Social Structure in Indian History* (Madison: University of Wisconsin Press, 1969), pp. 3–16.

[28]Eric Miller has made a similar point. Eric J. Miller, "Caste and Territory in Malabar," *American Anthropologist* 56 (1954): 410–20.

ants. Under these conditions, it is the tenants who directly manage production and who employ and direct the work of a large proportion of the local residents. In my definition, it is not land ownership per se, but rather power to employ and supervise directly the labor of others that makes for dominance.[29] When land is concentrated in the hands of a very few owners, they become distant figures with great prestige but little day-to-day control. The more households from a particular group that own holdings of a practicable size, where they can either work the land themselves or directly supervise the work of others, the more dominant that group becomes. Although a household cannot achieve direct control over others by working its own land, by being self-sufficient, it does contribute to the general prestige and position of the group to which it belongs. Other residents in the community are unable to dominate such a household, since it does not have to provide services for any other in order to support itself.[30]

In order to speak of a dominant caste in an area, therefore, that group must generally have more households owning or managing moderate amounts of land than any other group in the area.[31] If two or more groups are tied for this position, I would speak of them as rivals for dominance. Further fractionalization of land-management, by subcaste, would reduce the power of any one group even further. In most areas of Koṅku, however, there is no problem of rivalry. The Koṅku KavuNTars own at least eighty per cent of the land and they own it in small, individual holdings. Given such an advantage, no other caste can begin to challenge their position. However, in the few areas where CeTTiyārs and Mutaliyārs own a fair amount of land, they clearly do rival the KavuNTars for dominance in that particular place. This change in dominance relationships is expressed in the altered rules which govern interdining in these areas. Thus, in certain parts of Koṅku the Koṅku CeTTiyār do surpass KavuNTars in the social hierarchy. This is expressed by the fact that more groups are willing to eat from their hands than from KavuNTar hands at their local feasts.

In attempting to predict the strength of the right-left division in a particular region, the degree to which a single non-Brahman group has managed to dominate that particular area appears to me to be crucial. The essence of the right-left dichotomy lies in the rivalry for status of two sets of subcastes that operate with fundamentally different criteria. The first set takes pride in its right to land-management and in its concomitant

---

[29]I have benefited greatly, in the development of this definition, from discussions with David J. Elkins of the Department of Political Science at the University of British Columbia.

[30]It is possible that such a household would cooperate with other households belonging to the same group during the planting or harvest period, but this would be an equal, not a hierarchical, kind of exchange.

[31]A more precise formulation of this definition appears in the concluding chapter, pp. 268–69.

political power in a local territory. In the rituals they perform, the members of this set adopt textually prescribed ceremonies sparingly: their ceremonial focus places an emphasis on social interdependence and on various aspects of agricultural abundance. By contrast, the second set attempts to minimize its involvement in a particular place, especially where this entails relations of long-term economic dependence on other groups. Instead, this set stresses its material wealth, its ritual purity, and its connections with an all-South Indian scholarly and philosophical tradition. Wherever possible, its members will follow the ceremonies prescribed by textual sources.

For this kind of contrast in life-styles and value orientations to evolve in its most strident form, it appears that a clear division of regional caste roles is necessary. The Brahmans must maintain themselves as ritual specialists and teachers, while a non-Brahman group (or groups) has control over most of the land. Where this dichotomy in the traditional Hindu values between priest and king is reinforced by a dichotomy in actual caste and subcaste roles, there is an invitation to business and craft groups that are relatively independent of the land-owning community to claim that they are superior to the latter in ritual terms. Where the Brahmans themselves own and manage tracts of land, however, they tend to break down in practice, if not in principle, the traditional disjunction between ritual and royal roles. In such circumstances, of course, the Brahmans emerge stronger than ever; for they occupy the highest rung on both these social ladders. PiLLais, mentioned earlier, seem to be able to do the same thing when they are present in large numbers. Although such a situation may not end right-left rivalries completely, it must surely weaken them. Successfully coopting the top position in the two competing status hierarchies must necessarily bring the two sets of stairs closer together in the eyes of hopeful climbers. Now a non-Brahman needs both land and ritual purity in order to compete successfully for the highest positions. But where no group large enough to make its impact felt has succeeded in bringing the top rungs of the two ladders together, it is not quite clear how the two measure up. If members of the territorially dominant community have climbed to the top of one ladder, the obvious way for groups traditionally excluded from land ownership to challenge their prestige is to climb the other one, claiming that it is the taller of the two. Such appears to be the case in Koṅku, where a left-right opposition seems to have been a major feature of rural social structure for many years.

1

THE REGION: KOṄKU NĀTU

According to Koṅku bards, Tamilnadu is traditionally comprised of five great regions.[1] These are CōRa NāTu, PāNTiya NāTu, Cēra NāTu, ToNTai NāTu, and Koṅku NāTu respectively.[2] The first three regions are the most widely known, both for their famous royal families and for their valor in war. In all the old stories of adventure and conquest local poets mention these principal areas respectfully. Koṅku is always spoken of as a separate region, but as one ruled by an overlord loyal to one of the initial three. The fifth, ToNTai NāTu, is not well known in Koṅku folklore. It is most frequently spoken of as an area from which immigrants have come and it does not often figure in popular stories of battles and of heroism.[3]

Despite being overshadowed politically by its southern and eastern neighbors, in geographic terms Koṅku is better defined than any of the other famous four. The rural residents of Koṅku identify with their distinct physical surroundings and repeatedly refer to them in poetry. The

[1] Bards in Tamil are called *pulavar*. These men are asked to recite on request the genealogies of the more important local families, and are expected to know a certain amount about regional history. They also have a minor ritual role at festivals celebrated for Lord Civā and at the wedding ceremonies of most right-division castes. The pulavar claim that they belong to the Mutaliyār community. However, their role appears to be largely ascribed and I am not convinced that they form a distinct subcaste.

[2] ToNTai NāTu is better known in literary works as ToNTai MaNTalam. All five regions are referred to, at least obliquely, in the earliest existing body of literature for the area. This corpus, the Sangam works, dates back at least fifteen hundred years. N. Subramanian, *Sangam Polity: The Administration and Social Life of the Sangam Tamils* (New York: Asia Publishing House, 1968), pp. 112–13.

[3] I would predict that the inverse holds true also; i.e., that Koṅku is not well known in ToNTai NāTu folklore. Both of these areas appear to have defined themselves relative to the more powerful kingdoms of the South, at least from the tenth century onwards. They became territorial prizes to be warred over until finally they evolved into a kind of symbol of the variable fortunes of the other three. Koṅku was also conquered several times by armies based in Mysore. These northern kingdoms are not referred to in the local folklore as occupying a distinct social and cultural area, however. Such praise is reserved for kingdoms to the South.

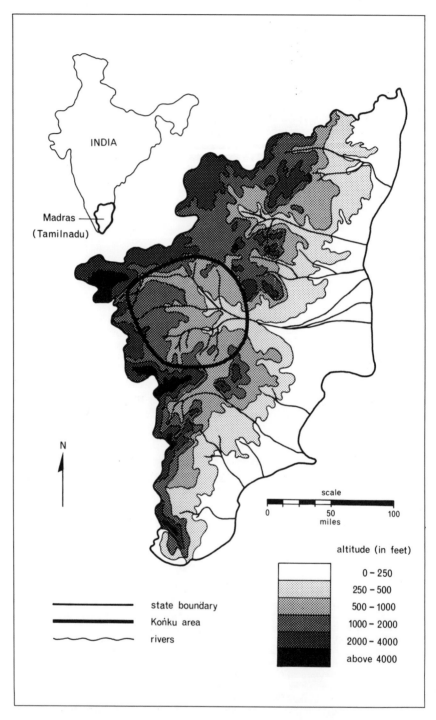

INDIA

Madras
(Tamilnadu)

N

scale

0   50   100
        miles

altitude (in feet)

0 – 250
250 – 500
500 – 1000
1000 – 2000
2000 – 4000
above 4000

state boundary
Koṅku area
rivers

Fig. 1.1.   Physiography of Madras State (Tamilnadu).

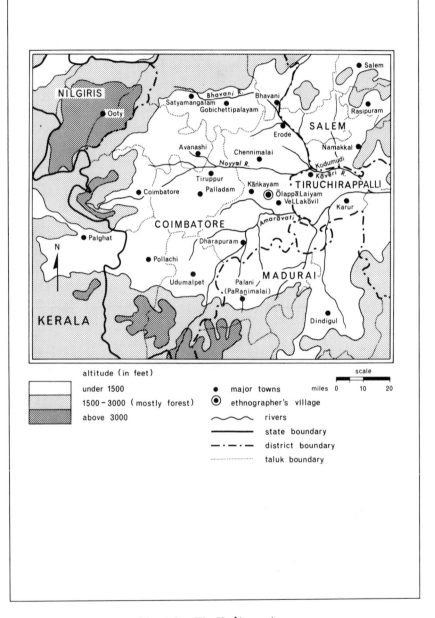

Fig. 1.2. The Koṅku region.

bards of the area reinforce this local feeling by reciting verses that provide a precise description of the mountain ranges bounding Koṅku on its four sides. According to this tradition, to the north lie the mountains of Talaimalai and Parukūrmalai. To the south, Koṅku is delineated by the range of mountains that stretch from Āṇaimalai to Varākamalai. In the west a line of hills runs north from VeLLimalai to the Nilgris, including a small but important gap at Palghat, and finally in the east, Koṅku is bounded by a mountain range composed of the Toppūrmalai, Cērvarā-yanmalai, and Kollimalai.[4] These ranges are shown in Figure 1.3. The southeast is the only direction in which passage is not impeded by high hills. Thus it is not surprising that many of the conquerors of Koṅku have come from this direction.

Interestingly enough, however, there is a traditional boundary for Koṅku, even on the floor of this southeastern valley. This is located at a place called Matukkarai, a famous point on the river Kāvēri about twenty-five miles east of Karur. Here, the Koṅku bards say that the CōRa, Cēra, and PāNTiya kings met to fight over the borders of their respective countries. Three Vināyakar temples located at Matukkarai are said to mark the traditional limits of these regions.[5] Thus the area to the north and west of these temples is remembered as Cēra NāTu, the area to the east as CōRa NāTu, and that to the south as PāNTiya NāTu. These three separate Vināyakar temples still stand. Inhabitants of the immediate area actively preserve the tradition surrounding the shrines.[6] In this demarcation, Koṅku is merged with Cēra NāTu. It may be that it was ruled by a Cēra king at the time the boundaries were fixed.

Besides the break in the mountains through which the Kāvēri flows, there are three important passes which have for centuries marked important trade routes into the area. Two of these lie roughly even with the plateau floor, but a true pass leads from the northeast corner of Koṅku into Mysore. At its midpoint, this access route rises to nearly 2,800 feet.[7]

The total area of the traditional Koṅku region, as just described, is about 7,500 square miles. It encompasses most of the present Coimbatore District, but also includes parts of Salem, Madurai and Tiruchirappalli.

---

[4]Taken from a poem recited by Informant no. 7. Similar details were obtained from Informant no. 22. These same verses appear in several early literary works. See K. V. Rangaswami Aiyangar, *Prof. K. V. Rangaswami Aiyangar Commemoration Volume* (Madras: G. S. Press, 1940), pp. 159–69.

[5]Vināyakar is an elephant-headed deity, also known as Ganesh or PiLLaiyār. He is considered the first son of Civā and is often found associated with settlement sites and boundaries in the Koṅku area.

[6]C. M. Ramachandra Chettiar, *Koṅku NāTTu Varalāṟu* [The story of Koṅku NāTu] (Annamalai: Annamalai University Press, 1954), p. 5; and field observations.

[7]Government of Madras, *Madras District Gazetteers, Coimbatore* (Madras: Government Press, 1966), p. 595.

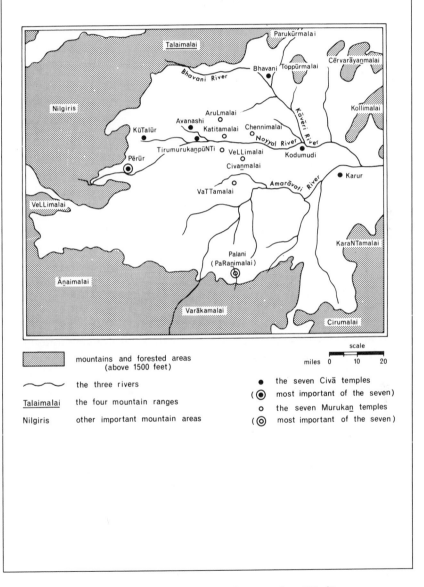

Fig. 1.3. The traditional sacred geography of Koṅku.

More specifically, the Koṅku area, as shown in Table 1.1, is comprised of the following present-day administrative units:

A. Coimbatore District (excepting the mountainous areas of Gobichettipalayam, Bhavani, Pollachi and Udumalpet Taluks)
B. Karur Taluk of Tiruchirappalli District
C. Palani Taluk of Madurai District
D. Namakkal, Tiruchangodu and Sankari Taluks of Salem District.[8]

TABLE 1.1
APPROXIMATE AREA AND POPULATION OF KOṄKU NĀTU, 1961

Administrative Unit	Area (sq. miles)	Population
A	5,000.0 (est.)	3,000,000 (est.)
B	610.4	345,162
C	624.9	288,809
D	1,285.3	909,206
Total	7,520.6	4,543,177

SOURCE: Republic of India, *Census of India, 1961*, Vol. IX, *Madras*, Part II-A, *General Population Tables* (Madras: Government Press, 1963), pp. 87–91 and p. 94.

NOTE: The letters in the first column of the table correspond to the list of administrative units given in the text.

Through the Koṅku plain flows the Kāvēri, one of the most important rivers in South India. This water course has its head far to the north, in Mysore. From its source, on the western edge of Coorg, it flows south into Koṅku, bending southeast at Bhavani to traverse the Koṅku plain. Two smaller rivers spring from the slopes of the Ghats on the western edge of Koṅku and a fourth rises in the southern Āṇaimalai range. These three tributaries meet the Kāvēri near the center of the region where they join forces and flow east towards the Tanjore (now Thanjavur) delta and the sea. Koṅku is thus a great shallow bowl, with water draining into it from three sides and escaping as a single, mighty flow from a gentle lip on its eastern edge.

The sacred geography of Koṅku constitutes a further aspect of its definition as a region by local inhabitants. Central to this geography are the three tributary rivers and seven prominent hills which rise dramatically out of the central plain. Seven points along the main rivers are also set aside as especially sacred and at each of these places a huge temple to Lord Civā has been constructed. These are jointly referred to as the *ēRu civālayaṅkaL*, or Koṅku's seven temples for Civā. All of these temples are old, several of them dating from the CōRa period.[9] They are generally situated at points where a great river and a tributary converge.

[8]See chapter 2, especially p. 65, n. 6 for an explanation of the terms "Taluk" and "District."
[9]The most important period of CōRa influence in Koṅku dates roughly from A.D. 900 to 1200.

Similarly, there are seven great temples dedicated to Murukaṉ, the second son of Civā, on the tops of seven sacred hills. In the South, Murukaṉ is the best loved of all the great Hindu deities. Indeed he was probably even more prominent in the earliest period for which we have literary records—roughly A.D. 100 to 400—than he is today. Many of the shrines dedicated to him in the Koṅku area are very old. The best known, PaRaṉimalai, is known to date back at least fifteen hundred years, as it is mentioned in the earliest collection of Tamil poems.[10] There is no collective name for these seven Murukaṉ temples which constitute a part of the sacred geography of Koṅku, however. Perhaps this is so because these seven shrines were arbitrarily selected from a much larger number, in an attempt to create a specific parallel for the seven which had been constructed in Civā's name during later periods.

In the case of the Civā temples, each temple name can be understood as linking a particular location with some specific aspect of the deity. The seven thereby serve as sacred links joining the various subregions of Koṅku into a united whole. In the case of the seven Murukaṉ shrines, however, the name of the deity refers only to its location on a particular mountain or *malai*. In contrast to Civā, Murukaṉ has always been associated with hills and peaked places.[11] Once a mountain is marked as sacred, therefore, it is Murukaṉ's pervasive association with it, as with all heights, that is stressed.[12] In this way, the particular and the universal, the valleys and the mountain tops, form in Koṅku two complementary sacred chains.[13]

Each of these groups of seven temples is organized around a leading or primary shrine: a single great temple in which all the Koṅku-linked manifestations of the deity converge. In the case of the Civā temples this shrine is to be found in Pērūr, while in the case of Murukaṉ an equivalent status is ascribed to the temple at PaRaṉi (or Palani). Each of these religious centers represents the pinnacle of the local organization of priests who serve

---

[10]The "TirumurukārrupaTai," one of ten idylls of the *PattuppāTTu* collection, was probably written somewhere between the first and fourth centuries A.D. See K. A. Nilakanta Sastri, *A History of South India,* 3rd ed. (Madras: Oxford University Press, 1966), p. 115.

[11]There are also early references to Murukaṉ riding the tops of the ocean waves.

[12]One well-known Koṅku mountain, in fact, is actually named Civaṉmalai (Civā's mountain) and yet the temple on top has been dedicated to Murukaṉ. Indeed this case is counted as one of the seven great shrines in Koṅku dedicated to Murukaṉ's name.

[13]In the Introduction it was suggested that the deities of right-division groups tend to have particular concerns linked to specific territorial claims, while left-division gods are associated with the relief of universal kinds of suffering. This seems to imply the existence of a special tie between the right-division communities and the river-based Civā temples, and of left groups with Murukaṉ and mountain peaks. Supporting evidence for such a pattern can be found, I think, in the differential usage rates of the two types of temples by members of the two divisions. I have not explored the matter in detail, but I suspect that wealthy KavuNTars are the most important patrons of the *civālayaṅkaL,* or temples for Civā. The prominent Murukaṉ temples, on the other hand, would appear to subsist on donations from a more mixed clientele, which may have a greater concentration of left-group members.

that deity in the Koṅku area. All priests who work in the local Civā temples look ultimately to Pērūr for direction and for decisions in ritual matters. All those who serve Murukaṉ, on the other hand, look to PaRaṇi.

These two leading male deities of Koṅku, and their temples, though complementary in themselves, are joined in opposition to the female Kāvēri, the third and final entity in the region's larger sacred pattern. The Kāvēri is said to carry water from the great river Ganges, and is in a sense the most highly revered element in the whole geography. Some say that it forms an underground connection with the Ganges itself.[14] Others claim that it has its origin in an overturned pot which contained water from this sacred source.[15] River water is considered to have an exceptional purificatory power in the Hindu world-view. The fact that the Kāvēri is treated as a sacred entity by local residents is part of this larger perspective.

One could go further and attempt to describe this formal geography in geometric terms. Viewed as a sacred order, a triangular relationship between the river and the two sets of temples would emerge. These same temples, in their role as secular, human-managed institutions, however, go to form supports on which this three-sided figure rests. Such a sketch illustrates the dualism Koṅku residents see in the organization of human affairs, and, simultaneously, the triadic pattern which emerges where those affairs are viewed as part of a larger whole. In fact it is common practice in Koṅku to use an even number—in this case "two"—in matters of administrative organization, but an odd one—in this case "three"—to refer to any divinely sanctioned, all encompassing order. The same idea will be illustrated again when the material presented in the first two sections of chapter 2 is discussed.

Despite its many small rivers, Koṅku is essentially an extremely dry plain. Thus crops must be irrigated from precious water supplies. Rain is infrequent and less dependable than anywhere else in Madras State.[16] Canal irrigation schemes are limited to the fields alongside the riverbanks. The only exceptions are a few big dam projects which have extended water resources in some areas in recent years. Most farmers, however, still depend on deep wells.

Koṅku peasants view these harsh living conditions with pride and boast of what they have done with scarce resources. In one well-known folk story a man refuses to marry an attractive bride from the southeast

---

[14]Informant no. 22.

[15]More specifically, Vināyakar, the first son of Civā, while in the shape of a crow, is said to have overturned the Akastiyar KamaNTalam which contained Ganges water (Informant no. 20). The name Kāvēri may also be related to the term *Kākanati* (from *kāka* or "crow"). See *A Dictionary Tamil and English,* 2nd ed. (Tranquebar: Evangelical Lutheran Mission, 1933), p. 223.

[16]Republic of India, *Census of India, 1961,* Vol. IX, *Madras,* Part IX, *Atlas of the Madras State* (Madras: Government Press, 1964), map 8.

A view of the Koṅku plain, showing some of the hills which border the area. This picture is taken from part way up Palani hill, one of the seven mountains of the region sacred to the god Murukaṇ.

The river Kāvēri, flowing across the Koṅku plain. This is the region's main water course. It is believed to have an underground connection with the Ganges and to be equivalent to the latter in its powers of ritual cleansing. The bathing and water-carrying activities in the foreground are typical. There are several traditional boats in the photograph, which are covered with skins.

delta area until he has built a complete irrigation system for himself. The consent to the match becomes final only after the hero's own homeland is made to turn a brighter green than that which the bride had known in her own childhood. This positive attitude towards hard work and grand achievements is characteristic of the rural population of Koṅku. Indeed, the Koṅku peasant's reputation for optimism and determination is widespread. In this particular respect Koṅku can be usefully compared with other dry but highly productive areas of India such as the Punjab and Rajasthan, and contrasted with the neighboring lush area of Thanjavur.[17] The 1961 census volume on Coimbatore, for example, discusses the district in the following terms:

> The district of Coimbatore in which the city is located leads other districts by its agrarian and industrial development recorded during the last 30 years. . . . But its economy is based on its sound agriculture built up by its hard working agriculturalists and supported by a number of irrigation projects constructed during the last decade. Its agrarian economy is further sustained by cottage industries which are practiced on a large scale in the district. Coimbatore has the highest standard of life in Madras State. Paradoxically it has not been blessed by nature. Its soils are not fertile. It has the least quantity of rain among all the districts and no valuable mineral deposit can be found. The development of Coimbatore district is, therefore, a tribute to the hard working people who inhabit the land.[18]

The pride which Koṅku residents have in their region is so great that several leaders of the area recently organized a special delegation whose sole job it was to bring the distinctive characteristics of Koṅku NāTu to the attention of the International Tamil Association. Some excerpts from a pamphlet prepared in 1968, when the association held its first meeting in Madras, will illustrate the extent of local feeling:

> It is hoped that this booklet will prove a distinct contribution to understand better the history of Kongu which is now occupying a 'pride of place' in the annals of Tamil Nad and India. . . . The Kongu country had existed as a separate entity like the Cholas, Cheras, Pandyas in the history of South India from ancient times. . . . The Kongu region has also flourishing commerce with foreign countries from ancient times. . . . In spite of frequent political changes, the country also made commendable progress in the field of Tamil literature, arts. . . . Kongunadu can claim to have given birth to able modern statesmen. . . . The singular progress in the industrial, agricultural and educational

[17]Such a comparison has already been suggested by Kusum Nair. Kusum Nair, *Blossoms in the Dust* (London: Gerald Duckworth & Co., 1962), p. 190.
[18]Republic of India, *Census of India, 1961,* Vol. IX, *Madras,* Part X-i, *District Census Handbook, Coimbatore,* 2 vols. (Madras: Government Press, 1964), 1:1.

sectors during the past two decades has resulted in the building up of a network of institutions which have become the glory of not only Tamilnad but also of India. . . . It can therefore be claimed with pardonable pride that no district has dedicated itself to the needs of the nation and has served so consistently and thoroughly as this region in Tamilnad.[19]

Particular features which are most often cited in support of this sense of regional identity will be discussed later. At this point it is sufficient to point out that in this geographically and socially distinct region, pride of place is strong.

HISTORY OF THE KOṄKU AREA

Surprisingly little has been written about Koṅku, despite its sociological and historical interest. The area has never been studied by an anthropologist or sociologist, and what ethnography is available consists largely of the observations of a few British officers.[20] As for history, the situation is rather similar. One contemporary Tamil work stands out as a pioneering effort.[21] A second work in English followed and made much of this material available to foreign scholars.[22] Prior to these two studies, there existed only local legend and the snippets of stories told by the pulavar or bards. Many of these, fortunately, have now been collected in soft-cover pocket editions which are available locally.[23]

The lack of interest in Koṅku on the part of most trained scholars is probably due to its variegated political history and its lack of glory as an

[19]Krishnamoorthy, Sengottu Velan, and Narayanan, *Kongu Nadu,* Second International Conference-Seminar of Tamil Studies (Coimbatore: Coimbatore District Reception Committee, n.d.), pp. 1, 10–11, 12, 26–27. (NOTE: "Kongu Nadu" is the usual Indian English spelling. In keeping with the system of transliteration used throughout this work, I spell this name as "Koṅku NāTu." For a fuller description of my transliteration system, see Appendix C.)

[20]During the period of English rule, census and district officers referred back and forth to one another's writings continually. Edgar Thurston summarized much of this material in his monumental *Castes and Tribes of Southern India,* 7 vols. (Madras: Government Press, 1909). This has, in turn, become a major source of information for the contemporary census work. Few original observations have been published since 1909.

[21]Ramachandra Chettiar, *Koṅku NāTTu Varalāṟu.* This work represents considerable research on the stone inscriptions found in the area.

[22]M. Arokiaswami, *The Kongu Country* (Madras: Madras University Press, 1956).

[23]Some of the more substantial and interesting of these works are: S. A. R. Ciṉṉucāmi KavuNTar, *Koṅku VēLāLar* [The VēLāLars of Koṅku] (Erode: TamiRaṉ Accakam, 1963); PaRaniccāmi Pulavar, *Koṅku Celvi* [The goddesses of Koṅku] (Coimbatore: Pudumalar Press, 1948); TiruvāNaṉ, *Maṅkalyam Tanta Makarāci* [The queen who gave away her wedding necklace] (Madras: Vāṉati Patippakam, 1960); K. K. KōtaNTarāmaṉ, *Koṅkunā-Tum CamaNamum* [Tidbits on Koṅku NāTu] (Coimbatore: Kōvai Nilaiya Patippakam, 1953); V. C. VeLLiyaṅkiri KavuNTar, *EṅkaL NāTTuppuram* [The story of our region] Coimbatore: Kōvai Nilaiya Patippakam, 1951); CivakaLai M. Cuppaiyā, *Koṅku NāTTu KōyilkaL* [The temples of Koṅku NāTu] (Madras: Pāri Accakam, 1967), and Pulavar KuRantai, *Koṅku NāTu* (Erode: Vēlā Patippakam, 1968).

independent empire. In any case, the details of various battles and of successive ruling families are not important to the general theme of this book and will not be summarized. Nonetheless a few important, if tentative, generalizations about Koṅku's history should be made. For example, the local nāṭu and kirāmam organization appears to have played an important part in previous centuries in knitting a diverse local population together both socially and ritually in the face of considerable political instability at higher levels.

Until the tenth century or so, Koṅku was a heavily forested area, its small population living largely by hunting and herding, rather than by direct cultivation of the soil. Even at this time, however, several important trade routes passed through the area.[24] One route originated on the west coast and entered Koṅku via the Palghat gap. From there, it turned east (via Kāṅkayam?) towards Karur and the Kāvēri delta. The traders appear to have carried such goods as spices, cloth, minerals, and gems on their treks, and this merchandise eventually reached places as distant as Rome and Egypt.[25] Just north of Kāṅkayam at PaTiyūr, for example, important quantities of beryl, white quartz, and aquamarine were mined.[26] These semi-precious stones were highly valued by the wealthy residents of urban centers in the Coromandel delta.

The great shrine to Murukaṉ at PaRaṉimalai is also mentioned in very early records.[27] This means that there must have been a route that passed along the southern edge of the Koṅku plain, enabling travelers to reach this important place of pilgrimage. Perhaps a third route led north from Koṅku as well, passing through the area now known as Satyamangalam.[28] Along each of the trade routes were resting places, associated in all likelihood with important agricultural settlements. Burton Stein, who studied the picture in some detail for other outlying areas, has described the situation as follows:

> The nuclear area as a center of power within the South Indian political system was the central element of that system until the thirteenth century. To that time, the Brahman- and Sat-Sudra-dominated nuclear areas were posed between the ambitious and expanding authority of the great Chola warriors and the always dangerous upland and forest peoples; and to that time the nuclear areas held their own against the former while continuously

[24] Arokiaswami, *Kongu Country*, pp. 284–90.

[25] Government of Madras, *Madras District Gazetteers, Coimbatore*, pp. 25–26, and Arokiaswami, *Kongu Country*, pp. 72–79.

[26] Republic of India, *Census of India, 1961*, Vol. IX, *Madras*, Part XI-D, *Temples of Madras State*, iii, *Coimbatore and Salem* (Madras: Government Press, 1968), p. 106. None of these mines is in operation today.

[27] See the Sangam poems, *Silappadikaram, Uraiperukkatturai*, and *Puran*, referred to by Arokiaswami in *Kongu Country*, p. 20.

[28] Government of Madras, *Madras District Gazetteers, Coimbatore*, p. 595.

pressing the latter peoples as forests were cleared and settled agriculture was established.[29]

Although the process that Stein describes had no doubt started in the Koṅku area well before the tenth century, it was greatly accelerated during the period of CōRa rule, because of the fact that the CōRas actively encouraged the settlement of outlying regions by people from the delta area. The folk tradition has recorded this social movement in terms of a personalized story:

> Once upon a time there was a handsome Cēra prince who married a CōRa princess, on the promise that he would lead an entourage of her father's men into the Koṅku area and create a new agricultural settlement there. The prince agreed and the CōRa king gave him an army of some eight thousand VēLāLar (the caste elsewhere in Madras State from which the KavuNTars claim descent). These men were to protect the prince and princess from attack by local hunters and raiders, and to aid in cultivation in times of peace. Certain clans soon distinguished themselves in local battles fought to protect the princess. As a result, the CōRa king rewarded them by giving them rights to some fine tracks of land. The clans which are named are among the prosperous KavuNTar clans in Koṅku today.[30]

Probably many such waves of settlers entered Koṅku under the auspices of successive kings, thus making the events described more complex and drawn-out than they are in the folk tradition. Nonetheless, the overall picture of the gradual settlement of Koṅku by groups related to the agricultural communities of the eastern littoral seems clear. Brahmans are mentioned in Koṅku, even at this early period. They were brought in to serve as priests at temple centers which were quickly constructed. Traders, merchants, and various service groups such as barbers and washermen are also mentioned as present during this period. Some of them had come into Koṅku from the north during the previous era of Ganga rule, the Ganga being a dynasty whose power center lay in northern Mysore.[31]

At the end of the CōRa period there was new unrest, and various usurpers tried to wrest power from the waning empire. Many Mutaliyārs are mentioned in inscriptions as having been employed as mercenaries to

---

[29]From Burton Stein, "Integration of the Agrarian System of South India," in Robert Eric Frykenberg, editor, *Land Control and Social Structure in Indian History* (Madison: The University of Wisconsin Press; © 1969 by the Regents of the University of Wisconsin), p. 185.

[30]This story is a summary of the following accounts: PaRaniccāmi Pulavar, *Koṅku Celvi,* pp. 132–33; PaRaniccāmi Pulavar, ed., *ŌtāLar Kuravanci enum Alakumalai Kuravanci* [The ŌtāLar clan story or the drama of Alaku Mountain] (Coimbatore: Kāntitācan Accakam, 1969); TiruvāNan, *Māṅkalyam Tanta Makarāci,* pp. 143–46; Government of Madras, *Madras District Gazetteers, Coimbatore,* p. 590, and Arokiaswami, *Kongu Country,* p. 55.

[31]PaRaniccāmi Pulavar, ed., *ŌtāLar Kuravanci,* pp. 38–41, and Ramachandra Chettiar, *Koṅku NāTTu Varalāru,* p. 114.

fight in the CōRa armies at this time. Later, it seems, some of them settled in Koṅku with their spoils and took to weaving and to business. Carpenters, blacksmiths, stone masons, and builders from other more developed regions must also have been in demand during this period.[32]

Whatever may have happened in terms of population movements during this early period, the tendency for non-agricultural castes to immigrate into Koṅku seems to have increased further in later epochs. In the fourteenth and fifteenth centuries there appears to have been an influx of Kannada-speaking people—largely businessmen from Mysore. After them—with the establishment of the Vijayanagar Empire—came waves of Telugu-speaking warriors and administrators.[33] About the seventeenth century, the first references to the right-left distinction, the great social division that was to split South Indian society for centuries to come, began to appear in the historical material concerning Koṅku.[34]

Because of its long history of wars and of repeated subjugation to neighboring kingdoms, it might be imagined that Koṅku has suffered great political and social instability over the centuries. At a closer look, however, it appears that many conquerors of the area were content with the prestige of victory and the proceeds of taxation. They worried little over the day-to-day affairs of the local populace. Within each nāTu, and even at the level of relations among these administrative units, the folk history of Koṅku emphasizes a surprising continuity of social traditions. It seems probable that nāTu and kirāmam organization has played a central role in defining the social, political, and ritual order of Koṅku at the local level for at least a millennium.[35]

The importance of the VēLāLar KavuNTar community as the major landowners in the Koṅku region, as we have seen, also appears very early. What is more, they always emerge in the position of heroes fighting valiantly against various antagonists. First they must fight the hunters and raiders in order to obtain their agricultural settlements. Later, however, they must oppose the many newer immigrant groups. The Ācāri, or artisans, in particular, resent their hold on the land and attempt to trick them. The development of a powerful, landed community aided by a few allies

---

[32]Ramachandra Chettiar, *Koṅku NāTTu Varalāṟu*, pp. 219–22.

[33]Ibid., pp. 339–45, and Robert Eric Frykenberg, *Guntur District 1788–1848* (Oxford: Clarendon Press, 1965), p. 3.

[34]For some general discussion of the historical development of this division elsewhere in the South, see Burton Stein, "Integration of the Agrarian System." For a more detailed discussion, see Arokiaswami, *Kongu Country*, p. 272.

[35]Similar findings have been reported for North India. See Winefred Day, "Relative Permanence of Former Boundaries in India," *Scottish Geographical Journal* 65, no. 3 (1949): 113–22, and Kashi N. Singh, "The Territorial Basis of Medieval Town and Village Settlement in Eastern Uttar Pradesh, India," *Annals of the Association of American Geographers* 58, no. 2 (1968): 203–20.

and service groups but envied and opposed by many of the technically skilled and later immigrants to the area can be said, therefore, to form the basic historical pattern—at least in the eyes of the local bards. With this background, the emergence of the right-left division as a major factor influencing differences in caste custom in the Koṅku area is not illogical.

One final example of the importance of the early agricultural settlers in establishing the tenor of major rivalries is provided by the great folk epic entitled *The Story of the Brothers*.[36] This epic is known by rural inhabitants in all parts of Koṅku, but its fame and popularity fade quickly beyond the region's boundaries.[37] This is not surprising since the story is specifically about the Koṅku area and is essentially a folk account of its history. The account presents this history in a heroic and semi-mythological form by recounting the story of one KavuNTar clan. In the story, the adventures of clan members are traced through four generations.[38] Because of the superhuman lives that these men lead, however, the span of time covered in the story is far greater than that which would be covered by four generations in an ordinary family.

The general progression of events in the story provides a sequence of historical situations that agrees in outline with what can be surmised about the early history of Koṅku from written sources. The epic begins, for example, with a description of a CōRa king encouraging people to settle in the upland parts of his kingdom. After a time, he awards land in this area to members of a particular KavuNTar clan, in return for favors performed. These settlers, on whom the story will focus, soon find themselves at war with the VēTTuvar—hunters who raid the settled areas. Finally the clan heroes win the struggle and their agricultural settlements expand.

The geography of the story is structured in terms of five nāTu divisions: 1) PonnivaLa nāTu, which belongs to the heroes; 2) TaṅkavaLa nāTu, which belongs to their *paṅkāLi,* or parallel relatives; 3) VāLavanti nāTu, which belongs to their *māman* or *maccāṉ*—cross relatives; 4) CōRa nāTu,

---

[36]There are also other important names for this epic story, and no one title is agreed upon throughout the Koṅku region. Some other common names are *KunruTaiyā KavuNTar Katai* and *Ponnar, Caṅkar Katai.* One recent attempt to abridge the story and render it in print in high Tamil prose has been printed as a cheap paperback under the title *PonnaRakarennum KaLLaRakar Ammāṉai* [The story of Ponnar, the KaLLar] (Madras: R. G. Pati Co., 1965). This last version is extensively abridged, and, as the title suggests, it may have been collected in an area where the KaLLar community is important, near Madurai. The history of the epic in this area to the south of Koṅku is not clear. I have done a considerable amount of work on this story and hope to publish a translation and analysis of it separately.

[37]In Salem District, north of Salem town, I found that the story was known only by immigrants from the Koṅku area. In Madurai District, I found no one who knew it south of the Dindigul gap. Although my inquiries were hurried they were enough to indicate a contrast with Koṅku, where the story is widely known.

[38]It may be noted that this pattern of telescoping the past into a four-generation depth is also used as a framework for remembering the history of land-holding in a single village. (See chapter 4, pp. 186–88.)

which is the residential area of the reigning king; and 5) VēTTuva nāTu, the region belonging to the enemy.[39] This geography fits with the general importance that nāTu divisions appear to have had in the traditional social and political organization of the Koṅku region.

More interesting still in terms of the general theme of this work, is the fact that the story concentrates so thoroughly on the history of a single VēLāLar KavuNTar family. It is their right to the land that is vindicated, and their struggles against rivals and enemies that are described. Other names come into the epic only briefly. While all the right division groups that serve the KavuNTar community are mentioned at one point or another, only two left division groups are referred to at all, the VēTTuvar (now VēTTuvar KavuNTars) and the Ācāri, or artisans. In both cases these groups are treated as treacherous and deceitful and as best avoided, or defeated in the case of the VēTTuvar, if it comes to a battle.[40] Although rivalries between brothers and between lineages within the VēLāLar KavuNTar group take up much of the story, the larger right-left opposition is always present in the background. It is a social fact, taken for granted and providing the scenery against which a specific story of land settlement can be played.

One final point, also connecting the story to the theme of this work, concerns the way in which the tale is presently retold. The people who take the greatest interest in this epic in Koṅku are not KavuNTars, as one would expect. They are drawn, rather, from the two other high-ranking right-division groups which do not directly serve the KavuNTar community, namely the Koṅku CeTTiyārs and Maramēri NāTārs. The first group regularly re-enacts some of the scenes of the brothers' story at its clan festival each year. The re-enactment is quite dramatic and several of the actors involved are "killed" annually during a mock battle. They are

---

[39]For an explanation of kinship terms such as *paṅkāLi, māmaṉ,* and *maccāṉ,* see Appendix F.

[40]Notice that this VēTTuvar group has now added the term "KavuNTar" to their earlier name in order to increase their prestige. As they possess rights to land, they feel that they are entitled to use it. Yet they are still considered to be members of the left division. Cases such as this one, where a single caste contains some subgroups belonging to each of the two over-arching divisions, lend strength to the argument presented earlier: this right-left opposition appears to have been rooted in rivalry stemming from the fact that land ownership and the social status accompanying it were originally an exclusive domain. As just described, much of *The Story of the Brothers* consists of accounts of how the right-division KavuNTar community fought to defend its territorial monopoly against the encroachments of other groups, many of whom belonged to the left division. Excluded from membership in the right division because they were considered rivals for land, as in the case of the VēTTuvar KavuNTars, or completely denied rights to land, left-division groups developed a parallel prestige structure within their own division. One might even think of the larger right-left bifurcation as a social blue print, writ large, of the factional struggles that develop between lineage brothers in local settlements and expand until they polarize an entire hamlet (see chapter 4).

returned to life at the end of the pageant, by the correct chanting of certain magical passages taken from the story itself.[41]

The second group, the NāTār, makes a great deal of the two brothers in clan and subcaste temples: it is very common to see images made of baked clay representing characters from *The Story of the Brothers* in local NāTār shrines.[42] Images of these characters can also be found in KavuN-Tar temples, but it is not common. Rather, KavuNTars commonly participate in the tradition surrounding the story by hiring someone to sing it. If too poor to pay for a performance themselves, they will join the audience eagerly when it is being sung at the request of some wealthier caste member. Singing the story all the way through is a ritual in itself, and provides an opportunity to make offerings to various deities—but never to the heroes of the story, directly—at the beginning and end of the performance. KavuNTars who pay for the singer and for these oblations obtain a certain status and religious merit by doing so.

The epic, itself, is extremely long. It requires about thirty-six hours or about fourteen nights to sing in full; it is always performed by a specialist who has studied the work with another singer for many years. These singers are generally barbers, but I have heard of members of other castes, usually groups that traditionally serve the KavuNTar community, learning to sing the story.[43] Thus the main communities involved in performing this epic, in worshipping its main heroes, and/or in simply commissioning it, are members of the right division. Left-division groups are much less affected by the story, and indeed most of them do not know the details of it well. As is the case with other parts of this body of folk history, the KavuNTars are participants in the prime events; it is only natural that their allies and dependents should be the ones to celebrate them most extensively.

No similar epic story exists involving the left-division castes. However, there is an interesting body of myths concerning the three highest-ranking communities in this bloc. Interestingly, they repeatedly stress the connection of these groups with the two neutral groups, the PiLLai and the

[41]I have actually seen this festival at TāyampāLaiyam, some miles southwest of Kāṅkayam. I do not know whether members of the Koṅku CeTTiyār group elsewhere in Koṅku perform the same rituals or celebrate the same festival.

[42]This identification of the NāTār with VēLāLar mythology can also be seen further south (in Tirunelveli), though the story here is somewhat different. Compare Robert Hardgrave, *The Nadars of Tamilnad* (Berkeley: University of California Press, 1969), pp. 19–20, with Thurston, *Castes and Tribes*, 7:362–63. ("Nadar" is the traditional English spelling, but in the present work the name has been transliterated from its Tamil spelling according to the system described in Appendix C, and thus is given as "NāTār" throughout.)

[43]Local priests (PaNTāram) and washermen (VaNNār) are the other two castes I encountered. I also met one member of a left-division community (a VēTar, or story-teller), who had learned to sing the story. However, he was a professional singer and this was simply one addition to a very large repertoire.

Brahmans. These myths are not celebrated by bards and indeed are not widely known among the local populace. They are, however, recorded on palm-leaf manuscripts and carefully preserved in a place where they can be referred to by leading members of the community.

In my fieldwork I managed to uncover only one such story, but there are many similar ones recorded by Thurston and others. The account I found belonged to the local KarNam's family. It was recorded on palm leaves and stored in the rafters of a relative's home. In fact, however, the story makes only a brief mention of the PiLLai themselves. The significance of this fact will be explained later. The manuscript begins with a long history of the gods and demons of another epoch. It is only in the second half of this work that the events condensed here are described. They are as follows:

> In KāvērippūmpaTTiNam there lived a NavakōTi CeTTiyār. He was a very wealthy merchant and had sixty thousand people working in his shops. One day someone dared to insult him by saying that, despite his wealth, he was really nothing but an orange seller. At this the CeTTiyār grew very angry and closed all his shops. Then the people could no longer buy spices and other necessary condiments. They suffered and complained to the king. The king approached the CeTTiyār and encouraged him to reopen his shops. Finally the rich merchant agreed on the condition that the king humble himself by dressing and dancing like a woman at an important festival. The king did this. Then the CeTTiyār reopened his shops and for a while the two were outwardly friends again. However, the king nursed a grudge and one day he told the CeTTiyār that he had had a dream in which the goddess PattirakāLi had appeared and demanded that the CeTTiyār give a feast for her.[44] Learning this, the sixty thousand CeTTiyārs got together and decided to give a feast inside the king's fort. They called the Brahman school teacher and asked him to bring all CeTTiyār children to the festivities. While the festival was in progress, however, the king sent his army to the fort and tried to kill everyone within it. Many died but the teacher and the children managed to escape through an opening at the back of the fort which issued onto the river Kāvēri. In order to escape they wrote a magical verse on a palm leaf which read:

>> The river Ganges never overflowed
>> A virgin (young girl) can never be destroyed
>> So to cross the Kāvēri
>> You, Krishna [KirusNa], show us the way.

> Then they laid this palm leaf on the swollen waters of the river, which magically parted to permit the children and their teacher to walk across. The army followed them as far as the river bank, but there gave up, realizing that this Brahman and his five-hundred pupils could not be destroyed.

[44]PattirakāLi is the local form of the great goddess KāLi, said to be the terrifying form of Civā's consort Pārvati.

The teacher and children then made their way to the palace of the famous PaTTakkārar at ParaiyakōTTai (ten miles north of Ōlappā-Laiyam) where they told the great KavuNTar family their story.[45] The PaTTakkārar then ordered that one boy be fed in each house which fell under his control. Later, after some years, the question of the marriage of these boys arose. To solve this problem the Brahman school teacher thought of a trick. He bought five-hundred silk bags, filled them with stones and placed them by the river, telling people that this was the wealth that the children had brought with them from KāvērippūmpaTTiNam. The people believed him and brought forth their KavuNTar daughters with offers of marriage. The ceremony took place and all the boys were married in one day. During the rituals the goddess PattirakāLi magically turned the stones in the little bags to gold. The young newly-weds, however, agreed to take only half of this inheritance themselves. The rest they decided to give to the Brahman teacher for his help. The teacher, however, declined the gift. Instead he gave the gold to the accountant (KaNakku PiLLai) who worked for the PaTTakkārar, on the condition that this money should be kept by him and used to finance the weddings of the children of the present couples. The KaNakku PiLLai wrote an agreement to this effect and all four PaTTakkārar of the region signed it. As a result, whenever a male descendant of these CeTTiyār–KavuN-Tar couples is married the KaNakku PiLLai is obliged to give them, as a gift, one measure of rice, one-eighth of a rupee, and a wedding necklace. These descendants call themselves the "five-hundred" CeTTiyār.

It is not hard to see that this story is really about the Koṅku CeTTiyār and how they managed to escape persecution by a king and become allied with the KavuNTar leaders of the right division. In the story the Brahman school teacher and the KaNakku PiLLai are essentially neutral figures. Their presence, however, is significant, in that it associates them with this kind of adventure. Furthermore, they are sympathetic to the persecuted CeTTiyārs and they try where possible to help them. The KaNakku PiLLai group owns the manuscript and strongly identifies with it. The parallel with stories that have been collected by Thurston from actual left-division groups should soon be clear.

Thurston has recorded some very interesting tales about various high-ranking communities of the left bloc. The three groups which he writes about—the non-Koṅku CeTTiyār, the Mutaliyār and the Ācāri—all appear to be mythologically connected, though he does not remark on this association. As in the account just given, all of these stories refer to a beseiged fort, a flood, some escapes, and, finally, a mixed marriage. Here

---

[45] *PaTTakkārar* is a hereditary title awarded to an individual by a king for military service, or for some virtuous deed or act of bravery. The PaTTakkārar referred to here would have been a member of one of the four titled families that controlled large areas of land in Koṅku NāTu and that were in positions of authority over the region as a whole. These families are described in detail in the next section in this chapter.

is one example, which highlights the Ācāri (Kammālan) community in this triad of events.

> In the town of Māndāpuri, the Kammālans of the five divisions formerly lived closely united together. They were employed by all sorts of people, as there were no other artificers in the country, and charged very high rates for their wares. They feared and respected no king. This offended the kings of the country, who combined against them. As the fort in which the Kammālans concealed themselves, called Kāntakkōttai, was entirely constructed of loadstone, all the weapons were drawn away by it. The king then promised a big reward to anyone who would burn down the fort, and at length the Dēvadāsīs [*sic*] (courtesans) of a temple undertook to do this, and took betel and nut in signification of their promise. The king built a fort for them opposite Kāntakkōttai, and they attracted the Kammālans by their singing, and had children by them. One of the Dēva-dāsīs at length succeeded in extracting from a young Kammālan the secret that, if the fort was surrounded with varaghu straw and set on fire, it would be destroyed. The king ordered that this should be done, and, in attempting to escape from the sudden conflagration, some of the Kammālans lost their lives. Others reached the ships, escaped by sea, or were captured and put to death. In consequence of this, artificers ceased to exist in the country. One pregnant Kammālan woman, however, took refuge in the house of a Beri Chetti, and escaped decapitation by being passed off as his daughter. The country was sorely troubled owing to the want of artificers; and agriculture, manufacturers and weaving suffered a great deal. One of the kings wanted to know if any Kammālan escaped the general destruction, and sent round his kingdom a piece of coral possessing a tortuous aperture running through it, and a piece of thread. A big reward was promised to anyone who could succeed in passing the thread through the coral. At last, the boy born of the Kammālan woman in the Chetti's house undertook to do it. He placed the coral over the mouth of an ant-hole, and having steeped the thread in sugar, laid it down at some distance from the hole. The ants took the thread, and drew it through the coral. The king, being pleased with the boy, sent him presents, and gave him more work to do. This he performed with the assistance of his mother, and satisfied the king. . . . The king provided him with the means for making ploughshares on a large scale, and got him married to the daughter of a Chetti, and made gifts of land for the maintenance of the couple. The Chetti woman bore him five sons, who followed the five branches of work now carried out by the Kammālan caste.[46]

Thurston's story gives an account of the origin of the Ācāri (Kammālan) community. His version mentions the anger and persecution of a king,

---

[46]Thurston, *Castes and Tribes,* 3:113–15. See also 3:315–17, 1:215–17, 2:93–94.

the fleeing of a few members, and the irregular union of one of them with a Chetti (CeTTiyār). The offspring of this mixed marriage became the founders of a new line of Ācāris. The Dēva-dāsīs, a subgroup of Mutali-yār, are also mentioned briefly in the role of seductresses. In another account of what is clearly the same story, which was published recently by a local poet of the Koṅku area, the CeTTiyār are prominent. Again there is a king in the role of persecutor, a few members flee, and, in the end, they enjoy an irregular union with a Mutaliyār woman. This time it is the CeTTiyār-Mutaliyār offspring who become the founders of a new CeT-Tiyār group. In a condensed translation, this final example follows:

> The PanniraNTān CeTTiyār (twelve-shares CeTTiyār) used to live in KāvērippūmpaTTiNam. However, they fled at the time of a great flood to Alakāpuri where a king asked for one of their girls in marriage. The CeTTiyārs refused this offer on the basis of caste. The king wanted to take revenge. However, the CeTTiyārs came to know of his anger and fled. Some of them escaped and one small boy went to a Kaikkōlar Mutaliyār house for refuge. The Mutaliyār protected him and he eventually married there and had eleven children. Later he wanted to divide his property, but it was awkward trying to divide it into eleven shares. Thus he went to a Civāyamalai and asked an elderly man there what to do. The man answered that he should divide the property into twelve shares. When the CeTTiyār did this the old man disappeared with the twelfth share. From a distance he called out that he was an orphan and deserved this much. Now he is worshipped as a god of this group, and one-twelfth of the income of these people is, by tradition, laid aside for him.[47]

These folktales indicate that a body of stories exists explaining the history of all the higher-ranking communities of the left division. Furthermore, this body of material appears to reiterate a small group of common themes, no matter where in the South it has been collected. Each account describes a tradition of reciprocal aid and sympathy existing between members of these communities. In addition, each story mentions an angry king (a leader of the right?) who time and again tries to destroy a particular left-division group. In every instance a few members of the persecuted community manage to evade the ogre. Their escape is associated with a flood or with the crossing of a swollen river.[48] Those who make it to the other side are forced to intermarry with another community and thus to start a new descent line. One group, the Koṅku CeTTiyār, even manages to ally itself with the right. Finally, the offspring of these irregular unions

---

[47]PaRaniccāmi Pulavar, *Koṅku Celvi*, pp. 150–52 (my translation). For an account of another CeTTiyār group which shows a certain resemblance to this one, see Thurston, *Castes and Tribes*, 5:258–62.

[48]However, no particular association with the deities of rivers or riverine basins is suggested.

manage to re-establish themselves on the basis of their skill in business or in one of the crafts.

The contrasts that exist between this all-South India mythology concerning high-ranking left-division members and the lengthy epic associated with the right-division KavuNTars and their dependents, are striking. The former stories make numerous references to classical mythology (see, in particular, the KaNakku PiLLai example).[49] And they refer almost exclusively to famous traditional urban centers such as KāvērippūmpaT-TiNam. The right-caste material, by contrast, has the character of a great folk epic. It is expressly tied to a local area and is oral with few references to literary sources. Furthermore, the right division has only one major story.[50] This is heavily focused on events within the KavuNTar community. The left bloc's mythology is more diffuse and a different version exists for each of the groups involved.[51] The folk history of the right- and left-division communities thus exhibits striking differences; as we shall see, these contrasts clearly parallel differences in their social organization to be described in later chapters.

TITLED FAMILIES OF KOṄKU

Another element, besides the sacred geography, serving to unite the Koṅku region are the four titled families or *PaTTakkārar*. These families are identified with the NāTu as a whole and their names frequently appear in local stories. In the past each of these families controlled large areas of land. They were considered to be the final court of appeal in cases of serious dispute and were in a position to demand military service from local residents in times of war. The four were clearly rivals for local influence, but in the folklore there is little mention of overt hostilities among them. Instead these leading families appear to have intermarried and to have formed a sort of minor aristocracy in the area.

All four titled families belong to the KavuNTar community. Their titles (*paTTam*) were granted directly from kings.[52] Politically they were considered to stand above the twenty-four nāTu divisions which will be discussed in the next chapter. All four families live in the central part of the

---

[49]There are also many such references in Thurston's accounts. I have edited them out for the sake of brevity.

[50]There are also many smaller stories dealing with the history of individual clans. These stories are much more numerous in the case of KavuNTar descent groups, than they are for the service communities of this division. They will be described in detail in chapter 2.

[51]The Nāyakkar, the VēTar, and the Mātāri, three low-ranking groups in the left division, do not share in this general all-South India mythology to the same extent. However, these communities do preserve an oral tradition about their ties to a particular region. The details will be taken up later.

[52]These overlords of very large areas such as the Vijayanagar empire are locally referred to as *rājās*. Most of these kings were based outside the Koṅku area and little information about them is provided by the folklore.

Koṅku area.[53] Three of them trace their descent from about the twelfth or thirteenth century, while the fourth family, that living at CaṅkaraNTāmpāLaiyam, claims a title awarded to it by the Vijayanagar kings in about the sixteenth century.[54]

Each family claims to have received its title as a reward for some special military service, or other distinguishing feats of prowess. Some details of their individual histories follow:

a) PaRaiyakōTTai PaTTakkārar (Payira clan) Family tradition traces their genealogy back to the 13th century. At about this time one of their ancestors in the male line is said to have been a general under JaTāvaramaṉ Cuntara PāNTiya. He distinguished himself in battle and was given land and the title Nalla Cēṉāpati Cakkarai Maṉrā-Tiyār as a reward.[55] The present family claims to be the thirtieth generation of descendants from this man.

b) KāTaiyūr PaTTakkārar (PoruLantai clan) Local poets and priests say that long ago the village where this family now lives was inhabited by men of the CēTa clan. A CēTa man, one day, begot an albino daughter. As the years passed by he found great difficulty in persuading an appropriate suitor to marry the girl. Finally a very poor man of the PoruLantai clan came forward and promised to marry her in return for a gift of land. The father, in desperation, made the promise. After the marriage, however, the brothers of the girl tried to prevent the transfer of land to her husband. A contest of strength was held and the man of the PoruLantai clan won. Later the victor's wife gave birth to two sons. One of them succeeded in capturing and controlling an elephant which had gone amuk. The reigning PāNTiya king was pleased with his prowess and awarded this man the title of PaTTakkārar.[56]

c) Putūr PaTTakkārar (CeṅkaNNaṉ clan) According to local tradition, a CōRa king was once at war with a Pallava king when a man of the CeṅkaNNaṉ clan came to the former's aid. When the CōRa king won he was grateful for the help he had received in his campaigns. The king thus rewarded the CeṅkaNNaṉ with the title of Pallavarāi-yaṉ PaTTakkārar and a generous stretch of land near the town of Kāṅkayam. Another story says that a man of this clan was awarded this title by a CōRa king named Pallava CōRaṉ. In this version, the rājā is said to have been pleased by the sight of the man's young son giving away a toy chariot made of gold to the poor.[57]

---

[53]This was one of the earliest areas of Koṅku to come under the plow and it has always retained its importance as a locus of regional political power.

[54]Two of these families, those living at Putūr and at KāTaiyūr, are now declining in terms of wealth and influence, while the descendants of the family in CaṅkaraNTāmpāLaiyam retain a position of some importance. The well-known family at PaRaiyakōTTai are, however, by far the most powerful of the four families at the present day.

[55]Cinnucāmi KavuNTar, *Koṅku VēLāLar*, pp. 326–28. Also in a personal communication from Informant no. 7.

[56]Ibid., pp. 181–82; and Informants nos. 7 and 35.

[57]Ibid., p. 328; and Informant no. 22.

d) CaṅkaraNTāmpāLaiyam PaTTakkārar (Periya clan) One version of the story about this family claims that a male ancestor named VēNāTaṉ was a general under a CōRa ruler named Karikāla. In this position he helped defeat a PāNTiya king. It is said that he was awarded the title of PaTTakkārar for his heroism in this battle. Another version argues that the title was obtained much later, during the Vijayanagar period as a reward for having sacrificed his only son to a goddess riding in a temple chariot during an important festival.[58]

These stories show that the people of the region believe the titles of their PaTTakkārar to be very old. They also demonstrate in detail techniques of intertwining local history with the campaigns of the great kings.

These paTTams are inherited in the male line. The general meaning of the term is something like the following: "to hold a title, or to have special power."[59] It suggests that its bearer has special rights in some local area. The term *PaTTakkārar* can perhaps be compared with the Gujarati word *Patidar,* originally a special title implying the right to pay tax directly to a king.[60] A similar parallel can be drawn between the four PaTTakkārar and the four *Tēvar* ("chiefs") of Pramalai Nad—located further south—which Dumont has described.[61] Thus the position of local titled families is clearly not unique to the Koṅku region.

The PaTTakkārar families serve as a modern illustration of the working of traditional economic ties in the Koṅku area.[62] These men, with their rights over large areas of land, were in contact with and able to utilize the services of the full range of castes. They are examples of the average landed family "writ large." It is expensive to maintain a full panoply of ritual servants, and these families have been able to continue to the present the traditional economic and ritual relationships which small landlords have long since been forced to relinquish.

The PaRaiyakōTTai PaTTakkārar may, indeed, be the only one of the four titled families which is able to continue operating with these traditional service agreements at the present time. These arrangements are not only expensive and cumbersome for the landowner, but also a source of friction with laborers, who demand more cash and more independence than in previous eras. It is my impression that both the PaTTakkārar's

---

[58]Government of Madras, *Madras District Gazetteers, Coimbatore,* pp. 589–90, and Cinnucāmi KavuNTar, *Koṅku VēLāLar,* pp. 324–25.

[59]The term is probably derived from the Sanskrit *patta,* meaning "frontlet, tiara, or diadem." See M. B. Emeneau and T. Burrow, *Dravidian Borrowings from Indo-Aryan* (Berkeley: University of California Press, 1962), p. 47.

[60]For supporting information on this possible parallel, see David F. Pocock, "The Movement of Castes," *Man* 55, Article no. 79 (1955): 71–72. The term has more recently been adopted as a title of the entire caste from which the privileged few were drawn.

[61]Louis Dumont, *Une Sous-Caste de l'Inde du Sud* (Paris: Mouton, 1957), pp. 142–44, 150.

[62]How far these traditional ties go back is not clear, but local folklore suggests that the rights and obligations defined by current PaTTakkārar practice have existed for several hundred years at least.

family and local residents are presently ambivalent in their attitude toward these traditional ties. Both would like to enjoy the security and the rights which were part of the older labor system, but both find the obligations rather onerous under present conditions.[63] Table 1.2 sets out these traditional interdependencies in some detail, as they exist in this specific case. It outlines in detail in relation to right, left and neutral subcastes, the services due to and rights claimed by the PaRaiyakōTTai PaTTakkārar. This family currently enjoys a position of hegemony over three kirāmams, or traditional revenue units.

It is clear that this system of allocation and exchange involves multiple rights. A man's duties are determined partly by the kind of service he renders and partly by the general status of his subcaste in the social hierarchy. This same association of features could also be stated the other way around; that is, the more onerous the service the lower the social status, the fewer the rights and the smaller the remuneration a man is able to claim. More important, however, for the general argument to be developed in later chapters is the contrast that is evident in the kind of rights in the production effort allocated to castes of the right and left divisions. From Table 1.2 it can be seen that the members of the right bloc are the only ones who enjoy specific claims to land, or who are tied by bonds of ritual service to those who do enjoy this privilege. Other communities—those who belong to the left division—do not have specific territorial ties, nor do they bear service obligations to leading families of the region.

Table 1.2 provides the details on these traditional economic relations. Brahmans and PiLLais—considered neutral in the division—are listed first. Second are the right subcastes in rough order of their social precedence. Following them the left subcastes are listed in similar fashion. It will be quickly noted that none of the higher-ranking communities of the left have rights to land or obligations of service to the PaTTakkārar's family. Only the lowest two groups of the left—the untouchable Mātāri and the Kuṟavar—are mentioned as having any specific rights and duties relative to the PaTTakkārar. Of these only the very lowest, the Kuṟavar, provide field labor on a daily basis. As I have indicated earlier, economic differentiation between the right and left blocs has traditionally been minimal among castes in the untouchable category—the Kuṟavar, Paṟaiyar, and Mātāri. Sentiment concerning divisional affiliation used to run high in such groups, but which subcastes actually held rights to a share in the annual harvest varied greatly from landowner to landowner, depending on custom in a given local area.

[63]For two excellent discussions of the economic implications of this kind of traditional labor system, see T. Scarlett Epstein, "Productive Efficiency and Customary Systems of Rewards in Rural South India," in Raymond Firth, ed., *Themes in Economic Anthropology* (London: Tavistock, 1967), pp. 229–52, and also Walter C. Neale, "Land is to Rule," in Frykenberg, ed., *Land Control and Social Structure,* pp. 3–15.

TABLE 1.2

TRADITIONAL RIGHTS AND SERVICES OF THE VARIOUS SUBCASTES VIS-À-VIS THE PAṬṬAKKĀRAR'S FAMILY AT PARAIYAKŌṬṬAI, 1966

Subcaste Name	General Occupation	Special Rights in the Kirāmam	Services due to PaTTakkārar Personally without Direct Remuneration	Indirect Remuneration from PaTTakkārar
Neutral Division:				
Aiyar Brahman	Astrologers and temple priests.	Rights to proceeds at Civā and VisNu temples and to tax-free land.	No special obligation. Would come when called.	None.
KaNakku PiLLai[1]	Accountants and Record Keepers.	Rights to tax-free land.	No special obligation. Would come when called.	None.
Right Division:				
Koṅku KavuNTar	Farmers.	Tenants on large tracts of land and rights to harvest therefrom.	Free field labor supplied, by family, in proportion to land occupied; or equivalent rent in cash or kind.	
			One adult man from each household to help PaTTakkārar with harvest during peak periods.	One noon meal per day supplied to men helping with harvest.
			Rights ceded to PaTTakkārar over any young bull calves born during the year (not now operative). The PaTTakkārar apparently selected only a portion of these for his own use and may also have made some reciprocal payment.	

OkaccāNTi PaNTāram	Priests at local temples. Also cooks, suppliers of eating leaves and makers of flower garlands.	Rights to festival proceeds at many local temples.	Two men a day (one from each temple group) to supply 60 eating leaves for PaTTakkārar's family. Also expected to heat water for bathing and to help with cooking. On call for other household tasks as well.	96 measures of grain a year given to the men of each of the two temple groups.
Koṅku UTaiyār	Potters. Also skilled in finer points of building construction.	Rights to supply potters' services to the inhabitants of the area and to reimbursement for these services. Also rights at temple and life-cycle ceremonies where similar services are required.	Obligation to supply all earthen pots required by the PaTTakkārar's family and also to supply skilled labor for plastering and building when needed.	96 measures of grain a year.
Maramēri NaTār	Tappers of the palmyra palm. Also skilled field laborers.	Rights to tap the palmyra palm trees and to distill sugar and toddy from the sap.	One adult man from each household to supply field labor for PaTTakkārar during the six months of the year when tree tapping is not done.	One noon meal supplied to each man while he is supplying field help.
Koṅku VaNNār[2]	Washermen.	Rights to wash the clothes of people in the area. Also rights at temple and life-cycle ceremonies.	One man a day to wash the clothes of the PaTTakkārar's family and the men providing services for him.	One noon meal supplied to man providing services. Also 96 measures of grain a year.
Koṅku Nāvitar	Barbers and country physicians.	Rights to shave and to practice the arts of curing and of spirit exorcism in the area for remuneration. Also rights at temple and life-cycle ceremonies where their services are required.	One man a day to shave the PaTTakkārar and his family. Also required to sweep and perform other menial household tasks.	One noon meal supplied to man providing services. Also 96 measures of grain a year.

TABLE 1.2 *Concluded*

Subcaste Name	General Occupation	Special Rights in the Kirāmam	Services due to PaTTakkārar Personally without Direct Remuneration	Indirect Remuneration from PaTTakkārar
Koṅku Paṟaiyar	Drummer and watch-man. Also errand boy.	Rights to drum at local kirāmam festivals and at Koṅku KavuNTar life-cycle ceremonies.	One man a day to serve as watchman.	One noon meal supplied to man providing services. Also 96 measures of grain a year.
Left Division:				
CōLi Ācāri	Artisans in precious metals, brass, iron, wood, and stone.	No particular rights.	No special obligation. Would come if called.	None.
KōmuTTi CeTTiyār[3]	Merchants.	No particular rights.	No special obligation. Would come when called.	None.
Kaikkōlar Mutaliyār[4]	Weavers.	No particular rights (temple dancers and musicians excepted).	No special obligation. Would come when called.	None.
VaTuka Nāyakkar	Well-diggers and builders.	No particular rights.	No special obligation. Would come if called.	None.
KūTai Kuṟavar	Watchmen, basket-makers, and fortune tellers.	Rights to act as guards for the kirāmam, to tell fortunes, and to supply woven baskets for remuneration.	One man (or more) each day to act as general messenger and as errand boy. Also required to guard the PaTTakkārar's house at night.	100 measures of grain a year.
Moracu Mātāri	Leatherworkers and field laborers.	Rights to carry off dead cattle and to provide leather for people of the kirāmam for remuneration.	One man from each household required, on call, to do fieldwork for the PaTTakkārar.	One noon meal supplied to men working on any particular day.

NOTES: The information in this table was supplied by an OkaccāNTi PaNTāram priest (Informant no. 20) who lives in one of the three kirāmams dominated by the PaTTakkarar at PaRaiyakōTTai and who, himself, is obliged to perform several days of service in the year, as part of a rotating arrangement within his own caste.

[1]In this instance KaNakku PiLLai is an occupational title only. The family is Kaikkolar Mutaliyār by subcaste. (See note 4.)

[2]The Koṅku VaNNār described here are members of the right division of the washerman community. Elsewhere in this book a left-division subcaste of VaNNār is described. This happened to be the traditional affiliation of the washerman families resident in OlappaLaiyam at the time of my stay. A right-division washerman group had lived there and served the Koṅku KavuNTar community until a few years previously. In its absence, however, the present left-division group moved in. These newcomers now serve both the right and the left castes in OlappaLaiyam for lack of a competitor, but previously, when ritual rules were followed more strictly, they would have only served those of the left. Similarly, the Koṅku VaNNār described in the table should, technically, serve only castes of the right in the PaRaiyakōTTai area.

[3]The CeTTiyār, like the Mutaliyār, were traditionally divided into right and left subgroups. The only community classified as right by my informants was that of the Koṅku CeTTiyār, none of whom lives in the PaRaiyakōTTai area.

[4]The Mutaliyār are a very large and diverse group. Besides being warriors (traditionally) and weavers (more recently), some subcastes perform important temple services. One affiliated group used to supply the Dēva-dāsis, or female temple dancers, and their male counterparts, the dancing masters and temple musicians. The latter profession persists, but the former was outlawed under the British because of the association with prostitution. Both right and left castes required the services of these groups at temple festivals and weddings. In some areas, but not in Koṅku, they seem to have been split into right and left subcastes to accommodate this demand. See Edgar Thurston, *Castes and Tribes of Southern India*, 7 vols. (Madras: Government Press, 1909), 7:128. In Coimbatore my informants classified all Mutaliyārs as left. Therefore I have represented them this way with the exception of one KaNakku PiLLai family which, because of its occupation, is defined as neutral (see note 1). For lack of a rival group, the Mutaliyār temple musicians do perform at wedding ceremonies of the right castes, at least at the present day. They also perform at the Māriyamman festival (see chapter 3), although they have no specific rights there and are dispensable in a crisis. I do not know in detail about the Pulavar or bard subcaste of Mutaliyārs; but there is no right-left distinction made among them at present. Thurston mentions the Coimbatore Pulavar group briefly in Thurston, *Castes and Tribes*, 6:235.

It is also important to notice the difference in type of payment received by members of the two divisions. In the case of the right subcastes these payments are fixed by tradition and are generally received in bulk at the time of the annual harvest. For the left subcastes, by contrast, payments are more flexible in amount and are paid on completion of the job. In the example, the six right subcastes fall under the former arrangement. Three of them, the Nāvitar (barber), the VaNNār (washerman), and the Paṟai-yar (drummer, watchman) send one man a day to the PaTTakkārar's house. These men provide their traditional skills when required, and other-wise act as handymen and as errand boys. Each of these groups is com-pensated by ninety-six measures of grain at the harvest, and by gifts of cloth (and sometimes staple food) at life-cycle ceremonies, whenever these should be performed by the PaTTakkārar's family. Only two groups have rights to work the land and/or to reap its produce directly. One of these is the KavuNTar community, the PaTTakārar's own community; the other the NāTār or palmyra-palm climbers. Both KavuNTars and NāTārs, however, are obliged to pay the PaTTakkārar a rent.[64] This may be paid in money, in labor, or in kind, in exchange for the right to direct cultiva-tion. KavuNTars obtain rights to the soil in this way, while NāTārs obtain rights to the sap, fruit, and leaves of palm trees by the same arrangement.

The responsibility of providing a man for the PaTTakkārar rotates among households within each of these communities and at the end of the year ninety-six measures of grain are divided by the local headman into household shares proportionate to the labor supplied.[65] The fourth group (PaNTāram or local priest, flower-tier, and leaf-plate supplier) supplies two men to the PaTTakkārar's household each day. One serves at the Māriyamman̲ temple—Māriyamman̲ is goddess of the kirāmam or reve-nue village and thus protectress of the local territory. The other serves at the temple dedicated to the patron deity of the PaTTakkārar's own clan. The PaNTāram are divided internally to match this division in services performed. Some households hold rights at one temple and some at the other. In this case each division is separately compensated by ninety-six measures of grain per year. In addition, members of each of these four groups are also compensated in smaller measures by KavuNTar tenant families and by other landowners in the area who make a similar use of

---

[64]In addition, the PaTTakkārar used to enjoy a right to receive from each household one bull calf born during the year. This right may be related to a very old custom of taxing cattle, probably as a compensation for grazing rights. There is a reference to such a tax in T. V. Mahalingam, *South Indian Polity* (Madras: Madras University Historical Series, 1955), p. 189. Of course, now—and in theory for some one hundred and fifty years since the earliest British Land Settlement in the area—anyone may own land outright. Those who have recently managed to obtain title to land are no longer obliged to pay rent to the PaTTakkārar's family.

[65]For details of how the inheritance of these kinds of rights evolve on individual families, see Appendix G.

their services. The total income of each of these subcastes is thus considerably greater than that shown by the one example in Table 1.2, taken singly.

If Table 1.2 can be interpreted as indicative of a system of land rights which was much more widely practiced in the past, then it would appear that the left communities do not have now, and probably never have had, the same degree of attachment to land and to landed families as did members of the right. This economic difference between the divisions can be seen most readily in the case of the high-ranking groups. At the bottom of the hierarchy the subcastes of the two divisions tend to converge in their economic arrangements, since they are alike in their dependence on the powerful landowners for employment. This economic convergence among the lower-ranking groups, furthermore, is clearly paralleled by a convergence in the social organization of these communities. A wide range of examples of this convergence will be discussed in later chapters.

CLIMATE, THE AGRICULTURAL CYCLE, AND FESTIVAL CALENDARS

Koṅku has repeatedly experienced famine because of lack of rain. Precipitation throughout the area is scanty and extremely irregular. Indeed, rainfall in Koṅku is less predictable than anywhere else in Madras. Annual precipitation often varies by as much as 35 per cent.[66] Furthermore, rainfall is not spread evenly throughout the year but comes rather in two peak periods. The first is in the form of thunder showers during the hot season; and the second is in the form of heavy rain during the northeast monsoon, and in years of high precipitation there are floods. The southeast monsoon, which falls between these periods, brings showers to some areas but only high winds to others.

This pattern of rainfall, in addition to variations in temperature, divides the year into four seasons for local residents. The first is the *veyyil kālam,* the hot or "sunny" season, lasting from the second half of February to the end of June. The second is the *Kārru kālam,* the windy season of July and August. The third is the *maRai kālam,* the rainy reason of September through November. And the fourth is the *paṇi kālam,* the "cold" season, which starts with December and lasts through the first half of February. None of these seasons begins or ends on a particular date. They are simply means of characterizing local climatic variations.

The rainfall pattern and the infrequency of rain are particularly important in Koṅku because of the kinds of soil found in this area. The land of

[66]Government of Madras, *Madras District Gazetteers, Coimbatore,* p. 16. Figures for average rainfall in such a situation are bound to be misleading. Nonetheless, a general figure for Coimbatore District—only 23.23 inches—will serve to illustrate that the mean over a number of years is always small. Contrast this with the Coromandel Coast area which has an average of forty to fifty inches a year. Republic of India, *Atlas of Madras State,* map 7.

Coimbatore District is "rather sandy, stony, and of the gravelly type."[67] More than 67.6 per cent of the soil of the Koṅku region contains a trace of iron and is reddish in color.[68] This type of soil is sandy, and, as a result, when it rains, the ground does not hold the moisture well. Rain water quickly drains through to an undulating rocky substratum, but can be collected in deep wells. Much of the agricultural wealth of the region consists of these wells and the garden patches that surround them. The value of land, therefore, is generally established by its proximity to a good supply of water for irrigation. Because of these geographic factors, planting and harvesting times are closely tied to the rainfall pattern and to the type of land under cultivation.

The best land in Koṅku is classified as *vayal,* well-watered and highly fertile. Vayal can be found only along river and canal banks and in places where the government has constructed large irrigation works. Such land is largely used for rice cultivation and for sugar cane. It is highly valued, and the owner of even an acre or two is assured a dependable income and a modicum of social status. Second best is *tōTTam* or garden land irrigated by a good, deep well. On this land, too, it is possible to grow rice, but cotton, tobacco, vegetables, and pulses are better suited to it and are generally preferred. Some of the wealthier families in each important settlement own tōTTam land. The majority of the fields are classified as *kāTu.* Of the three types of land described here, kāTu is the most dependent on the rainfall, as it alone lacks any means of irrigation. KāTu fields are sown at the first sign of heavy rain in the hope that the resulting moisture will remain long enough for a crop to mature. On this land are grown the hardy pulses and grains that are closely associated with various traditional agricultural rituals. Generally only one crop a year can be grown, although in good years a second crop may be reaped as well. Between growing seasons, the kāTu is left fallow and used for grazing. TōTTam and kāTu lands, therefore, are cultivated at slightly different times. Figure 1.4, which appears later on in this section, illustrates how the agricultural cycle, the planting and harvesting times for these lands; the crops yielded by them; the seasonal cycle; the rainfall pattern; and the times for holding certain festivals are all connected.

Three important staple cereals are grown in the Koṅku area: *kampu, cōLam,* and *rāki.* Of these three, kampu and cōLam can be grown on kāTu land. Kampu *(Penicellaria spicata)* is a small, greenish-looking millet; it grows quickly and is the crop given the most ceremonial importance.

---

[67]Republic of India, *District Census Handbook, Coimbatore,* 1:2. In some areas in the center of the Coimbatore District, one finds black cotton soil, which is considerably more fertile than the red type. The cotton grown in these areas supports a large spinning and handloom industry in the villages.

[68]Ibid.

A team of hired women planting *rāki,* a local millet. Women of all castes accept employment of this kind.

A young KavuNTar plowing. He is using a famous local breed of cattle for drawing-power, and a metal-tipped plow.

The traditional well-irrigation system in common use in the Konku area. The edge of a large and deep well is shown. The buckets are raised by means of a pulley system which is operated by a team of oxen driven down a steep ramp. The water, guided by the leather extensions to the buckets, flows into an irrigation channel.

CōLam *(Holcus sorgum)* resembles field corn in appearance and taste; it grows more slowly than kampu, but of the three cereals it gives the highest yield of both grain and straw. The third important cereal, rāki *(Eleusine coracana)* is a small, dark brown, very nourishing millet. As it requires transplanting and more irrigation than the other two, it cannot be grown on kāTu land. There are also many varieties of pulses which can be sown in kāTu fields, but all pulses do better under irrigation or garden conditions. It is in times of famine that the kāTu crops are most important as they are relatively dependable as a source of a subsistence diet.[69]

As the information given in diagram form in Figure 1.4 indicates, the movements of the sun and the cycle of the seasons, the agricultural cycle, and the ceremonial calendar are all interrelated to a certain extent. In festival terms, each year is punctuated by two major *nōmpus,* or family feasts. The first of these nōmpus takes place on the first three days of the month of *Tai,* or about the middle of January, and the second falls on the eighteenth day of the month of *ĀTi,* at the end of July or the beginning of August. Tai nōmpu marked the beginning of the year according to the traditional Tamil calendar, but now the new year officially commences on the first day of *Cittirai,* or in the middle of April.[70]

Since Tai used to begin the calendar year, it is not surprising that a ritual celebration of rebirth and rebeginning remains associated with the first part of this month, even though for official purposes the first month of the new year is now agreed to be April. The term *tai* actually means "green plant" or "young thing," and the Tai festival is overtly said to be for children, especially young girls. The first day of Tai nōmpu is officially called *caṅkarānti.* Caṅkarānti refers to the passage of the sun from one sign of the zodiac to another, a crossing that occurs at the time of the winter solstice. Though nowadays the solstice falls on 22 December and Tai nōmpu is held in the middle of January, it seems that the festival was once accu-

---

[69]Recently, however, more and more people in Koṅku have been demanding a regular diet of rice. Although the prestige of this grain is not recent, the consumption of it in large quantities probably is. Older residents in the area can still recall when rice was eaten only on important ceremonial occasions, perhaps two or three times a year. The period they refer to is not more than forty years ago. Even the wealthy were previously dependent on grains as a daily staple. Coimbatore is currently classified as a food-deficit area, but it is interesting to note that the deficit is only 19,000 tons per year in millet while it is 113,000 per year in rice (Republic of India, *District Census Handbook, Coimbatore,* 1:34). With modern transportation facilities, it is feasible to import in quantity; but one can surmise that, before the age of trucks and railroads, the population of Koṅku relied much more heavily on local produce.

[70]Officially the Tamil year now begins on the first day of Cittirai, in order to correspond with the current national Indian calendar, in which the year begins on 1 April. It is abundantly clear, however, that according to traditional Tamil calculations the year began on the first day of the month of Tai (January-February). See, for example, *Dictionary Tamil and English,* p. 564.

rately linked to this solar event.[71] The first day of Tai is the only day of the year when *poṅkal,* or festival rice, must be symbolically offered to the sun prior to general distribution.

The second major family feast day, ĀTi nōmpu, falls in late July. Here a traditional association with the summer solstice is not very clear, but could perhaps be documented with further research. Why this nōmpu occurs on the eighteenth day of the month rather than on the first is explained, locally, by reference to the *Mahabarata* story.[72] People say that the first eighteen days of the month of ĀTi mark the time of the great war the PaNTavas fought with their half-brothers over the inheritance of their father's kingdom. If we go back to about A.D. 400, to a time when the summer solstice would have coincided with the first day of ĀTi, it would seem fitting for men to associate the first eighteen days of the sun's return journey with a great battle. From the observer's point of view, of course, the sun would seem almost to stand still, in relation to the zodiac, during this period, as if its natural course of movement were threatened. One of the most climactic moments in the *Mahabarata* battle comes when the god VisNu throws his great disc or spinning wheel at the sun in order to darken the world. This symbolism would seem appropriate at the start of a six-month period during which the days will gradually become shorter.

These admittedly speculative suggestions concerning the original relation of the ĀTi festival to the movements of the sun are reinforced by the character of the nōmpu itself, which is centered on the worship of ancestors. While the month of Tai is thought to be very auspicious, ĀTi is full of dangers. Usually a waxing moon is a good sign, but in ĀTi even the bright half of the month is thought to be under certain nefarious influences. Apart from ancestor worship on the nōmpu day, the main concern in ĀTi is with the terrors of excessive increase. The Kāvēri river may spill over its banks during this month, and Pārvati, Civā's wife, is said to have first menstruated at this time.[73] Excess and overflow are further associated with the pollution of childbirth and with the heat which pollution is

---

[71]The traditional calendar does not seem to have taken into account the procession of the earth's axis. Thus the calculations which determined the time of the festival have had the effect of gradually delaying it, so that by now it is celebrated some three weeks "late" in solar terms. Since one complete solar procession cycle requires about 26,000 years, we can estimate from the above discrepancy that the traditional Tamil calendar was developed and put into practice some 1,600 years ago. If the same calculations were to persist for another 24,000 years, the solar and festival events should coincide once again.

[72]The *Mahabarata* is one of India's most famous pieces of epic literature.

[73]ĀTi is also the worst month of the year for childbirth. Some informants told stories of how women avoid intercourse during *Aippaci* and *Kārttikai* (nine months in advance) in order not to give birth during ĀTi. In general, it was stressed that during ĀTi childbirth is more dangerous than is conception. However, people admit that a child conceived during ĀTi may suffer from difficulties in later life. See Dumont, *Une Sous-Caste,* p. 374, for a description of a parallel belief elsewhere in the South.

thought to generate. It is in keeping with these ideas that ĀTi is a hot month in climatic terms, while Tai is a cool one.[74]

This polarization of the year by the two major nōmpus immediately suggests a more important organization of the entire ceremonial calendar into two great halves. During the first part of the year, from Tai to ĀTi, the sun is traveling northward and the length of the day is gradually increasing. During the second half, the sun returns on a southward course and the length of the day gradually decreases. Recent unpublished research suggests that this stress on a cosmic cycle of increase and decrease, on the sun becoming stronger and then weaker, and on the waxing and waning of the moon, can be seen as permeating the entire South Indian ritual complex.[75] On the philosophical level it corresponds to the Hindu textual tradition of yuga cycles, of cosmic flowering versus cosmic decay. Within the year, immense importance is attached to the division of the calendar into lunar fortnights, the fortnights into periods of day and night, and these units into even smaller cycles of auspicious and inauspicious time.[76]

When this notion of complementarity in the general structure of the cosmos is translated into a local festival calendar, the same kind of pattern reappears. Two polar points in the yearly cycle are marked by nōmpus, or family feast days, that are celebrated by all castes. The Brahmans are responsible for acting out an entire ritual cycle relating to the bright and dark halves of the year by the performance of a complex series of ceremonies at the great temples of the region. Leaving this matter to the "heads" of the social and ritual order, the right-division communities, particularly the KavuNTars, can then focus their own ritual concern on the first six months of the year—from Tai to ĀTi—taking a special interest in the local goddess Māriyamman̲ and her festival, which takes place in April. The planting ceremony which accompanies the seeding of the traditional kampu crop, just before ĀTi nōmpu, can also be counted as a KavuNTar concern. Left-division groups take little notice of these activities, and concentrate their interest on the complementary half of the year, the months from ĀTi to Tai. The higher-ranking members of these left subcastes, in contrast to their counterparts of the right, place great emphasis on the special offerings that are made to ancestors on the new moon day of *PuraTTāci,* the month of September-October. It is also customary for members of these communities to observe a partial fast, both during this month and during that of *MārkaRi,* or December-January. Such a

---

[74]For an extensive discussion of the significance of this hot-cool contrast, see Brenda E. F. Beck, "Colour and Heat in South Indian Ritual," *Man,* n.s. 4, no. 4 (1969): 553–72.

[75]Frederick Clothey, "The Murukan̲ Festival Cycle," a brilliant paper delivered at a workshop on South Indian Festivals, sponsored by the Association for Asian Studies, June 4–6, 1971, at Haverford College.

[76]See Appendix D for a description of auspicious and inauspicious moments, days, months, and years.

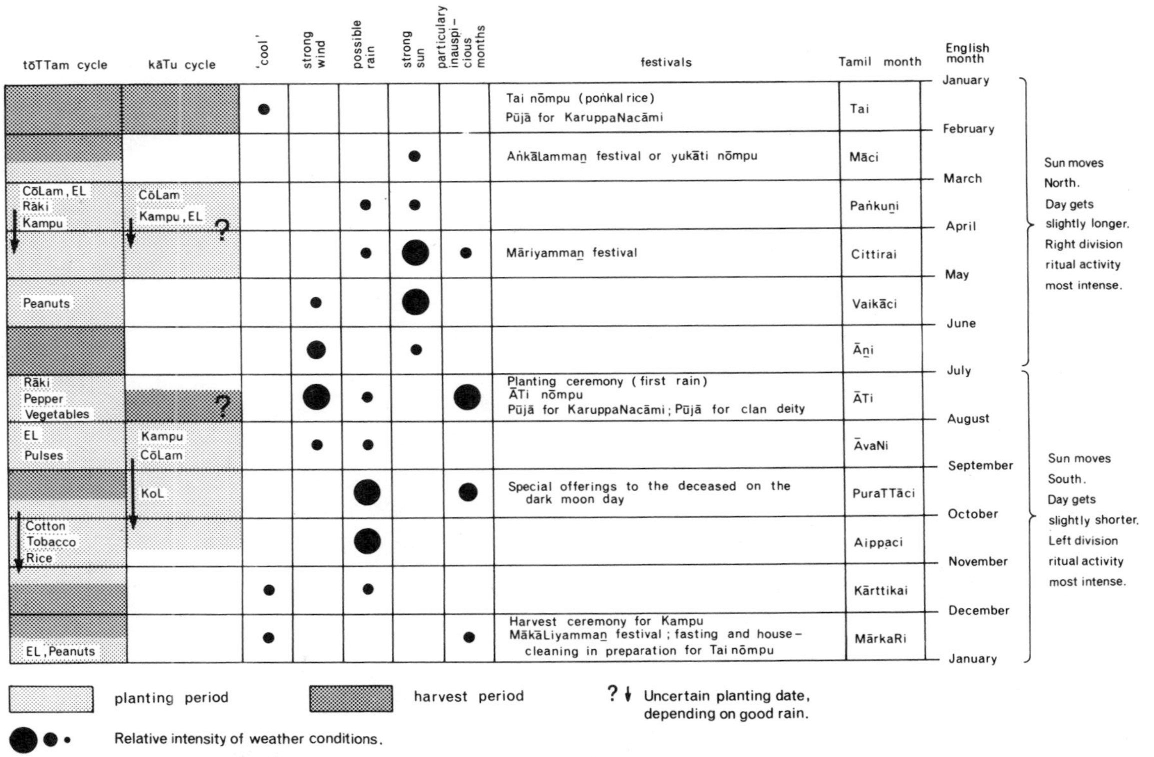

Fig. 1.4. The agricultural cycle and related festivals.

complementarity in the ritual concerns of the right- and left-division groups, however, is by no means complete. Some right subcastes also fast—or at least avoid meat—during the month of PuraTTāci, while many members of the left division are involved in a celebration for the goddess AṅkāLammaṉ which occurs in the month of Māci, or February-March.[77] At most, therefore, one can speak of a tendency for the ceremonial concerns of the left and right divisions to correspond with a ritual partition of the year into bright and dark halves. This pattern can also be viewed as supplementing or reinforcing the differences in the right- and left-division folk history described earlier.

THE CASTE POPULATION OF KOṄKU

The only information available on the proportional size of various caste groups in Koṅku can be found in the early census returns of this century. The 1901, 1911, and 1921 volumes, for example, all provide relatively detailed figures on this question. These are of some use in establishing the relative strength of different communities in the area, although it is risky to rely on the absolute figures provided. After 1921 a variety of objections were raised to recording census information by caste and thus later censuses evaded the use of many of these names. There is no reason to suspect, however, that the relative population of different groups has changed radically since 1921, particularly in rural areas.

The present population of the Koṅku area is about five million. Roughly 71 per cent of these people are rural residents, while the rest live in urban areas.[78] Many town-dwellers, furthermore, are recent immigrants

---

[77]One of the names for the day on which the AṅkāLammaṉ festival is held is *yukāti nōmpu*, or "the celebration for young women" (see Fig. 1.4). AṅkāLammaṉ herself is a goddess who is particularly linked to problems of childbirth and who is strongly associated with left-division groups. (A more detailed description of her and of this association is given in chapter 2, pp. 99–101.) As Pārvati, she was Civā's wife, and her festival is held at the same time as Civaṉrāttiri, Civā's night, when her husband is thought to pay her a brief visit.

More generally, one might speak of a division of the year into a bright half dominated by Civā and a dark half dominated by VisNu. Since AṅkāLammaṉ's festival focuses on Civā's visit, it is reasonable that it take place in the first half, during Māci. Both PuraTTāci and MārkaRi, on the other hand, the months of other, primarily left-division, ritual observances, are associated with VisNu. Furthermore, VisNu is frequently described as "dark-faced" in the mythology, while Civā is said to be the color of ash, or gray-white. Civā and VisNu are sometimes thought of as brothers-in-law. This makes them cross relatives in Tamil kin terminology (see chapter 5, pp. 213–20). In connection with this, it is interesting to note that members of each division have a custom of addressing those belonging to the opposite group as "brother-in-law" (see chapter 3, p. 120). It would make a very neat picture if one could say that left-division members are predominantly Vishnavite—VisNu worshippers—and that right-division members are for the most part Saivite—Civā worshippers. This does not seem to be the case, though, at least not at the present.

[78]Urban areas have been defined by the Census of India as population clusters of 2,500 or more. My estimate of 29 per cent is based on Coimbatore District figures. See Republic of India, *Atlas of the Madras State*, map 43.

whose families came to Koṅku during, or just prior to, the period of British rule.[79] The skills of immigrants who have settled in urban areas are also quite distinct. In rural Koṅku these newcomers have generally been unskilled laborers who are easily absorbed at or near the bottom of the status hierarchy. Such immigrants do not have much effect on prevailing patterns of peasant organization. Immigrants who are skilled workers or who belong to a profession, on the other hand, have gravitated to urban areas. There they have been incorporated into the local society at higher levels, and they have at times won for themselves considerable status. Hence the influence of immigrant populations on urban patterns of inter-action has been quite pronounced. Rural social traditions in Koṅku ap-pear to have been less disturbed by recent changes than their urban coun-terparts.

Table 1.3 provides a summary of the census information on castes in the Coimbatore District for the 1901–21 period.[80] Only castes discussed in the present work are listed.[81] For several small groups no information at all is available in the census returns and in some cases the subcaste referred to is not specified. Furthermore, it is clear from a comparison of the figures published for different years that the tally for some communities varied radically over time. This is attributable, in part, to the difficulties the cen-sus officials had in deciding which group names to combine and which to list separately. In some cases the changes may also represent an increasing concern on the part of members of some castes or subcastes to upgrade

[79]According to my calculations, 75 per cent of all Coimbatore District residents, born outside the area, presently live in urban centers. See Republic of India, *District Census Handbook, Coimbatore*, 1:10. Data on the previous century are not available.

[80]The Koṅku area, of course, is not quite co-terminous with Coimbatore District, but figures for the latter area represent the closest possible approximation under the circum-stances. Moreover, the boundaries of Coimbatore District have themselves been slightly altered in the post-British period, but these changes were so minor as to have no bearing on the present calculation.

[81]About 35 per cent of the castes named in the old census reports on Coimbatore are not discussed in this book. Many of these are small groups which are unknown in the District as a whole. A few—those with populations over 20,000—are reasonably important com-munities. The names of these latter groups, along with a brief description, follow. I did not encounter any of these groups in my travels through the area, and I know very little about them. As immigrants, many have probably found work in urban areas.

Balija:	Telugu-speaking traders. Mostly immigrants from southern Andhra, perhaps.
Devanga:	Telugu and Kannada-speaking weavers. They may be mostly immigrants from Mysore.
Kamma:	Telugu-speakers. Originally soldiers, but now largely agriculturalists. Perhaps immigants from the coastal districts of Andhra.
Kurumbam:	Tamil-speakers who live by hunting, gathering, and crude agriculture in the hill areas.
Palli:	Tamil-speakers. Mostly agricultural laborers and tenants. They may have emigrated from the Arcot and Salem Districts of Madras.
Pallan:	Tamil-speakers. A very low-ranking group of agricultural laborers. They could be immigrants from the southern half of Madras State.

TABLE 1.3
POPULATION DETAILS
(by caste)

Caste Name	Coimbatore District						(4) Author's Estimate of Percentage of District Population (Average of 1901, 1911, 1921)[1]	(5) Kannapuram Kirāmam (households)[2]		(6) ŌlappāLaiyam Settlement (individuals)	
	(1) Census of 1901	Per-centage	(2) Census of 1911	Per-centage	(3) Census of 1921	Per-centage		Number in 1966	Per-centage	Number in 1966	Per-centage
Neutral Division:											
Brahman (Tamil-speaking only)[3]	33,788	2.0	22,240	1.0	23,616	1.0	under 1.0	3	0.3	10	2.0
KaruNīkar PiLLai[4]	(Unknown. but probably under 1.0%)						1.0	1	0.1	10	2.0
Total	33,788	2.0	22,240	1.0	23,616	1.0	1.0	4	0.4	20	4.0
Right Division:											
KavuNTar (Vellala)[5]	629,540	31.0	639,557	30.0	694,906	31.0	31.0	590	53.0	217	44.0
PaNTāram (Andi)	35,160	2.0	39,594	2.0	38,344	2.0	2.0	16	1.0	10	2.0
UTaiyār (Kusuvan)	17,643	1.0	22,090	1.0	25,625	1.0	1.0	18	2.0	10	2.0
NāTār (Shannan)	70,655	3.0	76,907	4.0	72,923	3.0	3.0	75	7.0	34	7.0
VaNNār* (Vannan)	17,820	0.9	19,823	0.9	17,804	0.8	0.9	0	0.0	0	0.0
Nāvitar* (Ambattan)	16,549	0.8	19,674	0.9	20,323	0.9	0.9	22	2.0	6	1.0
Paraiyar (Paraiyan)	75,481	4.0	69,849	3.0	73,363	3.0	3.0	55	5.0	0	0.0
Total	862,648	43.0	887,494	42.0	943,288	42.0	43.0	776	69.0	277	56.0
Left Division:											
Ācāri (Kammala)	46,043	2.0	55,195	3.0	33,345	1.0	2.0	18	2.0	36	7.0
CeTTiyār[6] (Chetti)	100,544	5.0	64,428	3.0	47,989	2.0	3.0	5	0.4	7	1.0
Mutaliyār (Kaikolan)	56,249	3.0	61,227	3.0	83,000	3.0	3.0	24	2.0	30	6.0
Nāyakkar (Tottiyan)	34,237	2.0	26,643	1.0	28,505	1.0	1.0	23	2.0	26	5.0

Caste	Column One (no.)	(%)	Column Two (no.)	(%)	Column Three (no.)	(%)	Column Four (%)	Column Five (no.)	(%)	Column Six (no.)	(%)
VaNNār* (Vannan)	8,960	0.4	9,911	0.5	8,902	0.4	0.4	21	2.0	8	2.0
Nāvitar* (Ambattan)	8,274	0.4	9,837	0.5	10,162	0.5	0.5	0	0.0	0	0.0
Kuṟavar (Korava)	12,417	0.6	12,975	0.6	9,845	0.4	0.5	6	0.5	0	0.0
Mātāri (Chakkiliyan)	176,608	9.0	198,380	9.0	206,162	9.0	9.0	237	21.0	0	0.0
Total	443,332	22.0	438,596	21.0	427,910	19.0	21.0	334	30.0	107	22.0
Unclassified:											
NāyuTu (Telugu-speakers)	(Unknown but probably under 1.0%)						under 1.0	1	0.1	0	0.0
Tācar	(Unknown but certainly under 1.0%)						under 1.0	3	0.3	0	0.0
KōNār	(Unknown but probably under 1.0%)						under 1.0	1	0.1	0	0.0
Total (unclassified)							under 3.0	5	0.5	0	0.0
Total: all castes in table	1,340,068	67.0	1,348,330	64.0	1,394,814	62.0	65.0	1,119	100.0	404 / 493†	82.0 / 100.0
Total: census population	2,004,839	100.0	2,116,564	100.0	2,219,848	100.0		unknown		unknown	

SOURCES:

Column One: Presidency of Madras, *Madras District Manuals, Coimbatore,* 2 vols. (Madras: Government Press, 1898), 2:17.

Column Two: Dominion of India, *Census of India, 1911,* Vol. XII, *Madras,* Part II, *Imperial and Provincial Tables* (Madras: Government Press, 1912), pp. 2, 116–19.

Column Three: Dominion of India, *Census of India, 1921,* Vol. XIII, *Madras,* Part II, *Imperial and Provincial Tables* (Madras: Government Press, 1922), pp. 4, 118–23.

Column Five: Survey conducted by Informant no. 33 in 1966.

Column Six: Author's survey, 1966.

NOTES: Percentages in the table have been rounded to the nearest whole number, except in the case of fractions of one per cent.

[1]Column 4 represents an approximate average of Columns 1–3. It is intended as an approximation of the relative proportions of the various castes that make up the population of the District as a whole. The figures in this column can be compared with the percentages showing caste strength, by household, in Kannapuram kirāmam (Column 5) and with total caste membership in ŌlappāLaiyam settlement (Column 6); Columns 5 and 6 are two measures of the relative proportions of the castes listed, in the local area under discussion.

[2]Column 5 represents a count of house compounds, not of individual persons. ŌlappāLaiyam households are included.

[3]Figures for Tamil-speaking Brahmans only are given in the table. If Telugu- and Kannada-speaking subcastes were included they would account for another 0.8 per cent of the population.

[4]Caste names only are used for figures taken from the census returns. As these returns did not provide figures for the KaruÑikar PiLLai, the only amounts given are from the author's survey; and the subcaste name is used in this case.

[5]The names in parentheses are the caste names used in the census reports.

[6]All CeTTiyars have been classified as members of the left division in the census reports. The Koṅku CeTTiyār are the only group of merchants belonging to the right division in Koṅku, according to my informants, and they are a very small group not specifically identified in the census returns.

*Barbers and washermen are grouped together in the census returns, regardless of subcaste or division membership. I have allotted two-thirds of each group to the right division and one-third to the left in an attempt to approximate the numbers that serve these two groups.

†Twenty-two percent has been added to the total population of ŌlappāLaiyam to account for the untouchable Mātāri who live separately (and who were not surveyed in detail), but who form part of the local social order both in terms of ritual and in day-to-day relationships.

themselves by claiming new names with more prestige. None of these decennial differences, therefore, may be confidently said to represent actual changes in caste size. They are useful only in producing an average figure which can serve as some indication of the relative size of the various groups over a period of time. While the variation in the actual numbers recorded is considerable, it will be noticed that when the variation is considered as a proportion of the total it becomes small.

The table illustrates several important differences between the caste population of the right- and left-division groups. First, it clearly demonstrates the difference in their sizes. The right-division groups account for 43 per cent of the population of the region and the left-division groups for only 21 per cent. Thus the right division is roughly twice the size of the left. This same observation was made by early officials of the East India Company who encountered the two divisions in their trading activities.[82]

Indeed, this difference in relative size is symbolized in some of the traditional terms used to describe the divisions. Most commonly recorded is a description of the right group as the faction with eighteen members, and the left as that with only nine members.[83] Other numbers, such as 18-1/2 and 7, which suggest roughly similar proportions, have been observed in other areas.[84] This contrast of even with odd numbers has been carried over into ritual matters, where the right-division castes are said historically to have been allowed twelve posts in their wedding pavilions, and the left castes only eleven.[85]

Table 1.3 also serves to point out the absolute numerical strength of the KavuNTars in Coimbatore District, which, with the exceptions previously noted, corresponds geographically to the Koṅku region. This leading group constitutes about 31 per cent of the District's general population and 74 per cent of the total membership of the right division. All other communities in the right bloc are small by comparison. Higher-ranking groups of the left division, on the other hand, are more uniform in size than those of the right. In contrast to the KavuNTars in the right division, the largest left-division community—the untouchable Mātāri—is a group that ranks so low in the social scale that its numbers give it little influence on the character of the greater whole.

Furthermore, a comparison of the proportion of KavuNTars in the District population with their proportion, as measured by households, at

[82]H. D. Love, *Vestiges of Old Madras,* 3 vols. (London: John Murray, 1913), 2:25.

[83]See Dominion of India, *Census of India, 1911,* Vol. XII, *Madras* Part I, *Report* (Madras: Government Press, 1912), p. 150, and Benjamin Lewis Rice, *Mysore Gazetteer* (London: Westminster, 1897), Vol. I.

[84]N. S. Reddy, "Community Conflict Among the Depressed Castes of Andhra," *Man in India* 30, no. 4 (1950): 1–12.

[85]J. A. Dubois, *Hindu Manners, Customs and Ceremonies* (Oxford: Clarendon Press, 1906), p. 154.

the kirāmam level, suggests that this group is particularly important in rural areas. Although there are no published figures comparing the urban and rural distributions of any caste, my travels confirmed the impression that they constitute fully half of the population in some areas. Other communities directly or indirectly dependent on agriculture—the NāTārs, Nāyakkars, and Mātāris—are also proportionately more numerous in the villages of Koṅku than in urban areas.

The concentration of Ācāris (artisans), and Mutaliyārs (weavers), in ŌlappāLaiyam settlement, however, is part of a different pattern. These castes are very important in rural areas also, but instead of following the fairly even distribution pattern of agriculturally based groups, they show a tendency to cluster in well-established settlements. They prefer to be close to good transportation routes, and are often found near traditional temple centers. UTaiyārs (potters), PaNTārams (local priests and cooks), VēTars (story-tellers), and Paṛaiyars (drummers) also cluster around large temple sites where they can claim a share of the proceeds in return for services rendered on various festive occasions.

The KōmuTTi CeTTiyār are even more heavily concentrated in market centers than these groups are in the temple centers. Barbers and washermen, on the other hand, are personal service castes and are therefore thinly spread. These differences in settlement patterns reflect the more ritually conscious and in-group attitudes of the left-division communities, as well as their occupational specialization. Associated with their patterns of residence is the tendency of members of these groups to be relatively urban in their orientation. They tend to have thin, long-distance networks of a highly specialized sort, rather than a dense and generalized mesh of local connections.

The settlement patterns of these two blocs of castes are also associated with their propensity for travel. In ŌlappāLaiyam only 29 per cent of the adults in the right division had traveled beyond Koṅku in their lifetime, in contrast to 60 per cent of those in the opposite bloc who had made such a journey.[86] Of the neutral castes the proportion was 92 per cent, placing them in advance of both divisions. These statistics are based on too small a sample to be given great weight, but they support the general finding

---

[86]The actual breakdown in the figures, by subcaste, is as follows ("n" indicates the sample size in each case). Right subcastes: Koṅku KavuNTar, 18% (n 166); OkaccāNTi PaNTāram, 50% (n 8); Koṅku UTaiyār, 43% (n 7); Maramēri NāTār, 13% (n 23); Koṅku Nāvitar, 75% (n 4). Left subcastes: CōLi and Koṅku Ācāri, 44% (n 25); KōmuTTi CeTTiyār, 100% (n 3); Kaikkōlar Mutaliyār, 42% (n 19); VaTuka Nāyakkar, 15% (n 13); VaTuka VaNNār, 0% (n 5). Note that the right-division service groups are more mobile than the KavuNTars and NāTārs, communities that have direct rights in land. Among the left castes, the lower-status and poorer groups have traveled less extensively than their wealthier colleagues. The neutral Aiyar Brahmans score 88% (n 8) and the KaruNīkar PiLLai 100% (n 5). Though above the division in theory, these groups' interest in travel clearly resembles that of the high-status left subcastes. No untouchables were included in the sample.

that members of left-division communities are considerably more mobile than are members of the right. Clearly, the higher-ranking left castes come much closer to the example set by the two neutral groups.

To sum up, three important differences exist between the population of the right and left divisions in the Koṅku region. The right bloc is roughly twice the size of the left. Second, the right bloc is heavily dominated numerically by the land-owning KavuNTar community, while the higher-ranking groups of the left are small in size. Finally, right-division groups tend to be scattered relatively evenly through the countryside. They have representatives in nearly every touchable settlement. The higher-status left-division communities, on the other hand, cluster in only a few settlement areas of each kirāmam. They are usually found in the larger hamlets, near important temples, and along the transportation arteries that cross the countryside.

These are right-left differences that exist at the regional or all-Koṅku level. In ensuing chapters the same pattern of differences will be explored in terms of nāTu (subregion), kirāmam (revenue village), Ūr (hamlet), and kuTumpam (household) organization.

2

THE SUBREGION: KĀṄKAYAM NĀTU

TRADITIONAL NĀTU GEOGRAPHY

Within the Koṅku region as a whole, there are twenty-four nāTu divisions.[1] These nāTu divisions appear in inscriptions about Koṅku as early as the eighth century, or at roughly the time of Ganga rule in the region. It appears that they were initially laid out to accord with the location of powerful rural families and war leaders. Their boundaries therefore underwent changes from time to time.[2] Gradually, however, it seems that these nāTus acquired a ritual status and their locations became more or less fixed ceremonially. A map showing the now generally accepted positions of the twenty-four traditional nāTu areas appears in Figure 2.1.

Above the nāTu there seem to have been larger divisions of a shadowy sort at one time, although my informants did not know much about these. Thus Koṅku is spoken of as having been traditionally divided into VaTakoṅku and Teṉkoṅku or northern and southern halves.[3] It does not appear that any positions of caste leadership corresponded to this supra-division. Even the boundary between the two is unclear, though it may have been the Noyyal river. In the CōRa area, by contrast to Koṅku, these larger divisions seem to have had considerable importance, probably because the region itself was large enough to require it. Three divisions were used there rather than two.[4] One of them, PoṉṉivaLa nāTu, is repeatedly referred to in the Koṅku folklore.[5]

[1]This is widely known. Several important published sources are: C. M. Ramachandra Chettiar, *Koṅku NāTTu Varalāru* [The story of Koṅku NāTu] (Annamalai: Annamalai University Press, 1954), pp. 31–35; M. Arokiaswami, *The Kongu Country* (Madras: Madras University Press, 1956), pp. 221–22, and S. A. R. Ciṉṉucāmi KavuNTar, *Koṅku VēLāLar* [The VēLāLars of Koṅku] (Erode: TamiRaṉ Accakam, 1963), pp. 93–96.

[2]Arokiaswami, *Kongu Country*, p. 174, and Ramachandra Chettiar, *Koṅku NāTTu Varalāru*, pp. 109–11.

[3]Informant no. 7.

[4]T. V. Mahalingam, *South Indian Polity* (Madras: Madras University Historical Series, 1955), p. 304.

[5]In *The Story of the Brothers* particularly.

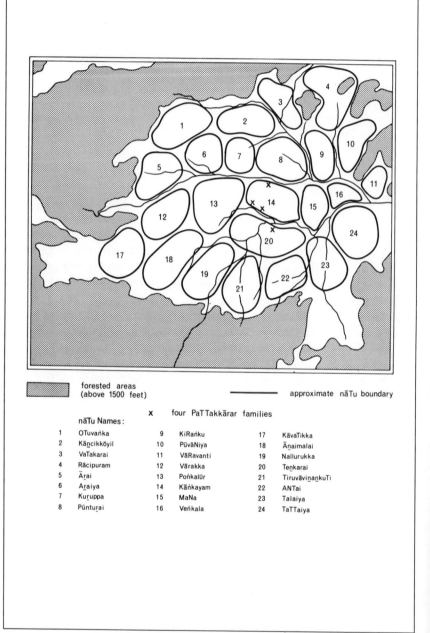

forested areas
(above 1500 feet)

approximate nāTu boundary

x   four PaTTakkārar families

nāTu Names:

1	OTuvaṅka	9	KiRaṅku	17	KāvaTikka
2	Kāncikkōyil	10	PūvāNiya	18	Āṇaimalai
3	VaTakarai	11	VāRavanti	19	Nallurukka
4	Rācipuram	12	Vārakka	20	Teṇkarai
5	Āṟai	13	Poṅkalūr	21	TiruvāviṉaṉkuTi
6	Aṟaiya	14	Kāṅkayam	22	ANTai
7	Kuṟuppa	15	MaNa	23	Talaiya
8	Pūnturai	16	Veṅkala	24	TaTTaiya

Fig. 2.1.   The approximate traditional political geography of Koṅku.

The nāTu divisions bear only a very general relation to the administrative divisions of the present day. The closest they come to matching the current organization of government offices and services is in their rough correspondence to the so-called Panchayat Union areas. There are currently some fifty Panchayat Unions contained in the area traditionally covered by the twenty-four nāTus. Much of this discrepancy can be accounted for by the breaking of traditional nāTu units into two. Kāṅkayam nāTu, for example, has recently been broken into two panchayat union blocks, called the Kāṅkayam and VeLLakōvil Panchayat Unions respectively. It is the earlier nāTu unit, however, which is still prominently featured in folklore, caste organization, and local ritual.

The Panchayat Union represents the highest organizational level for which some degree of traditional and modern administrative correspondence can be found. Above the Panchayat Union is now the Taluk, and above that is the District.[6] Both of these higher levels show a correspondence with previous British administrative boundaries, but to the best of my knowledge, neither of them was important in Koṅku prior to the British period. Modern Coimbatore District, for example, includes several mountainous regions which lay outside the old Koṅku area. Quite large parts of the Koṅku NāTu area, furthermore, have been allocated to Salem and to Tiruchirappalli by the State government.

While the correspondence between the Panchayat Union and the nāTu area is very rough, the parallel between the modern Panchayat territory and the traditional kirāmam area is often striking. Panchayat populations in Coimbatore today vary from about two thousand to five thousand people.[7] They represent the lowest level of present-day government organization. This fundamental revenue unit, strengthened by a strong local identity and reaffirmed by yearly ceremonies, is something which succeeding governments have not tampered with unduly. Where reorganizations by successful conquerors have occurred, they have generally affected only the highest administrative levels.[8]

[6] A Panchayat Union is made up of some ten local Panchayats and has a Chairman elected from among the Presidents of its member-Panchayats. A Taluk is a grouping of about ten Panchayat Unions for administrative purposes; and a District, consisting of some ten Taluks, is the highest level of administration below that of a State. Officials are appointed rather than elected to the administration at the Taluk and District levels.

[7] Republic of India, *Census of India, 1961,* Vol. IX, *Madras,* Part X-i, *District Census Handbook, Coimbatore,* 2 vols. (Madras: Government Press, 1964), 1:89.

[8] It is interesting to note that the official title of the Panchayat-level development officer or extension agent is Grama Sevak. Grama is simply the old English spelling of the traditional term *kirāmam.* Thus we have linguistic evidence of the official concern to equate traditional and modern at the lowest administrative level. At the next level of organization, that of the Panchayat Union, the official in charge of agricultural affairs is called a Block Development Officer. Here the parallel with the traditional nāTu unit has been ignored. There is no Tamil translation of the term, and in everyday speech this official is referred to by simply shortening his name to "the B. D. O."

The twelve kirāmams, or revenue villages, of Kānkayam nāTu and their approximate boundaries are shown in Figure 2.2.[9] Each of these kirāmams has its own Civā temple; and one of the twelve—the temple of Civaṇmalai—is spoken of as representing the nāTu as a whole.[10] Similarly, every other nāTu in Koṅku is said to have its leading Civā temple, though further research is needed to establish this with certainty. Kāṅkayam nāTu is famous for its association with three of the four PaTTakkārar families of Koṅku. This is consistent with the fact that this nāTu is centrally located, and that it was probably one of the earlier ones to be settled.[11]

ADMINISTRATIVE ORGANIZATION OF THE NĀTU AREAS

Corresponding to the spatial and ceremonial features of nāTu organization just described, is an elaborate traditional hierarchy of subcaste leadership.[12] Titles to positions of subcaste leadership are generally inherited in the male line, and the names of traditional political offices associated with the nāTu areas are still remembered by members of most groups. Common terms for the position of nāTu headman for Koṅku KavuNTars, for example, are *nāTTu KavuNTar, nāTTāmaikkārar,* or even just *nāTTār.* This man, often with a second man as a helper, was traditionally the one responsible for calling meetings in times of crisis or of dispute. Such meetings would resolve internal conflict and also decide subcaste policy on matters such as marriage, ritual, diet, and dress. Infractions could be punished by fine, or in extreme cases, by exile. Since nāTus are large areas, generally only the leaders of each sub-unit or kirāmam would attend these special gatherings.

To continue with the example of the KavuNTar community, at one time there were many lower-level leaders below the nāTu headman as well. At the kirāmam level, the responsibilities of office were mostly ceremonial in nature. The title used for this position was usually *muppāTTukkārar,* "a man who leads or goes first," to express the fact that this person was allocated the first place at local ceremonies and expected to represent the local area at nāTu meetings. The level at which local political power could

[9]A number of the boundaries indicated are approximate. As I was mainly interested in the principle, the only one I have traced in detail is that for Kannapuram kirāmam.

[10]This Civā temple at Civaṇmalai is distinct from the Murukan temple located on top of the mountain and said to be one of the seven Murukan temples of the region. The Civā temple, by contrast, is situated at the foot of the mountain.

[11]Kāṅkayam nāTu may have served as a place of intersection for two important trade routes, one that led north into Koṅku from Madurai, and one that led east across Koṅku from Kerala to Karur and then to other cultural centers in the Kāvēri delta. Government of Madras, *Madras District Gazetteers, Coimbatore* (Madras: Government Press, 1966), p. 588.

[12]Subcaste groupings are based on kin ties, and they serve as a convenient index to the local status hierarchy. They are the units within which ritual traditions are assumed to be uniform and within which a person is supposed to seek a spouse. (See the Introduction, pp. 2–3 for a more detailed explanation.)

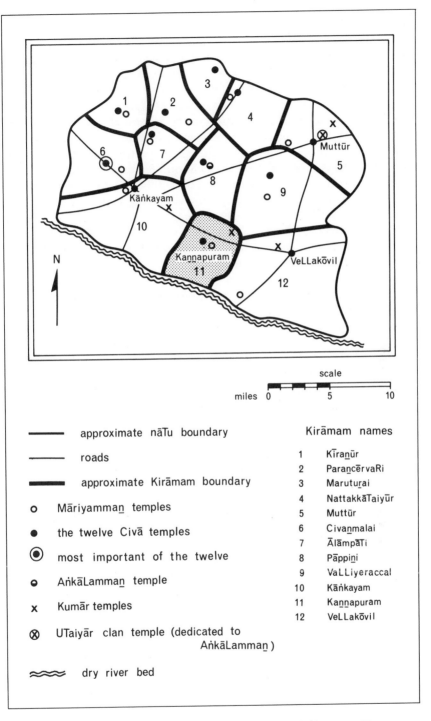

approximate nāTu boundary   Kirāmam names

roads

approximate Kirāmam boundary

o   Māriyamman̠ temples

●   the twelve Civā temples

◉   most important of the twelve

◒   An̠kāLamman̠ temple

x   Kumār temples

⊗   UTaiyār clan temple (dedicated to An̠kāLamman̠)

≈≈   dry river bed

1	Kīran̠ūr
2	Paran̠cērvaRi
3	Marutur̠ai
4	NattakkāTaiyūr
5	Muttūr
6	Civan̠malai
7	ĀlāmpāTi
8	Pāppin̠i
9	VaLLiyeraccal
10	Kān̠kayam
11	Kan̠n̠apuram
12	VeLLakōvil

Fig. 2.2.   The political and social geography of Kān̠kayam nāTu.

be wielded, however, was in the leadership of individual *Ūr* or hamlet areas. Here the hereditary leader of the KavuNTar community was generally called the *Ūr KavuNTar* or *kottukkārar*. Such men were often important local figures, wielding more real power but surrounded by fewer ceremonial trappings than their counterparts at higher levels.

This form of subcaste organization in the Koṅku region, as illustrated by the KavuNTar community, is not unique. Many other writers have mentioned, albeit in passing, what appear to be unmistakable organizational similarities in other areas of the South. Some information on these neighboring regions has been put together in Table 2.1 for comparison. In no one case is the data complete, but the over-all picture is impressive. Several major regions of the South appear to have had nāTu, kirāmam, and Ūr subdivisions.[13] At each level, local social identity was expressed in a temple and ceremonial complex, counterbalanced by a hierarchy of offices symbolizing local political leadership.

On examining the organization of the neighboring regions a repeated use of certain selected numbers to describe political divisions can be noted.[14] Each of these favored numbers appears to have held some ritual significance. Given numerical descriptions probably remained in use over long periods, even though the actual number of subdivisions was clearly subject to change with political circumstance.[15] All in all, multiples of six, or sometimes of four, appear to have been the most popular. Perhaps because of this principle of multiples, most numbers used for this purpose were even. By adhering to this tradition, the numbers used to characterize secular organization could provide a stable contrast with the odd digits preferred when sacred matters were described. For example, Koṅku residents always speak of the seven Civā or seven Murukaṉ temples, but of the four PaTTakkārar and the twenty-four nāTu divisions.[16]

---

[13]Actually, a similar sort of organization may also have been common in the North. Compare the terms *khap* and *ganwand* as used by M. C. Pradhan with the *nāTu* and *kirāmam* of this work. In Uttar Pradesh the jat *khap* is a clan territory containing eighty-four individual villages and extending over an area of some 228 square miles. M. C. Pradhan, *The Political System of the Jats of Northern India* (Bombay: Oxford University Press, 1966), pp. 91, 114, 116.

[14]For example, the eighteen nāTu of North Arcot, in Edgar Thurston, *Castes and Tribes of Southern India*, 7 vols. (Madras: Government Press, 1909), 4:428.

[15]For example, one informant (no. 22) listed fourteen current kirāmams in Kāṅkayam nāTu. Similarly it was generally conceded that there were now thirty-two ūr in Kannapuram kirāmam, in place of the original twenty-four. Yet in folklore and ritual, everyone continues to refer to the twelve and the twenty-four, respectively. Srinivas records a similar confusion over the number of nāTus in Coorg. M. N. Srinivas, *Religion and Society Among the Coorgs of South India* (1952; reprint ed., London: Asia Publishing House, 1965), pp. 13, 57–60.

[16]There are a few examples of the use of odd numbers to characterize the very largest political areas; see Eric J. Miller, "Caste and Territory in Malabar," *American Anthropologist* 56 (1954): 414–15, and Mahalingam, *South Indian Polity*, p. 304. These, it would appear, may have had more of a sacred than a secular significance.

TABLE 2.1

EXAMPLES OF TRADITIONAL POLITICAL AND ADMINISTRATIVE ORGANIZATION IN SOUTH INDIA

Rough Location According to Present Political Divisions	Traditional Region	Major Subdivisions	NāTu or Subregions	Kirāmam or Revenue Units	Ūr or Local Hamlets
(a) Coimbatore District plus parts of Salem and Tiruchirappalli Districts	*Koṅku NāTu* PaTTakkārar*	2 Subdivisions Unnamed (North and South)	24 Subregions *nāTu* NāTTāmaikkārar* Periyatanakkārar*	12 Revenue Units *kirāmam* MuppaTTukkārar*	24 (32) *Ūr* Ūr KavuNTar* Kottukkārar*
(b) Tiruchirappalli District	Edge of *Koṅku NāTu* PaTTakkārar*	Unknown	24 Subregions *nāTu* Periyatanakkārar* NāTTu KavuNTar*	Kottukkārar*	Unknown
(c) Tanjore and South Arcot Districts	*CōRa NāTu* (?)	9 Subdivisions *VaLanāTu*	78 Subregions *nāTu*	Unknown	Unknown
(d) Madurai District	A part of *PāNTiya NāTu* Tevar*	2 Subdivisions (?) Unnamed	8 Subregions (4) *nāTu* NāTTānmai* (?)	24 Revenue Units (12) *kirāmam*	Unknown
(e) North Arcot District	*ToNTai NāTu* (?)	Unknown	18 Subregions *nāTu* NāTTan*	Unknown	*Ūr* Ūran*
(f) Coorg District 4 pairs of headmen 4 appellate courts	*Coorg District* *Kombu*	12 Subdivisions *Kombu*	28 Subregions (35) *nād* Nād Takka*	Unknown	*Ūr* Ūr Takka*
(g) Koshikode, Trichur, and Palghat Districts (?)	*Cochin,* (and South Malabar)	*Chiefdom* Chieftain*	*nad*	*Dēsam*	Unknown
(h) Salem District	Mantiri*	Unknown	*nāTu* NāTTan*	Unknown	*Ūr* Kōlukkārar*

SOURCES: (a) Author's observation; (b) Edgar Thurston, *Castes and Tribes of Southern India*, 7 vols. (Madras: Government Press, 1909); 3: 417–18; (c) T. V. Mahalingam, *South Indian Polity* (Madras: Madras University Historical Series, 1955), p. 304; (d) Louis Dumont, *Une Sous-Caste de l'Inde du Sud* (Paris: Mouton, 1957), pp. 141–52, 288; (e) Thurston, *Castes and Tribes*, 4: 428; (f) M. N. Srinivas, *Religion and Society Among the Coorgs of South India* (1952; reprint ed., London: Asia Publishing House, 1965), pp. 13, 57–60; (g) Eric J. Miller, "Caste and Territory in Malabar," *American Anthropologist* 56 (1954): 414–15; (h) Republic of India, *Census of India, 1961*, Vol. IX, *Madras*, Part VI, *Village Survey Monographs*, no. 18, Alatipatti (Madras: Government Press, 1965), p. 53.

NOTES: The numbers indicate the number of units of a given order, while the numbers in parentheses indicate the possible alternate quantities. The names of units are given in italics, and the names of corresponding political offices are followed by an asterisk.

Given this over-all picture of territorial organization, it remains to describe what is known about right- and left-division differences at the nāTu level. This can be done only in a sketchy way, as much of the traditional organization has lost its significance in the past thirty years. Moreover, my informants were not all equally familiar with the traditional patterns of leadership in their individual communities. The description that follows, therefore, pertains to local political organization as remembered by selected subcaste elders. The period in question is that of about thirty to fifty years ago. Most of the offices described still exist in principle, but their significance has declined rapidly in the post-independence period. Elderly incumbents, for example, are not being replaced—particularly at the higher levels of the hierarchy. Village and kirāmam level organization, by contrast, has been more successful in surviving recent political changes.

In the case of the KavuNTars—the leading agricultural community of the right division—traditional territorial organization seems to have been most marked at its two extremes.[17] Thus at the level of the region as a whole, there were the PaTTakkārar or titled families who exercised considerable influence and to whom local residents still refer certain disputes for arbitration. The nāTTu KavuNTar or nāTu leaders, on the other hand, are now shadowy figures, who, although mentioned by some people, are difficult to find. In addition, there were—and still are—rather minor KavuNTar ceremonial leaders at the kirāmam level. Both of these sets of leaders seem to have had much less power and influence than either their PaTTakkārar superiors or the local Ūr headmen, perhaps because of endemic disputes between those qualified to hold these intermediate titles.[18]

As the only other right-division group with a direct tie to land, the NāTār developed an organization which resembles that of the KavuN-

---

[17]This description of KavuNTar organization, refers specifically to the Koṅku—or VēLā-Lar, as they are alternatively called—KavuNTars. This group constitutes by far the most important subcaste of KavuNTars in the region. However, there are also several smaller communities that use the KavuNTar title and which reside in the same general area. The first of these, the VēTTuvar KavuNTar subcaste, which is said to belong to the left division, is of some importance. Others are the UrāLi KavuNTars, the NāTTu KavuNTars, and the PiLLai KavuNTars. I am not certain about the right-left classification of these groups.

VēTTuvars are spoken of as rivals of the Koṅku KavuNTars in much of the folk literature, and particularly in *The Story of the Brothers*. They are described as hunters originally inhabiting forested areas; they were probably converted to farming at a relatively late date. Their major center is at Appiccimārmatam in the northern part of Koṅku. The VēTTuvar KavuNTars have their own PaTTakkārar and their own internal subdivisions, mirroring those of the VēLāLar KavuNTars on a smaller scale. Unfortunately I do not have detailed information about this group.

[18]Thurston mentions them as if they were commonplace, but I found that this was no longer the case. See Thurston, *Castes and Tribes*, 3:418.

Tars and which is similarly based on traditional territorial units.[19] However, the NāTār also exhibit important differences from KavuNTar tradition. They do not have any titles that are recognized at an all-Koṅku level and which could be considered to correspond to those held by the four KavuNTar PaTTakkārar. NāTār organization, by contrast, starts at the nāTu level. It is interesting that the title of the man in charge of the NāTār in this smaller area is also *PaTTakkārar,* the same name the KavuNTars use at the regional level.[20] Furthermore, the role of the NāTār PaTTakkārar in organizing meetings and settling disputes is similar to that of KavuNTars holding this title. Apparently, however, this position of NāTār PaTTakkārar has been losing its importance in recent years. When the last incumbent in Kāṅkayam nāTu died, he was not replaced.

At the kirāmam level a NāTār muppāTTukkārar plays a ritual role at the goddess' festival, just as the KavuNTar muppāTTukkārar does. At the Ūr level, there does not appear to be anyone holding such a hereditary office. In individual hamlets leadership is informal and is generally shared by the older and more respected males. Thus, organization among NāTārs appears to have been most developed in the intermediate range.[21] It was strongest at precisely those levels where KavuNTar organization was weak.

More surprising than any of these details is the fact that there are six subcastes of NāTār in Koṅku and that they share a common organization of a devotional kind.[22] Members of three subcastes are devotees of a spiritual preceptor, or "big guru," who resides in the Tiruchangodu area

---

[19]Here I refer only to the central area of Koṅku with which I am most familiar. There are pockets elsewhere in the region where the right-division Koṅku CeTTiyār and groups of Mutaliyārs also own land. In these areas these two groups probably have a more elaborate organization than where they do not own land. NāTārs in the Kāṅkayam area are in a sense a service caste, since they tap the trees that stand on KavuNTar property. However, they are the only people to have direct access to this resource and they are in control of the processing and distribution activities. Thus they have a large measure of independence in addition to a long-term association with particular stands of palms. They do not have to respond to the day-to-day demands of others. For this reason they do not have the ritual tie to the KavuNTar community possessed by the barber, washerman, local priest, potter, and drummer.

[20]One informant (no. 14) mentioned an *ēRu Periyatanam* or "great leader of the seven"; that is, someone presiding over seven nāTus. However, I was never able to confirm this assertion.

[21]Robert Hardgrave has found the situation to be similar in an area further south. See his *The Nadars of Tamilnad* (Berkeley: University of California Press, 1969), p. 99.

[22]The six are Matana cuvuntaran (Karumancerai or cinna matura), Kamala kētaran (KalyāNi), Kamalakēyūran (KīRāNi), Navanārikkuncaran (NāTTu), Kaṇakarēkan (Matura), and Kamalarōjanan (KirāmaNi). The first three follow the Periya KurukkaL of Karumāpuram, Tiruchangodu Taluk, and the second three are led by Cinna KurukkaL of Peruṅturai, Erode Taluk. My organizational information pertains to the first group. (*KurukkaL* is the title of a religious leader of a particular caste or community; its possessor has a right to collect dues on a periodic basis from members.)

in northeast Koṅku; and members of the other three are devotees of a "little guru" who resides at Peruntur̲ai, located roughly in the middle of the Koṅku area.[23] Thus there is a regional organization of sorts. These offices, however, are religious and the incumbents are held to be Brahmans rather than NāTār caste members. It is further claimed that the NāTār group once contained a seventh subcaste, the Koṅku NāTār, but that this has since died out.[24] This assertion is somewhat suspect, as seven is an auspicious number associated with the Kan̲n̲imār, the seven sisters or young goddesses who are said to protect all NāTārs. The assertion that the name of this subcaste was that of the region as a whole, however, is interesting. It indicates a concern to associate the caste firmly with this geographic area.[25]

The third caste of the right division to have a territorially based political organization consists of the UTaiyār, or potters, who, unlike the KavuN-Tars and the NāTār, do not have a direct tie to land. Here, therefore, I mean territory in the loosest sense—that is, geographical proximity without the structural implications of KavuNTar or NāTār territorial organization. The UTaiyār headman is traditionally referred to as a *Periyata-n̲akkārar*. This term, significantly, does not make any direct reference to territory but rather means something like "the most important relative, the big man." The stress here, then, seems to be on a notion of kindred. A Periyatan̲akkārar has authority over a marriage community or group of settlements which share common temples. Similarly, no particular UTaiyār organization exists at the Ūr, or hamlet, level. As a service community, the potters do not seem to have the same degree of attachment to a territory as the NāTār and KavuNTar groups already discussed. They are also relatively independent of the groups they serve.[26] This intermediate position, between being tied to the land themselves and being dependent through service on others who are, seems to have led the UTaiyār to focus on kin groupings as an organizational principle.

All the other subcastes of the right division are very closely tied to the KavuNTar community, with whom they interact on a day-to-day basis. As a result, none of these groups—the PaNTārams (local priests), Nāvitars (barbers), VaNNārs, (washermen), and Par̲aiyars (drummers, and sometimes guards or errand boys)—has any clear political organization, especially at the nāTu level. When there are disputes, the matter is taken to a

---

[23]Informant no. 11.

[24]Informant no. 11.

[25]Many NāTārs in Koṅku preserve folktales that link them to the Madurai region. Research on the group, however, indicates that they may have originally dispersed from a core area located even further south. Hardgrave, *The Nadars of Tamilnad*, pp. 19–21.

[26]Most pots and clay images are made for calendar festivals, though some special vessels are also supplied for household rituals, such as weddings. This work does not require day-to-day interaction with the community for which the service is supplied.

Cuntaramūrtti KurukkaL (Inf. 34),
a Brahman priest

K. Cuntaram (Inf. 20),
a PaNTāram

CeṅkōTTaiyaṉ (Inf. 29),
a KavuNTar

PāppammāL (Inf. 21),
a PaNTāram

Nācci, a Mātāri

respected KavuNTar family which will agree to serve as arbiter, or it is settled locally. Leadership in an individual settlement becomes the domain of a group of subcaste elders if more than a few families are present. Large concentrations of members of these castes in a single settlement are rare.

The only official title held in any of these service groups is that of *Arumaikkārar,* "the very auspicious person."[27] This is someone, male or female, who is still married to his or her first spouse, who has living children (generally male), and who has undergone a special ceremony of ordination. These Arumaikkārar serve as lay priests at the life-cycle ceremonies of their own subcaste community and are accorded a special respect in this connection. The position exactly parallels that of an Arumaikkārar in the KavuNTar community, although for the sake of brevity this has not been discussed. Indeed, all these service groups have exactly the same ritual traditions as KavuNTars in all life-cycle matters. These Arumaikkārar never have political authority, but are simply accorded a great respect in the community. An unlimited number of people residing in one settlement or belonging to one descent group may obtain and hold this title at the same time.[28]

With this summary of political organization among the different right subcastes in mind, it is possible to attempt a contrast with the left-division pattern and to generalize about all except the lowest-ranking groups. None of the socially high-ranking left-division subcastes has any territorially based organization at all. There are no official titles of leadership at any level for the KōmuTTi CeTTiyār (merchants).[29] The same thing is true of the VaTuka Nāyakkar (builders) and the PāNTiya Nāvitar (barbers).[30] Two other left-division groups, the Mutaliyār (weavers) and the Ācāri (artisans), are in a similar position. However, these two communities do have a certain degree of religious organization in the form of dedication to particular gurus or spiritual leaders. This is most pronounced in the case of the CōLi and Koṅku Ācāri, who belong to an all-South India

---

[27]There is one exception. The Paraiyar do have a muppāTTukkārar who performs a ritual role at the kirāmam level at the festival for the local goddess, Māriyamman.

[28]The UTaiyār, NāTār, and Mutaliyār groups also have Arumaikkārar, but the rituals they perform are somewhat different from those of the KavuNTar ceremony referred to here.

[29]The KōmuTTi CeTTiyār were classified as members of the left division by my Koṅku informants, though some sources record them as right-division members elsewhere. For example, Thurston, *Castes and Tribes,* 3:331, 340. According to Thurston, the Beri CeT-Tiyār, another left-division group, did have men who held the title *Periyatanakkārar* ("most important relative"), but no offices that referred directly to territorial units (1:213). I have no information on this point for the Koṅku CeTTiyār, who are classified as right-division in the Koṅku area. Another right-division CeTTiyār group, the Desayi CeTTiyār, are described by Thurston as having a territorially based organization in the North Arcot area (2:121–23 and 6:91), but I have not encountered any members of this group in Koṅku.

[30]Unfortunately, I have no information about washermen of either right or left division in this matter of subcaste leadership.

artisan organization having five subdivisions. According to my information, these groups are defined on the basis of descent—a person inherits group membership from his father—and not on the basis of occupation or of subcaste.[31] None of these gurus or their respective temples lie within the Koṅku area.[32]

The weavers have a rather similar arrangement, with a *cāmiyār* or guru for each descent group.[33] In the case of both the artisans and the weavers, these gurus travel about during most of the year, passing from one cluster of devotees to the next and collecting *kāNikkai* (dues) from each family. Assessments are made on a yearly basis and generally run somewhere between two and five rupees a household. They may be collected, however, at much longer intervals as the guru does not usually manage to visit each settlement in question each year. The money is used to support the guru and *pūjās* or devotional worship for the deity in the temple to which he is attached.

This sort of organization resembles that described for the NāTār, of the right division. However, there are two important differences. First, the gurus of these left groups belong to their own subcaste community. They are not held to be Brahmans as in the NāTār case, although they may claim Brahman-like status. And secondly, the organization is not limited to one region, but has an all-South India scope. Many or all of the shrines involved lie outside the Koṅku area.

The foregoing description leaves two low-ranking left groups to be discussed: the story-tellers (VēTar) and the leatherworkers (Mātāri or Cakkiliyar). These two groups have some interesting common features which distinguish them from those already described. Both the VēTar and the Mātāri have a moiety-type of subcaste organization which is, at least in

---

[31]The five occupational divisions are:
1. Taccu vēlai   —carpenter
2. Kallu vēlai   —stone mason
3. Poṇṇu vēlai   —goldsmith
4. KaNNāra vēlai—brass-smith
5. Kollu vēlai   —blacksmith.
SOURCE: Informant no. 50.

[32]*The Five Religious Leaders*	*Their Respective Temples*	*Names of the Descent Groups*
1. Kamalamūrtti meṉaṉa kuru	1. Chidamparam	1. Karimarisi
2. Paracamaya kōlari nāta	2. Tinnevelly Town	2. Janagirisi
3. Civaliṅkāccāri	3. Polu Taluk, N. Arcot	3. Munisvari
4. VeṅkaTāccalyia	4. Guntur Dt., Andhra	4. Sanagirisi
5. Virapirē mēntira	5. Cuddapah Dt., Andhra	5. Munugirisi

SOURCE: Informant no. 15. The five occupations, listed in n. 31, do not correspond neatly to this grouping in terms of five religious leaders.

[33]For example, the Alaṅkāram clan are followers of Paraṇcōti KurukkaL, who resides in Peruntalaiyūr, Gobi Taluk, while the CertukuTTai clan follows a second KurukkaL, who resides in Kumbakonam. Both KurukkaLs are drawn from the caste of their devotees and both periodically tour the area to collect a levy.

outline, related to named nāTu areas.[34] In both cases the entire set of clans in the subcaste is divided into two over-arching and ritually contrasted groups. The clans within each of these groups are considered to be "brothers" and marriage between brother clans is forbidden. Marriage with women of the other divison is thus ensured. Each moiety division is, furthermore, associated with a separate nāTu area, though since these moiety divisions remain unnamed, the correspondence must be implied by the location of temples and the references made to nāTu areas by informants. Each moiety has its own headman, and a set of two nāTus, each with one headman, form a pair. The two headmen are ranked, so that one of them is considered to serve as the ultimate authority in situations of dispute. In the case of the Mātāri groups, each headman is described as having an assistant, whose ceremonial role appears to counterbalance the political leadership of his superior. There are also Mātāri officials who serve at the hamlet level, and who are addressed as *Ūr Talaivar* ("local community headmen"). In the section on descent organization of the left groups, which appears later on in this chapter, specific examples are given of this system of moiety organization used by the VēTar and Mātāri subcastes.

To sum up, the major difference in right- and left-division political organization at the subcaste level is that the leading or dominant community of the right division, the KavuNTars, has a well-defined and territorially based organization that is strongest at the regional level and in the local settlement. At intermediate points, there appears to have been a rivalry for political status that has obscured the position of nāTu leaders. Two other right groups that are allied with the KavuNTars but which have a relative degree of independence from them are also organized on a territorial basis. Their formal leadership, however, is best articulated for the nāTu unit, or precisely the position in which KavuNTar organization is weak.

The subcastes of the right that perform daily services for KavuNTars, on the other hand, have no significant organization of their own. They look to the KavuNTars for leadership in the settlement of serious internal disputes.[35] This picture of right-division organization resembles a description recently provided by N.S. Reddy for Andhra. According to him, the right-division groups of this area also had a central organization with a

---

[34]There is only one group of VēTar, to my knowledge, but there are many subcastes of Mātāri. I refer here to the Moracu Mātāri, whom I know best. The Anappu and ToTTi Mātāri, whom I also interviewed, have similar moiety-type organizations and the Anappu, I am certain, have a system of political offices related to this division. (Informants nos. 5, 24, 25, and 41.)

[35]An excellent example of this is a case of a dispute between two subcastes of the PaN-Tāram community (local non-Brahman priests) some sixty years ago over rights to the proceeds of the local kirāmam festival. The matter was resolved by a leading KavuNTar family of the area which devised a system of rights to the proceeds in alternate years. (Informant no. 2.)

code of social behavior and a "supreme arbitrator."[36] Though one could not make quite such a strong statement about Konku, a similar type of situation does appear to have prevailed before 1947.

The organization of the relatively high-ranking subcastes of the left division resembles, in some ways, that of the service communities of the right. These groups, too, have no political organization of their own. However, the difference is that left-division members never refer their disputes to anyone, no matter how eminent, who belongs to another community in their division. Rather, each left subcaste always settles its own affairs internally by reference to a council of elder men. These men may be opinion leaders, but they bear no titles and their position makes no reference to territorial organization. Furthermore, their leadership is by general acclaim and is not inherited. The limitation of secular concerns to internal arbitration suggests, more generally, that left-division organization is more inward-looking than is right-division organization.

Some of these high-ranking left-division groups are devotees of wandering gurus, celibates drawn from their own community who are attached to famous South Indian temples, usually located outside the Konku region. This phenomenon occurs among the members of the right division also. Where it does, the gurus are drawn from the Brahman community and the organization therefore becomes an inter-caste affair where members of other groups may also be devotees of the same man. There is also a stronger reference to the Konku region and its territorial subdivisions in the guru organization of right-division groups. Left-caste religious organization, by contrast, is oriented towards all-South India centers. Thus, in both religious and secular matters, organization for the higher-ranking subcastes of the left division is less territorially tied than it is for counterpart groups in the right division.

Finally, the two lowest left-division groups have a moiety organization and an organized leadership that resembles in some respects the territorial organization of the right subcastes described previously. The differences are that the territorial reference is less explicit, and that there is considerably more emphasis placed on kin groupings in their leadership structure. Furthermore, the organization of these groups is entirely an internal affair, making no reference to higher-ranking communities of the same division. Thus the organization of the two lowest left-division subcastes lies half-way between the types of organization used by right-division groups and by higher-ranking left-division communities. It combines elements of both. This intermediate standing of the lowest-ranking left subcastes is probably due to their position of economic dependence on higher-ranking groups, particularly on the KavuNTar community. Thus, these lowest

[36]N. S. Reddy, "Community Conflict Among the Depressed Castes of Andhra," *Man in India* 30, no. 4 (1950): 7.

left-division communities are more intimately involved with the territorial divisions of their superiors and have a closer tie to the land generally than do their more independent left-division allies. In political and ceremonial organization, therefore, the right and left subcastes at the top of the local social hierarchy are more easily distinguished than are those right and left groups which fall near the bottom of the scale.

Brahman organization also lies somewhere between the patterns of higher-ranking subcastes of the left and right divisions.[37] Within the Aiyar Brahman community of Koṅku, there are a series of inherited titles which descend in the male line. These titles confer special rights on the bearer to collect a tax from residents of an area for the upkeep of kirāmam, nāTu, and regional shrines. These titles form a hierarchy corresponding to the territorial hierarchy of these shrines, and the incumbents, or *KurukkaLs*, perform certain of the more important rituals in these shrines each year.[38] Simultaneously, however, these Brahmans in Koṅku form part of an all-South India Aiyar organization where they are divided into five descent units attached to various great pilgrimage centers of South India.[39] In this respect, their organization resembles that of the left-division subcastes already described. The KaruNĭkar PiLLai group resembles this left-division pattern even more closely, as it has a similar set of gurus, but no territorial organization at all.

DESCENT ORGANIZATION OF THE RIGHT SUBCASTES

In the same way that Kāṅkayam nāTu has a well-defined sacred geography, each of the prominent land-tied subcastes of the area has a well-defined internal organization, and a corresponding hierarchy of kin-group temples or shrines. For each level in the clan and lineage organization of the area there are corresponding deities for whom periodic festivals are celebrated. Each of the temples at which these festivals are celebrated serves to express and emphasize the unity, or expected cooperation of the members of the group with which it is associated. Thus in the case of the Koṅku KavuNTars, for example, there are subcaste temples where representatives of different clans worship together, clan temples where mem-

---

[37]I speak here only of Aiyar Brahmans. I know little about Aiyangar organization.

[38]See p. 71, n. 22, for an explanation of the term *KurukkaL.*

[39]These divisions are: 1) Īcānam (Āticivāccāri), 2) Tarpurucam (Akōracivāccāri), 3) Vāmatēvam (Nampūtiri), 4) Catyū jātam (PaTTar), 5) Akōram. (The names given here are those of the various forms of Civā's *lingam,* a word that refers to the main symbol for this deity. In the case of the first four, each is followed by the name, in parentheses, of the Brahman social grouping that has a special relationship with that particular form; I do not know the name of the grouping associated with the fifth form.) The second group has a particular tie to the seven Civā temples of Koṅku, and the third probably refers to the Nambudiri Brahmans of Kerala. I am not familiar with the other three, but they, too, may have some territorial reference. This information was supplied by Informant no. 11. However, the names of these divisions were unfamiliar to another informant (no. 34).

bers of different lineages worship together, lineage temples where member households worship together, and household shrines where members of one cooking unit worship together.[40] In general, it may be said that sub-caste temples are linked to organization at the kirāmam level, clan temples to organization at the Ūr level, lineage temples to individual settlements, or ūr, and household shrines to organization at the kuTumpam level. Not all clans and lineages belonging to the Koṅku KavuNTar subcastes, how-ever, have their own separate set of temples. A full complement of levels or tiers seems to develop only when a particular subcaste, clan, or lineage becomes numerically and economically dominant in a given area. Without large numbers differentiation is not practical, and without territorial rights to assert there is little to be divided. Where a group is both large and locally dominant, however, the kind of kin-group differentiation described can become nearly indistinguishable from the territorial subdivision seen to accompany it.

By looking at the order of clan rights in a series of local kirāmam areas it has been possible to collect some information on the pattern of KavuN-Tar clan distribution within the nāTu area. The map shown in Figure 2.3 delineates four major KavuNTar clan areas within Kāṅkayam nāTu and will serve as an example. Other, lesser clan areas overlap these, but their distribution is not shown in an effort to focus the discussion on the prin-ciple involved.

Each kirāmam has, in addition to its Civā temple, a sacred center dedi-cated to a local *amman,* or goddess, who is recognized as the patroness of all the locally resident Koṅku KavuNTar clans.[41] Here—in principle—each local clan will have its own ancestral stone or stones. The order in which these stones are worshipped at the time of a subcaste festival illus-trates the accepted ranking of these descent groups in terms of political and economic dominance at the time when the ceremonial order at the temple became fixed. Such orders can be the source of bitter factional fighting, and the sequence is sometimes altered as a result of a dispute. Thus these rules of precedence on festive occasions are not fixed for eter-nity. They can be changed, in recognition of changing power realities. Such alterations of the ceremonial rules, however, are only a means of in-stitutionalizing accepted facts. The innovations originate in power strug-gles, and are later incorporated into the ceremonial idiom.[42]

---

[40]The definition of the terms clan, lineage, and household, as used throughout this study has been given in the Introduction, pp. 3–4.

[41]Not to be confused with the temple dedicated to the kirāmam goddess, who is often called Māriyamman.

[42]For example, as Table 2.2 shows, the CeṅkaNNan clan enjoys first ritual precedence in Kannapuram kirāmam. However, it has now lost nearly all its land, and many of its mem-bers have emigrated elsewhere. They continue to retain their ceremonial priority, but could now easily be challenged by the ŌtāLar clan, which still ranks officially second.

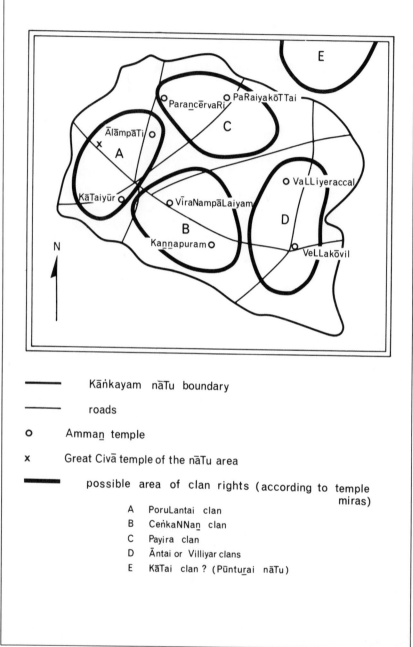

Kāṅkayam nāTu boundary

roads

○   Ammaṉ temple

×   Great Civā temple of the nāTu area

possible area of clan rights (according to temple miras)

A   PoruLantai clan
B   CeṅkaNNaṉ clan
C   Payira clan
D   Āntai or Villiyar clans
E   KāTai clan ? (Pūnturai nāTu)

Fig. 2.3. Traditional clusters of KavuNTar clans in Kāṅkayam nāTu.

Kāṅkayam nāTu is traditionally said to have contained twelve kirāmam areas. Each of these has a local amman shrine which is used by the Koṅku KavuNTars as a subcaste temple.[43] For the purpose of simplification, only eight of the twelve are shown on the map in Figure 2.3. The order of clan rights at these temples—as given by a local poet who specializes in remembering such matters—is shown in Table 2.2.[44] Note that in each of the four areas delineated the dominant clan has a claim at two different temples.[45] This suggests that major clans can dominate an area that encompasses several kirāmams, but that a clan's precedence must be established in each of these kirāmams independently. This pattern points to the kirāmam as the primary organizational level at which clan identity and clan ranking find expression. I call these temples in which clan precedence is established subcaste temples, as their membership is drawn from the subcaste as a whole.

Beneath these subcaste temples in the territorial hierarchy are separate temples belonging to individual clans. These clan temples appear to be linked to Ūr or hamlet areas and are used by representatives of various lineages within the clan on special occasions. Each of them tends to be located near the Ūr, or hamlet, where a certain clan predominates and where most of its members reside. For example, the CeṅkaNNan clan, which previously dominated Kannapuram kirāmam, has a separate clan temple dedicated to KariyakāLiyamman—which is not shown in Figure 2.3—in addition to the subcaste temple to the same goddess mentioned in Table 2.2.[46] This clan temple is located in the southern half of the kirāmam near KōyilpāLaiyam, in the residential section where most of the clan members are concentrated. The subcaste temple, on the other hand, is in the center of the kirāmam, right next to the Civā and Māriyamman temples for the area. The clan temple dedicated to KariyakāLiyamman is now in great disrepair, as opposed to the subcaste temple to the same goddess, which is well kept up. The former is used only very occasionally, as many important CeṅkaNNan families have now emigrated elsewhere, while at the latter, several ceremonies are performed each year. The KaNa-

---

[43]There is some disagreement about the actual number of kirāmams, which seems to have risen, at some point in history, to fourteen. The poet whose work has been used in constructing the map in Figure 2.3 includes fifteen ammans in his list, indicating a process of still further division at work. The matter becomes extremely complex when examined in detail, and thus necessitates a simplified approach in an exposition of principles involved, which is the main interest here.

[44]In Table 2.2 only the first three clans named in the ritual sequence are shown. Some temples have a list which includes up to fifteen names.

[45]Some clans have a major claim at as many as three of these kirāmam-linked subcaste temples in the Kāṅkayam area.

[46]Clan temples tend to be simple in layout, and do not have stones installed to correspond to each subdivision as is the case for subcaste temples. A simple square enclosure with a central deity is sufficient at this level, although clan temples can be more elaborate in some instances.

TABLE 2.2
SOME IMPORTANT TEMPLES OF KĀNKAYAM NĀTU AND THE ORDER OF KAVUNTAR CLAN RIGHTS

Area of Map	Kirāmam	Name of Goddess	KavuNTar Clans (in order of their right to receive offerings blessed by the deity)		
			I	II	III
A	KaTaiyūr / ĀlampāTi	KariyakāLiyamman / ĀlampāTiyamman	CeTar / *PoruLantai*	*PoruLantai*	— / —
B	Kāṅkayam (now ViraNampāLaiyam) / Kannapuram	Āyiamman / KariyakāLiyamman	PeruṅkuTi[1] / *CeṅkaNNaṉ*	*CeṅkaNNaṉ* / ŌtāLar	Turar / KaNavāLar[2]
C	ParancervaRi / PaRaiyakōTTai	KariyakāLiyamman / Anuramman	*Payirar* / *Payirar*	Cempiyar	ŌtāLar
D	VaLLiyeraccal / VeLLakōvil	ARakanācciyamman / VeLLakōvilammaṉ	*Villiyar* / Kurukular[3]	Celvar / *Antai*	*Antai* / Villiyar

SOURCE: Information for this table was drawn from PaRaniccāmi Pulavar, *Koṅku Celvi* [The goddesses of Koṅku] (Coimbatore: Pudumalar Press, 1948), pp. 70–122 and combined with material gathered in my own inquiries.

NOTES: The table represents a simplification and is intended only to illustrate the general pattern of single-clan dominance within a given territory. The names of clans which appear to have exercised particular influence in a given area at some time in the past are given in italics.

The letters in the first column of the table correspond to the areas labeled on Figure 2.3, which shows where the temples are located.

Note that the order of clan rights listed by the local poet does not correspond very satisfactorily with the actual order of clan shrines at two of these temples, as described to me by their local priests in 1965. See Figures 2.4 and 2.5 for comparison with the table.

In every case, except that of Kāṅkayam, the name of the kirāmam and the name of the Ūr where the goddess's temple is located are the same. In the case of Āyiamman, the temple is located in ViraNampāLaiyam, an Ūr which used to be part of Kāṅkayam kirāmam, but which has now split to form a separate kirāmam under its own name. Thus, in principle, the temple of each of the goddesses listed is located in that Ūr after which the kirāmam has been named.

[1]The famous clan of *The Story of the Brothers.*

[2]The author of the work on which this chart is based says that the third clan with rights at this temple are the Patariya, the KaNavāLar being fourth. However, the present priest at the temple—Informant no. 20—says that this group has now forfeited its claim by not attending the festival for many years. This is not surprising since no member of this clan is now known to reside in the area.

[3]This name probably refers to a non-KavuNTar group.

vāLar clan, which presently dominates the ŌlappāLaiyam and Kaṇṇapuram hamlet areas, also has its own clan temple which is dedicated to the Kaṇṇimār, or seven sisters. This temple, by contrast to that of the CeṅkaNNaṉ clan, is located in Kaṇṇapuram hamlet and is in fair condition.[47]

At a lower level than the kirāmam, that of the Ūr, the KaNavāLar clan is divided into two lineages, each of which worships its own female founder. These lineages are said to be descended from the first and second wives of a single male ancestor. For the most part, members of the lineage founded by the senior wife reside in one settlement, while members of the lineage founded by the junior wife reside in another. Both wives are said to have committed suicide after their husband's death, but an important distinction between their final actions remains. The first wife is said to have jumped into a well, and the second to have thrown herself on a fire.[48] The descendants of the latter hold a yearly festival at a substantial lineage temple erected in ŌlappāLaiyam and dedicated to her. The descendants of the former hold their ceremonies on a different day, under a tree near Kaṇṇapuram village, as they have no lineage temple of their own.

It is interesting that at all three levels of Koṅku KavuNTar organization just described (that is, at the subcaste, the clan, and the lineage level) the associated temple is dedicated to an ammaṉ, or female. These women are definitely goddesses, but many have suggestively human origins. The principal deity of the KavuNTar subcaste in Kaṇṇapuram is KariyakāLiyamman. At the clan level, furthermore, the CeṅkaNNaṉ worship at another temple dedicated to the same goddess, while the KaNavāLar worship the Kaṇṇimār or seven sisters, and their male guardian, KaruppaNacāmi. These sisters are at once a generalized form of actual clan women who have died before puberty, and a recognized divinity in their own right.[49] Finally, as already mentioned, there is the case of a KaNavāLar temple which was erected to honor one of the co-wives of a single male ancestor, and which serves to distinguish a local lineage from the descendants of the other co-wife.

The emphasis on women in these subcaste, clan, and lineage temples is particularly clear in the case of the KaNavāLar. It is less striking but still a common pattern in the case of other local KavuNTar clans. Two general

---

[47]The KaNavāLar clan owes its dominant position to a combination of numerical preponderance and economic influence in this area; they are the largest KavuNTar descent group in ŌlappāLaiyam, and jointly they own more land than any other clan in this settlement.

[48]Informants nos. 42 and 51. Generally suicide by fire has more prestige than suicide by drowning. As the first wife would have more prestige than the second wife by virtue of her primary position, one would expect the story of suicide by fire to be associated with her, rather than with the second wife. Why the precedence of the two wives should be reversed in this manner—it was the first wife who jumped into the well—is not known.

[49]This most interesting group of sisters will be discussed at length in later volumes on folklore and ceremony in Koṅku.

themes can be said justly to characterize the spirit of these internal sub-caste divisions. First, internal differentiation within the KavuNTar community is nearly indistinguishable from territorial subdivision. Second, the marker of this differentiation is generally female. Women, one might say, appear to serve as the crucial or nodal points around which subdivisions within the KavuNTar descent group are seen to occur.

A woman can come to play a part in male descent-group formation in two important ways. For one, a man may have sons by more than one wife. If these half-brothers find themselves at odds in adult life, as is very often the case, they may decide to include references to their respective mothers in describing their relation to their clan ancestors for the benefit of later generations. When a man has several wives, therefore, these women can be used as reference points for the formation of new linages and ultimately of new clans. The role of a woman whose husband comes to reside uxorilocally can be similar. Here a temptation exists for the woman's father to pass property through her to his grandsons. These boys may then experience friction in later life with their own father's brothers' sons over claims to additional property in the male line. These factors can also serve to differentiate two male lines, one which stayed on the traditional family land and the other which went to reside uxorilocally. The latter would logically become identified with the name of the woman from whom the sons in that new line inherited.

The theme that women serve as dividers of a descent group is a common one in Koṅku. This division, furthermore, can occur at any of several levels, that of caste, subcaste, clan, or lineage, depending on the rivalries involved. Such stories are particularly associated with the dominant KavuNTar community. The following is taken from the folk history of the PaTTakkārar's family in KāTaiyūr as an example of why a particular clan shrine has been dedicated to VeLLaiyamman (a white or albino girl).[50] The story is from the temple priest.[51]

> Long ago in KāTaiyūr there was a clan of Cēra KavuNTars who had an albino daughter. No man among the respectable families of the area would come forth to marry her. However, at the time there was a poor man of the PoruLantai clan from Ātikarumāpuram who happened to be wandering around KāTaiyūr. The men of the Cēra clan tried to persuade him to marry their daughter by offering him some land. He accepted. After the marriage, however, the girl's parents died. Meanwhile the girl had already given birth to three sons and was pregnant with a fourth. At the same time, her jealous brothers tried to take away the land their father had given to their sister's husband. When the brothers killed the husband the girl tried to argue, but they only attempted to intimidate her and force her to leave the village.

[50]See the discussion of another albino girl in a different context, in chapter 3, pp. 122–23.
[51]Informant no. 35.

A fairly typical image of the Kannimār, carved from black stone. This group of young virgin sisters is very commonly worshipped at local clan shrines.

KaruppaNacāmi, or the "black god," who generally serves as protector in temples for the Kannimār, and also as guardian of local fields.

Men dividing up betel leaves as symbolic of shares held by local families in an important subcaste temple. The annual festival at the temple is just about over.

Finally a village council was called to discuss the matter. At the meeting the brothers told their sister that they were prepared to give her land and money if she would meet one condition. The council members asked what this was and the brothers demanded that she take a VeTattalā (babool) tree which was felled ten years before in a field, sharpen one end of it, and drive it into the ground with her hands. Each time she hit the tree to drive it into the ground it must spread out branches and provide leafy shade.

To everyone's surprise the sister agreed to the condition. First she gave birth to her fourth son. Then her brothers brought the tree in question from the field. The girl bathed and walked clockwise around the Civā temple near their home. Then she took the tree and drove it into the ground, as her brothers had asked. It bounced back out of the ground twice and then on the third try, sprouted a leafy head of branches. As this happened she sang a song saying that the male branches of the tree would be cut off and die, while the female branches would grow and bear fruit. Her brothers were frightened and ran away. The girl's sons grew to great strength and the fourth was able to control an elephant belonging to the PāNTiya king which had run amuk. The king was greatly pleased and gave the son the title PaTTakkārar of Koṅku. Later the girl (VeLLaiyamman) was made a goddess and a shrine was erected to her memory inside the KāTaiyūr Civā temple.

This story illustrates not only the magical power that the women of a clan are said to possess, but also how, according to tradition, they may use this power to form new descent-group branches. Either a woman's own sons may establish distinct descent lines when one of them goes to reside uxorilocally or these men may decide to differentiate themselves jointly from the sons of a co-wife. This latter is perhaps the more common pattern. We have just seen how within the KaNavāLar clan of Kannapuram kirāmam there is a division into two distinct groups on precisely these grounds. Each group has its own shrine, dedicated to the wife of the common male ancestor from whom both are descended.

A similar legend, using women to explain the history of a social division, may also serve to provide a background to the over-all right-left distinction as it applies to the region as a whole.

A Kammālan who had two sons—one by a Balija woman, and the other by his Kammālan wife—was unjustly slain by a king of Conjeeveram, and was avenged by his two sons, who killed the king and divided his body. The Kammālan son took his head and used it as a weighing pan, while the Balija son made a pedler's carpet out of the skin, and threads out of the sinews for stringing bangles. A quarrel arose, because each thought the other had got the best of the division, and all the other castes joined in, and took the side of either the Kammālan or the Balija. (These then became the right- and left-division antagonists, respectively.)[52]

[52]Thurston, *Castes and Tribes,* 3:117–18.

The presence of a woman, therefore, serves as a classic explanation of a social separation, be it within the descent group or within society as a whole.

The architecture of these subcaste and clan temples, furthermore, bears out the same theme of social division in a spatial idiom, as illustrated in the maps in Figures 2.4 and 2.5 of the Āyiammaṉ and ARakaṉācciyam-maṉ temples. The female in a subcaste shrine generally faces north; this particular compass orientation is the one most often used for shrines dedicated to the deceased. At these shrines the ancestral stones or images of individual clans are lined up in one or more rows in front of the goddess in a way implying direct lines of descent. The most important clan—the one with the first ceremonial rights—generally has its shrine closest to the main deity, as if it had been born first, just as the representative of this clan would stand nearest to the deity during any important ritual.[53] Shrines belonging to other castes, by contrast, stand at the end of the line, or just outside the inner walls. The position of these less important shrines exactly parallels that taken by members of many service castes when worshipping at KavuNTar subcaste temples. Instead of establishing independent sacred structures to express parallel divisions within their own community, members of such castes tend simply to worship at the clan or subcaste temple of whatever powerful landed family they have traditionally served.

Two examples of the way in which the local histories of particular descent groups are remembered by members of such service groups are as follows:

Local History of PaNTāram Descent Groups[54] Long ago there was a descent group of OkaccāNTi PaNTārams from a place called Cēlūr-putūr who came to reside in Kaṉṉapuram kirāmam. These men had the right to perform the rituals at the temple for the kirāmam goddess, Māriyammaṉ. After some time, however, they became dissatisfied with this job and left the area. The reason may have been that the KavuNTar community demanded too much work.

Then the leading KavuNTar family in the Ur of Kaṉṉapuram called in a second group of OkaccāNTi PaNTārams who had previously been living in KomarāNTicāvaTi and KoRalipāLaiyam. This new group was then given the rights to perform the ceremonies at the Māriyammaṉ temple. After a time, however, a second leading family from RaTTivalacu, another Ur in Kaṉṉapuram kirāmam, became dissatisfied. It claimed that the PaNTārams were always being called

[53] Both Figures 2.4 and 2.5 are constructed from my own observations recorded on visits to these temples in 1965. Note that the clan precedence orders described to me by the priests of these temples differs considerably from those provided by the local poet in Table 2.2 on page 82. I do not know why the line of clan stones, in Figure 2.4, should be ordered from the perspective of a secondary deity.

[54] Informant no. 20.

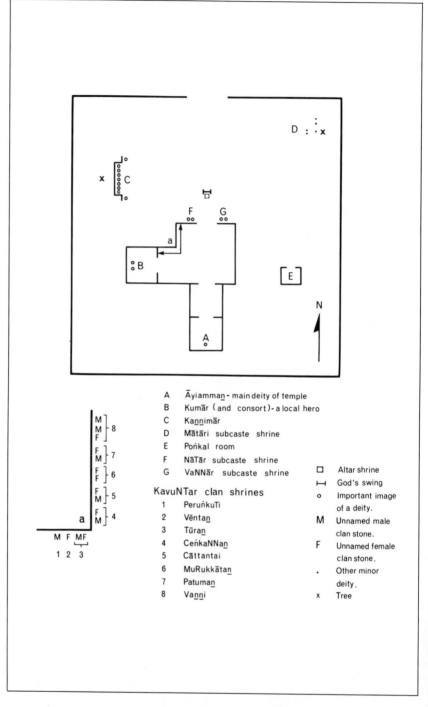

A   Āyiamman̠ - main deity of temple
B   Kumār (and consort) - a local hero
C   Kan̠n̠imār
D   Mātāri subcaste shrine
E   Pon̠kal room
F   NāTār subcaste shrine
G   VaNNār subcaste shrine

KavuNTar clan shrines

1   Perun̠kuTi
2   Vēntan̠
3   Tūran̠
4   Cen̠kaNNan̠
5   Cāttantai
6   MuRukkātan̠
7   Patuman̠
8   Van̠n̠i

☐   Altar shrine
⊢   God's swing
o   Important image of a deity.
M   Unnamed male clan stone.
F   Unnamed female clan stone.
.   Other minor deity.
x   Tree

Fig. 2.4.   The Āyiamman̠ temple at VīraNampāLaiyam.

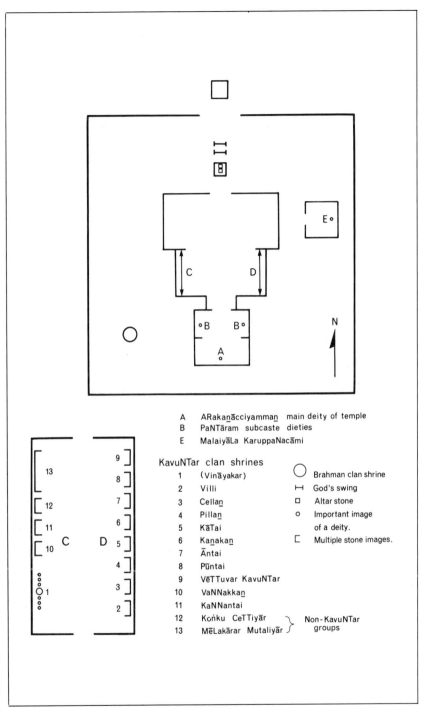

A   ARakanācciyamman main deity of temple
B   PaNTāram subcaste dieties
E   MalaiyāLa KaruppaNacāmi

KavuNTar clan shrines
1   (Vināyakar)
2   Villi
3   Cellan
4   Pillan
5   KāTai
6   Kanakan
7   Āntai
8   Pūntai
9   VēTTuvar KavuNTar
10   VaNNakkan
11   KaNNantai
12   Koṅku CeTTiyār ⎤ Non-KavuNTar
13   MēLakārar Mutaliyār ⎦ groups

○   Brahman clan shrine
⊢   God's swing
□   Altar stone
○   Important image
     of a deity.
⊏   Multiple stone images.

Fig. 2.5. The ARakanācciyamman temple at VaLLiyeraccal.

by the Kaṇṇapuram KavuNTar family and never had time to give the RaTTivalacu KavuNTars any personal service.

Thus the leading RaTTivalacu KavuNTar family called in its own group of OkaccāNTi PaNTārams from VeruvōTampāLaiyam, west of Dharapuram. This occurred about one hundred years ago, and the genealogy of this group is still known. The present priests are members of the third generation. Initially, the second group of PaNTārams called in resisted sharing their rights at the Māriyammaṇ temple with the third group. However, the KavuNTar family in RaTTivalacu was very influential and managed, after some difficulties, to provide for a share of the kirāmam festival for its own priests.

Local History of Paraiyar Descent Groups[55] Originally all the Paraiyar families in Kaṇṇapuram kirāmam were members of one clan. They shared the work of drumming without any formal division. Then in a time of famine and great hardship elsewhere, which may have been about two hundred years ago, a man of a second clan came to the village. At this time the Paraiyars of Kaṇṇapuram were themselves overburdened with work, as the population of the kirāmam had grown and there were many festivals to drum for. Therefore they offered the newcomer a share in the work if he were to stay and help. He agreed and the division was formally made. After a time the original clan also split into two subdivisions. Thus there are now three divisions of Paraiyars in the kirāmam and work is divided equally among them. Responsibility for outlying hamlets was allocated on the basis of a general territorial division of the kirāmam into three areas. The most important settlements, however, are internally divided according to the pattern of KavuNTar clans within them. There are three major KavuNTar clans in these settlements, and one division of the Paraiyars is responsible for drumming at the life-cycle ceremonies of each of them. The work of drumming for the Māriyammaṇ festival each year, however, remains undivided.

These examples suggest that the tie between particular families within a service caste and an individual KavuNTar household is often stronger than their identification with families in their own caste community. Thus, KavuNTar internal divisions become the adopted internal divisions of their closest servants. The latter, in a very real sense, have none of their own. This generalization applies in particular to the PaNTārams (local priests), Nāvitars (barbers), VaNNārs (washermen), Paraiyars (drummers) and in some cases to Mātāris (untouchable laborers and leatherworkers).

Only two right-division castes, apart from the KavuNTars, can be said to have an independent descent-group organization and a separate hierarchy of local clan shrines. These are the NāTārs (palmyra-palm tappers) and UTaiyārs (potters).[56] These two castes have strong local ties, and yet

---

[55]Informant no. 1.

[56]A third group, the Koṅku CeTTiyār (merchants), should also be mentioned here. However, I have very little information about them. The one clan festival of this community I attended was an impressive affair. (It was celebrated in the month of Māci (February–March)

are relatively free of KavuNTar dominance. They do not generally work under direct KavuNTar surveillance, either in their houses or in the fields. Thus few traditional ties exist between members of these castes and individual KavuNTar families. Their position is less one of dependence than of symbiosis or complementarity. Therefore it is not surprising that their pattern of internal descent-groupings should be found to be separate from but similar to that of the KavuNTar community.

The NāTār provide another example of a right-division caste with an elaborate set of internal descent divisions. Although the NāTār have only a middling prestige in Koṅku, they have at times controlled considerable wealth. They do not own land directly, but they take long-term leases on stands of palmyra palms and sometimes coconut palms. They are able to make a good living from the products of these trees, a certain amount of which they give back to the KavuNTars as rent. Before prohibition the NāTārs in the Kāṅkayam area made a considerable profit on alcohol distilled from the sap of these palms and some of them lived in well-built, respectable homes. However, they are traditionally more mobile than the landowning KavuNTars and tend to move in drought years to areas where the sap in the trees still runs.

The Maramēri (tree-climbing) NāTār are the most important subcaste of this community in the Kannapuram area. The headman or Periyatanakkārar of the subcaste tells an interesting story of how the group came to settle in this location.[57]

Long ago the NāTārs lived in a country called TiruvāTa which was ruled by a *rāja*. In this country there was a great lake with a dam and one day that dam broke and all the fields flooded. To repair the dam

by the Koṅku CeTTiyār of TāyampāLaiyam.) The ceremonies focused on the reenactment of part of the folklore surrounding their ancestors. (The story reenacted was that of *The Brothers*, the great local epic concerning the settlement of the Koṅku region. The heroes of this story are KavuNTars. However, they are celebrated as ancestors by this particular group of Koṅku CeTTiyārs in support of a claim that they were originally KavuNTars, who broke with this caste and became known as "CeTTiyārs" when they decided to enter business.) The temple in which these heroes are worshipped is primarily dedicated to the Kannimār. As such, it has the appearance of a clan temple, similar to that mentioned as belonging to the KaNavāLar KavuNTars in Kannapuram. The same group also worships occasionally at a temple dedicated to a woman named MīnāTci near Kannapuram. This is probably an old caste temple, similar in function to the KavuNTar Āyiamman temple previously described but more modest in scope.

MīnāTci, of course, is also the name of the great goddess of Madurai, and I am not convinced that this temple is dedicated to her. No one I asked knew the history of the shrine, except to say that it once belonged to some Koṅku CeTTiyārs who have since moved from the area. It is more likely to have been constructed in memory of some female ancestor of the local lineage named MīnāTci, particularly since the goddess stands at the south end of a line of three images, the other two of which are unnamed males. All three images face east. Further research might uncover more temples and fill out this picture of a descent hierarchy among Koṅku CeTTiyārs, paralleling that of the KavuNTars in the Kāṅkayam area.

[57]Informant no. 14.

the rājā ordered one able-bodied man to come from each house and to bring a shovel. All the other communities sent men except the Nā-Tārs. At this the king was very angry and he ordered them, as a penalty, to set their heads under an elephant's foot and be crushed to death. One NāTār followed the rājā's orders, but his relations, two brothers and a brother-in-law, instead fled with their wives and children to Koṅku.

When this little group of travelers arrived on the south side of the place called VīracōRapuram, they found a forest full of Karuvēlā trees. Here the three families set up camp and began to cook. However, a very wealthy man living in VīracōRapuram saw smoke rising from the forest. He mounted a bull and came to see who these people were. When he met them he invited the travelers to use a shelter for the night which was east of the road leading south from the village. (This man knew full well that people who slept in this shelter never lived to see the next day.) The NāTārs, unsuspecting, accepted his offer and lifted their baskets of belongings to move. However, when they raised them they quickly discovered a stone in one basket weighing it down. They threw the stone away only to discover another and this experience was repeated several times. When they had reached the shelter, they threw this magic stone away for the third and final time. [The storyteller explains that the stone was really a god whom people now call ONTivīraiyaṉ or "the single brave man."] Where the stone landed a shrine was later constructed.

The reason why people camping in this shelter used to lose their lives was that there was a *muni* ("frightening giant") living just to the west of the same road. This muni used to come and kill anyone camped there during the night. That particular evening, however, the party of travelers heard a *paLLi* ("wall lizard") cry out a warning sound about midnight. The elder brother of the group woke up and, frightened, shook his younger brother until he awoke also. The latter was well versed in the art of seeing into the future. He looked up the signs in a special book and predicted that they would all die if they stayed in the shelter until morning.

Just then the three men heard shouts and sounds like a man rushing towards them through the night. It was the muni on the rampage and he was drawing near. However, just in time, the god manifested earlier in the magical stone stood up and fought the muni off. The elder brother tried to help. He caught hold of the muni's hair and managed to pull out his teeth.[58] He then carried the giant to the west of the road and set him down facing east. He then drew seven straight lines in front of him, saying that if he never crossed these lines he would receive sacrifices and be fed.

The next morning, a group of KavuNTars from VīracōRapuram came to see if the NāTārs were dead or alive. They found them calmly smoking cigars and were much impressed. After a while the NāTārs told these KavuNTars their story. The men from the village then asked what work the NāTārs could do and the latter answered that they could climb trees. The KavuNTars were pleased and offered

[58]After a man's two upper front teeth have been pulled, he no longer has the power to practice sorcery.

them a chance to stay and to climb trees on their fields without paying rent. One of the NāTārs then climbed up a tall tree upside down, just to show off. The descendants of this man still live around VīracōRapuram.

The story emphasizes the relative independence of the NāTār, and their strong ties to the local territory. It also suggests that their settlement in the present spot was sanctioned by the Maramēri subcaste deity. A temple dedicated to their particular goddess, ATaṉcāramman, now stands on the spot where the magic stone is said to have landed. ATaṉcāramman is associated with an area where rights to the palmyra palms are claimed, and there is no separate story about her. The temple, shown in Figure 2.6, is to the Maramēri NāTār what the Āyiamman subcaste temple, previously described, is to the Koṅku KavuNTar community. There are said to be sixty-three clans of Maramēri NāTār now associated with the former.[59] Each clan sets up a small stone, which perhaps represents that clan's individual deity, at the time of the subcaste festival, and offerings are made to all these stones in a set order.[60] The ATaṉcāramman subcaste temple also has a number of lesser temples associated with it where clan ceremonies take place annually. The ones I managed to identify were:

X_1 Mūppar Clan X_4 Vāttiyār Clan

X_2 CappāNi Clan X_5 KiNarupāva Clan

X_3 Rāvuttar Clan

Every one of these shrines is dedicated to the seven sisters, and to their guardian, KaruppaNacāmi.

Two of the Maramēri clans, in particular, appear to have had a long history of dispute over who should enjoy the first rights at the subcaste festival. One clan, the Mūppar, now holds the right to secular leadership of the subcaste, and the office of Periyataṉakkārar belongs to this descent group. The other clan, the CappāNi, holds the right to the office of ATaṉcāramman temple priest. At one time, the Mūppar clan was divided over whether it should continue to cede first rights at the festival to the CappāNi, or rather construct its own subcaste temple nearby. The discontented element won, and a second temple (Y), a simplified replica of

---

[59]Actually I only discovered five. Sixty-three merely serves as an impressive and auspicious formal number. Interestingly, sixty-three is the equivalent of twenty-one multiplied by three. Mention of twenty-one gods in a temple is rare in Koṅku, but Dumont suggests that it may be common further south, in the same area from which these NāTārs are said to have come. I found one such example, the AṅkāLamman temple in Karur. See Louis Dumont, *Une Sous-Caste de l'Inde du Sud* (Paris: Mouton, 1957), pp. 357-66. The choice of an odd number is appropriate here, since it refers to the ideal of sixty-three stones (representing deities) which are installed at the time of the festival.

[60]A full festival occurs only once every ten years or so, at a time when the palmyra sap is running particularly well.

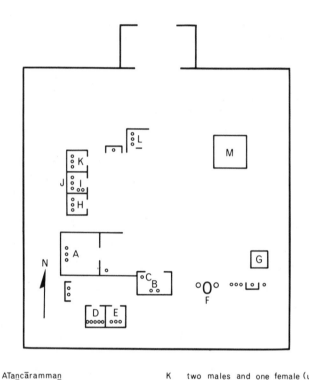

A   ATaṉcārammaṉ
B   The Two Brothers
C   TaṅkāttāL
D   five stones (unidentified)
E   three male figures (unidentified)
F   Pāramakāmuṉi
G   temple well
H   Taṉṉāci plus one male and one female figure

I   FF of present priest, and FFB of same
J   three female figures (unidentified)

K   two males and one female (unidentified)
L   IruLappaṉ
M   structure to hold festive cloths during large subcaste gatherings

O   Male and female figures who serve as assistants to Pāramakāmuṉi

o   Important image of a deity

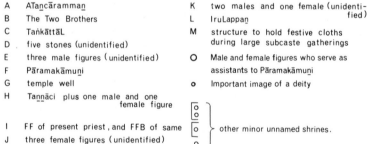 other minor unnamed shrines.

Fig. 2.6.   A Maramēri NāTār subcaste temple.

the first (X), was constructed.[61] At this new temple (Y), the CappāNi clan took precedence, and then it acquired its own subsidiary Mūppar clan temple (Y₁). Other clans, however, apparently did not follow suit. In recent years the factional feeling between the CappāNi and the Mūppar has subsided, perhaps because the former have unanimously ceded ceremonial rights to the latter at temple X. Temple Y and clan temple X₁ have now fallen into disuse, whereas all the other temples listed are still kept up. Y₁ now replaces X₁ as the Mūppar clan temple associated with the big complex dedicated to ATancāramman.[62]

The last of the right-division castes with an independent set of descent-group shrines and festivals are the UTaiyār or potters. As they are a relatively small caste, and a few families can serve a wide region, one clan of UTaiyār has territorial claims over the entire Kāṅkayam nāTu area. A second clan, similarly, has rights to the neighboring nāTu of Pūnturai. Each clan supports a large temple in its own nāTu at which a yearly festival is held. Rights to the priesthood at each temple are held by clan members, but the festival is a subcaste affair which a number of different clan groups attend.[63]

The Kāṅkayam UTaiyār temple, however, is dedicated to the seven sisters, thus following the clan rather than the subcaste pattern. Probably it was once a clan temple which has now grown to subcaste proportions. This view is supported by the fact that about fifty years ago a split occurred in the Kāṅkayam nāTu clan, following a quarrel between three brothers. The descendants of each brother now celebrate their own festival at the temple and provide their own priest.[64] Rights rotate on a yearly basis. Thus any one descent group will gather for a celebration once in three years.[65] What were probably once lineages—groups in which all members shared certain ritual restrictions during the period of mourning the death of any one of them—have now grown to clan proportions. This means that members no longer share these mourning restrictions as an entire body, but only with members of their own subdivision.

[61]See Figure 2.6.

[62]I have pieced this history together from the accounts of Informants nos. 12, 13, and 14. I am not certain that it is correct in every detail but it serves to illustrate the principle of NaTār descent groupings which clearly lie behind these extensive temple complexes.

[63]There are other subcastes of UTaiyār in the Koṅku region, but I did not obtain any information about them. In the Kāṅkayam–Pūnturai area the Koṅku UTaiyār subcaste predominates. Similarly, there are other subcastes of NaTār in the area.

[64]Here is a glimpse of the descent-group division process. It would be interesting to know if these men are actually half-brothers or whether women are involved in some other way in the split as it is occurring.

[65]In 1965, I attended the festival celebrated by the UTaiyār subcaste whose membership includes the potters who reside in ŌlappāLaiyam. That year fifty-two out of a possible sixty households paid the four-rupee levy for festival expenditures. Of these families twenty-six also contributed a goat for sacrifice. The coconuts and other food offerings blessed by the deity were similarly divided into fifty-two shares and redistributed at the end of the ceremonies.

Now that several clans share festival rights, this sacred center is quickly acquiring the characteristics of a subcaste temple. The situation at present is one of organizational transition. Celebrations at the clan temple have already come to resemble a subcaste festival for the nāTu area. Simultaneously, the divisions within the clan which were once just lineages, have now subdivided and taken on an individual clan-like quality. One might predict that the nāTu descent grouping will soon be characterized as a cluster of three "brother" clans, each of which will eventually acquire a name and a smaller, physically separate shrine of its own.[66]

In the foregoing description of descent-group organization of the right-bloc subcastes, it has been seen that each of three relatively high-ranking and independent right communities—the Koṅku KavuNTar, the Marameri NāTār, and the Koṅku UTaiyar—has an elaborate descent-group organization of its own. In the case of the KavuNTars, this organization is closely tied to a notion of territorial rights and the points of subdivision are clearly associated with kirāmam, and Ūr units.[67]

For the NāTār and the UTaiyar the relation of descent-group organization to territory becomes at once more generalized and more vague. The NāTār subcaste temple is located in a spot where palmyra palms are plentiful. Their history of residence in the area, furthermore, would seem to suggest that their spatial and ritual organization corresponds more to the cluster patterns of these trees than to kirāmam and nāTu units per se. The elaborate development of their temples seems related, therefore, to the detailed allocation of territorial rights, but not directly to kirāmam and Ūr units. The UTaiyar have taken another tack. Their temple organization is overtly related to the nāTu territorial unit, but with them lesser divisions into kirāmam and Ūr areas seem to be unimportant. Hence with all three groups there is some relation between descent organization and politico-territorial units. This pattern is best developed in the KavuNTar case, but both the NāTār and the UTaiyar also play on this dimension in their own ways and to a lesser extent.

The remaining right-bloc subcastes—PaNTāram, Nāvitar, VaNNār, and Paṟaiyar—are mainly service groups. Individual families within these groups generally have a strong personal tie to some important KavuNTar household which they have traditionally served. Ties to these powerful

---

[66]This has just recently happened in the case of another UTaiyar subcaste which also claims rights to Kāṅkayam nāTu. This group, centered in the Muttūr-VeLLakōvil-VaL-Liyeraccal area of the nāTu, has recently split into three, and each segment is currently constructing its own temple. The second of these new temples was only completed in 1969. (From Informant no. 20, by letter.)

[67]Leach discusses the same sort of situation in his book on land tenure in Ceylon, except that he refers to endogamous micro-castes rather than to exogamous descent units. See E. R. Leach, *Pul Eliya, A Village in Ceylon: A Study of Land Tenure and Kinship* (Cambridge: Cambridge University Press, 1961), p. 303.

families rather than direct ties to territory tend to serve as points of internal differentiation. Often the founder of a descent group will have originally been invited to settle in the area at the request of a leading family in need of additional service. The story of the PaNTāram descent groups given earlier is a case in point. The descendants of that initial settler will then be expected to identify with that family's clan and subcaste temples and to participate in the festivals performed there. I know of no examples of independent descent-group organization in these communities.

The organization of right-division subcastes at the nāTu level and below is both elaborate and important.[68] Furthermore, the hierarchy of KavuNTar descent-groupings and KavuNTar shrines is more closely tied to territorial concepts than that of any other community in the region.[69] At the same time, it is precisely KavuNTar descent-group organization that is currently the most neglected.[70] The KavuNTars spend little money on the upkeep of their temples nowadays. In the past this disregard, and the decline in periodic festivals which accompanied it, could be partly blamed on the bitter feuding which used to be endemic in the KavuNTar community. Most of these feuds, however, are now past history. Probably the lack of interest in descent-group activities among KavuNTars today is associated with a gradual shift of emphasis away from collective ritual toward the affirmation of individual family status. Thus, households, rather than lineages and clans, are now becoming the primary units in local battles for prestige. Although this change is most noticeable in the KavuNTar community, other groups are sure to follow their lead.

DESCENT ORGANIZATION OF THE LEFT SUBCASTES

A striking contrast can be noted between right- and left-division communities in the matter of descent-group organization. Among those of the right division there exists an elaborate hierarchy of clan and lineage groupings, each one publicly affirmed by the construction of a separate temple to which members come to jointly celebrate important festivals. This hierarchy, as we have seen, is most elaborate in the case of the high-ranking KavuNTar community. but it is mirrored in its main features by other relatively independent, high-ranking groups of the same bloc. The service communities share in this organization in a vicarious manner, by

---

[68]Morgan Maclachlan and Alan Beals have hinted that the same sort of pattern may prevail among land-tied castes of southern Mysore. See their article entitled "The Internal and External Relationships of a Mysore Chiefdom," *Journal of Asian and African Studies* 1, no. 2 (1966): 87–99.

[69]Adrian C. Mayer has made a similar observation concerning the extent of Rajput clan organization in Malwa. See his *Caste and Kinship in Central India* (London: Routledge and Kegan Paul, 1960), pp. 164–66.

[70]With some notable exceptions. For example, the Āyiamman subcaste temple near Kāṅkayam is currently being rebuilt.

participating in the festivals that their employers organize. Among the high-ranking left-division groups, by contrast, there is no descent-group structure at all. In particular, there are no lineages, clans, or subcastes that come together for periodic festivals and there are no temples owned by or specifically linked to such descent divisions.

This characterization applies to the three highest-ranking left-division groups: the CōLi Ācāri, the KōmuTTi CeTTiyār, and the Koṅku Ācāri. It also applies to the Aiyar Brahmans and to the KaruNīkar PiLLai, two subcastes which stand technically above the division. All of these communities have a set of clan-like groups, called *kōttirams,* which trace their descent through the male line, but the names of these groups have little purpose beyond showing a mythological connection with some sage of the classical literature.[71] In theory each kōttiram forms an exogamous unit, at least to a depth of seven generations. However, in fact I found that marriageability in these groups was calculated according to the cross-parallel rules of Tamil kin terminology and not according to kōttiram names.[72]

Members of these groups sometimes do assert a connection between their kōttiram or descent group and some particular deity. However, the temple dedicated to this deity is always a sacred center used by all communities, where a Brahman or a PaNTāram—but never a man of the subcaste in question—will serve as priest.[73] Families of these three high-ranking left groups and of the two neutral communities make a pilgrimage to the temple traditionally visited by their family whenever any important life-cycle ritual is performed. However, joint ceremonies financed by an entire lineage, clan, or subcaste are never organized, and other groups are quite free to worship at the temple simultaneously. Among the several subcastes that may worship at such temples, there is no tradition of prece-

[71]In my experience, the subcastes of these communities always claimed to have a fixed and auspicious number of kōttirams (five, seven, or nine), and these all had elaborate Sanskirt names that people had difficulty remembering. Compare the formality in Koṅku of naming left-caste clans after classical sages with Mayer's comment concerning the carpenters of Malwa, who, according to their local genealogist, are divided into twenty-seven clans named after different sages. (See Mayer, *Caste and Kinship,* p. 166.)

In the case of the Ācāri, there are two, cross-cutting types of division, that of subcaste and that of an all-South India occupational classification (goldsmiths, stone masons, etc.), as mentioned on pp. 74–75 of this chapter. Membership in both is inherited in the male line and is unaffected by present-day pursuits. I have the impression that each subcaste within an occupational class forms an endogamous unit. Within these units, there is a seven-generation restriction on marriage between members of the same kōttiram. Since the total number of kōttiram names is limited, however, one finds the same ones used over and over again in a number of these different marriage communities.

[72]A description of the Tamil kin terminology is given in chapter 5, pp. 213–29.

[73]At KavuNTar caste temples (and also sometimes at KavuNTar clan and lineage temples) there may be a PaNTāram priest, but he is hired and is treated as a dependent, whereas in temples frequented by the left-division castes, a PaNTāram is treated as an institutional employee, and not as one loyal to any particular family.

dence or first rights. All that is necessary is that within a given household group the oldest members receive the first portion of whatever has been blessed by the deity.

Just as in the case of the right-division communities, the Brahmans and the four other groups discussed here tend to name females when asked about their *kula teyvam* or clan deity. Unlike the right groups, where each caste and clan deity has a distinctive, local name, however, the goddesses listed by the Brahman, KaruNīkar PiLLai, KōmuTTi CeTTiyār, and Ācāri groups are well known throughout South India. Furthermore, unlike the deities of the right division, these left-division deities are not associated with a particular territorial area, and the temples dedicated to them draw devotees from far and wide. Only the particular tract of land immediately surrounding their temples is associated with them, and usually they are described as a special manifestation of a great goddess of some distant pilgrimage point, such as Conjeepuram or Madurai.[74]

In my own enquiries, the clan goddess most frequently named by the relatively high-ranking left-division communities, the KōmuTTi CeTTiyār and the two Ācāri groups, was AṅkāLamman. There is a very long story recounting the events of AṅkāLamman's life, some of the details of which are significant in explaining her association with these groups.[75] AṅkāLamman was born in heaven as Pārvati, but after she reached maturity, she was banished by her husband, Civā, because he was displeased with her conduct. Once she entered the human world her name changed to AṅkāLamman, and she began to wander from place to place. On her travels she collected devotees of various castes here and there by chance encounter. The story told about her is essentially a detailed account of how she acquired her following. A small example, drawn from the extensive cycle of stories which surrounds this goddess, is given below:

> AṅkāLamman continued her wanderings for many years. However, one day she decided it was time to have a proper temple constructed where her devotees could worship her. The thought of a very wealthy Ācāri came to her mind. She knew that he had both the means and the skills appropriate for this task. He was a very powerful government official, a *Tashildar,* or top-ranking administrator at the Taluk level, and she knew that he was afraid of no one. He was so wealthy that he had a palace surrounded by eight walls, but he also had the sorrow of having only one son. AṅkāLamman decided to persuade him to build her temple and asked her priest to go to him to make the request.

[74]F. J. Richards has provided a suggestive parallel here in his article "Village Deities of Vellore Taluk, North Arcot District," *The Quarterly Journal of the Mythic Society* 10, no. 2 (1920): 116.
[75]The story is sung by a VēTar (drummer, story-teller) every year at the time of her largest festival. I obtained it from Informant no. 16. I plan to include a much more detailed account of its text in a subsequent volume.

The priest filled a special ceremonial pot with ash from the burning ground as a sign of his goddess and set off. When he reached the palace he asked to see the Ācāri, but the latter refused to be summoned by anyone. So the priest had to make his way through seven gates, and past seven guards, in order to confront the man in person. When the priest told the Ācāri that AṅkāLamman had asked that he build her a temple the man became angry. He told his assistants to tie up the priest and beat him. The priest pleaded for mercy with his punishers, however, and was released after a light beating. As the priest ran away, the wealthy Ācāri shouted after him that he would not build a temple for a goddess of the burning ground. He told the priest he should instead pull out AṅkāLamman's teeth—a common remedy for suspected sorcery—and beat her to death.

The priest told all of this to the goddess but she responded by asking him to return to the Ācāri's house. She promised him some special *mantras* ("magical verses") which she told him to place in various spots around the palace. The priest did this. Then AṅkāLamman caused the house to fall into darkness in the middle of the day. She also gave the Ācāri's only son a severe stomach ache. The Ācāri quickly sent a servant to fetch a light from a window ledge, but this woman was bitten by a scorpion. Then a second girl, sent to get firewood, was bitten by a snake. Finally, the Ācāri began to suspect that all these misfortunes might be due to the goddess AṅkāLamman, whose teeth he had earlier said should be pulled. At that very moment an old woman, who was the goddess AṅkāLamman in disguise, made her way to the house, and, in telling the Ācāri's fortune, confirmed his interpretation of events. He then asked this woman if the stomach ache, the scorpion sting, and the snake bite would be cured if he agreed to accept AṅkāLamman as his *kula teyvam,* or clan goddess, and to build a temple for her. AṅkāLamman agreed to this bargain, but threatened to visit the Ācāri with further difficulties if he did not carry through with the promise of the temple, and in addition if he did not name all his succeeding children after her.[76]

This is just one small incident in AṅkāLamman's lengthy career, but it serves to illustrate how her mythology is broken into individual subsections, each one dealing with a particular community of the left division. Usually the goddess picks on a group whose skills she can use, and in all cases she resorts to some form of guile or trickery to extract a promise of worship and service from them.

The account I collected includes, in addition to this tale of the Ācāri, a story about a CeTTiyār, a CempaTavar (fisherman), and a VēTar.[77] Dumont, in addition, has recorded a similar story linking the Nāyakkar with the same goddess, and Thurston says that members of the Mātāri caste

[76]From Informant no. 16.

[77]The CempaTavar are generally classified as a left-division group in the literature and were categorized as such by my informants. I have little information about this community, as none of its members resides in the Kāṅkayam area.

sometimes act out her story.[78] This collection of mythological stories is thus similar in form to the group of stories about the origin of the left-division groups in general, as discussed in chapter 1. It is almost as if, in order to compensate for a lack of a developed economic interdependence such as the one characterizing the communities of the right, a mythological fabric had been repeatedly constructed to attempt to knit these left-division groups together.

One further group, the Mutaliyār, resembles the three left-division, and two neutral, subcastes just described, except in a few particulars. For one thing, they use the term *kūTTam* instead of *kōttiram* to describe descent groupings within their community.[79] In addition, the Mutaliyār do not have a fixed number of descent groups, nor have they named these units after classical sages. Instead the Mutaliyār kūTTams have names that sound very much like those that KavuNTars or other right-division castes might select, for example, names that refer to the heroic attributes of some lineal ancestor or to some animal or vegetable species in the environment.[80] And finally, the Mutaliyār use their clan names to determine marriageability. Thus, these names have a practical importance in regulating exogamy, and are not a mere formality. In the lack of individual clan shrines and festivals, however, and in the frequent mention of AṅkāLamman as a generalized family deity, the Mutaliyār resemble the neutral and the other high-ranking left-division groups already described.

In respect to descent-group divisions, as in the case of so many other features of caste tradition, the Kaikkōlar Mutaliyār stand in an ambivalent position. Officially, they are members of the left division. As a result of the vagaries of history, however, many members of this group fought loyally for right-division kings and were granted land in Koṅku for their heroism.[81] As a result, it seems, the Mutaliyār have developed split loyalties. Many members of the group have come to identify with right-division leaders and have adopted some of their attitudes, mannerisms, and traditions. Yet they retain a recognizable trace of their left-division ancestry.[82]

---

[78]Dumont, *Une Sous-Caste*, p. 391, and Thurston, *Castes and Tribes*, 4:315.

[79]The Kaikkōlar (also called Ceṅkuntam) and MēLakārar Mutaliyār subcastes are referred to here. I do not have details on any others.

[80]Not all KavuNTar clan names have any clear meaning. I refer to those that can be reasonably interpreted, often by informants themselves.

[81]K. V. Raman, *The Early History of the Madras Region* (Madras: Amudha Nilayam Ltd., 1959), p. 176; H. D. Love, *Vestiges of Old Madras*, 3 vols. (London: John Murray, 1913), 2:29, and Arokiaswami, *Kongu Country*, p. 273. The same kind of historical background was also suggested by the various military poems which Informant no. 31 could recite.

[82]It is also possible to explain a certain amount of this Mutaliyār ambivalence, which will be pointed out again in later chapters, by suggesting that their name is a catch-all term which lumps together groups having a very different ancestry; that is, some with right-division, some with left-division, and some with neutral ancestry. Certainly this is the case if one considers the wide application of the name "Mutaliyār" in other areas of Madras State.

Below the Mutaliyār in wealth and prestige are three other left-division communities: the VaTuka Nāyakkar (well-diggers), PāNTiya Nāvitar (barbers), and VaTuka VaNNār (washermen).[83] The first of these, the Nāyakkar, call their descent groups *kūTTams,* and the naming pattern for these descent units resembles that just described for Mutaliyārs. The barbers and washermen, by contrast, call their descent units by the names of the particular nāTus in which they have been traditionally employed. Unlike other left-division castes, both the Nāyakkar and left-division VaN-Nār have a tradition of lineage shrines where occasional ceremonies are celebrated by a localized branch of some more widespread clan. At the clan level as a whole and at the subcaste level, however, there are no corresponding ceremonial foci, as there are for right-division groups. Here the pattern of worship by individual households belonging to these clans at the shrines of generalized clan goddesses strongly resembles that of the high-ranking left-division communities already described.

The descent-group organization of only two left-division groups remains to be described. These—the VēTar (temple drummers and hunters) and the Mātāri (leatherworkers and field laborers)—are the lowest ranking castes of this entire bloc. Both groups show a strong association between clan groupings and the nāTu territorial area. The VēTar (drummers), like the other left-division service groups, the Nāvitar and the VaN-Nār, use nāTu names to identify their internal clan divisions. However, there are no VēTar currently resident in Kāṅkayam nāTu. The VēTar who now drums for the important AṅkāLamman festival held at MaTaviLā-kam in Kāṅkayam nāTu each year is brought in for the occasion from the neighboring MaNa nāTu.

The VēTar of the MaNa area have a tight moiety system of organization which merits a few words of description. The VēTar who are ritually associated with MaNa nāTu form an exogamous group. Their marriage partners are drawn from a second, affinal nāTu, called Pūnturai, which is ritually and administratively linked to MaNa nāTu. Each half of this paired nāTu unit has its own VēTar subcaste temple dedicated to AṅkāLamman. Furthermore, of these two territories, Pūnturai is known as the "head" or *talai* nāTu. The headman of the subcaste resides there, and he, or his representative, must be given first place if any subcaste-wide ceremonies are held. The assistant headman is drawn from MaNa nāTu and is a cross relative of the headman himself.[84] Both titles are inherited. The headman's representative, on the other hand, is always a parallel relative. Figure 2.7

---

[83]This description refers primarily to the VaTuka Nāyakkar and the VaTuka VaNNār subcastes; I have no detailed information on the left-division Nāvitar, but I presume that their organization resembles that of these other two groups.

[84]The headman is responsible for approving all marriage arrangements; and he and his representative should be present at all life-cycle ceremonies, for example, weddings and

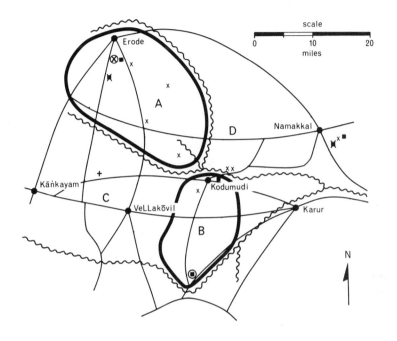

scale

0   10   20
miles

⊗   Headman's village (Pūntuṟai) and temple to AṅkāLammaṉ

x   other villages where Headman's parallel relatives reside

⊙   Assistant Headman's village (CūTāmaNi) and temple to AṅkāLam-
                                               maṉ

■   other villages where Headman's cross relatives reside

✷   villages where both parallel and cross relatives reside

+   AṅkāLammaṉ temple of Kāṅkayam nāTu where Assistant Head-
                                              man now drums

━━━━   approximate boundary of parallel/cross nāTu areas

A   Pūntuṟai nāTu   B   MaNa nāTu
      (Parallel relatives)   (Cross relatives)
────   roads

∿∿   rivers   Other Neighboring Areas:

●   towns   C   Kāṅkayam nāTu

                                 D   KiRaṅku nāTu

Fig. 2.7.   VēTar territorial distribution.

outlines the nāTu areas involved and gives the location of the headman's village as well as the villages of his cross and parallel relatives. Periodic festivals in which all the members of the nāTu unit participate do not occur at either of the main subcaste temples. Instead, individual families worship separately at these centers.

Here we see the principle of social division into opposed halves or moieties worked out with neat symmetry so as to correspond both to nāTu areas and to the parallel-cross kin classification discussed later, in chapter 5. This very special elaboration on the basic dualistic or right-left theme occurs, in Koṅku, only among left untouchable groups. The VēTar exhibit certain organizational features—an emphasis on AṅkāLammaṉ and on individual worship—which reflect the practice of higher-ranking members of the left division. In basic structure, however, they differ strikingly from them and are much closer to the Mātāri untouchables who rank just below them.

Of all the left-division groups of which I have any significant knowledge, the Mātāri, who are also called Cakkiliyar, are the lowest in prestige.[85] They are a very large caste, the members of which are traditionally considered to be leatherworkers, but who in fact form the great body of unskilled agricultural laborers in the area. The Mātāri are divided into a number of subcastes. All of those whom I encountered spoke either Telugu or Kannada at home, but Tamil in the presence of other castes.[86]

All three Mātāri subcastes on which I collected information, the Moracu, the Aṉappu, and the ToTTi, had clans that were organized into paired, unnamed, exogamous moieties. Each of these clans had a headman and each moiety of clans had a head clan. Within each moiety, furthermore, there was a marked division of ritual and secular functions. The clearest example I have is from the Aṉappu, a subcaste found around the town of Karur.[87] The organization of this subcaste takes the form shown in Table 2.3.

---

funerals. The headman is also responsible for mediation in times of dispute between members of the Pūnturai and MaNa areas, or of dispute within Pūnturai nāTu itself. The assistant headman, drawn from MaNa nāTu, is responsible for mediation when the conflict is contained within his own territory; that is, MaNa nāTu.

[85]A small caste of Kuravars (basketmakers) rival the Mātāri for status. The two groups are roughly equal in their efforts to assign each other the lowest rank of all in the local hierarchy. The Kuravar are a migratory caste, and I have little information about their social organization. I was given a rather confused picture by Informant no. 23. Although I have reason to suspect that they have a moiety-type organization, with each half having its own temple, I am not confident of this interpretation.

[86]I was told by Informant no. 20 that a subcaste called Koṅku Mātāri, which may be Tamil-speaking only, does exist in the area. However, I did not manage to locate it. It is possible that a Kannada-speaking group sometimes calls itself by this name.

[87]I spent just over a week interviewing Mātāris in Karur, as any intimate contact with untouchable communities closer to ŌlappāLaiyam was socially difficult, because of my general association with the higher-ranking groups of this area.

TABLE 2.3

HEREDITARY LEADERSHIP AMONG THE AṆAPPU MĀTĀRI OF KARUR

(by clan)

Moiety A (Ritual Superiority)			Moiety B (Secular Superiority)		
Clan Name	Ritual Precedence	Hereditary Title	Clan Name	Ritual Precedence	Hereditary Title
PōTTanār	1	*Kāppiliyan* (Ritual leader of entire community)	ETuppanār	2	*PakaTai* (Secular leader of entire community)
CōLanār	3	*MaNiyam* (Secular leader of the moiety)	TiTTanār	4	*Kōlukkāran* (Ritual leader of the moiety)

NOTE: The information on which this table is based was supplied by Informant no. 24. The analysis in this condensed table form, however, is my own. I believe that my interpretation represents the organization of this subcaste accurately, but more intensive fieldwork would be needed to substantiate it in detail.

The names of the four clans mentioned in this table seem to hang together as a unit. "CōLanār" seems to refer to a provider of *côLam*, an important food grain; "PōTTanār" to someone who ritually husks it; "TiTTanār" to someone who rituallly places it; and "ETuppanār" to someone who takes it away. This would correspond to a symbolic division between ritual and secular tasks within each moiety and also to the subcaste as a functioning unit in which each clan has an assigned task basic to the sustenance of the group as a whole.

Each moiety division has a general association with a nāTu area. The association is not as explicit as in the case of the service communities just discussed, as there is no tradition of exogamy for the Mātāri by nāTu area. However, when the distribution of moiety-linked temples is mapped, a rough correspondence with these traditional territorial areas emerges. For lack of sufficient information on this matter for the Aṇappu Mātāri, I use here an example from the Moracu subcaste. My informants from this group spoke of their traditional affiliation with two nāTus, Kāṅkayam and Teṅkarai respectively.[88] Of these, Teṅkarai is spoken of as the head or talai nāTu and the ritual headman of the group comes from there. The assistant headman, by the same reasoning, comes from the secondary nāTu, Kāṅkayam. The clan with hereditary rights to each of these offices is also located within the respective nāTu from which their leader is drawn. Kāṅkayam nāTu and Teṅkarai nāTu, and the location of the main temples in these regional moieties, are shown in Figure 2.8. Though this picture of the VēTar and Mātāri castes is sketchy, it is enough to suggest that their regional organization is of great interest and worthy of further research. Clearly both groups have an elaborate, descent-based internal structure. Furthermore, this structure is directly associated with traditional nāTu areas. The focus here has been on their organization at the clan and moiety level. I am confident that if one looked into the matter in more detail a pattern of lineage temples, linked to residential areas, would also emerge.

In summary, the leading communities of the right division have an elaborate descent-group structure. Their organization is intimately linked to the nāTu territory, as in the case of the NāTār, and to its kirāmam and Ūr subdivisions. The service groups of this division, however, are organized around the divisions within the dominant community rather than around subgroupings of their own. The neutral subcastes and those of the left division with the most prestige, by contrast, have no significant descent-group organization and no tradition of local temples. Instead, they worship, on an individual family basis, at the temples of the better-known deities of the region. Lower-ranking groups of the left division have a more elaborate internal organization and local subcaste temples reappear. Finally, the lowest communities of all in this group, present a new and most interesting variation—moiety organization.

Previous generalizations in other works to the effect that lower-ranking subcastes tend to have a more elaborate internal organization than higher-ranking ones, therefore, are not entirely borne out by data from the Koṅku area.[89] What is clear from the present material is the importance of a

---

[88]Informants nos. 25 and 26.

[89]I refer in particular to E. A. H. Blunt, *The Caste System of Northern India with Special Reference to the United Provinces of Agra and Oudh* (London: Oxford University Press, 1931), pp. 106, 125–29; L. S. S. O'Malley, *Popular Hinduism* (Cambridge: Cambridge University

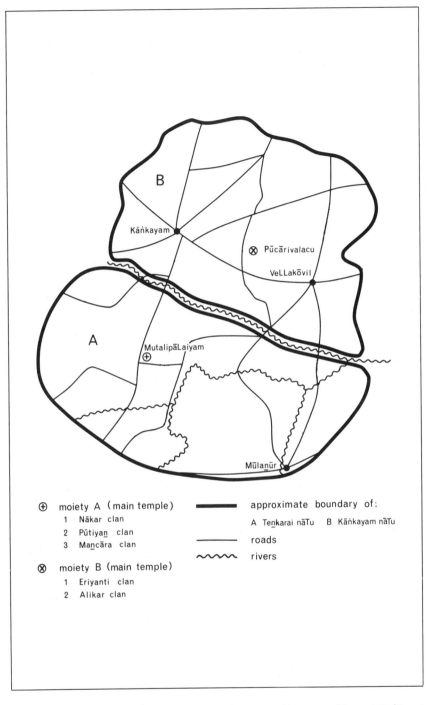

Fig. 2.8. Main temples of the Moracu Mātāri in Kāṅkayam nāTu and Teṅkarai nāTu.

second factor: the question of division membership. The right division—those groups which have rights in land—has an elaborate internal descent structure which is intimately linked to local territorial boundaries. The left division—those who live by various traditional and specialized skills—place little emphasis on descent and have no important ties to territory. This generalization is most applicable, however, to the higher-ranking members of each category; for status in the social hierarchy clearly does play a secondary role in determining a group's internal organization. The lower-ranking service communities of the right division, as a result of their dependence on the KavuNTars, tend to a great degree to mold their own organization around these division leaders. In the same way, lower-ranking service groups of the left division also make some reference in their organization to the territorial divisions of the right subcastes to which they too are subservient. According to this logic, it is not surprising that two of the lowest-ranking communities of the left division—the Mātāri and the VēTar, who form the bulk of the left population in the countryside—reflect KavuNTar organization more than any other group in their division.

TABLE 2.4
TENTATIVE NāTU MOIETY ALIGNMENT

Moiety A	Moiety B
1. Pūnturai nāTu	2. Kānkayam nāTu
3. Tenkarai nāTu	4. MaNa nāTu

Finally, a few generalizations about nāTu organization are possible. Although the information gathered is far from complete, it appears that ritualized marriage ties between nāTus may have once constituted an over-arching pattern, common to a number of castes. For example, Pūnturai nāTu appears to have been traditionally linked with MaNa nāTu in the case of the VēTar, while Kānkayam nāTu is linked with Tenkarai in the same way for the Mātāri. We also have a hint that the VēTar of MaNa nāTu considered those of Kānkayam nāTu to be brothers; the former appear to have had the right to succeed the latter as drummers at the temple there, once the Kānkayam VēTar were no longer resident in the area. This suggestion is reinforced by the fact that, in the case of the VēTar, both MaNa nāTu and Kānkayam nāTu enjoyed a ritualized marriage tie

Press, 1935), p. 74, and Louis Dumont, *Homo hierarchicus* (Paris: Gallimard, 1966), p. 230. Kathleen Gough makes a similar statement, although she simply contrasts Brahmans with non-Brahmans. E. Kathleen Gough, "The Social Structure of a Tanjore Village," *Economic Weekly* 4 (May 24, 1952): 532, 534. In fairness to these authors, however, one must agree that they all refer primarily to the number of hereditary offices and not to descent-group organization per se.

with the head nāTu, Pūnturai. Information about the UTaiyār indicates a similar ritualized marriage tie between Kāṅkayam nāTu and Pūnturai nāTu as far as that group is concerned. These hints suggest the pattern outlined in Table 2.4, where the nāTus themselves may have, at one time, reflected a moiety-like pattern, the organizational implications of which were shared by many communities. We know that representatives of neighboring nāTus were once expected to attend all important ceremonies, and that the order of their ritual precedence was fixed according to the numbers that appear in Table 2.4.[90] These scraps of information suggest that a traditional pattern of ritual and secular leadership may once have existed at the nāTu level, perhaps developed by KavuNTars before their present clan system became fixed. Several service castes still retain traces of this earlier order, as do the very lowest-ranking communities of the left. The higher-ranking members of this second division, by contrast, were oriented towards an all-South India pattern of organization and do not seem to have participated to any extent in the local nāTu superstructure. Finally, if such a local, territorially defined moiety organization did exist, it may well have resembled the organization that can still be found today within certain of the lowest-ranking left-division groups.

[90]The order is still explicitly retained in the wedding ceremony (Informants nos. 33, 48, and 49).

3

THE REVENUE VILLAGE: KAṈṈAPURAM KIRĀMAM

The *kirāmam*, or revenue village, is in some ways the most significant unit of social organization in Koṅku today. This is the area with which people generally identify themselves when they meet strangers, and it is the territory within which several important seasonal festivals are celebrated. It is also the level of local council or Panchayat authority. During the British period, this revenue area was frequently referred to as a "village" in government documents, and this nomenclature has been retained by the Indian census authorities to this day. The term is most unfortunate and has caused endless ethnographic confusion in recent decades.

In its Indian usage, the term village has carried the traditional English connotation of a "minor municipality with limited corporate powers."[1] In rural areas of the South this normally meant an administratively defined area (*kirāmam*), containing a number of hamlets (*Ūr*). Hamlets, in turn, were groupings of individual settlements (*ūr*).[2] Settlements, which collectively made up a hamlet, were simply the physical locale of one or more houses. To prevent confusion I will continue to use these terms in their traditional sense to describe the current scene.

In Koṅku today, small settlements are often single-caste groupings, while, except in the case of untouchables, larger ones are generally multicaste affairs. Hamlets, by contrast, are necessarily multicaste units. A hamlet must contain all of the castes necessary to assure the continuance of ordinary productive activities and to provide the basic ritual services. Both hamlets and villages have a clear social personality, and these invariably find expression on ritual occasions. Settlements, on the other

[1] W. Little, H. Fowler, and J. Coulson, *The Shorter Oxford English Dictionary* (Oxford: Clarendon Press, 1964), p. 2357.
[2] Note that I capitalize *Ūr*, when referring to a hamlet area but use the lower-case *ūr*, when individual settlements are discussed.

hand, are rather arbitrary groupings with only minor sociological significance.[3]

A village in the technical sense used here, then, is not a settlement site but a revenue area. A kirāmam, as this unit was traditionally referred to in Tamil, refers to an area that can extend to some twenty square miles and within which the population may be concentrated in one or two settlements or scattered through many.[4] It is this area, not the individual settlement, that is of foremost social and ritual significance.

Each kirāmam has its own sacred geography, just as the nāTu and region have a sacred geography. First and foremost, a kirāmam has its own Civā temple.[5] The festivals at this temple and the Brahmans who direct them link the kirāmam to the sacred geography of the nāTu as a whole. This linkage has been outlined in Figure 2.2, chapter 2. Furthermore, most kirāmams have a VisNu temple, a KariyakāLiyamman (locally PattirakāLi) temple, and at least one temple dedicated to Murukaṇ. All of these are cared for by Brahmans, and left- and right-division groups worship at them. However, none of them is central to the religious activity of the local population at large, especially to that of members of the right division.[6] They serve, rather, to tie the nāTu to the leading deities of literary Hinduism. Their presence satisfies formal requirements more than emotional ones, to judge from the mild popular interest which they are generally accorded.

To complement this set of temples dedicated to the great or official deities and their wives, is a set of lesser temples dedicated primarily to independent females. It is these that form the hub of local devotional and festival activity. The most important of these goddesses is the *kirāma tēvi* who protects the inhabitants of the kirāmam area. In the Kāṅkayam nāTu area, this goddess is usually Māriyamman. Ten of the twelve kirāmams of Kāṅkayam nāTu have a Māriyamman temple and in all but one of these she is the focus of kirāmam ritual activity.[7] The eleventh kirāmam, Maruturai, is small and probably shares one Māriyamman temple with the neighboring kirāmam of NattakkāTaiyūr. The twelfth kirāmam, Pāppiṇi,

---

[3] David J. Elkins of the University of British Columbia first gave me the idea of using the traditional English nomenclature of village, hamlet, and settlement to make this three-tier distinction stand out clearly.

[4] Kirāmams which include a town generally cover a smaller area than heavily rural ones. The population of a revenue village rarely exceeds 10,000 and the average size, for Coimbatore District, is only 2,815. Revenue units average about 6.5 square miles in area. Republic of India, *Census of India, 1961,* Vol. IX, *Madras,* Part X-i, *District Census Handbook, Coimbatore,* 2 vols. (Madras: Government Press, 1964), 1: 83, 89.

[5] Kaṇṇapuram kirāmam is said to have had five Civā temples originally but all but the most important of these are now abandoned and in considerable disrepair. (See Fig. 3.2.)

[6] With the possible exception of Murukaṇ, for whom the local populace of Kaṇṇapuram has recently organized a devotional club.

[7] In the tenth kirāmam (VeLLakōvil), Māriyamman takes second place at the time of the kirāmam festival, but only in relation to a local hero, Vīrakkumār.

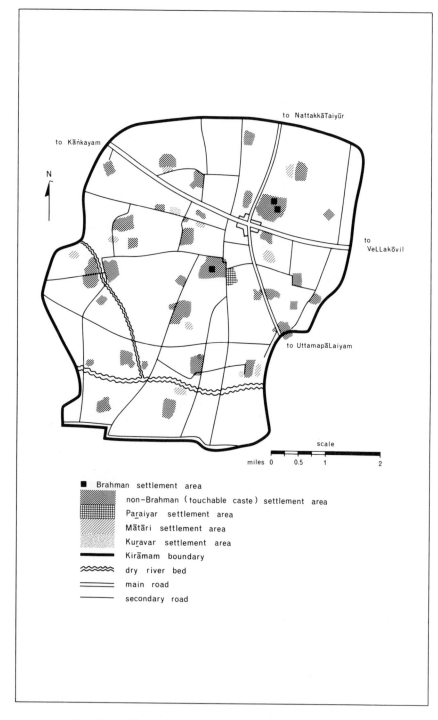

to NattakkāTaiyūr

to Kāṅkayam

N

to VeLLakōvil

to UttamapāLaiyam

scale

miles 0   0.5   1   2

◼   Brahman settlement area

   non-Brahman (touchable caste) settlement area

   Paṟaiyar settlement area

   Mātāri settlement area

   Kuṟavar settlement area

━━   Kirāmam boundary

〰〰   dry river bed

══   main road

──   secondary road

Fig. 3.1. The settlement pattern of Kaṇṇapuram kirāmam.

TABLE 3.1
KANNAPURAM KIRĀMAM CASTE POPULATION, 1966
(by household)

Caste Name	Number of Households	Percentage of Population
Neutral Division:		
Brahman	3	0.3
KaNakku PiLLai	1	0.1
Right Division:		
KavuNTar	590	54.0
PaNTāram	16	1.0
UTaiyār	18	1.0
NāTār	75	7.0
Nāvitar	22	2.0
Paraiyar*	55	5.0
Total for Division	776	70.0
Left Division:		
Ācāri	18	1.0
CeTTiyār	5	0.4
Mutaliyār	24	2.0
Nāyakkar	23	2.0
VaNNār	21	2.0
Kuravar*	6	0.5
Mātāri*	237	21.0
Total for Division	334	29.0
Total for Kirāmam	1,114	100.0

NOTES: These figures were obtained from Informant no. 33, whom I employed briefly for the purpose of making this survey. They are the same figures as those given in Column 5 of Table 1.3. That table, however, listed data for some unclassified groups. These have not been included here; for since the groups are very small and I have little information about them, they are not discussed in the text.
*Outcastes. The 1961 census gives the proportion of "scheduled castes" in the Panchayat at only twelve per cent. This is misleading, as the proportion of outcastes is actually about twenty-six per cent. The reason for the census figure being low is that those who have officially been "converted" to Christianity are no longer counted as members of a scheduled caste according to census definition.

has an AṅkāLamman temple that may serve as a substitute. AṅkāLamman and Māriyamman are considered to be rivals and I am told that their temples are never found close together.[8]

In this chapter, and in the chapters that follow, Kannapuram serves as the major example of a kirāmam area in Kāṅkayam nāTu. Figure 3.1 shows the physical outline of the settlement pattern for this kirāmam. As it is discussed in detail in these chapters, it is important to begin with a few facts about the social make-up of this area. In 1961, Kannapuram had a total population of 4,706, according to the census enumerators.[9] The distribution of this population, by caste, is given in Table 3.1.

Kannapuram kirāmam (now PaccāpāLaiyam Panchayat) is a revenue unit. It may be defined also as the area that cooperates to provide a great yearly festival for its patron goddess, Māriyamman. This kirāmam is too

[8] Informant no. 10.
[9] This figure was obtained from the headmaster of the local school. He had kept a record of the official census count in one of his classroom registers.

large a territory for all of its populace to interact with any frequency, and so it has been further subdivided into Ūr. These are the units which are significant in terms of day-to-day cooperation. An Ūr is an area which contains all of the major occupational groups or castes needed to carry out agricultural work and the affairs of daily living. Normally it will include landowners, service castes, a few artisans and merchants, and a sizeable body of laborers. These groups may all live in one settlement, or they may be dispersed in small clusters over, say, an area of one square mile. Each Ūr area—like the kirāmam as a whole—is guarded by a goddess. In Kaṇṇapuram, this goddess is known as MākāLiyamman (a form of Pattira-kāLi) and each Ūr in this kirāmam area has its own temple dedicated to her. Figure 3.2 outlines the sacred geography of Kaṇṇapuram kirāmam.

There are two important yearly events, furthermore, in which many kirāmam residents participate. One is the *muyal vēTTai,* or the annual hare hunt. In Kaṇṇapuram this hunt takes place in late June, during the first half of the Tamil month of *Āni.* It is an event for men only, but beyond this an able body and good health are the only requirements.[10] The ages of those who participate vary from fifteen to sixty and over. All who join are proud, while those who have been ill or otherwise preoccupied regret missing the fun. The hunt is not restricted by subcaste or by traditional division membership. Indeed, every household in the kirāmam is expected to send a man for at least one of the three days.[11]

The most important communal event in Kaṇṇapuram each year, however, is the Māriyamman festival. This celebration always takes place in the month of *Cittirai* (April-May).[12] Its precise timing is arranged so that the climax will occur on the Thursday closest to the night of the full moon. Each household is expected to bring a tray of rice flour lamps carried by its women.[13] These are presented to the goddess as an offering during the

---

[10]For the hunt, men gather at the *kaTai vīti,* the part of the kirāmam where the shops are located. Generally they form a group of several hundred. The men start the hunt together, but soon they begin to fan out in two's and three's in order to better flush the hare. The only weapon used is a big stick with which the hare may be stunned on the run. Many succeed in stunning one hare during the chase, but the very nimble may collect two or three. After the stunning, the hare is killed by cutting its throat with a knife. At sundown, the men return to the kaTai vīti, where they stand around in discussion. Finally, each returns with his catch to his own home.

[11]Note the parallel this description provides with that given by M. N. Srinivas in *Religion and Society Among the Coorgs of South India* (1952; reprint ed., London: Asia Publishing House, 1965), pp. 61–2, 203, 240.

[12]Other months during which Māriyamman festivals are traditionally celebrated in neighboring kirāmams include *Paṅkuni* (March-April), *Aippaci* (October-November), and *Kārttikai* (November-December). All these are months during which a certain amount of rain may be expected. Paṅkuni and *Cittirai* (April-May) correspond to the "hot" season—rain comes only in thunder showers late in the day—and it is my impression that these are the more popular months for the goddess' festival.

[13]These lamps are made by mixing rice flour with sugar and water and forming small balls of this substance, each with a depression in the middle. In the depression is poured a

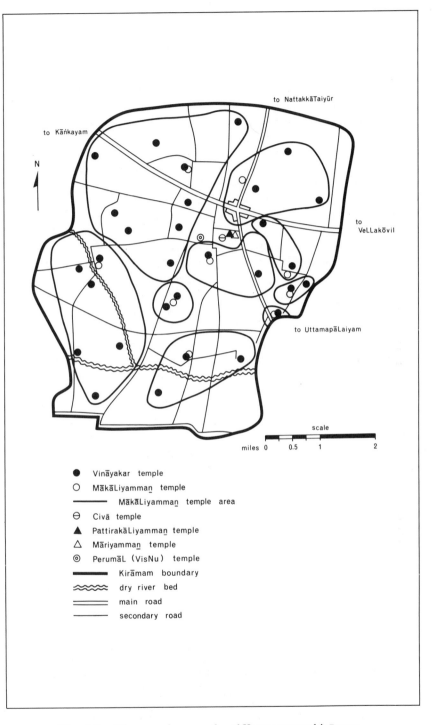

Fig. 3.2.   The sacred geography of Kaṉṉapuram kirāmam.

festival period. The men also participate in this festival. They form groups to collect the river water of the Kāvēri in special pots and bring these back to the goddess on the ends of long poles.[14] In some areas the sense of community participation in the festival is so strong that it is reported that outsiders are excluded altogether.[15] In such situations, great care is taken to see that the intruder does not lay his hands on any of the offerings that have been made to the goddess.

During the many nights of the Māriyamman festival, other ceremonies are being performed simultaneously at the Civā and PattirakāLi temples nearby. These latter rituals, however, are familiar only to the Brahman priests and a few ritual representatives of other castes in the kirāmam. Except for one climactic night when the temple cart carrying Civā and his bride is pulled once around the entire temple complex, there is little participation in the events at these two other temples by kirāmam residents, although a few subcastes of both divisions do have ritual duties to perform at them. From the point of view of excitement and activity, the events of the Māriyamman temple both begin and end the festival period. Ritual events continue at the Civā temple until the following Sunday, but for most kirāmam residents, the Thursday of the full moon marks the climax of the entire cycle. Ceremonies at the PattirakāLi (KariyakāLiyamman) temple, similarly, pass almost unnoticed. Authors of works concerned with other areas of South India also mention the importance given to Māriyamman in festival cycles involving other deities.[16]

In Kaṇṇapuram a big cattle fair is now held simultaneously with the Māriyamman festival. It is one of the four or five important cattle fairs held in Madras State each year, and people come from hundreds of miles to attend it. It is a great affair for the kirāmam, and the fields surrounding the stores on the main road are inundated for a week with campers who have brought their wares and their animals for sale. However, the fair is unconnected with the ritual events at the temple and nothing similar takes place during Māriyamman festivals elsewhere.[17]

---

little ghee and the whole is lighted by inserting a small wick. This lamp is known as *mā viLakku,* which, I believe, means "lamp of the goddess." Generally a woman carries fifteen or twenty of these on one tray.

[14]These pots of water, when mounted on long poles, are referred to as *kāvaTi.*

[15]In Kaṇṇapuram strangers may not boil poṅkal rice for the goddess. In other kirāmams, restrictions have traditionally been more severe. For example, see Edgar Thurston, *Castes and Tribes of Southern India,* 7 vols. (Madras: Government Press, 1909), 4:335–44.

[16]See Louis Dumont, "A Structural Definition of a Folk Deity of Tamil Nad: Aiyanar the Lord," *Contributions to Indian Sociology* 3 (1959): 80, 86, and H. Whitehead, *Village Gods of South India* (London: Oxford University Press, 1916), pp. 92–93, 101, 107. I have extremely detailed information on this festival complex, but it is largely irrelevant to the theme of this book and will be published in a subsequent volume.

[17]According to Informant no. 9, the Kaṇṇapuram fair was started only about 1900, at the suggestion of the PaRaiyakōTTai PaTTakkārar, who wanted to interest businessmen from

The image of Māriyamman dressed up for the annual festival.

A PaNTāram priest, possessed by the goddess as he removes the fire pot from the *kampam,* or ritual tree stump (see illustration below, right), and attempts to replace it by a cool, green one.

The *kampam,* or white tree stump, set up in front of Māriyamman's shrine during the festival and said to represent her lover. The stone at the base of the tree trunk serves as its ritual substitute between festivals. The tiles on the stump prevent it from being burnt by the pot of fire which is placed on top of it each night. This fire represents the anger of the goddess. The women are pouring water in order to "cool" the tree stump, symbolic of the object of her fury.

The most important aspect of the Māriyammaṉ ceremonies for the purpose of this work, is the fact that each and every locally resident subcaste of the right division has a ritual duty to perform at the festival. By contrast, no left-division community has any ceremonial responsibility in relation to this goddess.[18] Furthermore, in previous centuries—presumably—no left-division women were allowed to bring rice flour lamps or any other offerings inside the festival area. It will be remembered from the Preface that in order to demarcate the boundary of the area within which the presence of left-division women was forbidden, a special string of leaves, called a *tōraNam,* was tied across the path leading to the temple. This restriction, if it did once exist, has now been relaxed, but the archway of leaves is still tied in the customary place.

The distinctive ritual contributions that each subcaste of the right bloc is expected to make to the Māriyammaṉ festival are as follows: A Koṅku KavuNTar, belonging to the clan with ritual seniority in the kirāmam, helps with the felling of an important tree to be used in the ceremonies and receives the first blessings of the god when the ceremonies are over; a Maramēri NāTār must sacrifice the goats and sheep required for the festival and must also contribute ten rupees to cover, in theory, the expense of the first seven days of the festival.[19] An OkaccāNTi PaNTāram is responsible for performing all of the ritual oblations or pūjās required and also for speaking for the goddess, when possessed by her, and for carrying a pot of fire around the temple each morning.[20] A Koṅku UTaiyār is responsible for supplying the important ritual pots for the well water and the fire, and a Koṅku Paraiyar must provide the drumming necessary for many of the festival events. In addition, the Koṅku Nāvitar subcaste is responsible for shaving the men just listed, and the Koṅku VaNNār must

---

a wide area in his superior breed of cattle. His exhibition of livestock is still the most impressive one at the fair. The November, 1969, issue of a local journal published in Kāṅkayam and called *Nakara VaRi KāTTi* ("The City Signpost") confirmed this local tradition that the cattle fair was started about 1900. However, it did not give the source of its information. I have also found references to the fair for the years 1912–16 in the Madras Presidency, Department of Agriculture, *Madras Agricultural Calendars 1911–17* (Coimbatore: Agricultural College and Research Institute, 1918), but not for 1911 or earlier.

[18]One minor exception is the MēLakārar subcaste of Mutaliyārs, which provides music for the ritual, but whose presence is not essential to the proceedings.

[19]This role of the NāTār as sacrificer indicates the close alliance and symbiotic relationship between KavuNTars and NāTārs in agricultural matters. In the past there used to be buffalo sacrificed as well.

[20]It is interesting to note that one particular subcaste of PaNTārams, the Ayaṉ, also have special ritual responsibilities at the PaRaṉimalai Murukaṉ temple (the most important Murukaṉ pilgrimage center in Koṅku). This community has exclusive rights to draw the water used by the Brahman priest in his daily offerings to this great deity. On the basis of their traditional right, members of this PaNTāram subcaste reason that they must have been the original priests of Murukaṉ in the Koṅku area, and they suggest that the Brahmans probably took over many of their duties in regard to this god only at a later period. (Informant no. 20.)

A view of the main temple complex of Kannapuram kirāmam. Civā and Pārvati, the divine married couple, are enshrined here, along with their sons, Vināyakar and Murukan. The celebration of Civā's wedding is an important annual event.

An UTaiyār and two helpers ready to perform the *kirāma cānti*, just before the beginning of the annual marriage ceremonies for Civā and Pārvati. This man will circle the entire temple compound, throwing bloodied rice to the evil spirits said to hover around the kirāmam in order to pacify them and to encourage them to leave. The task is believed to be so dangerous that two helpers must hold on to him lest the spirits try to carry him off along with his rice offerings.

The men of Kannapuram kirāmam as they return from the annual hare hunt.

carry the *pantam,* or traditional torchlight, each night.

The foregoing description makes clear that each and every locally resident right-division subcaste is vital to the celebration of the Māriyamman festival, while the left-division groups are in the main entirely irrelevant. The presence of a member of each of these right-division castes at the proper points in the ceremony is essential. Matters can be held up for hours if they do not make a well-timed appearance. When the correct, traditional representative of a group is unavailable, a lineally related kinsman may substitute in his place. If one of the right-division communities refuses to participate entirely, however, the festival will come to a standstill. This whole emphasis on the right division's association with Māriyamman is in keeping, of course, with her association with local territory. It is also in keeping with the mythology of this goddess. Stories about her emphasize that all the communities that serve Māriyamman were originally born from a pot of fire which Civā gave to the goddess and which she held for a time in her right hand.[21] These stories suggest an underlying tradition of brotherhood among the right-division communities. In a ritual context, this tradition is expressed by the interdependence of the duties performed by each of the castes in ceremonies at the Māriyamman temple. It is also expressed in day-to-day interaction. For example, members of all the right-division subcastes of the middle range—OkaccaNTi PaNTārams, Maramēri NāTārs, Koṅku UTaiyārs, and Koṅku CeTTiyārs—tend to use the term *ANNan* or *tampi* ("brother") when speaking to one another, while they generally reserve the term *maccāṉ* ("brother-in-law") for addressing the members of counterpart groups in the left division.[22] Significantly, then, this tradition of brotherhood, which is based on mythology, is manifested both on a religious level in the organization of ceremony, and on a secular level in customary forms of address.

To return to the sacred geography of the kirāmam as a whole, one further point requires mention. Kirāmam borders are ritually significant and are referred to during the yearly Māriyamman festival. On a special night, just before the climax of the festival events, a short ritual to clear the kirāmam of evil spirits is performed. This ceremony, called *kirāma cānti,* brings calm and "coolness" to the area.[23] The proceedings involve circling

---

[21]Informant no. 22 and also M. Arokiaswami, *The Kongu Country* (Madras: Madras University Press, 1956), p. 272. This pot of fire is symbolized at the yearly festival by the earthen vessel full of burning embers which is placed on top of the forked tree stump each evening and which is carried around the temple by a PaNTāram priest who is possessed by the goddess.

[22]Mutaliyārs are sometimes included in this group which tends to extend parallel kin terms to one another. Here is yet another indication of the Mutaliyārs' ambivalent position between the two divisions, which is suggested elsewhere in this study.

[23]Calm is thought to be cooling, in contrast to agitation, which is heating. For a lengthy discussion of the significance of temperature in the Koṅku area, see Brenda E. F. Beck, "Colour and Heat in South Indian Ritual," *Man,* n.s. 4, no. 4 (1969): 553–72.

the temple with burning torches, shouting loudly, and throwing blood and cooked rice to the hovering spirits. The fire and noise are said to frighten the greedy beings away for an entire year. Thurston has recorded several similar descriptions of kirāmam festivals where rice mixed with blood is thrown in the air during a procession through a village; what remains of the mixture is always deposited beyond the boundary of the habitation site.[24] In Kannapuram the great temple complex represents the kirāmam for this ritual purpose. To circle it is symbolically to protect the entire area and ritually to demarcate its borders.[25]

Thus the kirāmam area is marked by sacred geography. It is also a clearly demarcated ritual and social area, and one with which residents have a strong sense of identity. This unity is acted out in an important cooperative endeavor each year: the annual hunt. At a second and even more important event, the Māriyamman festival, the interdependence of the right-division castes in a social and economic context is expressed ritually: in the ceremonies for the goddess, each of these castes performs a particular, and essential duty. Moreover, at this time the mythological brotherhood of all the right castes is ritually reaffirmed. Left-division castes have no parallel duties at the festival, and in the past their women were probably excluded from these festival activities entirely.

Because of the differing economic base which the two divisions enjoy, right castes are bound to figure more prominantly than left castes where questions of territorial organization are concerned. The aspects of kirāmam life which give this unit a distinct social and ritual identity are also closely associated with them. Within the right division, however, the only caste to figure prominently in the dynamics of descent-group territorial dominance are the KavuNTars. We now turn to a study of this particular relation on the kirāmam level.

CLAN HISTORIES AND LOCAL KIRĀMAM RIGHTS

In previous centuries, kirāmam territories were often controlled by a few families that belonged to a single powerful lineage within the dominant clan and caste. In general, authorities at the nāTu level granted such families the right to manage land and labor resources and to arbitrate disputes in a given kirāmam area; in return, the families promised to turn

---

[24]Thurston, *Castes and Tribes,* 4:335–36, 342–44. This same tradition of the ritual demarcation of kirāmam boundaries with blood or with substitute red-colored symbols was apparently once common in North India as well. M. Elphinstone, *History of India: Hindu and Moghul Periods,* 1:36, as quoted by Winefred Day in her article, "Relative Permanence of Former Boundaries in India," *Scottish Geographical Journal* 65, no. 3 (1949): 114.

[25]There is a nice parallel between this and a story told about Civā and his two sons. The sons were to compete to see who could circle the world more quickly. While the younger son (Murukan) set out across the sea at a run, the elder (Vināyakar) simply walked once around the place where his parents were seated and won the race hands down.

over the land revenues to the authorities and to supply them with mercenaries in times of war.[26] Once in power in a particular kirāmam, a family had the right to supervise local labor organization and to establish local rights and duties. The following discussion will be phrased in terms of clan dominance in a given area, but what is actually meant is the local dominance of one or more lineages belonging to that clan. Kaṇṇapuram kirāmam provides one example of this pattern of clan dominance and the rights related to it. A KavuNTar clan named CeṅkaNNaṉ is said to have originally controlled this area; and in local folklore the history of this clan is traced back to the CōRa period, around the twelfth century A.D., when one early member of this group was awarded land near the town of Kāṅkayam.[27] Their main place of residence was called Putūr, but this family's lineal relatives were widespread in the area and they came to dominate Kaṇṇapuram as well.[28] CeṅkaNNaṉ clan members still enjoy the first rights at the Kaṇṇapuram Civā and KariyakāLiyammaṉ temples today.

Sometime during the period of Muslin invasions from the North in the fourteenth century, a man of the CeṅkaNNaṉ clan living in CukkuTTipāLaiyam—a settlement in Kaṇṇapuram kirāmam—is said to have had a wife who gave birth to only one child, an albino daughter. No one could be found to marry this girl and finally a man of the ŌtāLar clan was brought in for this purpose from a kirāmam which lay about ten miles to the north. This ŌtāLar was allowed to settle in the kirāmam on the condition that he would reside uxorilocally and supervise the cultivation of land belonging to his father-in-law. Over a long period of time, this man's clan, through further marriage ties in the area, came to acquire considerable strength in the Kaṇṇapuram kirāmam territory. This transfer of dominance, however, did not take place until most CeṅkaNNaṉ descendants had been eliminated as a result of seven generations of bitter feuding between the two groups. Many CeṅkaNNaṉ migrated during this period to a sparsely settled area on the western edge of Koṅku, where they can be

---

[26]Good historical material on this subject is still very scanty. These statements are based on research in other regions. Suggestions made in these articles have been combined with information supplied by local informants who were knowledgeable about the traditional kirāmam pattern in the Kāṅkayam area. For discussions of the situation elsewhere, see the following: Eric J. Miller, "Caste and Territory in Malabar," *American Anthropologist* 56 (1954): 410–20; Bernard S. Cohn, "Political Systems of Eighteenth Century India," *Journal of the American Oriental Society* 82 (1962): 312–20; Louis Dumont, "The Functional Equivalents of the Individual in Caste Society," *Contributions to Indian Sociology* 8 (1965): 94–97 in particular, and E. Kathleen Gough, "Caste in a Tanjore Village," in E. R. Leach, ed., *Aspects of Caste in South India, Ceylon and North-West Pakistan* (Cambridge: Cambridge University Press, 1960), p. 28. The one published source on Koṅku I have found which is relevant to this question is F. A. Nicholson, *Manual of the Coimbatore District* (Madras: Government Press, 1887), p. 5.

[27]This is the story of the Putūr PaTTakkārar also mentioned in chapter 1.

[28]S. A. R. Ciṉṉucāmi KavuNTar, *Koṅku VēLāLar* [The VēLāLars of Koṅku] (Erode: TamiRaṉ Accakam, 1963), p. 328.

found to this day.[29] The story of the feud, as told by local residents, is as follows:

The ŌtāLar who had been asked to reside uxorilocally turned out to be a very irascible man. No sooner had his father-in-law settled him on the land, than the young man decided to move off his newly acquired fields and into an abandoned house some distance away. He refused to give an accounting of financial matters to his wife's father, gave him some second-rate horses (which insulted the latter) and finally had the audacity to beat his father-in-law for complaining. At this treatment, the CeṅkaNNan became furious and ordered his men to kill the son-in-law. They succeeded in this but soon the father learnt that his young daughter was pregnant by her deceased husband. When she gave birth to a son her father's heart softened and he turned over to her and the child the gifts of property he had made to the couple at the wedding, but had reclaimed at the height of the dispute. After some years, the young boy grew up and came to learn the story of how his father had been killed. The young man became angry and in a moment of rage, killed his own mother's brother, the original father's son. (The old CeṅkaNNan had died by this time.) But the wife of this murdered man was also pregnant and thus a son of his now grew to maturity. In this way a feud developed between the families that lasted for seven generations. At the end of this period, a descendant of the CeṅkaNNan group came to Kaṇṇapuram and killed a man he thought to be the last surviving male of the unhappy line generated by the irascible ŌtāLar son-in-law. He then declared the blood feud to be at an end. At this moment the goddess of Kaṇṇapuram spoke, saying that there yet remained a man of the ŌtāLar clan among them. A search was conducted, but to no avail as no one realized that the goddess was referring to an unborn child. Thus the final descendant escaped notice and when he became adult his wife gave birth, in turn, to three sons. (From here the informant is able to give an actual genealogy of the ŌtāLar families in Kaṇṇapuram kirāmam, coming to himself, now an old man, in the seventh generation.)[30]

The ŌtāLar now have second rights at the Kaṇṇapuram Civā temple at the time of the festival.[31] Third in this ritual order of precedence is another

---

[29]These CeṅkaNNan remain loyal to their old lineage temple in Kaṇṇapuram and continue to send contributions for its upkeep to a PaNTāram priest (Informant no. 39) in ŌlappāLaiyam. There are now 114 adult CeṅkaNNan males in the Pollachi, Palani, and UTumalai areas who can be called upon for contributions. By contrast, there are only 24 ŌtāLar males in these areas whose history can be traced in a similar fashion. Furthermore, most of the latter appear to have left Kaṇṇapuram more recently, long after the feud had come to an end.

[30]Different versions of this story were told to me by Informants nos. 36, 37, and 38. The most elaborate one was recounted by Informant no. 36 and is the story summarized here. There are more stories as the genealogy approaches the modern period. In the first incident connected with this elaborate clan genealogy, the arrival of the British in the area is mentioned. Calculating back seven generations from the present informant, one arrives at precisely this period; that is, about 1800. For another account of lineage feuds, see Louis Dumont, *Une Sous-Caste de l'Inde du Sud* (Paris: Mouton, 1957), pp. 139–41.

[31]The same order of rights holds for the Māriyamman temple festival as well.

important local clan, the KaNavāLar. This is the most important descent group in the Ūr of ŌlappāLaiyam, and it will be described in some detail in chapter 4. Here, however, it is important only to note how this clan fits into the history of KavuNTar descent groups in the kirāmam as a whole. The story of the KaNavāLar's arrival in the area is as follows:

> At one time there was a severe famine in Koṅku. During this period some members of the KaNavāLar clan were wandering in the area with their herd of cattle. They found a damp river bed near Kaṇṇapuram and settled there to graze their herd, building only a few rough shacks. One week the villagers of ŌlappāLaiyam decided to perform a drama to be held on consecutive nights. On the third night they suddenly discovered that they had no more clarified butter, which was needed to light the big torches, or *pantam,* for the stage. They went to the group of men along the river bed to ask for some butter, but the latter refused, saying that they would only supply the butter if they were given the rights to some land in return. The villagers finally agreed to this condition and thus members of the KaNavāLar clan were able to settle permanently in the area.[32]

These stories about the ŌtāLar and the KaNavāLar clans both emphasize the importance of the acquisition of rights to land as a prior condition to obtaining rights of ritual precedence at local kirāmam temples. However, there is one important difference in these two accounts. In the first case, that of the ŌtāLar, these rights were acquired in exchange for an agreed uxorilocal marriage; but in the second they were acquired in the exchange for a material substance of ritual importance, clarified butter. The implications of this difference continue to the present day in the realm of marriage arrangement. The first two clans—the CeṅkaNNaṉ and ŌtāLar—have repeatedly intermarried, except during their feud which lasted for seven generations. They can be described as having had a marriage "alliance" in the strict sense of this term.[33] The ŌtāLar, indeed, remember this genealogical history in great detail. Furthermore, the account always starts with the initial marriage of an albino daughter with an ŌtāLar from the northern edge of the nāTu. This alliance pattern, as remembered for succeeding generations from an ŌtāLar genealogy recounted to me, is shown in Figure 3.3.[34]

It can be seen immediately from this diagram that while the CeṅkaNNaṉ have continued to "give women" to ŌtāLar resident in certain settlements of the kirāmam, they also began to "receive" women from ŌtāLar of other settlements, at least five generations ago. Thus the "alliance" was

---

[32]Informant no. 38.
[33]See Louis Dumont, *Hierarchy and Marriage Alliance in South Indian Kinship,* Occasional Papers of the Royal Anthropological Institute, no. 12 (London, 1957) for a discussion of the notion of "alliance" as developed by its leading proponent.
[34]Informants nos. 36 and 38.

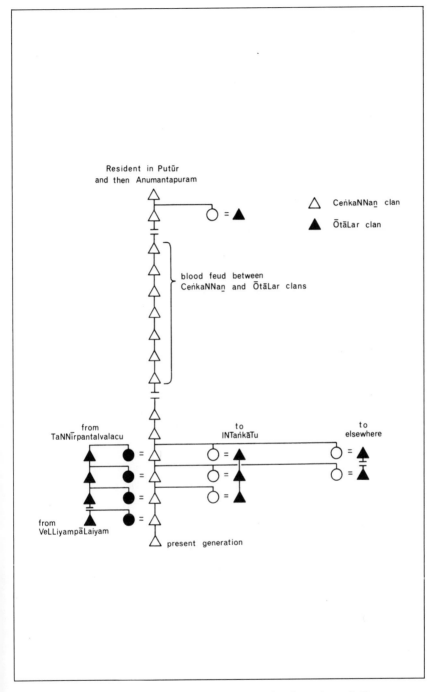

Fig. 3.3. The genealogy of the first lineage of the first clan of Kaṇṇapuram kirāmam, showing a marriage alliance, over time, with the second clan of the same kirāmam.

asymmetric locally, but symmetric over the kirāmam territory as a whole. Actual MBD marriage, although important in theory, was not always carried out.[35] Terminological MBDs—certain distant relatives for whom the same term is used as for an actual MBD—were often substituted in practice. Unfortunately, however, my informants did not know the genealogies well enough to specify precisely where these substitutions had occurred. The KaNavāLar, in contrast with the ŌtāLar, have not intermarried with the CeṅkaNNan clan at all. They have consistently imported brides into the kirāmam who were born of other KavuNTar clans. Some of these clans have since taken up uxorilocal residence in ŌlappāLaiyam and gradually acquired small land holdings nearby. They have not managed to supplant local KaNavāLar dominance of this Ūr as the ŌtāLar managed to supplant CeṅkaNNan dominance in the wider kirāmam area.

As the largest landowners in Kannapuram kirāmam, the ŌtāLar are also by far the most powerful politically of all KavuNTar descent groups in the area. A count of *periya kuTumpams*, or powerful families, in the kirāmam suggested that seventeen out of a total of forty-five, or 38 per cent, were members of the ŌtāLar clan.[36] In addition, the ŌtāLar largely control the local Panchayat, as they occupy five of the nine KavuNTar seats. The elected Panchayat president, furthermore, is an ŌtāLar by descent. Thus, it is clear that, to date, this clan has successfully perpetuated its position of relative dominance in the kirāmam area.[37] The CeṅkaNNan who were once even more powerful than the ŌtāLar have now largely moved away.

In addition to the elected Panchayat officials already described, there are two important appointed officials: the MaNiyārar, or local revenue collector, and the KarNam, or local accountant and keeper of the land register. Both are hereditary posts. The MaNiyārar's position has been traditionally held by an ŌtāLar family; the KarNam post by a KaruNīkar PiLLai.[38] Traditionally both these families received a certain amount

---

[35]Throughout the rest of this study, especially in the sections on genealogy, kinship terms are coded as follows: B (brother), D (daughter), F (father), H (husband), M (mother), S (son), W (wife), and Z (sister). Thus MBD is the code form of "mother's brother's daughter."

[36]This count was made for me by Informant no. 33. Four more families were of the CeṅkaNNan clan, and three belonged to the KaNavāLar clan. Two other clans can boast two *periya kuTumpams* each, and four others just one.

[37]The same thing, of course, happens on a larger scale at the Panchayat Union level, since the highest-ranking of the Panchayat presidents is generally elected chairman of this wider body. Kannapuram kirāmam is part of the VeLLakōvil Panchayat Union whose chairman is an extremely wealthy KavuNTar of the Payira clan, and a lineal relation of the PaTTakkārar of PaRaiyakōTTai. The situation of neighboring Panchayat Unions is similar, but I am not familiar enough with local politics elsewhere to generalize about all of the Koṅku region.

[38]By present law, these positions are open to competition by examination from other local residents. The competition, in theory, takes place at the time of retirement or death of the incumbent. However, I have never heard of one of these positions being contested in the Kāṅkayam area by a man who had not been raised in an accountant's family.

of tax-free land in exchange for their services, but now they receive simply a small government salary. Together these men have five assistants who also receive a small stipend in return for acting as messengers and errand boys for these appointed officials.[39]

Both the MaNiyārar and the KarNam are in a position of considerable power. The MaNiyārar, for example, has the right to appropriate a man's personal property and place it on the market for sale if he does not pay his property taxes within four days of the announced deadline. The Kar-Nam is in a privileged and knowledgeable position when it comes to the transfer of land. He is the only person with full access to the local records and he is likely to have knowledge of attempted evasions of the land ceiling act, as well as of the possibility of forthcoming sales of land in payment for debt. Thus he is in an excellent position to pressure local residents, and to release information about land available for purchase as his own advantage dictates. Although neither the MaNiyārar nor the Kar-Nam may be members of the Panchayat, they wield more political influence, perhaps, than any of their elected counterparts.

As noted at the beginning of this discussion, it is more accurate to describe dominance at the kirāmam level in terms of one or two lineages belonging to a certain clan than in terms of the clan itself. A clan's membership may be widespread, and thus the eminence of one of its lineages in one area by no means assures a similar status to other lineages resident elsewhere. Thus the dominant position acquired by certain lineages of the ŌtāLar clan in Kaṇṇapuram kirāmam has not significantly raised the status of members of that clan who remained in the northern part of the nāTu. Moreover, during times of hardship—feud or famine—descent groups have tended to emigrate from prior kirāmam locations to seek new and more favorable locations elsewhere. For example, as mentioned previously, during the feud between the CeṅkaNNaṉ and the ŌtāLar, many members of the former clan left Kāṅkayam to settle on the western edge of Koṅku; but the first rights they had enjoyed in the first kirāmam area were not transportable. Internal divisions, due to rivalries within given kirāmam areas, are also common.[40] They too can result in the departure of members of a clan and consequently in changes in the power structure within a given area.

When a descent group divides into two or more lineages, each newly formed group will establish a separate lineage temple. If the division has been the result of a split within one locality, the new temple will be dedicated to a new deity—generally female—who in some way is thought to have served as a nodal point for that division.[41] If the new temple is

---

[39]One of these is a KavuNTar. The other four are Paraiyars.
[40]See chapter 4, pp. 196–202.
[41]See chapter 2, pp. 83–86.

established as a result of migration, however, lineage members will generally attempt to duplicate the one they left behind.

For example, when the CeṅkaNNan migrated in large numbers to the western edge of Koṅku they constructed a new temple where they settled, but they dedicated it to their original clan deity. In order to construct this duplicate, no image or handful of earth was carried from the location of the original. However, the group did not see itself as cut off permanently from the old shrine by this move. The new temple will always remain secondary to the old, and its devotees retain responsibility for the former's upkeep through regular donations collected annually by the priest in charge, and also for making pilgrimages to the original spot whenever feasible. It is understood, furthermore, that the god will never have the same degree of *cakti* ("power") in its new temple as at the old site.[42]

In general terms, therefore, there is a clear relationship in Koṅku between locality and descent. The place where the descent group first separated from a larger ancestral unit to become a discrete lineage is important. This specific territorial reference point is part and parcel of the identity of any KavuNTar lineage group. Yet the territorial component is elastic, so to speak, since if the group has to move, the original tie continues to be of importance for some time. Eventually, however, a group that has moved will give rise in its turn to new lineages, whose members will worship at still newer temples. At this point the old territorial tie will be discarded and a new one acquired.

One territorially specific deity cannot be moved under any circumstances. This is the so-called nāTTu stone, or *nāTTukkal,* which can be found in every settlement.[43] This stone, to which obeisance is paid on all life-cycle occasions, has an absolute identity with local territory. Its importance in ritual is shared by all right-division castes.[44] It must never be transported. When a new settlement is constructed, a new nāTTu stone is always installed.

This situation, as described, falls halfway between that of two other groups. The Kallar (to the South) are one extreme in which locality and descent group appear to be completely undifferentiated.[45] At the other extreme are the various castes of Malwa (to the North), where these two

---

[42]Informant no. 20 clarified this notion of decreasing power relative to distance from the original site by citing the following two examples: Murukan, who is believed to have his greatest power on the great hill at Palani; and Christ who, he thought, must surely have his greatest power at the spot where he was crucified.

[43]See the next chapter for a further discussion of this stone.

[44]Though some low-ranking left-division groups also pay obeisance to the nāTTukkal, most neutral and high-ranking left castes simply ignore this stone in their ritual.

[45]Louis Dumont, *Une Sous-Caste,* pp. 327, 336, 359, 393; idem, "Distribution of Some Maravar Sub-castes," in Bala Ratnam, ed., *Anthropology on the March* (Madras: The Book Centre, 1963), pp. 299, 304. Also see Robert Hardgrave, *The Nadars of Tamilnad* (Berkeley: University of California Press, 1969), pp. 37–39.

concepts seem to be kept quite distinct.[46] In Koṅku the presence of the nāTTu stone provides for the possibility of separation of residence from descent.[47] Once installed, a particular stone will never be moved, but, as already stated, a duplicate can be placed at the entrance to a new settlement or neighborhood area when necessary. Table 3.2 presents in summarized form a comparison of the extent to which lineage and neighborhood shrines may be moved from their locations, for locally dominant castes in two Southern districts and one Northern one. There is a definite progression here from locality and descent being undistinguished to a situ-

TABLE 3.2
COMPARISON OF MOVABILITY OF LINEAGE AND NEIGHBORHOOD SHRINES
IN DIFFERENT PARTS OF INDIA

	Caste	Area	Lineage Shrine	Neighborhood or Locality Shrine
(a)	Kallar	Madurai Dt., Madras	Outside. Can be moved only with surrounding earth.	Absent.
(b)	KavuNTar	Coimbatore Dt., Madras	Outside. New shrines can be constructed without earth from the old, but the latter are never moved.	Present. Never moved.
(c)	Khati and Rajput	Dewar Dt., Madhya Pradesh	Inside. Can be moved at will with the household.	Present. Moved only "painfully."

SOURCES: (a) Louis Dumont, *Une Sous-Caste de l'Inde du Sud* (Paris: Mouton, 1957), pp. 327, 336, 359, and 393; (b) Author's observation; (c) Adrian C. Mayer, *Caste and Kinship in Central India* (London: Routledge and Kegan Paul, 1960), pp. 184–93.

ation where they are clearly separated, and a parallel progression from shrines that can be moved only with their physical surroundings to ones that can be duplicated. Finally, there are shrines which have no physical component and can be moved with ease. Whether this suggests a general North-South contrast or merely caste differences in the conception of locality, remains to be studied.

In the foregoing discussion of the kirāmam as a whole, special attention has been given to the organization of the high-ranking right-division communities relative to this territorial unit. In the final section of this chapter, the untouchable groups of the area will also be discussed. As will soon be seen the differences between the two major outcaste communities, as

[46]Adrian C. Mayer, *Caste and Kinship in Central India* (London: Routledge and Kegan Paul, 1960), pp. 184–93.
[47]For a most interesting and detailed discussion of this issue, see Louis Dumont, "A Note on Locality in Relation to Descent," *Contributions to Indian Sociology* 7 (1964): 71–76. This interpretation of the Koṅku material is further supported by local folklore which insists that the nāTTu stone was established exactly at the time when the nāTu areas stopped serving as units for exogamy, and thus when territory, in fact, became separated from the notion of descent.

exhibited by their response to the increased pressure for schooling, and to pressure from Christian missionaries for conversion, suggests a reversal in the pattern of attachment to kirāmam-based traditions at the bottom of the right-left hierarchy.

CONTRASTS BETWEEN THE LEFT AND RIGHT UNTOUCHABLE COMMUNITIES

Although I never had much opportunity to work intensively with the Mātāri and Paṟaiyar groups in Kaṇṇapuram kirāmam, I did acquire some general impressions concerning the differences between these two main untouchable communities. These impressions help to elucidate some of the stress factors associated with being low on the ladder in an over-all social organization which serves to group higher-ranking communities into two opposed categories. These general perceptions will be outlined in this section.

Even the casual observer will quickly notice the visual differences between the several Mātāri residential sites in Kaṇṇapuram kirāmam and the one Paṟaiyar area. Not only is there an important difference in the absolute size of these two subcastes locally, but there is also a difference in their spatial placement. The Paṟaiyar living area is close to the ritual center of Kaṇṇapuram. It is here that the kirāmam temples at which this group holds hereditary rights are located. The Mātāri living areas, on the other hand, are scattered throughout the kirāmam and often difficult to reach except by foot. The Mātāri in these separate areas belong to different subcastes, and there is little evidence of interaction among these distinctive groups.

Even more striking, perhaps, are the differences in the appearance of cleanliness and comfort in the living quarters of these two communities. The Paṟaiyar have wide, clean streets, and many homes of plaster and tile construction. Their settlement includes a fine-looking church, and an open plaza with a few trees. The Mātāri settlements, by contrast, are full of dirty, narrow lanes; and the houses are mostly unplastered, uneven, and thatched. No churches are located near any of these settlements, and a long walk is generally necessary to get to school, to the roadside shops, or to the local dispensary, as all such amenities are centrally located. These contrasts suggest that the Mātāri community is the poorer and more marginal of the two, but they also lead one to suspect that members of this group take less pride in what little they do possess. The same contrast was noticeable in the way the Mātāri interacted with me as ethnographer. They were always more obsequious in their behavior and evidenced less pride in their traditional customs than did Paṟaiyars of similar age and local status.

Differences of the same nature can be observed in the local folklore, which often refers to these two groups. In the great epic of the Koṅku area, *The Story of the Brothers,* for example, a Paṟaiyar is one of the heroes. His role is largely that of a low-status, but super-powerful sibling of the two KavuNTars for whom the story is named.[48] Furthermore, local mythology treats all the right-division castes as brothers. They are said to have been born of the same pot of fire and merely assigned different worldly duties by the goddess whom they were born into the world to serve. The Paṟaiyar are proud of their role in the annual Māriyammaṉ festival.[49] In their view of right-division ideology, they do not deserve to be outcastes.

It is also important to note that the Paṟaiyar take pride in the fact that, until their conversion to Christianity, they observed precisely the same life-cycle ceremonies as did the higher-ranking members of their division.[50] Even in day-to-day matters, the right division promotes an air of deliberate cooperation. There is more sharing of food and more necessity for the presence of representatives of all the castes within the division on festive occasions than there is among left groups. The Paṟaiyar also forbid widows to remarry and insist that these women wear pure white, just as the KavuNTars do. Hence there is a sense in which the Paṟaiyar can be said to be the mythological and ritual equals of others in their division. Taking all this into account, one can argue that the Paṟaiyar are untouchable only because the right division, in order to conform to Brahmanical standards, had to have some outcaste group of their own. The Paṟaiyar believe that they were simply unlucky that this lot of untouchability fell to them. Their very integration into the organization of the right-division community has made them resentful of their low status within it.

The Mātāri, by contrast, exhibit substantial differences in their relationships with the more prestigious communities of the left division. Here the mythology stresses the ranked relationship existing between the Mātāri and the other subcastes of their bloc. Often this idea is expressed by the use of the terms "father" and "son" as modes of address, and less frequently by using the terms "elder" and "younger brother." Thus many Mātāri subcastes—both Telugu- and Kannada-speaking groups—refer

---

[48]There is some historical evidence that the Paṟaiyar may not have been as degraded at one time as they are today. Tiruvalluvar, one of the great Tamil Saivite saints was a Paṟaiyar by caste, for example, and there are also early poems mentioning Paṟaiyar as the name of a noble clan. See P. T. Srinivasa Iyengar, *History of the Tamils from the Earliest Times to 600 A.D.* (Madras: Madras University Press, 1929), p. 16 and Thurston, *Castes and Tribes,* 6:82, 88, 107–8. A similar relationship between Jats and Sweepers is mentioned by M. Pradhan for Uttar Pradesh. See M. C. Pradhan, *The Political System of the Jats of Northern India* (Bombay: Oxford University Press, 1966), p. 49.

[49]Thurston suggests that they claim similar ritual rights at festivals throughout the South. See his *Castes and Tribes,* 6:83–4, 86.

[50]Except, of course, that they substituted men of their own community for the position of barber, washerman, and priest. See chapter 4 for details.

to themselves as the *jāti piLLai* or "children" of the Nāyakkar.[51] Stories which describe the connection between the Mātāri and the Nāyakkar are quick to emphasize the dependence of the former on the latter. One story which I collected, for example, describes how the Nāyakkar brought the Mātāri into the area with them as servants.[52] Another example can be drawn from the story of the folk hero Maturaivīraṉ, a tale of adventure which is famous all over the South.[53] In this great epic, the son of a ruler of Madurai (or Maturai) is cast into the forest as a babe, because of his birth at an inauspicious moment. Then he is found and raised by a Mātāri couple. The child grows up in this servant family, but eventually marries the daughter of a local Nāyakkar king. He then goes on to perform many heroic feats, all of which are explained by the fact of his true royal ancestry. His humble upbringing among the Mātāri provides many opportunities for the story-teller to contrast their lives with that of the Nāyakkar kings.

More important, however, is the frequent emphasis on the Mātāri as beef eaters and leatherworkers. I give below two stories of this genre, both told to me by Mātāris themselves.

1) *VaTuka Subcaste of Mātāri*[54] Once there lived a ToTTi Nāyakkar and his younger brother. One day there was not enough food in the house and so the younger brother had to go out to search for work. Six or seven days elapsed. The younger brother became hungry and the roads leading back to his elder brother's house were flooded because of heavy rains. Finally, he ate a young calf in desperation. When he returned to his elder brother's house the latter came to learn of what his younger brother had eaten. He asked him to leave the family as a result. Thus, the elder brother's descendants became Nāyakkars and the younger brother's descendants became Mātāris. However, the two groups retain a memory of their former relationship and to this day, the Mātāri have a right to claim their status as younger brothers.

2) *Moracu Subcaste of Mātāri (Story of the VēTTuvar Karuppa-Nacāmi Temple, VīracōRapuram)*[55] Once, long ago, three Moracu Mātāri men from VīracōRapuram left on a journey to Uppamaṅkalam, near MaNappārai, which is east of Karur, to buy skins. They

[51]See Dumont's discussion of similar data from elsewhere in *Homo hierarchicus* (Paris: Gallimard, 1966), p. 55. The term can also have a derisive aspect, referring to the possible illegitimacy of the "children."

[52]Thurston recounts similar tales which associate the Mātāri with the KōmuTTi CeTTiyār, *Castes and Tribes*, 3:325–31.

[53]I have the impression that this folktale is known throughout the Tamil-speaking area, but do not have precise information to document this. Several printed versions exist and I have met people from outside the Koṅku area who know the story. The Mātāri greatly revere this folk epic and shrines dedicated to its main heroes are common in their settlements.

[54]Informant no. 40.

[55]Informant no. 6. Note that the story links the Mātāri to the VēTTuvar KavuNTars, another left-division caste in the Koṅku area.

belonged to the Pūtiyan, Eriyanti, and Alikar clans, respectively. Although these men spent a whole week in their search, no goat or cattle skins were available for purchase. So, they set off for home empty handed. Half-way, however, they found a shrine in a field, at the foot of a tree. In front of the god of this shrine an offering of cooked rice and meat had been set out on leaves. The three Mātāris were very hungry; so they surreptitiously ate this offering. Continuing their journey, they next discovered several skins lying across a fence of the same field. These, they realized, had been left to dry by the men who had made the sacrifice to the god. Each Mātāri picked up two of the skins and the men continued their journey.

After a time, however, one of the men discovered that his skins were unusually heavy. He called to his *māman* (MB) but the latter was simply amused that his cross-relative was not able to carry his share. Finally the poor man set his skin down, opened it, and discovered that he had been carrying a big stone inside the hide. Throwing this stone away, he set off again with the others. Then a second man began to find his skins heavy. Laying them down, he too found a stone of the same size. This, too, was thrown away, but the experience was then repeated for the third man. The stone [explains the story-teller] was really the god to whom the offerings had been made under the tree.

During this time, the god of the shrine had gone to the VēTTuvar KavuNTar priest who had originally prepared the goat offering. The god told this man how these three Mātāris had come and eaten his offering. He complained that he wanted offerings from these men as well, and that the priest should give them the proper utensils so that they, too, could prepare something for him. Meanwhile, the three men had been walking steadily. Finally, they reached the town of VeL-Lakōvil. There one of their number died and had to be buried to the north of the settlement. Finally, the two remaining men completed the final rites and then returned to their homes in VīracōRapuram. When they arrived, however, they discovered that they had lost the power of speech. Their relatives, discovering this, became very worried. Finally they resolved to follow the men back to the field where they had discovered the shrine.

When they reached this tree for the second time, they discovered the VēTTuvar KavuNTar priest waiting there for them. He presented the Mātāris with all the articles necessary to perform an oblation or pūjā. Having completed this, the two Mātāris and their relatives returned to VīracōRapuram. There they asked an old KavuNTar headman where they could install a new god. The headman answered that they must place it far enough from the village site so that the sounds of pounding and grinding grain could not be heard. Thus the Mātāris selected the bank of the stream bed to the south of this settlement, where they built a shrine and placed an image of the god in it, facing east. Next to this deity, named VēTTuvar KaruppaNa-cāmi, they also made a shrine for his younger sister, VīratankaL.

Both of these stories refer openly to the Mātāri's degraded status. Furthermore, both link it to the eating of something forbidden, in the one case, beef and in the other, the offering of goat meat stolen from a shrine.

The consequence in the first story is ostracism from the family, and in the second, ostracism from the village. These stories are different in degree from those which Paṛaiyars tell about themselves. The former tend to accept their low status as deserved, while the latter stress the injustice of their rank and attempt to explain it by some quirk of fate unrelated to their own past actions. Both groups are ambivalent about their low status, of course, but in the case of the Mātāri, I have the impression that their low position is more fully internalized, and that members of this community are prone to a strong sense of self-inferiority. Paṛaiyars repudiate the assertion made by the higher-ranking groups that they eat beef, while the Mātāri do not repudiate the same accusations.[56] Mātāri traditions concerning widowhood, and also their ceremonial rights, establish only a partial link with more prominent subcastes of their own division. For example, according to Thurston, Mātāris have the right to be invited to a

TABLE 3.3
LITERACY IN THE KOṄKU REGION

	Area	Percentage of Literates
(a)	Coimbatore Dt.	30.0
(b)	Dharapuram Taluk	25.0
(c)	Kaṉṉapuram (officially PaccāpāLaiyam Panchayat)	28.0
(d)	ŌlappāLaiyam Settlement	31.0

SOURCES: (a) Republic of India, *Census of India,* 1961, Vol. IX, *Madras,* Part X-i, *District Census Handbook, Coimbatore,* 2 vols. (Madras: Government Press, 1964), 1:296; (b) Ibid., 1:12; (c) Ibid., 2:614; (d) Author's census material.

KōmuTTi CeTTiyār wedding, and they expect to receive a formal invitation. Sometimes they are also asked to bless a KōmuTTi bride's wedding necklace.[57] However, they also accept important differences in their behavior from that of higher-ranking groups and do not boast of exact duplication of the ceremonies performed by these communities.

The same pattern of differences appears if we turn to the figures on literacy for right- and left-division groups in Kaṉṉapuram—actually ŌlappāLaiyam settlement—and to similar statistics on the proportion of literates in different communities in 1911 for the Madras Presidency as a whole.[58] The figures for literacy in Kaṉṉapuram kirāmam, shown in Table 3.3, compare very favorably with the figures on literacy for the region as a whole, particularly if one considers that they describe a situation in a rural community, fifty miles from the nearest city and eighteen miles

[56]Thurston refers briefly to a similar repudiation of beef elsewhere. See his *Castes and Tribes,* 6:116–17.

[57]Ibid., 3:327.

[58]Unfortunately, no breakdown of literacy figures by caste is available at the District level. This is true even for 1911, the last year for which a breakdown, by caste, for any administrative unit in the South is available.

from the nearest large town.[59] The reasons for this relatively high literacy rate are two-fold. For one, Kaṇṇapuram has long been an established cultural center, housing an important temple complex; and second, there has been a good school in the area since at least the turn of the century.

In addition to these figures for literacy of the kirāmam area as a whole, it is important for the purpose of this study to break the calculation down, where possible, by caste and subcaste. By doing this, a very striking difference between groups affiliated with the right and the left divisions can be observed, as shown in Table 3.4.

Note first that the average rate of literacy among the higher-ranking groups of the left division in ŌlappāLaiyam is roughly twice that recorded for equivalent communities of the right. Furthermore, this differential would appear to have remained relatively stable over a fifty-year period. While literacy rates in the area as a whole have more than tripled since 1911, the high-ranking left-division groups have managed to maintain their relative educational advantage, and perhaps they have even increased it. Such a finding is not unexpected, since members of the left with the most prestige are precisely those groups who are most dependent on their specialized skills and on contacts over a wide area for a livelihood.

However, I do not think that the occupational preferences of these communities are sufficient to explain their keen interest in literacy. The right-division UTaiyār, for example, are a similarly specialized group, and yet they do not show the same enthusiasm. The above figures, are, rather, a further demonstration of what has been argued throughout this work: that the high-ranking left-division groups identify more strongly than their right-division counterparts with an all-South Indian textual tradition. This tradition revolves around great mythological, ritual, and philosophical writings of the past. Literacy forms a major route of access to this specialized, religious knowledge; and the communities of the left with the most prestige, I think, have greatly prized scholarship for this reason.[60]

What is even more interesting about Table 3.4 is the suggestion of reversal in the relative percentage of literates among low-ranking groups in the two divisions. The right-division Paṟaiyar appear much more committed to education than are the left-division Mātāri.[61] This same pattern may also be present among some of the lower-ranking touchable communities.

---

[59]Of course, ŌlappāLaiyam is only five miles from the important market center of Kāṅkayam.

[60]This might appear to contradict the fact that most people say they want an education in order to "get a good job." What they often mean is that literacy will give them access to a white-collar occupation which can be defined as "good" in traditional religious terms. Just as in the West, more money can usually be made in services or in blue-collar trades than in highly intellectual pursuits.

[61]The contrast between Paṟaiyars and Mātāris in this regard is well known to local residents. School teachers are particularly aware of the difference.

TABLE 3.4

LITERACY BY COMMUNITY

Caste or Subcaste Name	Madras Presidency in 1911[1]		ŌlappāLaiyam in 1966[2]	
	Percentage Literate	Sample Size	Number Literate	Sample Size
Neutral Division:				
Brahman	42.0	480,063	9	9
KaNakku PiLLai (Kanakkan)	27.0	63,360	7	7
Right Division (upper and middle rank):				
KavuNTar (Vellala)	13.0	2,535,791	44	184
PaNTāram	9.0	66,868	2	9
UTaiyār (Kusavan)	5.1	153,127	5	9
NāTār (Shannan)	9.2	641,976	4	29
Percentage Average for Division	9.3			
Left Division (upper and middle rank):				
Ācāri (Kammalan)	13.3	559,205	12	28
KōmuTTi CeTTiyār (Komati Chetti)	27.0	498,295	4	4
Mutaliyār (Kaikolan)	11.2	368,347	15	26
Percentage Average for Division	20.0			
Low-ranking Groups:				
Nāyakkar (Odde)	0.6	550,109	1	21
VaTuka VaNNār	unknown	. . .	1	5
Koṅku Nāvitar	unknown	. . .	1	4
Paraiyar*	1.4	2,363,802	6,775	35,923
Mātāri* (Madari & Chakkiliyan)	0.5	526,451	9,002	300,075

SOURCES: The calculation for 1911 is based on the figures from the Dominion of India, *Census of India, 1911*, Vol. XII, *Madras*, Part II, *Imperial and Provincial Tables* (Madras: Government Press, 1912), p. 80. Unfortunately, they represent an average for the entire Madras Presidency. The figures for 1966 are based on my own census of ŌlappāLaiyam settlement.

NOTES: The names in parentheses are those used by the census enumerators for Madras Presidency. With the exception of Komati Chetti, these are caste rather than subcaste names.
[1]Figures from 1911 are given because the census for that year provides the best breakdown available to date of the population in caste terms. It is not entirely clear what definition of literacy was used, but the count was probably based on an interviewer's question phrased something like this: "Can you read or write?" In general, the census figures are stated in terms of adult population; that is, people over fifteen years of age.
[2]I have included in my figures for ŌlappāLaiyam settlement, 1966, everyone resident in the settlement who was over fifteen years of age, or a total of 335 individuals. I counted a person as literate if he had completed the 5th grade, or if he was "self-educated" to the same standard. This criterion puts the total number of literate persons at 105, and thus the literacy rate for ŌlappāLaiyam at 31 per cent. If I had used the 3rd grade as the standard, the literacy rate would have risen to 42 per cent. It must be remembered that this figure of 31 per cent characterizes a touchable caste settlement. When untouchables are included in the calculations, this "average" is depressed under 25 per cent.
*Since there were no outcastes resident in ŌlappāLaiyam settlement, and since scheduled caste figures on literacy are available at the District level, I have included 1961 census figures on "scheduled" castes (that is, non-Christian Paraiyars and Mātāris only) for comparison. The figures given are for the rural population of Coimbatore District. In urban areas of the District, the proportion literate increases. (The literacy rate rises to 21 per cent from 19 per cent for Paraiyars, and it rises to 17 per cent from 3 per cent for Mātāris. Note that the difference between the two groups is maintained to a certain extent.) The figures are from the Republic of India, *Census of India, 1961*, Vol. IX, *Madras*, Part X-i, *District Census Handbook, Coimbatore*, 2 vols. (Madras: Government Press, 1964), 1:339.

The Nāyakkar who are members of the left, for example, have a very low literacy rate while the Koṅku Nāvitar, or barbers, who belong to the right division, are surprisingly educated for their status.[62]

This reversal of the pattern of literacy in the lowest reaches of the social hierarchy can be explained, I think, in terms of the difference in attitudes just discussed, which these two important untouchable groups seem to exhibit toward their low social status. A leveling influence appears to be at work among the members of the right. Those with low rank in this division want very much to achieve equality with those of higher rank and to underplay status differences. Their interest in education as a modern route to steady employment is one way of claiming equality. Among the low-ranking castes of the left division, by contrast, a sense of distance from the upper castes of the same group could explain the lower value they attach to literacy. If the Mātāri see themselves as truly low on the social scale, then it is easy for them to become resigned and to believe in the hopelessness of any effort to "catch up."

This interpretation of the difference in literacy rates between the untouchable left-division and untouchable right-division groups is further supported by the experience of the Christian missionaries in their attempts to convert members of these two distinct communities to a new and foreign faith. Despite the fact that the Mātāri (left) had much less invested in the local status quo than did the Paraiyar (right), they proved much more difficult converts to an alien but essentially egalitarian creed. The Paraiyar were more open to the call for social change and to the doctrine of man's equality before God than the Mātāri were. The latter, far more isolated from the currents of the larger society around them, had no margin of self-worth to gamble, and feared conversion would only bring them ignominy and further degradation. It appears that on the whole, the Mātāri preferred to be left alone.[63]

In their approach to outcaste groups, missionaries have not given much attention to the prominent rivalries between the Paraiyar and Mātāri communities. In general, they have sought instead to play down the intense competition that has existed between them. From available accounts, therefore, it would appear that a more or less equal pitch has been made to both groups.[64] When the first Christian missionaries arrived in the

---

[62] My sample is very small, of course, but my impression from talking with other Koṅku Nāvitars is that their interest in literacy is considerably higher than, say, that of the left-division barbers or washermen. Unfortunately, my sample is not large enough to demonstrate this statistically.

[63] A. Andreen, *Annual Report for the T.E.L.C. Pioneer Board* (Pollachi: Lutheran Church, 1954), pp. 1–2.

[64] S. Rajamanikam, "Factors in the Growth of the Christian Movement in the Ex-Methodist Area of the Tiruchirappalli Diocese and their Relation to Present-Day Problems" (Thesis for B.D. degree, United Theological College, Bangalore, 1950–51), pp. 5,

Koṅku area, about 1850, they had already had the bitter experience of attempting to convert high-caste Hindus in other areas of the South, with little success. About the time that they began to move inland to more remote areas, therefore, they made a major change in strategy. In particular, they began to concentrate on preaching to members of the untouchable communities.

The missionaries of the late nineteenth century reasoned that with the lowest-ranking groups, teachings about a Christian Savior and the equality of man before God would strike a sympathetic note. Here, they thought, was a potential for mass conversions which had not caught on in their prior work with the elite. Many Mātāri conversions were made under crisis conditions, such as famine, when there was hope for some quick gain. Many of these professions of faith, however, have not stood the test of time. Through the years, it would seem, the Mātāri have not had the self-confidence to stand up as different. Hence members of this group have tended to "slip back" into the traditional "pagan" ways much more easily than their Paraiyar counterparts.[65] The Paraiyar, by contrast, have gained a considerable amount in education, in medical attention, and in mobility, from their contact with the Christian church—not to mention the spiritual benefits those within the faith claim for them. Whatever differences initially existed between the Paraiyar and the Mātāri, therefore, have probably been reinforced by the impact of a foreign creed.

To conclude, this chapter has argued for the importance of the kirāmam as a local organizational unit for right-division groups. Furthermore, it has described the degree of dominance which these communities have, both in the political arena and in ceremonial activities at this local level. And finally, it has been argued that the different values which are stressed by members of the left and right divisions make for some unexpected contrasts among the lowest-ranking groups of the two blocs. The emphasis which the higher-ranking subcastes of the right place on ritual cooperation and alliance in dealing with local affairs seems to have had the effect of making the lowest groups in this division very resentful of their inferior

---

10–12, 14–15, 22–26, 28; and Rev. L. Bechu, *Story of the Coimbatore Mission* (Bangalore: Paris Foreign Mission Society, 1948), pp. 76–78.

[65]Andreen, *Annual Report,* pp. 4–5, and Rajamanikam, "Factors in the Growth of the Christian Movement," p. 31. With the help of the Swedish Lutheran Mission, *Tranquebar Almanac* (Tranquebar: Tranquebar Publishing House, 1964) and Reverend J. Ulrici, I have made a rough count of Lutheran congregations in the Coimbatore District at the present time. Out of a total of about 104 congregations, a full 63 per cent are Paraiyar while only 29 per cent are Mātāri, despite the fact that Mātāris are about three times as numerous in the area as a whole. Another 5 per cent of the Lutheran community are converts from other low-caste groups and only 3 per cent are from what could be called high-caste backgrounds. From informal discussion with Catholic and Methodist churchmen in the area, I gather that the composition of the congregations of these other major Christian groups is similar.

status. Among the subcastes of the left, by contrast, the ritual separation of groups is more marked and hierarchy has received a greater stress. In consequence, the lowest-ranking groups of this division are socially more isolated. At the same time, they are less energetic, less optimistic, and less confident, in the struggle to raise their own position in relation to others in the same locality. This partially accounts for the fact that in Koṅku the Christian missionaries have had greater success with the Paṟaiyar than they have had with the Mātāri outcaste community.

The next chapter will focus on the dynamics of division organization at the Ūr, as opposed to the kirāmam, level. There, the patterns of competition utilized by the two blocs of subcastes in the struggle for local rank will be analyzed in some detail.

4

THE HAMLET: ŌLAPPĀLAIYAM
AND NEIGHBORING ŪR AREAS

THE EFFECTIVE COMMUNITY AND ITS RESIDENTIAL NEIGHBORHOODS

Kaṇṇapuram kirāmam officially includes thirty-two ūr or distinct settle-ments.[1] This count is affirmed each year at the Māriyammaṉ festival when a delegation of women from each of these thirty-two settlements is ex-pected to present an offering of lighted oil lamps, called *mā viLakku,* to the goddess. Without the aid of this ritual convention it would be difficult to determine empirically how many distinct settlements exist in any given kirāmam area. To begin with, only touchable caste areas are included in the official, temple tally. Furthermore, small clusters of dwellings contain-ing only a few families may or may not be counted, depending, it would seem, on whether or not the settlement has its own Viṉāyakar temple. Some all-NāTār clusters have such a temple and so are counted, while isolated KavuNTar households do not and are omitted from the tally. As with higher levels of organization, the definition of local residential units turns ultimately on ritual criteria.

Viṉāyakar, the elephant-headed deity, is known all over India as the first son of Civā. In Koṅku he is always considered unmarried.[2] At the same time he is almost always found flanked by *nākakkals* ("cobra stones"), a representation of divinity that has strong female associations in other contexts.[3] Viṉāyakar is thought to be the "remover of obstacles" and must be worshipped before any temple or household ceremony begins. Participants in festivals and life-cycle rituals always worship this god in

---

[1]Earlier, the official number was twenty-four, which was the count in several old poems and songs about the kirāmam area.

[2]This is generally true elsewhere in India as well, but I understand that there are a few exceptions.

[3]This may seem surprising, given the general European association of snakes with male or phallic symbols. A lengthy discussion of contrary associations in a South Indian context will be included in my study of folklore and ceremony in the Koṅku area.

their local hamlet before proceeding to the shrine or household where the major ritual activity is centered. The bride and groom must visit the groom's local Vināyakar temple several times during the course of the wedding ritual. However, major festivities never take place at a Vināyakar temple itself. It serves, rather, as a point of reference or a beginning to whatever else occurs.

Larger than the settlement proper and smaller than the kirāmam, is the "area of day-to-day cooperation." No separate term exists for this unit. It too is called an *Ūr* in local speech.[4] Such areas generally include at least one outcaste cluster, and settlements belonging to several different touchable groups. This grouping of settlements, whose population interacts on a daily basis, and within which all the essential service communities, such as barbers and washermen, are generally found, I call a hamlet. This larger Ūr of cooperation is more important than the individual settlements just described. It is ritually defined as the area whose population worships the *Ūr teyvam*, MākāLiyamman. She is the goddess who protects the hamlet area.

In Kaṇṇapuram kirāmam are nine Ūr or hamlet goddesses. The location of temples dedicated to these goddesses in some of the settlements in the kirāmam is shown in Figure 4.1. At the yearly ceremony for each of the nine goddesses, females from every household in the hamlet are asked to bring mā viLakku to her temple.[5] Untouchables who reside within the hamlet area are also expected to attend, but are asked to stand at a respectful distance from the focus of ceremonial activity. In this as with all other features, the ceremonies performed at MākāLiyamman temple festivals follow very closely the rituals performed at the annual Māriyamman festival, but with reduced pomp. The parallels are, indeed, so close that no separate discussion is necessary.

At the kirāmam or village level, it will be remembered, there is both an important Māriyamman temple and a less used but still important KariyakāLiyamman shrine. Māriyamman is a specific goddess whose story and festival are familiar to all local residents. KariyakāLiyamman, by contrast, is a more generalized goddess. She is said to be the manifestation of Civa's female consort, Cakti or Pārvati, in her terrifying and destructive form. As such she is generally appealed to in times of local illness and misfortune. At the Ūr level, MākāLiyamman would seem to combine these aspects of Māriyamman and KariyakāLiyamman as separately manifested at the kirāmam level. This goddess can be viewed as a localized and simplified embodiment of both these great female divinities of the kirāmam as they

---

[4] I capitalize the word "ūr" when referring to a hamlet in order to distinguish it from its other meaning, "settlement."

[5] Three of the nine temples had not held a festival for some years. In each case, the cancellation of festivities was due to factional fights within that particular goddess' area. For more details see pp. 196–202 of this chapter.

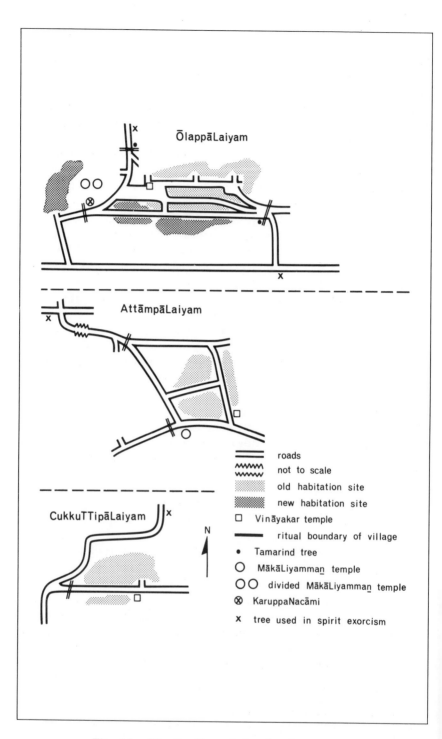

Fig. 4.1. The ritual boundaries of settlement sites.

relate to the Ūr area. Furthermore, like Māriyamman, MākāLiyamman is thought to have special rain-providing powers; thus she receives special worship in times of drought.

In addition to an Ūr goddess who is worshipped on festival occasions, ritual boundaries exist which help to protect the Ūr area from evil influences. On the main road leading to ŌlappāLaiyam, for example, there is believed to stand a big *muṇi,* or giant, who demands a blood sacrifice at the time of the Ūr MākāLiyamman festival. The sacrifice of a chicken or goat is made when the procession carrying the sacred pot from the temple well passes the muṇi's locale.[6] He demands blood before letting the procession proceed, as a return for his work in protecting the Ūr area from malevolent beings during the year to come.

Within the settlement or Vināyakar area proper, there are further spatial subdivisions that receive ritual recognition. The first of these is the neighborhood, often designated by its compass orientation, but also in some places by its caste or subcaste population. Each neighborhood is ritually distinguished by its separate *nāTTukkal* or nāTTu stone. Thus in ŌlappāLaiyam there is the residential area proper, with its nāTTu stone, and also *merku ūr* or "West ŌlappāLaiyam" with its independent ritual focus. These nāTTukkals, or neighborhood stones, are always inconspicuous and are generally imbedded at the side of a road or path at the point where various streets of that neighborhood converge in the direction of the ūr Vināyakar temple.

In earlier times, according to Konku KavuNTar tradition, all males of this subcaste who resided in a given nāTu area were treated as "brothers." They formed an exogamous unit. After a few generations, however, it is said that the original principle of territorial exogamy bogged down in a hopeless tangle. According to the folk tradition, a huge council of elders was finally held to discuss this problem, and it was decided to identify and name a number of individual male descent groups.[7] Since this meeting the KavuNTars have practiced clan rather than nāTu exogamy, and the nāTTu stone was established, marking this separation of territory from descent. Today the nāTTukkal stone is important only in marriage and funeral rituals.[8] The stone is said to represent the nāTu headman, who can no longer make it a practice to attend these ceremonies.

---

[6] The well used for both Māriyamman and MākāLiyamman should not lie in the direction of a burning ground and should not be the major drinking well of the settlement. Usually, it lies just outside the settlement area in a field. The well may, however, be used for agricultural purposes.

[7] Informants nos. 7, 22, and 38 told me this story independently. See also references to the nāTTukkal in H. Whitehead, *Village Gods of South India* (London: Oxford University Press, 1916), pp. 40–41, and Edgar Thurston, *Castes and Tribes of Southern India,* 7 vols. (Madras: Government Press, 1909), 3:408.

[8] A few of the neutral and higher-ranking left-division groups ignore this stone in their life-cycle rituals. They are the Brahmans, the KaruNīkar PiLLai, the KōmuTTi CeTTiyār,

Beneath the neighborhood exists still one further unit of territorial significance before we reach the level of individual households. This is the
teru, or street. Here the marker of ritual unity is a *tōraNam* or decorative
archway of leaves which is tied whenever a wedding is celebrated by any of
the member households. This archway is always constructed at the end of
the street nearest the Vināyakar temple. Thus all participants in the festivities must pass under it on their way to the home where the celebration will
be held. In theory, the archway seems to mark off the residential area of a
particular clan or lineage within the caste neighborhood on this festive
occasion. In fact, however, residence is governed in part by economic and
spatial constraints and clan, not to mention caste, areas are not neatly
segregated in these terms. Thus the archway marks the unity of a "street"
but not necessarily the unity of a lineage during the marriage celebration.[9]

Two other minor roads leading into the settlement also have ritual
boundaries drawn across them which residents can locate. They are
marked by particular trees, fixed upon by tradition, which are said to be
attractive to troublesome spirits, called *pēy*.[10] When such a spirit is exor-
cised from a local victim it is explicitly led across one of these two boundaries and asked to remain in one of these trees. The victim, after various
purification rituals, is then asked to jump over a small fire lit at the boundary point, before re-entering the *ūr* area.[11] Similarly, a bier used to carry
the corpse of a deceased resident is given a half-turn counterclockwise at
this point before it is taken to the graveyard, probably to confuse evil
spirits who might try to retrace the steps of the funeral party and haunt *ūr*
residents. Just as certain protections cease at the *ūr* boundary, omens cease
also at this point to have significance. Many sights or occurrences are
thought to have predictive value if they are noticed while one is still within

---

the CōLi Ācāri, the Nāyakkar, and the Teluṅku Mātāri. Other left-division groups and all
of the right-division castes include obeisance to this stone in their ceremonies.

[9]The tōraNam described is used as a marker of larger social groupings as well. Thus at
the time of the Ūr festival, an archway of leaves is tied over the path leading from the
Ūr Vināyakar temple to the MākāLiyamman festival area. All the residents of the
Ūr are expected to pass under this archway on their way to the celebration. And similarly,
during a Māriyamman festival there is a leafy arch tied over the path leading from the
Ūr Vināyakar to the Māriyamman temple. All women carrying mā viLakku must pass
under this string of leaves on their way to the kirāmam festival. Margosa leaves are a favorite
for this purpose, as they have both cooling and cleansing properties.

[10]The trees are usually found growing on government land, at the edge of a public
thoroughfare, as owners of private land would object to a tree on their property being
used in this manner. Otherwise, there is no specification of botanical variety, although
tamarind trees are favorites. In ŌlappāLaiyam there are only two such trees, one marking
the boundary to the north and the other to the east. The only other access road to the settlement, the main road, is guarded by MākāLiyamman and her associated muni.

[11]The ritual associated with spirit exorcism is elaborate. Only a few excerpts from it are
given here. The main body of the description will appear in my study of ritual and folklore in
Koṅku, to follow.

the ūr area. Once outside these ritual barriers, however, the same events cease to have any auspicious or inauspicious connotation.[12]

Exactly as at higher organizational levels, the sacred geography and ritual boundaries of the ūr site are important. Even within the unit of local cooperation, territorial divisions, neighborhoods and streets, are found to have their corresponding ceremonial markers. As we shall see in chapter 5, this principle holds true right down to the level of the individual household. Each significant social grouping in rural Koṅku has some ritual or ceremonial expression.

INDIVIDUAL SETTLEMENT AREAS

Within the ŌlappāLaiyam MākāLiyamman̠ temple area there are three main population centers: ŌlappāLaiyam settlement, the roadside shops, and an untouchable area, or *cēri*. This three-fold cluster of settlements is the equivalent of a hamlet or "effective local community" as I have used the term in the preceding discussion. It is important to note that the average size of such areas in the Koṅku region is small, as compared with other parts of the South. This can be explained partly by the fact that the region is dry and the produce of the land is sparse. Conditions do not favor heavy concentrations of population.

Comparing average hamlet size in various regions is a difficult task. McKim Marriott has made one attempt using the same concept that I employ, namely the size of an average "effective community" rather than the average sizes of individual settlements. By this phrase I assume he refers, as I do, to that unit of population which regularly interchanges services, labor, and payments within itself.[13] As a key to comparable "effective community size" in the Koṅku area, it seems reasonable to study the pattern of MākāLiyamman̠ temples in Kan̠n̠apuram kirāmam. If it is assumed that this local distribution represents a rough average of the number of such temples to be found in other kirāmams or revenue villages in the region, then a rough size of the "effective community" can be calculated by dividing the average Panchayat population for the area by this number. When used with the census figures for 1961, this method yields an "effective community" of 313 persons for the District of Coimbatore, or of 406 for the Dharapuram subdivision in which Kan̠n̠apuram falls.[14] The contrast with Marriott's estimate of 813 persons for the rice-growing Coromandel Coast is striking.[15] In 1965, the population of the hamlet of

[12]Informant no. 20.

[13]McKim Marriott, *Caste Ranking and Community Structure in Five Regions of India and Pakistan* (Poona: Deccan College Postgraduate Research Institute, 1965), pp. 36–38.

[14]Republic of India, *Census of India, 1961,* Vol. IX, *Madras,* Part X-i, *District Census Handbook, Coimbatore,* 2 vols. (Madras: Government Press, 1964), 1:89.

[15]Marriott, *Caste Ranking and Community Structure,* p. 36.

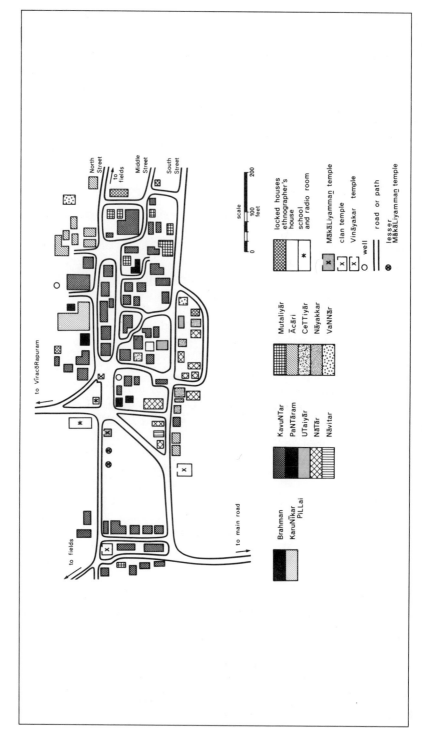

Fig. 4.2. ŌlappāLaiyam settlement site, 1965.

which ŌlappāLaiyam was a part was about six hundred, somewhat above the average as calculated for the region as a whole.

Each of the three major settlements within the ŌlappāLaiyam hamlet— or MākāLiyamman̠ temple area—will be described briefly.

(1) ŌlappāLaiyam Settlement ŌlappāLaiyam proper had a resident population of 404 and when I made a census count in 1966.[16] It is the largest ūr in Kan̠n̠apuram kirāmam and includes representatives of most of the important castes of the region. The living cluster itself shows a certain rationale in its internal settlement pattern. Figure 4.2 shows the location of household compounds, by caste, in 1965. Note that there are three main streets running through the area from west to east, locally referred to as *VaTakku vīti* ("North Street"), *NaTu vīti* ("Middle Street"), and *Ten̠ vīti* ("South Street"), respectively.

All of the vegetarian families, save two, live on the north side of North Street. This is, in general, a wealthy and respectable area. The CōLi Ācāris, who live at the far north-eastern end of North Street, inhabit a rather isolated quarter by themselves. Their houses face inward on each other, rather than outward onto the main thoroughfare. This residential pattern correlates with their ambiguous status in other respects. Ācāris, a left-division group, claim to be higher in the social hierarchy than they are admitted to be by the rest of the local residents.[17]

The homes of members of the main landowning caste (KavuNTar) are evenly distributed on both sides of Middle Street. The entrances to almost all these houses face north. Those that are entered from North Street are generally those of wealthier families; those entered from Middle Street, poorer. However, there is no hard and fast rule in this regard. The wealthiest family of all lives at the eastern extreme of the area. Their house actually blocks Middle Street entirely so that people are obliged to detour around it. The Mutaliyārs, who are largely weavers, also live at the eastern end of the settlement.

In general, as one moves to the western and southern extremities of ŌlappāLaiyam, one encounters more and more low-caste dwellings. This is in keeping with the fact that the north and east are considered the most auspicious and desirable directions. South Street, in fact, used to draw a fairly clear boundary between the landholding KavuN-Tars and the lower, service communities. However, at the present day, this boundary is gradually being transgressed, particularly at the west end of the settlement area. The two Kon̠ku Ācāri families that live at the southwest extremity of the living cluster are meat-eating and of a different subcaste from the community on the northeast periphery, which is CōLi Ācāri. The Kon̠ku Ācāris live on land recently purchased from the government at a low price. In fact, most of the houses in this area, and all the houses in the cluster further to the west, have been built in the same manner on government allocated land, within the last forty years.

[16]One family of six has been omitted from this count. They were recent immigrants who claimed to be Telugu-speaking NāyuTus by caste. I learned little about them and they are not included in any of my cross-caste comparisons.

[17]See pp. 164–68 and 176–77 of this chapter.

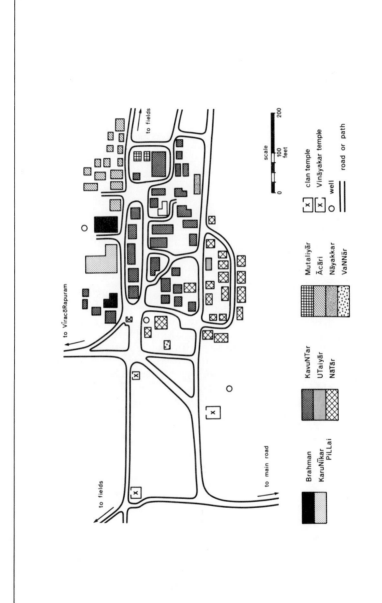

Fig. 4.3. Approximate ŌlappāLaiyam settlement site, 1900.

While the houses on the southwestern extremity of the old site represent mostly newcomers to the settlement, the "western area," as it is called, is largely a spill-over of landowning families from the main site. Land for building has become very scarce in the old living area, and thus a new settlement has sprung up on what was previously public land. A comparison of Figure 4.2 with Figure 4.3, which depicts the settlement as it was in 1900, will show that it was very likely smaller, more homogeneous, and more clearly divided, castewise, at that time. It would seem that the living site then was more clearly dominated by three large groups, the KavuNTars, the Ācāri, and the NāTār, although there is the possibility of selective recall on the part of informants on this matter. Still, this historical map can at least be said to represent local residents' view of their own village in the past. Clearly the Ācāri and the NāTār were once proportionally larger groups in the population than now. As a result of poverty, a large number have recently been forced to emigrate to more promising areas.[18] The KavuNTar community, on the other hand, has managed to retain its dominant position in the settlement as a whole.

At the same time that two previously numerically dominant groups have lost ground, others have improved their position. Most of the newcomers are immigrants from the immediate kirāmam area. They represent trade and service communities that were previously settled in other hamlets nearby. They have moved to ŌlappāLaiyam as a result of disputes elsewhere or because demand for their skills has been growing faster in ŌlappāLaiyam than in other parts of the kirāmam.

(2) The Roadside Shops About a quarter of a mile south of ŌlappāLaiyam proper, a large cluster of stores is strung out on both sides of the main Coimbatore-Tiruchirappalli road. ŌlappāLaiyam *KaTai vīti*, as this area is called, is the center for business activity in the kirāmam. This street of stores, which is shown in Figure 4.4, serves as a sort of nerve center. By listening to conversation here, one readily gains an idea of what is going on in the kirāmam as a whole. Buses to all the major towns in the area stop here; and the local post office, library, and Panchayat office are all located in the same cluster. Radios play continually at KaTai vīti, although individual settlements also have receiving sets, and cinema posters are prominently displayed. News from the outside world generally filters through this center before traveling to surrounding hamlets. This is the only place in the kirāmam where there was an interest in politics in 1965 and

---

[18]The NāTār have lost ground economically, because of the prohibition laws introduced soon after Independence in 1947. The prohibition laws were revoked in Madras in August, 1971, just before this book went to press. NāTārs once had a monopoly on the sale of liquor, since they were the only group skilled in tapping the tall palmyra or toddy palm. The CōLi Ācāri are also poorer now than they used to be, and many families live in the ramshackle remains of what were once quite fine houses. Their loss vis-à-vis other groups is not so easily explained, except perhaps in terms of intensified discrimination against them on the part of other castes in the area. For a further discussion of this phenomenon, see chapter 5, pp. 259–60.

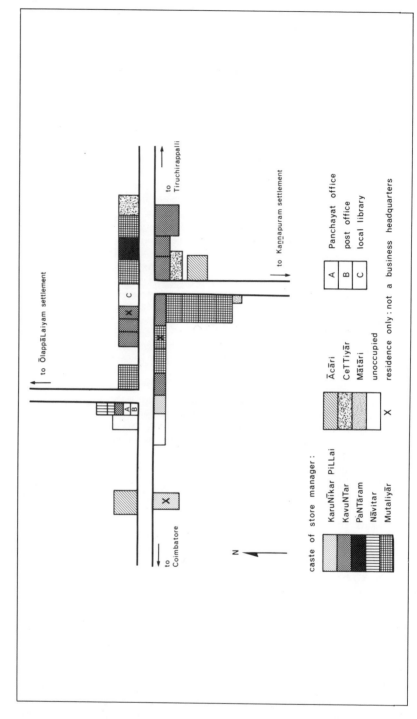

Fig. 4.4. ŌlappāLaiyam kaTai vīti.

where men could identify the names and platforms of the various regional parties.[19]

The people who run the roadside shops are more worldly and better informed than other villagers. At the same time, KaTai vĩti shop-keepers are somewhat mistrusted. Thus, despite their urbanity, or per-haps because of it, they do not serve as important opinion leaders for the surrounding area. Rivalries between the various shops, further-more, were common. Interestingly, these did not seem to affect in a significant way the rivalries present between cultivators elsewhere in the kirāmam area. People from ŌlappāLaiyam tended to patronize some shops more than others, but this was so because the keepers of these shops were better known through patronage in the past and through residence in the same settlement, rather than because rivals in other contexts would not bring themselves to patronize the same merchant.[20] These shopkeepers sold a small amount of goods on credit, but were not in a position to compete with the more influential landed money-lenders of nearby settlements. They had acquired very little land as a result of investments of the profits of their businesses. They were by no means the wealthy of the area.[21]

Of the twenty-five roadside shops at KaTai vĩti in 1965, a third were financed by KavuNTars and a third by Mutaliyārs. On the whole, the Mutaliyārs were the most successful. The remaining third were fi-nanced variously, mostly by people offering the services of their tradi-tional caste occupation. CeTTiyārs did not play a significant role in the local business community. Two-thirds of the shop owners were born in the kirāmam, while four others established themselves through their wives' kinsmen. Only seven had no direct kin connec-tions in the kirāmam, but even in these cases, the owner or his father was born no more than four miles from the shopping center. Thus, there are no real "outsiders" attempting to practice business at KaTai vĩti.

In 1968, an assistant conducted a resurvey of this shopping area to assess any changes in social composition which might be occurring.[22] The survey indicated a high turnover rate in shop ownership, but very little change in the basic social composition of the area. Hence, in three years, a quarter, or six, of the original shops surveyed had gone out of business, while six new ones had appeared in their place. Of those that had gone out of business, two had been established for a full ten years, while others had held out only a year or less. Half of those that disappeared were managed by men who were born outside the kirāmam area. All of the operators of the new stores, by contrast,

---

[19]This was in 1965–66. However, there were signs that political interest was increasing and that others apart from shopkeepers would soon become involved. The 1967 national elections were, at this time, already a topic of conversation.

[20]These statements are based on a personal survey made of every shop on the street in 1965.

[21]This picture forms an interesting contrast with the shopkeepers of Teretunne described by Nur Yalman in *Under the Bo Tree* (Berkeley: University of California Press, 1967), pp. 51, 196.

[22]Informant no. 20.

were drawn from settlements within this local unit.[23] Thus, if any trend can be established, it is that fewer strangers are trying their hand at business in this local center than was the case before. Finally, there is no sign of a change in caste composition of the shopping area. Four of the newcomers are KavuNTars; one is a Mutaliyār; and the last is a traditional artisan, an Ācāri.

The four coffee shops at KaTai vīti make an interesting study in caste interaction. Food restrictions which prevail in all the other local settlements of the area are eased considerably in this cosmopolitan center. All the coffee shops are run by KavuNTars, Mutaliyārs, or PiLLais—all high-ranking groups. Brahmans in the area, with one exception, refuse to patronize them; but all other groups will accept both coffee and cooked rice in these restaurants without reservation.[24]

Until about 1962, I am told, untouchables were asked to sit on the floor in these shops, instead of sitting on benches; and they were served drinks in separate glass tumblers. They were asked to wash these tumblers themselves and to dispose of their own eating leaves. Now, however, untouchables are served beverages in the same metal tumblers as others, and they may even sit on benches; but if there is a crowd, they are forced to yield their place to men of superior social rank. The only distinction that continues to prevail among customers at these shops is a differential expectation on the part of the store owner as to which groups will pick up their own eating leaves. In general, KavuNTars and those belonging to vegetarian groups, such as the PiLLai, the CōLi Ācāri, and the KōmuTTi CeTTiyār, may leave their eating leaves for the hotel owner or his help to remove. In the cases of the middle-ranking groups, such as the Mutaliyār, the PaNTāram, the NāTār, and the ŪTaiyār, the situation is ambivalent. A man may or may not remove his own leaf depending on his self-assurance or desire to challenge others. For the lower-ranking communities such as the Nāyakkar, Nāvitar, VaNNār, and the untouchables, there is a definite expectation that a man will remove his own leaf. But a shopkeeper has no way of enforcing this custom, and in the case of a rude customer, may get stuck with the unpleasant task of removing such low-ranking refuse himself.

(3) Pūcārivalacu Cēri (The Untouchable Hamlet) As in the case with other cēris in the region, this untouchable settlement contains members of only one subcaste, the Moracu Mātāri. Note that it lies to the west of the main—touchable—living site. The west and south, which are the two least auspicious directions, are generally allocated to the lowest-ranking members of a community. Within the cēri area, which is shown in Figure 4.5, there are members of two distinct clans. The Eriyanti settled the area first and the Nākar moved in later as uxorilocal newcomers. This latter descent group has generally been allocated the southwest corner of the site, farthest of all from the touchable caste areas.

---

[23]I refer here to six cases, as in the seventh (an Ācāri), I do not have adequate information on this point.

[24]Contrast this with the discussion of food exchange on pp. 156–57 and 162–71.

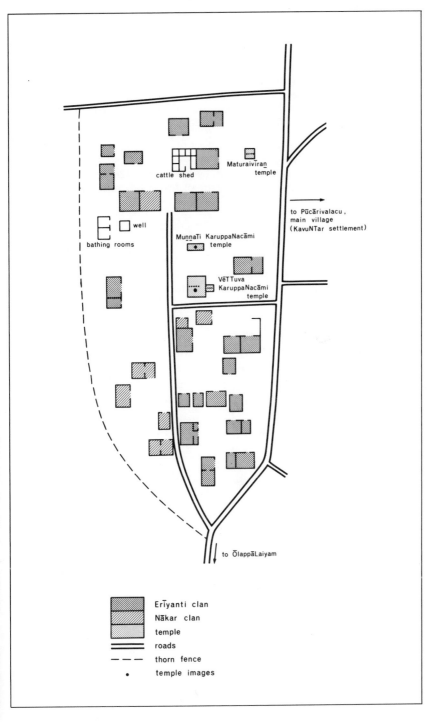

Fig. 4.5. Pūcārivalacu cēri site (a Moracu Mātāri untouchable settlement).

The cēri, just like the main residential site, has its own sacred geography. Each of the two descent groups has its own lineage temple, and the Eriyanti, as the original settlers, have the larger of the two. This temple is dedicated to VēTTuvar KaruppaNacāmi—which may suggest a tie with the left-division VēTTuvar KavuNTars—and the MunnaTi KaruppaNacāmi stone, which stands in front of it, is part of the same complex. The second clan, the Nākar, has a separate temple dedicated to Maturaiviran, a well-known folk hero associated with the Mātāri caste as a whole. Finally, like the touchable caste living site, the cēri has distinct and ceremonially significant boundaries. Roads mark the area on three sides, and a thorn fence provides the fourth boundary. Furthermore, all the major entrances to the site are guarded by the deities just described.

Three elements together make up the ŌlappāLaiyam MākāLiyamman ritual area: ŌlappāLaiyam proper; KaTai vīti, the roadside shops; and Pūcārivalacu cēri, the untouchable area.[25] This is the unit of day-to-day cooperation within which most ordinary social interaction occurs. An analysis of this interaction is provided in the discussion of local ranking patterns that follows.

THE LOCAL RANKING OF SUBCASTE GROUPS

Anthropologists have been aware of the extreme emphasis on hierarchical ordering in Indian society for many years. A number of essays have been published on the nature of this ideological supposition.[26] Also, several attempts have been made to translate this general attitude into studies of observed behavior.[27] Generally, these studies have been made in rural areas, within the confines of a single kirāmam, or revenue unit. For a long

---

[25]A few KavuNTar houses in Pūcārivalacu proper are also included in this Mākā-Liyamman unit.

[26]Émile Senart, *Les Castes dans l'Inde: Les faits et le système* (Paris: E. Leroux, 1894); C. Bouglé, *Essais sur le Régime des Castes* (1908; reprint ed., Paris: Alcan, 1927); E. A. H. Blunt, *The Caste System of Northern India with Special Reference to the United Provinces of Agra and Oudh* (London: Oxford University Press, 1931); G. S. Ghurye, *Caste and Race in India* (London: Kegan Paul, 1932); A. M. Hocart, *Caste: A Comparative Study* (London: Methuen, 1950); J. H. Hutton, *Caste in India, Its Nature, Function, and Origins* (Cambridge: Cambridge University Press, 1946), and Louis Dumont, *Homo hierarchicus* (Paris: Gallimard, 1966).

[27]S. C. Dube, "Ranking of Castes in Telangana Villages," *The Eastern Anthropologist* 8, nos. 3 and 4 (1955): 182–90; McKim Marriott, "Interactional and Attributional Theories of Caste Ranking," *Man in India* 39, no. 2 (1959): 92–107; Pauline M. Kolenda, "A Multiple Scaling Technique for Caste Ranking," *Man in India* 39, no. 2 (1959): 127–47; Adrian C. Mayer, *Caste and Kinship in Central India* (London: Routledge and Kegan Paul, 1960), pp. 33–40, ff.; Stanley Freed, "An Objective Method for Determining the Collective Caste Hierarchy of an Indian Village," *American Anthropologist* 65 (1963): 879–91; Karigaudar Ishwaran, "Goldsmith in a Mysore Village," *Journal of Asian and African Studies* 1, no. 1 (1966): 50–62, and McKim Marriott, "Caste Ranking and Food Transactions: A Matrix Analysis," in Milton Singer and Bernard Cohn, eds., *Structure and Change in Indian Society* (Chicago: Aldine, 1968), pp. 133–71.

time it was simply assumed that subcastes would be more easily recognized and ranking attitudes more clearly defined in small intimate communities. Recently, evidence has been assembled to show that this is indeed the case.[28] The following details were collected with the intention of adding to this growing body of studies of ranking in India.

Within Kaṇṇapuram kirāmam there are essentially two levels of sub-caste interaction. First, is the day-to-day interaction of the people who reside within the "area of cooperation," and second, the more formalized interaction of their caste representatives at the yearly kirāmam festival. The day-to-day interaction is individualized, many-faceted, and somewhat flexible; while the second, more formalized pattern is highly ritualized and apparently extremely stable. Ūr-based interaction is more responsive to, and expressive of, the attitudes and motives underlying a particular, local-ized, ranking pattern. The kirāmam festival patterns, on the other hand, set out a broader and more generalized code. This broad statement or ideological framework of interaction has already been discussed in chapter 3. Here we will focus on the Ūr and on what the complexity and inconsis-tencies of daily interaction reveal about the underlying dynamics of caste hierarchies in the individual hamlet.

A great variety of occasions arise in a small community in which the attempts of subcastes to establish rank in relation to one another can be observed. Food passes between some groups but not between others, and guests of a given community are invited to sit on the porch of some homes but in the courtyards of others. Ranking is also implied in the forms of address used between groups, and by subtle body gestures that accompany conversation. For example, a man of one community may cover his mouth when speaking, or stoop slightly and look at the ground, while another from a caste that claims superiority to the first may stand erect, fold his arms on his chest, and look straight ahead. Adjustments in clothing can also serve as indicators of status. Women generally draw the end of their sari over both shoulders when in the presence of superiors. Men, similarly, lower their long skirt-like *vēsTi,* principal garments, so as to cover their calves when they wish to indicate deference.[29]

---

[28]Victor S. D'Souza, "Caste Structure in India in the Light of Set Theory," in *Current Anthropology* 13, no. 1 (1972): 5–14.

[29]It appears that the rules of clothing adjustment vary, depending on whether rank on a purity-pollution scale, or on a master-servant scale is taken as the primary point of refer-ence. (See the end of this section for a discussion of ideas which underlie this notion of pollution.) For the former, the body is covered as an indication of deference, but for the latter it is uncovered to indicate readiness to perform some service or menial task. Thus household servants tie their vestments up when carrying out their duties, as do priests while performing oblations to a god. Guests at a home or devotees at a temple, on the other hand, attempt to cover their limbs during their visit. A more extreme example of the same logic would be the old tradition, now somewhat out of fashion, in which untouchables were expected to cover their mouths when addressing men of clean, or touchable, status.

Each of these ways of implying relative status will be referred to here as a particular medium employed by local residents to express subcaste rank. Hence, the rules of food exchange constitute a medium, as do the rules for seating guests. Other media include the rules of excrement removal, and those of tonal and semantic modifications in address. In addition, subdivisions can be made within most of these categories. For example, the rules of food exchange on informal occasions differ slightly from the rules of exchange on formal, festive occasions.

Within each medium, there exist two roles to play: that of host and that of guest. This is clearest in the matter of food exchange, but the same roles apply also to seating and to excrement removal. "Master" and "servant" may be substituted for "host" and "guest" respectively as a more appropriate pair of terms when what is provided by the giver is somehow onerous or demeaning to the receiver. This subtle shift from host to master and from guest to servant is indeed critical in local reasoning about rank. Being in the position of receiver is always tricky; for a degree of indebtedness, and hence of servility, can always be implied.[30]

Because of fear of the implications of being a receiver, castes that are trying to raise their rank in the local setting may refuse to interact in situations in which their acceptance of the giver's hospitality would be expected. As a result, a few groups in some media have quite a different rank as hosts and as guests. They may succeed in giving to very few, and hence rank low in one dimension, but at the same time refuse to receive, and hence rank very high according to the complementary criterion. In previous studies on ranking by Marriott, these two dimensions, as I call them, have been "summed" by subtracting the number of points lost as a receiver from the total gained as a giver.[31] I will treat each dimension separately, as in their discussions of such data with me, local informants did not suggest that these two perspectives should be directly "averaged" or "combined." Invitations, refusals, and counter-refusals are commonplace, however. The dynamics of this kind of behavior will be discussed at a later point.

Two major, day-to-day expressions of rank will be considered first: the rules of food exchange and those of seating. Food exchange is the critical medium for demonstrating the relative rank of subcastes in purity-pollution terms. Seating, on the other hand, is the important medium when master-servant patterns in day-to-day labor relationships are considered.

---

[30]The classic discussion of this problem, of course, is provided by Marcel Mauss' essay, *The Gift,* trans. I. Cunnison (London: Cohen and West, 1954). More recently, McKim Marriott has made its relevance to "score-keeping" in the "game" of caste ranking very clear. See his "Caste Ranking and Food Transactions," p. 154. It is interesting to note that this danger of implied inferiority as a guest runs counter to the classical Indian doctrine of *varataTcanai,* or of the lowly position of the giver of the bride in relation to her receiver.

[31]Marriott, "Caste Ranking and Food Transactions," pp. 154-6.

Local subcastes are ranked somewhat differently in these two media, and within each medium they are ranked somewhat differently again, according to whether the interaction is taking place on an ordinary or a festive occasion.

Figure 4.8, which appears later in this section, provides details on the rules of exchange of cooked rice by subcaste of host and of guest. In cooking, rice absorbs water. This water carries with it the full pollution quotient of the cook who has handled it. Hence people avoid accepting cooked rice from anyone whom they consider to have a higher pollution quotient than themselves. The data is taken directly from twenty-five interview response sheets, in which one male and one female of each of twelve subcastes, and one male from a thirteenth, answered the question, "Will you accept cooked rice from the hand of a . . . [*subcaste name*]?" Each person was asked about sixteen individual subcastes, in a random order established prior to the interview.[32] Figure 4.7, which also appears later in this section, provides details on the rules of seating, also by subcaste of host and guest. This figure is based on the results of the same interview and represents respondents' answers to a second question, "Will you invite a . . . [*subcaste name*] to sit on your porch?"

Seating, as I use the term, is distinct from rules about entry. All touchable subcastes are allowed entry into the courtyard and porch areas of the homes of all other touchable subcastes.[33] However, where these various groups may sit once they have entered the living area is determined by other criteria. People who provide regular services—maids, barbers, cooks, washermen, and similarly employed persons—are allowed to enter various parts of the house, as needed, to perform their assigned tasks. In moments of repose, however, these people are expected to seat themselves on the floor of the inner courtyard. True guests, by contrast, are invited to sit with the host on a raised porch area or in one of his receiving rooms. The inner courtyard of a house is always slightly lower in level than these reception areas, so that this servant-guest distinction is always accompanied by a vertical difference in placement. For clarity, the areas of a house referred to are illustrated in Figure 4.6.

---

[32]The interviewees were all residents of the ŌlappāLaiyam hamlet area. As much as possible, each person was interviewed in private, although no one showed particular sensitivity concerning this issue. In a few cases, I failed to distinguish between subcastes. Hence some additional cells were later filled in by correspondence with Informant no. 20. To the best of my knowledge the answers accurately reflect actual practice in the area in 1965.

[33]In practice, however, men of high caste have little reason to enter the houses of those distinctly beneath them. A Brahman, for example, will enter the home of a barber only when asked to perform a particular domestic ceremony, and a KavuNTar may never have occasion to enter a barber's home at all. A KavuNTar who has come on business to such a home—to request a vote, for example—will stand, or sit on a cot if necessary, in the courtyard, but he will not enter the interior of the house.

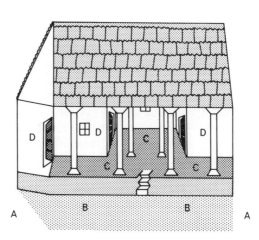

classification	space	Tamil term	seating possibilities
A	exterior space (beyond entrance)	veLi vācal	plain floor
B	inner courtyard	uL vācal	plain floor
C	reception hall and porch	cāvaTi or tiNNai	chair , cot , straw mat, and plain floor
D	kitchen (and inner rooms)	(camaiyal) vīTu	normally none

Fig. 4.6. Areas of ritual significance in a Koṅku house. (This drawing was provided by Informant no. 20.)

The importance of the master-servant relationship, as opposed to questions of purity-pollution, in this matter of seating can be seen from two examples. A PaNTāram cook, as the first example, is allowed to enter the kitchen of a KavuNTar house when he has work to perform, but he is not allowed to sit on the raised porch areas of the same house in moments of repose. Even though the house owner may eat food cooked by him and he is thus his employer's equal in purity-pollution terms, the cook is distinctly inferior in terms of a master-servant scale.

As the second example, a guest of an inferior subcaste on the purity-pollution scale will be invited to sit in a position equal to that of the host, regardless of rank, if the guest is sufficiently wealthy or powerful to demand this position of equality. I have seen this happen when government officials of low caste origin paid visits to the Ūr area. A KavuNTar host will seat such men, even if they are untouchables by origin, at the same level as himself. However, the same host would never agree to accept food which had been cooked in the local, private home of such an official.[34] Here the Ūr host must grant equality in the dominance-servility sphere, but retains his superiority in purity-pollution terms.[35] In the details of Ūr seating rules as provided in Figure 4.7, as in all these diagrams, it must be understood that normal or expected subcaste behavior is represented. A few subcaste members always deviate from standard practice, either by being more restrictive or more liberal in their personal habits, but these nonconformists exist in very small numbers. They are not generally sanctioned for their actions and have been left aside for the purposes of this discussion.

A certain amount of explanation is necessary to aid the reader in his examination of these figures on food and seating arrangements. A key to individual subcaste names and the corresponding numbers used is given below. The order of subcastes provided here was also used to construct the table on caste groups which appears in the Introduction.

A	1. Aiyar Brahman	C	10. Maramēri NāTār
	2. KaruNīkar PiLLai		11. VaTuka Nāyakkar
	3. CōLi Ācāri		12. Koṅku VaNNār
	4. KōmuTTi CeTTiyār	D	13. VaTuka VaNNār
B	5. Koṅku KavuNTar		14. Koṅku Nāvitar
	6. Koṅku Ācāri		15. PāNTiya Nāvitar
	7. Kaikkōlar Mutaliyār		16. Koṅku Paraiyar
	8. OkaccāNTi PaNTāram	E	17. KūTai Kuravar
	9. Koṅku UTaiyar		18. Moracu Mātāri

[34]If an ŌlappāLaiyam KavuNTar pays a visit to the office of a government official of a low-ranking subcaste, he may feel obliged to adopt a servile attitude in recognition of this man's control over some good which he desires. He might even agree to take food at this official's urban residence, while he would never attend a wedding feast in this man's village dwelling. Hence purity-pollution rules can be compromised for power considerations anywhere except in the inferior man's own private, local home.

[35]If a poor, local Brahman and a high government official of low-caste origin were to visit a KavuNTar home simultaneously, and there was only one chair, the host would likely

The letters reflect the rank order of groups of subcastes as guests at a Brahman feast, as Brahman feasts provide one of several common frames of reference for evaluating social status in the Ūr area. Within ranks, subcastes have been numbered according to the judgments of Informant no. 20.[36] These numbers are intended to provide the unfamiliar reader with a fixed point from which to consider the various rank orders discussed.[37]

The numbers along the edges of each matrix serve simply as a shorthand for subcaste names. The rows in the middle of each figure provide a list of all the relevant subcastes according to how they are ranked in the particular transactions described. The subcaste that is highest in rank appears at the top of each scale. This technique of rank-ordering subcastes is an adaptation of Guttman scaling methods.[38] The only difference lies in the fact that here the subcastes have been scaled according to responses concerning interaction with other subcastes, rather than on agree-disagree items as in most attitude scaling.[39]

This unusual situation, in which the cases and the items refer to the same universe, and only the dimension of giver and receiver differentiates them, entails a number of self-reciprocal cells. All such cells are marked with a cross (X) when the interaction is allowed or positive, and with a circle (O) when the interaction is not allowed or negative. A person may accept food from other members of his own subcaste, for example (positive), but he may not agree to pick up excrement produced by members of his own community (negative).

---

offer it to the official. Even a Brahman can be placed symbolically in a second position, therefore, when dominance and not purity is the type of rank being expressed.

[36]This man, a very thoughtful and articulate informant, was asked to rank-order the subcastes in question, using a set of 3″ × 5″ index cards.

[37]Unfortunately, the rank order I use here does not correspond to the one which appears in my doctoral dissertation "Social and Conceptual Order in Koṅku: A Region of South India" (Oxford: Institute of Social Anthropology, 1968), available through the University of Chicago microfilm library, and in my article "The Right-Left Division of South Indian Society," *Journal of Asian Studies* 29, no. 4 (1970): 779–98. This is so because my earlier attempts to discuss ranking centered on discovering some over-all hierarchy which would average out the different positions that different subcastes hold in different media and different dimensions. I have recently abandoned this attempt at combining rank orders based on differing criteria because of the methodological assumptions required to decide how much weight to give to each criterion for combining them. The names of the different subcastes are available in each case, however, so that the interested reader may easily compare the analysis presented here with that which appears in my earlier writings.

[38]See Louis Guttman, "The Basis for Scalogram Analysis," in Stouffer et al., *Measurement and Prediction,* Studies in Social Psychology in World War II, vol. 4 (1949–50; reprint ed., New York: John Wiley and Sons, 1966), pp. 60–90, and Warren Torgerson, "Deterministic Models for Categorical Data," chapter in his *Theory and Methods of Scaling* (New York: John Wiley and Sons, 1965), pp. 298–359.

[39]David Elkins, of the Department of Political Science at the University of British Columbia helped clarify for me the nature of Guttman scaling, and suggested this presentation of the data. McKim Marriott has also been most helpful in suggesting ways to clarify discussion of this material.

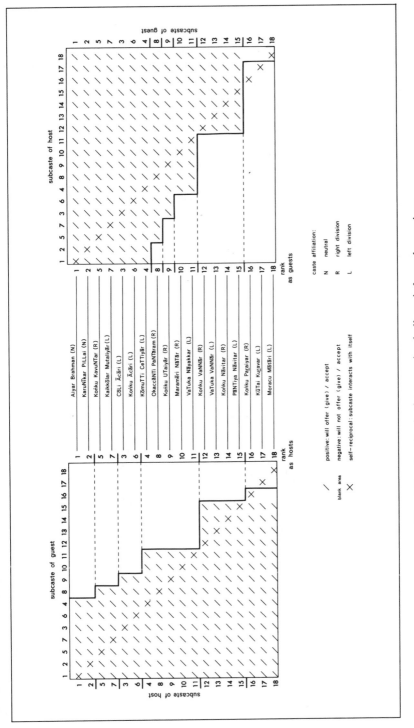

Fig. 4.7. Seating in the reception hall, on informal occasions.

In each figure a heavy line indicates differences in the total number of positive interactions experienced by each subcaste. In drawing this line, if a self-reciprocal cell was not contiguous with the shaded area—the other positive responses, I compensated for it by including one blank space inside the boundary line. On each figure, the matrices have been drawn so as to form an even, step-by-step diminution of the shaded or positive response area. This provides the scale order.[40] The dotted horizontal lines mark the steps in each scale. All subcastes falling between these horizontal lines form an undifferentiated bloc in terms of that dimension of that particular matrix. Within such a bloc the subcastes have been ordered by their assigned number as already explained, except where some shuffling has allowed a reduction in the discrepancy between two orders that are being compared.

First, let us consider the rank of subcastes in the seating medium, a scale that is heavily influenced by master-servant relationships (see Fig. 4.7). Notice that the seating does not show any reversals in rank order when the dimensions of giver and receiver are compared. In both cases, one finds the KavuNTars (no. 5) and the two subcastes that are best able to sanction this powerful group (nos. 1 and 2) at the top of the hierarchy.[41] Next, following the KavuNTars are those communities which are relatively independent of this land-owning group in their day-to-day affairs (nos. 3, 4, 6, and 7). Below them are two ritual service groups, the cooks (no. 8) and the potters (no. 9), which are directly allied with the KavuNTars and which have a hand in KavuNTar food preparation. Below them are two subcastes of skilled laborers, ranked in order of their involvement with agricultural production. Then come the washermen and barbers, groups which perform menial personal services, and finally the untouchable laborers. It is possible to argue, I think, that this ranking comes as close as is possible, to a scale of the relative power and dependence of the various subcastes in the Ūr area on the KavuNTar community. That is to say, the two groups above the KavuNTars (nos. 1 and 2) have superior ritual and legal powers; the groups immediately below (nos. 3, 4, 6, and 7) are rivals that exhibit a balance resulting in independence; and those near the bottom (nos. 8, 9, 10, 11, etc.) rely to an increasing degree on the patronage and goodwill of the KavuNTar group (no. 5).

Now let us turn to the food medium and consider several scales that are heavily influenced by dietary and ritual ideals (see Fig. 4.8). If we look initially at the behavior of the various subcastes as guests it becomes clear

[40]See Torgerson, *Theory and Methods of Scaling,* p. 314.
[41]Brahmans (no. 1) can sanction KavuNTars by refusing to perform certain crucial life-cycle ceremonies for them. Members of the KaruNīkar PiLLai subcaste, as accountants and keepers of the land records, can control legal transactions and also count on government backing in times of dispute.

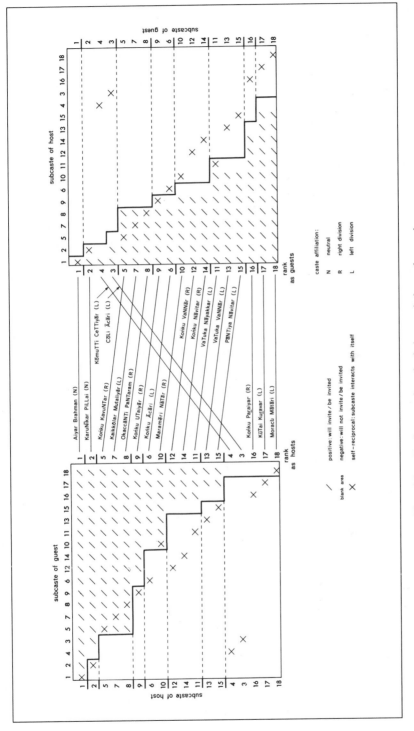

Fig. 4.8. Exchange of cooked rice, on informal occasions.

that the vegetarian subcastes rank the highest (nos. 1, 2, 4, and 3), KavuN-
Tars and groups from which these landlords will accept food (nos. 5, 7,
and 8) are second. Third come subcastes nos. 9 and 6 (the Koṅku UTaiyār
and the Koṅku Ācāri), two groups which do not resemble KavuNTars
closely in their life-cycle rituals, but which provide important ritual
services for them: the Koṅku Ācāris build funeral biers and repair plows,
while the Koṅku UTaiyārs make pots for ceremonial use. Both groups try
hard to keep on good terms with the KavuNTars, taking pride in these
landowners' patronage when it comes to ritually significant matters. To
show their respect for KavuNTar power and their desire for good relations, both subcastes in this third category agree to take food from the
same subcastes that the KavuNTar community does. Furthermore, when
they can afford to hire a PaNTāram cook, they reciprocate by inviting
these important groups to their own weddings. Fourth in the hierarchy of
guests in this food medium are the NāTār, who provide palmyra sugar
for KavuNTar life-cycle ceremonies, and two personal service subcastes
that traditionally work for the KavuNTar community. Fifth are the other
low-ranking service groups that are not ritually allied with KavuNTars,
and, finally, there are the outcaste communities.

One very interesting difference in this rank order emerges when the position of subcastes as food hosts is separately considered. As shown in Figure 4.8, groups 3 and 4 rank strikingly lower in this dimension than they
do as guests, making it quite difficult to generalize about a uniform hierarchy expressed by food exchange as a whole. The superficial reason for
their low rank as hosts is easily ascertained: no other group, not even the
untouchables, will accept cooked rice from these two groups, though the
former would willingly serve them if they came. The fact that these two
groups refuse food from the KavuNTars isolates them from the rest of the
community, since other groups respond by reciprocally refusing food
from their hands. To understand this situation in greater depth a further
set of transactions involving curds and the removal of soiled eating leaves
must be considered. The basic data are contained in Figures 4.9 and 4.10.[42]
Some of the most important details from these figures are further summarized in Table 4.1.

With the help of the summary of Figures 4.9 and 4.10, the low position
of CōLi Ācāris and KōmuTTi CeTTiyārs as food hosts can be explained.
The latter group refuses to accept cooked rice from all but Brahmans,
an action which many consider haughty and antisocial. Other groups

---

[42]The data for these two figures were obtained from Informant no. 20. They represent his report of actual behavioral norms in ŌlappāLaiyam in 1968. The interviews on which the
earlier figures were based were conducted in 1965, but I am not aware of any significant
changes in interaction having occurred during this three-year period.

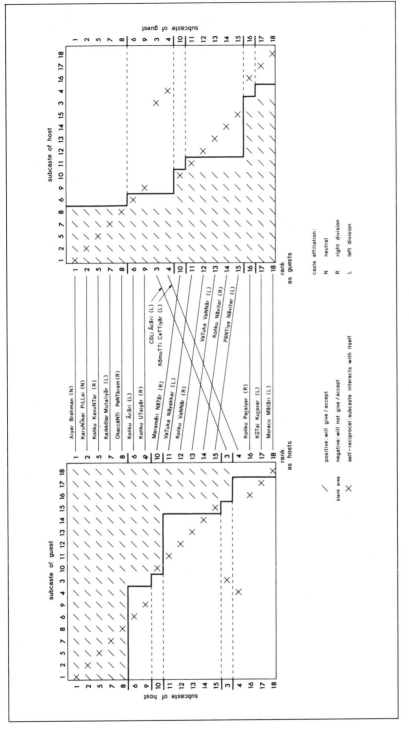

Fig. 4.9. Exchange of curds.

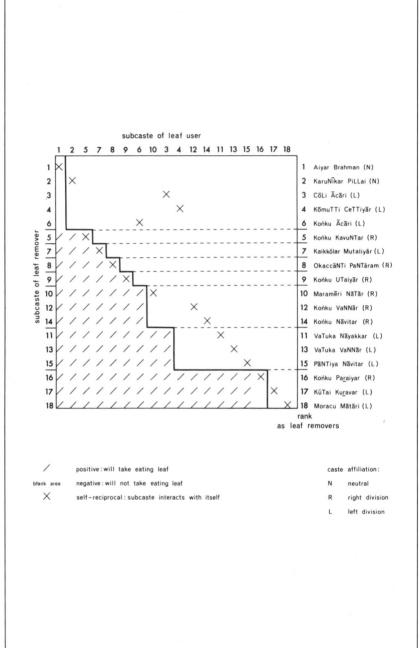

Fig. 4.10. Removal of eating leaves.

TABLE 4.1
SUMMARY OF IMPORTANT DETAILS CONTAINED IN FIGURES 4.8, 4.9, AND 4.10

(1) Subcaste Name	(2) Cooked rice accepted from	(3) If necessary, eating leaves will be disposed for	(4) Reciprocal treatment received by (1)
KōmuTTi CeTTiyār (no. 4)	Brahmans only	No one	Not a single group will accept curds or cooked rice from them.
CōLi Ācāri (no. 3)	Brahmans (and from PiLLais on ordinary occasions)	No one	Two left untouchable groups take curds, but no one will take cooked rice from them.
Koṅku Ācāri (no. 6)	Brahmans, PiL-Lais, KavuNTars, Mutaliyārs, and PaNTārams	No one	Nine low-ranking groups take curds. Three left touchable groups and all untouchables take cooked rice from them.
Kaikkōlar Mutaliyār and OkaccāNTi PaNTāram (nos. 7 and 8)	Brahmans, PiL-Lais, KavuNTars, Mutaliyārs, and PaNTārams	Brahmans, PiL-Lais, KavuNTars, Mutaliyārs, and PaNTārams	All groups take curds. All non-Brahmans, except PiLLais, CeTTiyārs, and CōLi Ācāris take cooked rice from them.
KaruNīkar PiLLai (no. 2)	Brahmans only	No one	All groups take curds. All non-Brahmans except CeTTiyārs take cooked rice from them.

reciprocate by refusing to accept either rice or curds from them.[43] Although there is only one household of this subcaste in the area, the feeling that its members should be boycotted runs high.[44]

The CōLi Ācāri are only slightly more lenient in their pattern of food acceptance, taking cooked rice from Brahmans and, on ordinary occasions, from PiLLais. In return for this slightly more moderate stance, two left untouchable groups accept curds from this subcaste. Considerably less

[43]Informant no. 20 has repeatedly expressed this attitude with the phrase, "They do not accept food from us, we do not accept food from them." Although he does not explicitly insert the term "therefore," the fact that they do not take his subcaste's food is always mentioned first. When he discusses subcaste no. 9 and the groups ranking below it, by contrast, he uses the phrase "We do not take food from them because they are lower [*kīR jāti*] than we are." He does not use this term when speaking of subcastes nos. 3 and 4, although he has often commented that they are "like outcastes" because no other group will accept cooked preparations from them.

[44]This curious position of the KōmuTTi CeTTiyār group (no. 3) has also been noted by J. H. B. Den Ouden in his article, "The Komutti Chettiyar: Position and Change of a Merchant Caste in a South-Indian Village," *Tropical Man* 2 (1969): 45–59.

rigorous in their food habits are the Koṅku Ācāri (no. 6), who accept cooked food from five leading communities in the area. Nine subcastes agree to accept curds from them, and six of these also accept cooked rice.

In this situation one might well ask why members of the Brahman and PiLLai communities, who exhibit the same attitudes, are not given the same reciprocal treatment that the KōmuTTi CeTTiyār and CōLi Ācāri receive. The answer is that the Brahman and PiLLai behavior is accepted as appropriate: recall that both groups were traditionally above the left-right division. Only those subcastes which are not classified as above the division are resented when they attempt to emulate those in this neutral category. The game of reciprocal non-engagement appears to be strongly associated with a larger pattern of right-left rivalry. It does not occur between castes which are not members of opposed divisions.

One further action indicates a group's true willingness to compromise on the rules of purity in deference to the practical issue of power. This is the readiness, if forced by economic circumstance, to pick up the used eating leaves of KavuNTars and the two other communities with which this group maintains reciprocal dining rights (see Fig. 4.10). An occasion to pick up such leaves does not generally occur unless one works as an employee in another's house, as occasional guests generally will dispose of their own leaves out of politeness. The significant difference here lies between members of subcastes nos. 3, 4, and 6, who would never accept such work, no matter how poor, and members of groups nos. 7 and 8, who will.[45] This attitude of deference to local power relations, at the price of some lessening of subcaste purity, gains the latter two groups full acceptance in the local food exchange hierarchy. With these groups the pattern of reciprocal refusals does not appear.

It is interesting to observe that this clear pattern of refusals and counter-refusals occurs exclusively in the food exchange medium. It is in this arena, of course, that arguments concerning purity are the most relevant. It is also the one arena in which Brahman standards are explicitly used as a yardstick for rank measurement. A claim to superior ritual purity, rather than to a superior economic position, is the favorite taunt of those left-division groups which wish to bypass the power alliance formed by the practical, dominance-oriented right-division communities.

This argument, which suggests that reciprocal refusal is the major strategy used by the right alliance for dealing with attempted upward mobility on the part of non-members, is reinforced by observations on the type of jockeying for status that occurs among untouchable groups, as shown in

---

[45]Refusal to pick up an eating leaf says, essentially, that that person or group refuses to acknowledge an inferior status. This is why the women of a household will agree to pick up the eating leaves of the men, but the men will not reciprocate.

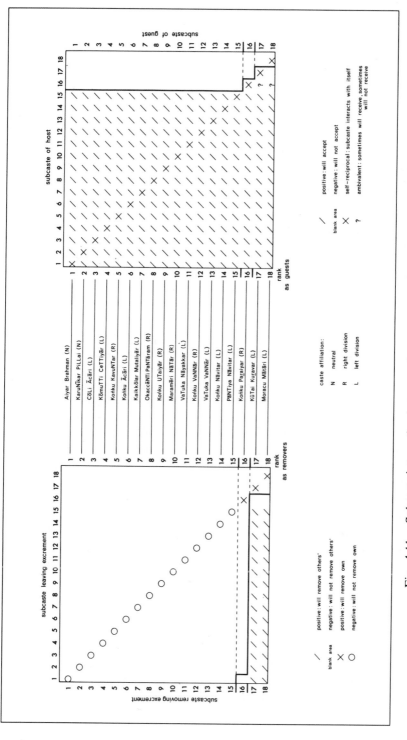

Fig. 4.11. Subcaste interaction in terms of excrement removal and betel exchange.

Figure 4.11.[46] The left-division subcastes nos. 17 and 18, for example, will remove human excrement from the household of any touchable community, while right subcaste no. 16 (Paraiyar) steadfastly refuses to perform this service. The same group (no. 16) attempts to reinforce its claim to superiority by refusing betel nut from the subcastes that do agree to this work. Their objections, however, are significantly different from those of their hamlet superiors. This time the punitive response of group no. 16 is based on the charge that nos. 17 and 18 are excessively polluted, rather than that they are haughty and excessively "pure." Thus it is seen that the punishment for extreme pollution closely resembles that used to counter an extreme emphasis on purity.

In the diagram that appears in Figure 4.12, the reader can compare these various aspects of food exchange which have been discussed.[47] Of these, the rules governing the acceptance of curds appear to hold some special interest. Here is an arena in which the great contrast between subcastes nos. 3 and 4 as givers and as receivers of food is more moderate; overtones of economic considerations appear, furthermore, in the process of compromise. In the same vein one may observe that the rank discrepancies exhibited by no. 6 are less than those observed for nos. 3 and 4. This finding accords with a milder denial by the former of the community's local power hierarchy. Milk is, in principle, resistant to pollution as long as no water is added, since it comes directly from the cow without human intervention. After churning or warming, however, according to Informant no. 20, there is a sense of human modification. This is what makes people hesitant to accept milk products in houses where they will not accept cooked food. The transmission of pollution by handling pure milk is thought to be much less than that conveyed when water is added.

Where KavuNTars are economically dominant and control the source of milk, Brahmans, PiLLais, and high-ranking left groups will stretch their principles by necessity. The same principle of flexibility would also seem to explain their relative leniency where curds are concerned. They will submit to this mild form of food contamination by touch where water has not been added and where their only source of curd is the KavuNTar community, or those other subcastes from which KavuNTars will accept food. If a Brahman source of milk products were available, however, it would be preferred by these groups.

---

[46]The source for Figure 4.11 is the same as for Figures 4.7 and 4.8 (see p. 157).

[47]In Figure 4.12, the short dotted lines that break up the vertical columns indicate rank categories within a particular medium. No rank distinctions exist among members of any given category in any one column. The numbers falling within any one category, therefore, have been given in standard numerical order, except in cases where a reordering prevents two lines from intersecting because the castes are assigned to different rank categories in two neighboring columns. Thus "3" follows "4" in the final column because "4" falls in the rank category above "3" in the preceding column.

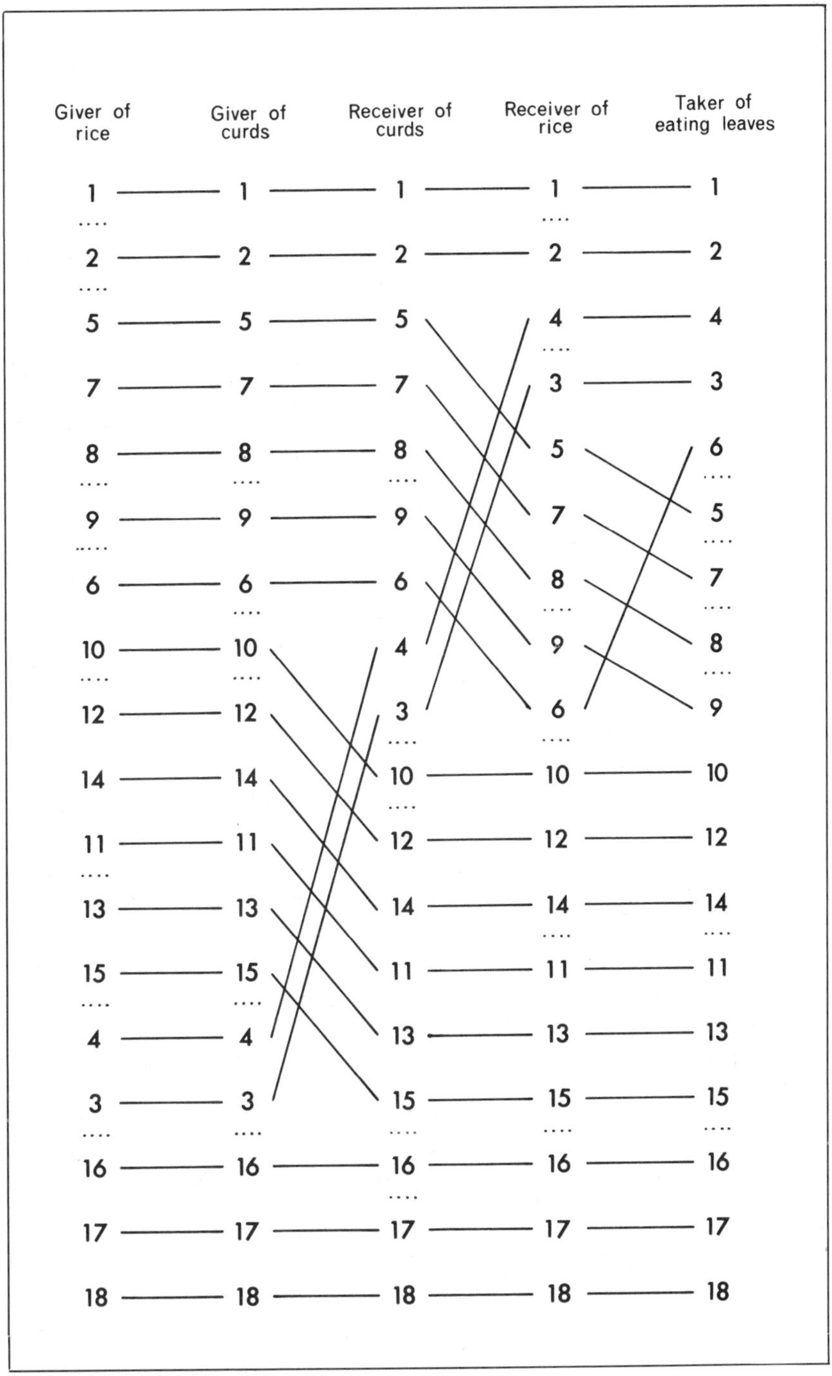

Fig. 4.12. Comparison of how subcastes are ranked in various subdivisions of the food medium.

Finally, patterns of food transaction, which exhibit giver-receiver differences, and seating hierarchies, which do not, can be seen to merge in the
area of the formal feast. This is the consequence of introducing a third
factor, which is not present in informal situations: a set order in which
groups are served.[48] Normally there are a number of sittings at a feast.
The first sitting will accommodate the relatives and subcaste associates
of the host's own group, plus members of any superior groups who agree
to accept cooked food at that house.[49] As shown in Figure 4.13, this first
sitting (A) is followed by several others (B, C, D, etc.), each accommodat-
ing persons of lower status than the preceding one. Within each sitting,
certain subcastes are seated in separate lines (B_1, B_2, B_3). There is no overt
ranking of these lines, but in general those with the most prestige are
accorded the best location, which is nearest the kitchen.

Such feasts provide occasions for a formal statement of rank, and appear to be more resistant to change than are the customs of informal food
transaction. Thus in 1965, the CōLi Ācāri (no. 3) would accept cooked
rice from KaruNīkar PiLLais (no. 2) only on informal occasions. I predict
that in a few years they will also begin to accept food formally, at feasts.
Of the two media, seating and food, seating would seem to allow for the
more rapid adjustment to changing economic circumstance. It is my impression that when changes in ranking occur, they appear first in informal
seating arrangements and only later in the realm of informal food exchange. Once these informal changes become generally accepted, they will
be ratified at a formal feast. Thus we see a possible ordered progression
of any particular innovation through several contexts and media.[50]

The order in which Ūr subcastes are feasted by different communities
is illustrated in Figure 4.13. As the principles on which this figure is constructed are somewhat novel, they need a special explanation. The number
of the guest subcaste is indicated from left to right horizontally on the top
margin, while the letters (A, B_1, B_2 etc.) in the horizontal bars indicate the
group and line with which that subcaste will be seated at any particular
dinner. The numbers identifying the subcaste of the host are indicated
vertically along the left-hand margin. Which subcaste will attend a given
feast can be ascertained by referring to the shaded area in any particular
bar.[51] Note that the Brahman feast is the only one that all subcastes
of the Ūr will attend. It is, therefore, the only one at which an over-all

---

[48]Formal feasts generally occur at weddings and other major life-cycle events.

[49]The host himself, and the members of his immediate family will dine only at the end of
the feast. If they have employed cooks and servers, then these people will dine at the last
sitting, eating inconspicuously inside while the untouchables are being fed without. If there
are no servants, then the males of the house will be served by a young female, and she will
dine alone, last of all.

[50]This suggestion, however, needs to be tested through further research.

[51]Fig. 4.13 is a condensation of a detailed description provided by Informant no. 20.

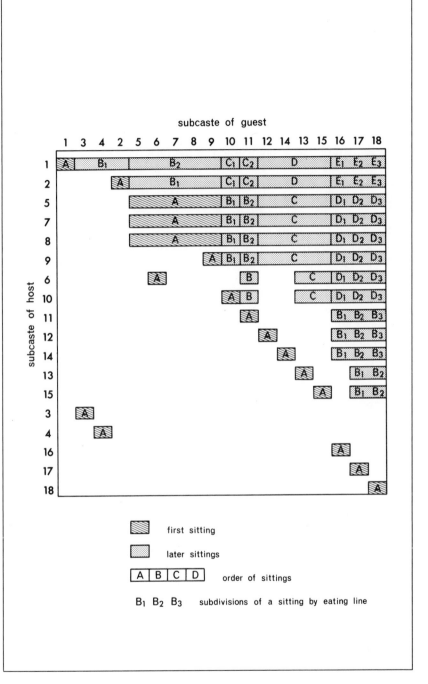

Fig. 4.13.   Number of sittings provided by hosts at formal subcaste feasts.

seating order is established. Moreover, there is no disagreement among communities as to where the breaks between sittings should occur.

Hence there exists a general consensus on precedence at feasts. This is not surprising, since they are semi-public occasions which, when the host is a Brahman, can involve the entire community. Interestingly, there are two further publicly agreed-upon orders of precedence which operate in another set of circumstances. At every local temple festival, a fixed order has been established in which food, ash, and colored powders that have been blessed by the god are supposed to be handed out to participants. One order is in force at the temples of the local goddesses, Māriyamman and MākāLiyamman; another prevails at the great temple of the kirāmam dedicated to Civā. These festivals provide additional public occasions at which the major communities of the area are openly ranked. The two orders of precedence at temple festivals are listed beside the feasting order for comparison in Figure 4.14.

Note that not all of the subcastes previously discussed are listed in the temple-precedence columns. The reason for this is that a number of castes do not claim rights at these temples and are not generally present for the ceremonial distribution, although this does not mean that they do not worship at these temples on other occasions. In particular, all of the high-ranking vegetarian castes (nos. 2, 3, and 4) drop out, along with the left-division barbers and washermen.[52] The Kuṟavar—an untouchable group of basket-makers—are also absent. The remaining "short list" of sub-castes that claim rights at the Civā temple is almost identical to the list of those which hold claims at the temples of the local goddesses. Yet the rank ordering of these groups in the two contexts is significantly different.

Note that the rank order at the Civā temple does not invert the feasting order at any point. At the temples for the local goddesses, by contrast, the KavuNTars move into first place. They are immediately followed by the NāTār, a group that is important agriculturally and which has very old and firm rights of precedence in these particular ceremonies. Next come the Mutaliyār, and the Koṅku Ācāri, both of whom have become allied with KavuNTars in the food hierarchy; they sit together freely at feasts. From these differences it seems clear that the KavuNTars and their local associates enjoy here a statement of their power and importance that differs significantly from their supposed level of purity in matters of food exchange.[53]

---

[52] These two communities might be called on to participate, if no right-division equivalent is available.

[53] An example of an attempt to bring these diverse rank orders more into line is described on page 198. Here a group of relatively poor KavuNTars split off from their wealthier sub-caste co-members and argued that Mutaliyārs should receive precedence over NāTārs at the local MākāLiyamman festival. This would have brought this festival into closer alignment with the established rank order at the Civā temple. The challenge resulted in breaking the

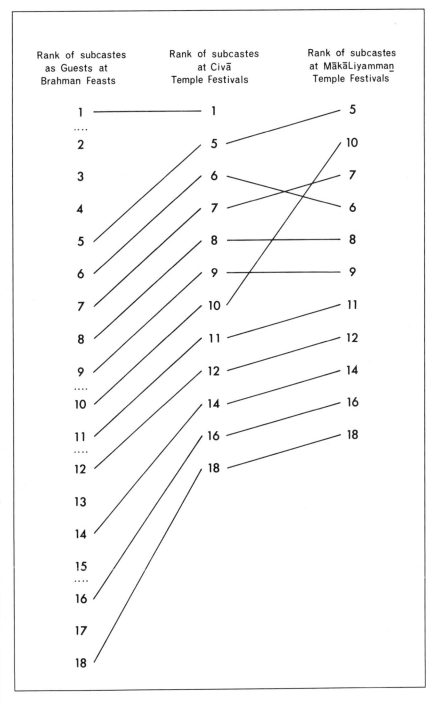

Fig. 4.14. Comparison of how hamlet subcastes are ranked on various public occasions.

The presence of this group of ritual allies or associates who cluster around a powerful, landed community resembles the situation Adrian Mayer has described for Malwa.[54] In both cases one finds a public solidarity expressed by a small group of relatively high-ranking communities. Rather than a one-dimensional statement of association, in Koṅku there are different patterns of alliance in different settings. In terms of food exchange the KavuNTars, Mutaliyārs, and PaNTārams recognize one another as equals. In terms of seating, however, PaNTārams rank in a lower category because of their position as household servants of the other two. And in the matter of Ūr temple precedence, NāTārs are ranked next to the KavuNTars, despite their lack of commensal equality. Furthermore, all of the subcastes with "Koṅku" attached to their name have important ceremonial roles vis-à-vis the KavuNTar community and are treated as associates of this group on certain occasions.

By contrast with this loosely knit group of allies, which are clustered around the subcaste with local economic power, there are four subcastes who consciously remain apart. These are the four vegetarian communities: the Brahmans, KaruNīkar PiLLais, KōmuTTi CeTTiyārs, and CōLi Ācāris. These four groups interact extensively with one other, though clearly the last two have a secondary status. They are the ones to make visits to the homes of the former two groups and to be received on their exterior porch. They are also the ones to accept food even though their friends in the former two groups do not accept food from them. There is a sort of "stand off" relationship between these four and the network of previously described allies. It is as if the same set of public interactions were being observed from two perspectives. The four vegetarian groups consider purity-pollution criteria the crucial element in evaluating status and believe themselves to be the group with first rank in the hamlet area. Diet and Brahman-style life-cycle ceremonies are taken as the measure of this extreme purity.

KavuNTars also grant first place in the status hierarchy to Brahmans, but having disposed of the first rung of the ladder, this landed group reverts to power as the major criterion of status. PiLLais are granted second place by this group because of their control over land records; next or third, the KavuNTars place their own group, and under themselves the assortment of communities which serve them and are dependent on them to a greater or lesser extent. The status of the CōLi Ācāri is thus much lower in the eyes of the KavuNTar community than it is to the vegetarian subcastes just described. KavuNTars accord more respect to the Koṅku Ācāri, who eat meat, but who perform ritual services for them, than they

---

worshippers at the local MākāLiyamman temple into two opposed factions, but the desired inversion in the order of precedence has been dropped in favor of a no-ranking rule.

[54]Mayer, *Caste and Kinship,* pp. 37–38, 44–47, 81, 88.

do to the vegetarian counterparts of this subcaste, the CōLi. Unfortunately, I did not obtain a general ranking of subcastes, without reference to particular media, either from a KavuNTar or from a member of one of the vegetarian communities while I was in the field. However, Informant no. 20, who is a PaNTāram by caste, has provided such a ranking using 3″ × 5″ cards.[55]

This ranking appears in the center of Figure 4.15. Notice that it provides a compromise between the rank order actually observed at feasts and that observed at ceremonies for the local goddesses. I would estimate that this informant's judgments resemble closely those that a KavuNTar would make; but, being a priest by profession, he may place slightly more emphasis on matters of purity than a KavuNTar would.

In making his ranking, Informant no. 20 commented several times on the relative power of the various groups in the local area. At times, however, he fell back also on a general argument concerning relative purity. "Members of that subcaste are impure," he would say. "There is no other way to explain it." This kind of reasoning seems to provide evidence that the KavuNTars and their allies do not discount the question of purity entirely in making judgments about relative prestige, but that they do modify such an evaluation by bringing to bear information about relative power in the local setting.[56]

The ultimate importance of notions of purity can be further seen from the fact that Informant no. 20 did not once try to justify his judgments about rank order in terms of interaction rules. According to his paradigm or conceptual frame, the position of the various subcastes is more or less given. Interaction rules primarily confirm or express what is essentially a predetermined status position. While clearly recognizing the contradictions that result from this sort of notion, in practice he consistently refused to invert the causal arrow and suggest that local interaction rules arise from a game situation in which the stakes are increments in group prestige. For him, Brahmans are born into the top position and untouchables into the bottom one. These two opposed positions define the scale when it is conceptualized, even though considerations of power frequently enter into actual behavior.

The way in which Informant no. 20 discussed questions about the transfer of pollution in specific contexts was similar. Here, too, the basic paradigm that he used could not be made to fit exactly with day-to-day realities. Yet the larger explanation provided to justify such actions remained

---

[55]This ranking was elicited without any hints as to what criteria to use.

[56]I was fortunate in being able to bring Informant no. 20 from India to Vancouver during the calendar year 1971 and hence was able to consult him directly in drafting the final pages of this section. All discussion of these issues was in Tamil, as he was barely able to converse in English even about elementary matters at the time.

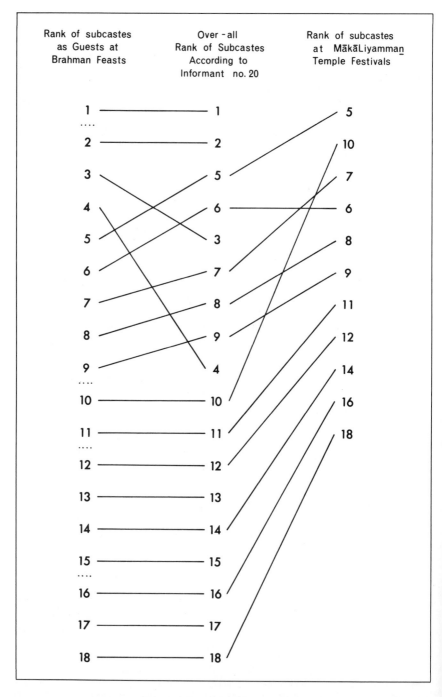

Fig. 4.15. Relative subcaste rank as judged by Informant no. 20, compared to the ranking of guests at Brahman feasts and to the ranking of participants at the festival for the hamlet goddess MākāLiyamman̲.

unshaken. Substantive pollution can be transferred in two basic ways. Contact of dry, uncooked foodstuffs with a man's hands, clothes, or house transfers a minute percentage of his total pollution quotient to the goods touched, during the period they remain in his presence. Untouchables have a total quotient so high that the percentage conveyed in touching any clothing or raw food makes Brahmans unable to receive these goods directly because Brahmans have a particularly low pollution quotient. Non-Brahmans, who have a somewhat higher natural pollution level, can receive raw food stuffs from untouchables without further raising their own level of impurity. Since the pollution that goods acquire by touch disappears when the polluting presence is removed, a non-Brahman can purchase such goods from an untouchable and sell them immediately to a Brahman without the latter raising objections.

Water, by contrast to dry touch, allows a man's full pollution quotient to be transferred to the foodstuff in question. If the water is absorbed, as in cooking, then the transfer becomes permanent. Hence, once foods have been cooked, they can only be eaten by subcastes with the same or a higher pollution quotient than that of the cook. Moreover, since a house can transfer pollution levels equal to that of touch, only those groups whose members one can touch without increasing one's own pollution quotient can provide acceptable environments to eat in, even if a special cook belonging to a higher-ranking group has been invited to prepare food. Brahmans have to bathe to remove the pollution acquired by touching a non-Brahman; hence a Brahman can never eat in a non-Brahman house even if a Brahman cook has been hired for the occasion. Similarly, no man of touchable status can eat in an untouchable's house, even if a cook of an acceptable subcaste has been hired. Eating food in the home of someone with a pollution quotient higher than one's own requires pilgrimage to the great temple centers of the South and months of penance to remove, whereas pollution acquired simply by touch can be removed with a bath.[57]

It is interesting to pursue this matter of pollution theory further, and to ask certain difficult questions about how the distinction between dry and wet touch is maintained in practice. Pressing the question, I found many instances of behavior that Informant no. 20 was at a loss to explain in terms of his general theory. For example, all the subcastes of the hamlet, including Brahmans, use brown sugar distilled from the sap of the palmyra

---

[57]That is, Brahmans can remove with a bath the pollution acquired by touching a non-Brahman. But if a Brahman should be touched by an untouchable—except in some neutral context like a bus—a special pilgrimage would be required. If a non-Brahman should touch an untouchable, however, a bath is sufficient to remove the pollution acquired. Since the inadvertent touch of an untouchable is always possible under present-day conditions of travel, it has now become the accepted practice for a Brahman merely to bathe after all such journeys before he enters his house.

palm. This sugar is prepared by the NāTār community by boiling the sap and then setting it out in molds that have been lined with wet cloths. These cloths need not be particularly clean and the water which moistens them is enough to convey the NāTār's quotient of impurity to the sugar. Yet no local group refuses to purchase or use the sugar on account of this detail.

Pressing the matter in still another direction, one can ask, for example, about foods fried in butter, or boiled in milk, without the addition of water. In principle these cooked foods should contain only the amount of pollution conveyed by "dry touch," and yet they are classified with cooked rice in the rules of food exchange. Here there seems to be something about cooking, per se, that conveys more impurity to the substance than mere touch, but this intermediate step is not recognized in the paradigm used by Informant no. 20. Similarly, any raw foodstuffs carried by an untouchable to the home of a non-Brahman and presented as a gift would not be accepted. However, the same produce could be bought from this man were he to set up a roadside stand. Something about the personalized mode of transfer increases the impurity of the product, but this too is not recognized explicitly in the informant's general theory. Despite pressure on these details, he refuses to alter the paradigm.[58] The dry-and-wet touch principle is the only explanation that the local culture provides.

Thus, many types of interaction in the hamlet area express rank. Some such interactions are private or semi-private, but others are explicitly public and formalized. Seating and food exchange, for example, provide two major ways of expressing in public the relative status of various subcaste groups. Seating is closely linked to power or dominance criteria and varies little in the host and guest dimensions. Food exchange, on the other hand, is directly related to notions of substantive purity. Refusals to eat from the hands of others cause two left-division subcastes to be ranked very differently in the host and guest dimensions of this medium. Both of these communities are well regarded by Brahmans and interact repeatedly with them. They ally themselves with these Brahmans and a second high-ranking neutral group, the KaruNĪkar PiLLai, and try to remain apart from the rest of the hamlet community. These same groups, however, are put down soundly by the allied strength of the right communities who believe that their superior power and their ties to local territory afford them the second place.

Finally, the substantive theory that says that some men are simply born Brahmans, some non-Brahmans, and some untouchables always seems to come to the fore when the set of community interactions is conceptualized

---

[58]This is not, it seems, a simple contrast between gift and purchase; for the same untouchable could accompany the non-Brahman to a store and pay the merchant for the goods in question and the non-Brahman would gladly accept.

as a whole. In this sense, matters of purity and pollution can be said to encompass considerations of power.[59] This over-arching paradigm finds direct expression in ceremonial contexts.[60] Nevertheless, it is partially shunted aside in favor of practical considerations where day-to-day matters are concerned. This ultimate recourse to substantive, purity-pollution arguments confirms the presence of what earlier writers have called a "caste system" in the hamlet area. When recourse to such ideas is no longer common, and interaction itself becomes defined as the causal factor in rank ordering, only then can we say that caste, in the traditional sense, does not persist.

LAND OWNERSHIP PATTERNS AND THE OCCUPATIONAL STRUCTURE

The caste system is frequently described as a prime example of a social order with a high degree of status congruity.[61] By this is meant a social order in which a person's, or a group's, general economic status tends to be correlated with his ritual status as defined by formal interaction rules. According to this theory, there should be a high degree of resemblance between rank orders in terms of the local seating and food-exchange hierarchies in ŌlappāLaiyam, and a rank order established in terms of the average total assets or average yearly income for each subcaste. In fact, however, the range of economic conditions within each subcaste is too wide to permit such a resemblance. In calculating an average annual income, or an average total of assets, for households of particular subcastes, no rank order meaningfully related to other rank orders previously discussed can be seen to emerge. We have already seen in the previous section that even in the related dimensions of seating and informal food transactions, rank orders are not consistent.

A household's total assets, as I have defined them for use in Figure 4.16, can be calculated by adding together the market value of all land, buildings, and animals owned, plus any cash savings, and then subtracting debts from this total.[62] Since very few households in ŌlappāLaiyam have

[59]"Englobant" is the term proposed by Dumont, *Homo hierarchicus,* pp. 103–8, and 274–77.

[60]Even in the ranking of subcastes enforced at temples to local goddesses it is argued that groups come forward in an order which expresses the degree of their association with that deity, ultimately a substantive notion regarding limited access to super-human powers. If Brahmans *are* present at one of these ceremonies, they will be accorded first place.

[61]Thomas O. Beidelman, *A Comparative Analysis of the Jajmani System* (Locust Valley, New York: Association for Asian Studies, 1959) and Martin Orans, "Maximizing in Jajmani Land: A Model of Caste Relations," *American Anthropologist* 70 (1968): 875–97.

[62]The data used were collected in a detailed economic survey of all households in ŌlappāLaiyam which I made in 1966. In a few cases I estimated holdings for a household where I suspected a lack of candor. The crosses (x) indicate estimates for a subcaste as a whole, in

substantial savings or business investments, this turns out to be almost entirely a measure of real estate holdings. The main point of Figure 4.16 is to illustrate the tremendous diversity in real wealth among households within one subcaste, a diversity almost as great, in the case of the KavuN-Tars, as that existing among the averages taken for each of these groups as a whole. The vertical lines in the diagram represent the range of assets owned by various households within a single subcaste. The length of each horizontal bar on these vertical lines is determined by the number of households which have assets of the same specific, total value. (Each "segment" of a horizontal bar represents one household.)

There are two further details of interest concerning Figure 4.16. The Brahmans (no. 1) and other primarily ritual-linked occupational groups (nos. 8, 9, 12, 13, 14, 15, and 16) show much less internal variation in wealth than do other communities.[63] This would seem to reflect the relatively uniform and traditional payments that such groups receive for their services in rural areas. Where a group is involved either in agriculture or in a skilled trade, by contrast, there is much more room for variation in employment demand and in rates of return. The other finding to be noted is the unusually low position of subcastes nos. 3 and 4, in view of their specialized skills and high ritual prestige as vegetarians. Their depressed condition probably reflects a certain local discrimination against these groups in the economic realm, paralleling that observed in the previous section in questions of food exchange.

The marginal economic position of nos. 3 and 4 (KōmuTTi CeTTiyārs and CōLi Ācāris) is less marked, however, when income rather than assets is considered. This may be so because discrimination takes the form of fewer opportunities for local investment, rather than reduced reimbursement for skills supplied. Such an interpretatio would fit the larger pattern of right-division resentment of these two leading left-division groups, the resentment taking the form of preventing the latter from forming a territorially specific power base.

In general, the distribution of yearly income, as shown in Figure 4.17, exhibits a pattern similar to that for total assets, both by subcaste and by

---

those cases where I did not collect sufficient first-hand information. Conversion to cash values was made according to the following average prices (1966):

1 acre irrigated land	= Rs. 9,000	1 bull or cow	= Rs. 400
1 acre dry land	= 4,000	1 calf	= 100
Each room in the house	= 500	1 buffalo	= 200
1 sheep or goat	= 50	1 buffalo calf	= 50
	1 chicken = Rs. 5		

[63]This finding is probably exaggerated somewhat by the small sample sizes for these groups.

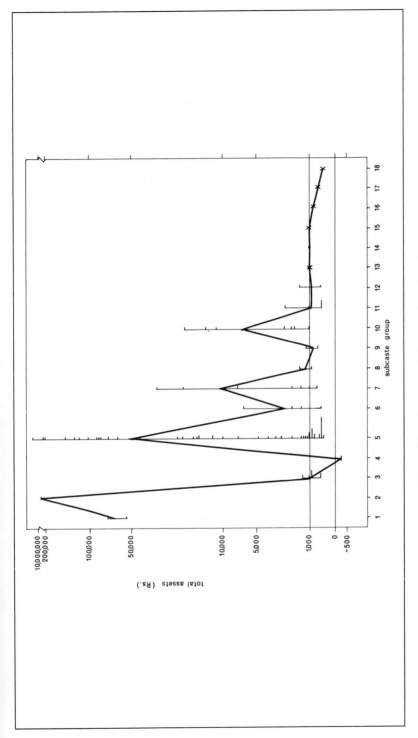

Fig. 4.16. Average total assets, by subcaste.

household, but with the disparities reduced in scale.[64] Furthermore, the ritual service communities do somewhat better vis-à-vis other groups when income is considered than they do in terms of assets. Not surprisingly, the position of nos. 3 and 4 is altered most strikingly. In food exchange, these two groups do much better as guests than as hosts; correspondingly, in the economic realm, they do much better as wage earners than they do as property owners. In Figure 4.17, the vertical lines represent the range of the annual income received by different households within a single sub-caste. The length of the bars on these vertical lines represents the number of households which have the same level of income. (As in Fig. 4.16, each "segment" of a horizontal bar represents one household.)

The people resident in ŌlappāLaiyam settlement together own about 630 acres of cultivable land, or 5 per cent of the arable land of the entire kirāmam.[65] The fact that they account for 9 per cent of the touchable population of the kirāmam, however, means that the residents of Ōlap-pāLaiyam own slightly less land, on the average, than the people of other settlements own. There are two reasons for this: first, several of the kirāmam's wealthiest landlords live elsewhere in the area; and second, a large cluster of artisan and weaving communities, generally landless castes, are found in ŌlappāLaiyam, while this is not the case in other settlements of the kirāmam.

The 630 acres owned by ŌlappāLaiyam residents are by no means even-ly distributed among them. My information on land ownership shows that less than one per cent of the male heads of households currently control about 35 per cent of the total acreage. Another 7 per cent account for the ownership of an additional 40 per cent of the land. Grouping these to-gether, 8 per cent of the heads of households control about 75 per cent of the settlement-owned acreage. A further 28 per cent of ŌlappāLaiyam's households have a bare subsistence holding, or less. This leaves 64 per cent of the households in ŌlappāLaiyam landless. The lion's share of the land, therefore, is effectively controlled by a few dominant, wealthy families. ŌlappāLaiyam is not an exception in this matter, nor is it by any means an extreme example. Others have already published similar figures for

---

[64]Income estimates are taken from the same economic survey as are the data on assets. In some cases, informants gave cash estimates of their income (which I then checked against food expenditure and other living expenses), but in others, income was stated in terms of crops harvested in an average year. In these instances, I have made a conversion to cash values according to the going market price. (See Appendix E for details.) A few people received monthly or yearly payments in kind. These were converted into cash values by using the same price scales; crosses (x) indicate estimates where no data were collected. Furthermore, a few of the larger incomes included in the table represent informed estimates made by myself and local collaborators. Wealthier families in the area were understandably hesitant to disclose the full extent of their resources.

[65]One man also owns some land in another kirāmam.

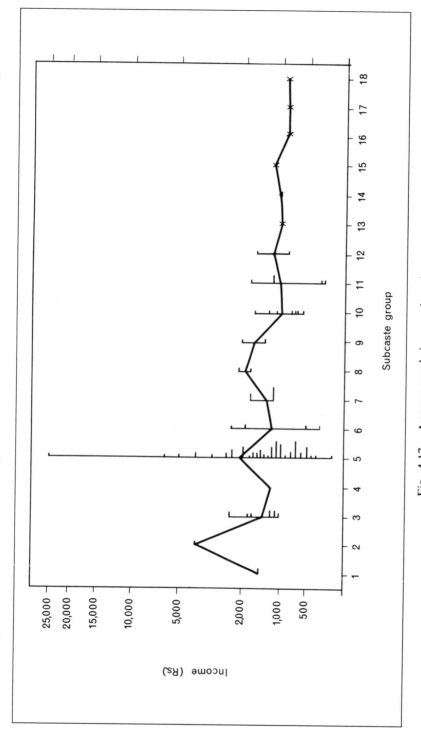

Fig. 4.17. Average yearly income, by subcaste.

elsewhere in India.[66] The figures would reveal an even greater imbalance if the untouchable population were to be included in these calculations. Unfortunately, I do not have comparable figures for these groups. The distribution of land ownership by subcaste is also significant. Nearly three-quarters of the land-owning households referred to above belong to the KavuNTar subcaste. Together, this group controls 89 per cent of Ōlappālaiyam-owned lands. The other 11 per cent of the acreage was, at the time of my survey, held by other subcastes in the proportions shown in Table 4.2.

The map in Figure 4.18 shows KavuNTar land ownership, by clan, for the residents of Ōlappālaiyam village. It will be clear immediately that the first clan to settle at this site, the KaNavāLar, continue to control some 75 per cent of the land belonging to the subcaste as a whole. The other two clans with historical claims on the other parts of the kirāmam,

TABLE 4.2
LAND-HOLDING IN ŌLAPPĀLAIYAM
(by subcaste)

Subcaste Name	Percentage of Total Acreage	Number of Households
Aiyar Brahman	5.0	2
KaruNīkar PiLLai	4.0	1
Koṅku KavuNTar	89.0	32
Kaikkōlar Mutaliyār	1.0	2
Marameri NāTār	1.0	3
Total	100.0	40

NOTE: The term "household" is used in the sense of a cooking unit even where land was registered officially as undivided among several such units.

the CeṅkaNNaṉ and ŌtāLar, are also represented.[67] One anomaly, the big KaNNantai holding, can be explained as the result of the uxorilocal residence of the husband of a rich KaNavāLar female a generation ago. His sons have now inherited her land title. As far as I know, the only other clans that own land in this particular area, the Āntai and the Mu-Rukkātaṉ, have obtained their local toehold by contracting similar marriages.

Furthermore, the KaNavāLar clan is clearly in a dominant position within the Ōlappālaiyam KavuNTar community as a whole. The genealogy of the clan is remembered in terms of the division of an initial clan

[66]Republic of India, *All India Rural Household Survey*, Vol. II, *Income and Spending* (New Delhi: Government Press, 1963) reports that in 1963, 1 per cent of all rural households owned 18 per cent of the total rural wealth and that 2.8 per cent of all rural households together enjoyed a little more than 50 per cent of the total rural income. Dumont suggests a similar picture for an area near Madurai. See Louis Dumont, *Une Sous-Caste de l'Inde du Sud* (Paris: Mouton, 1957), p. 122.

[67]The CeṅkaNNaṉ clan area represents a recent purchase from the ŌtāLar. It is not clear whether the CeṅkaNNaṉ have traditionally held land in this part of the kirāmam.

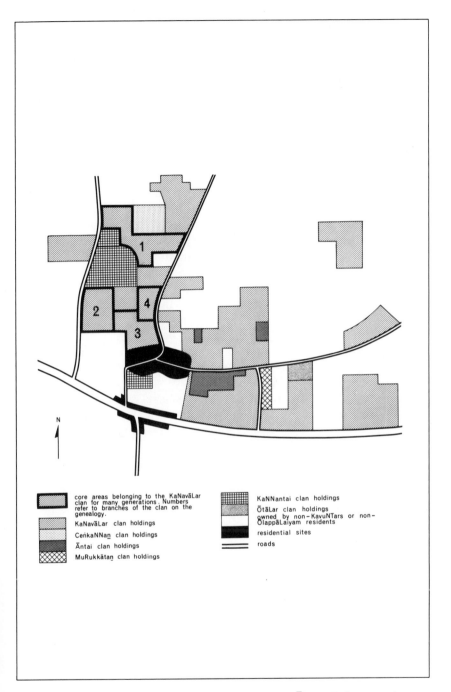

Fig. 4.18. Land ownership, by clan, in and around ŌlappāLaiyam settlement, 1965. The numbers on the areas belonging to the KaNavāLar clan correspond to the branches of the clan in the genealogy in Figure 4.19 as follows: (1) VeLLiyan̲ TōTTam, (2) KuTTai KāTu, (3) KuTTai TōTTam, and (4) NaTu TōTTam.

territory among four brothers. The site of these original holdings can still
be traced to a core area northwest of the settlement area. As is clear from
the genealogy, given in Figure 4.19, each branch of this important clan
still retains its association with its own particular inherited plot. The way
in which the internal structure of the descent group is remembered, moreover, clearly illustrates the importance of these *paṅku* ("shares") in
KavuNTar thinking.

Several older men of the settlement, Informants nos. 43, 44, 45, and 46,
told me that in the time of their FFFF or *muppāTTaṉ*, the original KaNavāLar clan lands had been divided into four shares.[68] In the time of the
FFF or *pāTTaṉ*, these four shares were further subdivided according to
the number of male descendants of each of the four "brothers." These
subdivisions were again divided when they passed into the hands of the
FF or *appāru* of the present generation. The story always has a depth of
four generations, the history of the first two being one of simple subdivision, and that of the last two—from FF to the present—one of rich detail.
The history of these later generations, unlike that of the earlier, is a complex story involving several adoptions and transfers of land. If these kinds
of adjustments occurred in earlier periods as well, no trace of them is left,
as here the history is recorded as one of simple subdivision. No one informant could trace the history of all four shares, but each had a good
knowledge of his own family's subdivision.

It is not surprising that this KaNavāLar genealogy is consistently "col-
lapsed" to a depth of four generations, although the clan has probably
inhabited the site for considerably longer. The terms used to refer to the
F and FF of ego's grandparents, *pāTTaṉ* and *muppāTTaṉ* are both very
vague. In addition to these specific relatives, they may refer also to all the
ancestors of the clan; that is, to men who "lived long ago." The epic of
The Brothers who settled in Koṅku is also structured in terms of the history of four generations. For most purposes, probably, four generations is
the greatest genealogical depth to which the term *paṅkāLi*, meaning "lineage brothers," or literally, "those who share," can be pushed.

Finally, some of the land in the KaNavāLar core area is still cultivated
according to a rule of rotation, following a very old tradition of land
use which has been reported only sporadically elsewhere in the South.[69]

---

[68]See Appendix F for a list of Tamil kinship terms by subcaste, and chapter 3, p. 126, n. 35
for a description of the code used for these terms throughout this study.

[69]Dharma Kumar, *Land and Caste in South India* (Cambridge: Cambridge University Press,
1965), pp. 14–18; B. H. Baden-Powell, *The Indian Village Community* (1896; reprint ed.,
New Haven: Human Relations Area File Press, 1957), pp. 366–74; T. V. Mahalingam, *Ad-
ministration and Social Life Under Vijayanagar* (Madras: Madras University Historical
Series, 1940), pp. 209–10, and C. S. H. Stokes, "The Custom of Kareiyid or Periodical
Redistribution of Land in Tanjore," *The Indian Antiquary* 3 (1874): 65–69. For Ceylon, see
Gananath Obeyesekere, *Land Tenure in Village Ceylon* (Cambridge: Cambridge University
Press, 1967), pp. 18–36, and Yalman, *Under the Bo Tree,* p. 98.

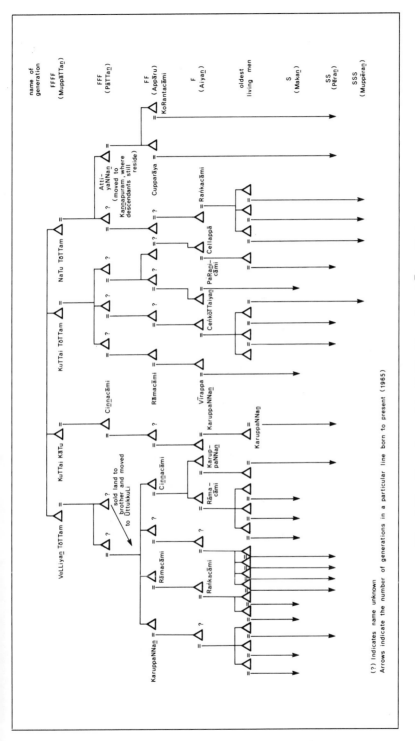

Fig. 4.19. Genealogy of the KaNavāLar clan of ŌlappāLaiyam.

According to this tradition, the land inherited by several brothers is held in common. Each brother then cultivates a portion of it, the portions being rotated periodically. Here the period is every two years. This arrangement is considered fairer than an outright division, since the land in question may be unevenly fertile: this way, each man has his turn with the fertile and less fertile areas. As the number of descendants increases, however, this kind of rotation eventually becomes cumbersome. Finally, then, the land is permanently divided into shares, and the rotation begins again on a smaller scale. This has probably occurred several times in the past in the KaNavāLar core area. With the permanent division of land, quarrels among the inheritors frequently arise. As we shall see in the next section, these family disputes seem to provide a seed from which rivalries within the settlement can grow.

While some KavuNTars in the region are landed and wealthy, there are many more who are poor. More than half of the KavuNTar community in ŌlappāLaiyam, in fact, is landless. It is more significant, however, that even under such conditions KavuNTars have clung to pursuits related to agriculture. Community opinion supports this by assuming that KavuN-Tars are not skillful in business and trade. Table 4.3 provides a detailed breakdown of the actual occupations of members of the KavuNTar community. From the table it is clear that only 16 per cent of the KavuNTar households in ŌlappāLaiyam are wealthy or at least economically established, while the proportion that are subsistence farmers and coolies is more than three times as large, or about 60 per cent of the group's membership. Most of these people are barely able to support their families, let alone to save. About 80 per cent of those classified in the subsistence group, in fact, have debts of one kind or another. Despite this economic squeeze, very few KavuNTar households have turned to non-agricultural pursuits.

Apart from agriculture and related pursuits, spinning and weaving are perhaps the most common occupational choice for KavuNTars to make. This preference does not show up well in the figures for ŌlappāLaiyam settlement, but in the nearby Ūr of Kaṇṇapuram a government-sponsored spinning center operates. Of the thirty-two workers employed at this center, a full three-quarters are drawn from the KavuNTar community.[70] Hand-spinning and weaving have long played an important part in the rural economy of Koṅku. Cotton is grown on the black soil in the area, and income from its cultivation provides a supplement to food crops in a

---

[70]Of the thirty-two workers, thirty are women. The remaining two are KavuNTar men. Of eight non-KavuNTar women, three are PaNTārams, two are NāTārs, one is a Koṅku VaNNār, one is a Paṟaiyar, and one is a Mutaliyār. Note that the Mutaliyār is the only representative of a left-division group. Thus, the spinning center is to date essentially a right-division institution, dominated by the KavuNTar group.

CuppiramaNiyam Mutaliyār selling household necessities at a local roadside shop.

Kāṅkappa Pulavar (Inf. 9), who is a local poet, reading a palm-leaf manuscript as part of a local ceremony.

Periyacāmi UTaiyār (Inf. 48) preparing a large cooking vessel on his potter's wheel.

PaRaniyappan Nāvitar (Inf. 33) giving a traditional-style haircut to a local KavuNTar.

TABLE 4.3

KAVUNTAR OCCUPATIONAL STRUCTURE, ŌLAPPĀLAIYAM, 1966

(by primary occupation of household)

General Category of Occupation	Percentage of Total	Specific Category of Occupation	Percentage of Total	Number of Households
Wealthy Landlords	2.0	Household controlling a large group of tenants and workers.	2.0	1
Established Farmers	14.0	Household employing at least one other KavuN-Tar as well as regular out-caste laborers.	6.0	4
		Household which hires outcaste laborers only, but on a regular basis.	8.0	5
Subsistence Farmers	46.0	Household eking out a living on its own holding, without hired labor.	28.0	19
		Household which works as a tenant on another's land.	6.0	4
		Household doing animal or cart business.	12.0	8
Coolies	13.0	Household supporting it-self by doing agricultural labor on a daily or month-ly basis.	20.0	13
		Household supporting it-self by doing coolie labor on the roads.	2.0	1
Non-agricul-turalists	25.0	Weaver	6.0	4
		Storekeeper	6.0	4
		Laborers in a town	4.0	2
Total	100.0		100.0	65

region where rain is scarce and the harvest unreliable. In recent years, the state government has been attempting to support and encourage the local hand-spinning and weaving industry by subsidizing it. This has encour-aged many KavuNTars to turn to weaving at the same time that Mutali-yārs, the traditional weaving community, have been switching from this occupation to involvement in business.

Of all the communities in the area, the barbers and washermen have stuck the most consistently to their traditional occupation. The demand for these services is quite constant and there is no competition from other groups trying to share in the trade.[71] Furthermore, these are the two occu-pations in which the traditional fixed payments in kind are most common, perhaps because the tie between the service-providing family and its em-

[71]This is not quite so true in urban areas, where men of higher castes often own the shop in which barbers or washermen do business.

ployer is of an intimate and enduring nature. Despite the disadvantages of such a personalized service tie, where one can be called to work at any time, this arrangement does assure a basic minimum of food and clothing for a family in time of hardship and famine. It is a dependable trade because as long as an important landed family can continue to command services, it will not cut off its support from these all-important groups.

The general economic implications of these special service relationships have recently been discussed by T. Scarlett Epstein in an excellent article.[72] She concludes that the tradition of fixed payments in kind is a means of maximizing subsistence security in an unpredictable environment, rather than a means of maximizing production and profit as in most so-called modern economies. An example of the payments received by two VaN-Nār families in ŌlappāLaiyam during the year 1965–66, in return for their washing services, as shown in Table 4.4, makes this subsistence function particularly clear.

The standard traditional payment by a large, landowning KavuNTar family to a service caste is sixteen *vaLLam* or one *moTā* of grain a year.[73] Many families, however, are too poor to make this full payment; therefore, the principle that poor KavuNTar families pay less for services, but also receive services less regularly, has been generally adopted. Many KavuNTars now substitute small amounts of cash for this grain.

The service communities also exchange services without payment among themselves. Thus a barber will shave a PaNTāram and a PaNTāram in turn will provide him with eating leaves for his guests. In general, payment in kind is considered the best insurance against famine or inflation. On the other hand, cash is highly desired in order to make purchases in the market economy.

As the information in Table 4.4 shows, washermen are generally better off where they are paid in kind, by a fixed number of measures of grain, than where a cash agreement is made. If income from yearly and festival payments is added together, it can be estimated that each of these two families receives roughly 200 vaLLam of grain and 200 rupees in cash, per year. This income will just support a small family at a subsistence level.

Of the remaining communities, most continue to follow their traditional occupations for lack of viable alternatives, but keep an eye open for opportunities to innovate, particularly through the education of their children. Most Brahmans in the rural areas, for example, continue to serve as priests in the local Civā and VisNu temples. The meagre income from this source is supplemented by earnings from *iṉām* or temple lands to which

---

[72]T. Scarlett Epstein, "Productive Efficiency and Customary Systems of Rewards in Rural South India," in Raymond Firth, ed., *Themes in Economic Anthropology* (London: Tavistock, 1967), pp. 229–52.
[73]See Appendix E for an explanation of the units of measure used in Koṅku.

TABLE 4.4(a)
PAYMENTS MADE TO A WASHERMAN, 1965–66
(yearly basis)

Subcaste Name	Number of Households	Payment in Rupees	Payment in Kind
Koṅku KavuNTar	1	5.00	
	2	6.00 (each)	
	3	8.00 (each)	Occasional noon meals (?)
	1	10.00	
	1	12.00	
	4	—	12 VaLLam grain (each)
	6	—	12 VaLLam grain (each)
Koṅku Ācāri	1	10.00	—
Kaikkōlar Mutaliyār	1	9.00	—
	1	12.00	—
OkaccāNTi PaNTāram	1	—	Any required eating leaves or priestly services.
Koṅku UTaiyār	1	—	Any required pots.
Marāmeri NāTār	2	—	1 MaNaṅku sugar (each)
VaTuka Nāyakkar	1	5.00	—
	1	9.00	—
	1	12.00	—
Total	28	120.00	144 VaLLam grain, plus occasional noon meals, sugar, pots, and eating leaves.
Total for a second washerman	26	145.00	135 VaLLam grain, plus sugar, rent, and noon meals.

NOTES: These payments are generally made at the time of the Māriyamman festival in April–May. See Appendix E for a definition of a VaLLam and a MaNaṅku, and their equivalents.

TABLE 4.4(b)
ADDITIONAL SPECIAL GIFTS EXPECTED BY WASHERMEN ON THE
OCCASION OF LIFE-CYCLE CEREMONIES

Marriage . . . . . . Rs. 2-1/2 and 4-1/2 VaLLam of rice at a marriage within the village. Rs. 10 and 1 VaLLam of rice at a marriage elsewhere. A man's upper cloth and lower cloth and a woman's sari are often additional gifts expected at this time.
Death . . . . Rs. 5 and 8 VaLLam of rice.
Girls first
menstruation . . . Rs. 2 and 4 VaLLam of rice.

NOTE: Payments in kind are reduced in favor of cash at weddings taking place outside the village. Intimate servants attached to particular families also receive gifts of cloth from time to time (especially at the two nōmpus or big festivals of the year). Sometimes the families of such service castes are also given rent-free housing and/or they are allowed to graze animals on their master's fields.

these priests have a claim, and which they generally lease to KavuNTar tenants. Some Brahmans practice astrology and some run vegetarian restaurants in small towns. PaNTārams, the local non-Brahman priests, also subsist on payments for their temple services, supplementing this by hiring themselves out as cooks, especially on festive occasions. Their other traditional sources of income—supplying eating leaves to the KavuNTar community and tying flower garlands—are no longer in much demand. PaNTārams, like many others, are beginning to look to education and to the towns to supplement such meagre means of livelihood.

Similarly the PiLLai have retained their traditional occupation of accountancy. The Ācāri continue to pursue their hereditary and relatively profitable metal and woodworking trades. Blacksmiths and carpenters manage to earn a dependable living at these occupations, but the goldsmiths are in harsh straits economically. Not enough people in the rural areas can afford to buy gold to keep these men employed, and they now subsist largely as workmen for wealthy jewelers—usually CeTTiyārs— in nearby towns.

Another traditional artisan group, the UTaiyār or potters, regularly supplements its income with plastering and skilled house-construction work. To date most men of this community retain their traditional skill, but practice it only during the festival seasons when new earthenware is in high demand. Because of current competition from the pots made in towns, the potters' interests have clearly shifted toward skilled masonry. The number of able young potters is rapidly decreasing.

The Nāyakkar, the group of well-diggers and earth-movers, are in a position similar to that of the blacksmiths and the carpenters. Their services are frequently required and they have a certain amount of specialized skill. Because of this, all Nāyakkar households in ŌlappāLaiyam continue to pursue their traditional occupation, supplementing it with road crew work when skilled construction jobs are not available.

Finally, there are the untouchable communities. The Paraiyar, like the PaNTāram, can no longer support themselves from their ritual services alone. Some work as local coolies, while many have migrated to the tea plantations in the hills. The most ambitious among them seek employment in town. The bulk of the outcaste population, however, consists of Mātāris. As a group, these people are in a subsistence position. Their traditional skills in making sandals and large leather bags for drawing water now face modern, industrial competition; at present, most Mātāris must depend entirely on unskilled agricultural labor for a bare living. This work is somewhat seasonal and it is very poorly paid.[74] The Mātāri as a whole are so numerous, so despised, and so near the subsistence level that they have not been able to force up the price of labor fast enough to keep up

[74]See Appendix E for details.

with the general rise in prices. The Kuṟavar are in a somewhat better economic position than the Mātāri because of their specialized basket-making skills, their small numbers, and their willingness to migrate when local opportunities are reduced.

Thus a majority of persons in ŌlappāLaiyam continue to pursue a traditional subcaste occupation. Qualifying this general picture, however, are certain important right- and left-division contrasts in occupational aspiration. A growing interest in education and the resultant opportunities for town living is evident among the leading communities of the left. The right-division KavuNTars, by contrast, have been slower to respond to new opportunities for schooling and for town employment. This contrast is in keeping, of course, with the territorially based power of the KavuN-Tar community. The KavuNTars are generalists in a local setting, while the higher-ranking left-division groups seek to develop specialized skills that will intensify their network of ties over a wide region.

When one considers middle- and lower-ranking subcastes, this picture of differences is almost reversed. The right-division service communities, particularly the PaNTāram and the UTaiyār, place a heavy emphasis on schooling and on new job opportunities. Even the Paṟaiyar, or right-division untouchables, share this outlook. As the description in chapter 3 pointed out, the pride that all of these groups take in their alliance with the landed community makes them somewhat dissatisfied with their current status and supplies them with the self-confidence to attempt something better. Lower-ranking left-division groups, such as Nāyakkars and Mātāris, by contrast, stick to their current occupations with tenacity. They are economically and socially more vulnerable than these other groups and clearly have less margin for experimentation and less innovative confidence than their right-division counterparts.

FACTIONAL DIVISION AT THE COMMUNITY LEVEL

Factional feeling, at the kirāmam and Ūr levels, tends to build around the personal rivalries of prominent men within the KavuNTar community. Sometimes disputes involve men of two competing clans, but often they spring from animosities that exist within the most prominent clan or lineage. (See Figure 4.20 for details on KavuNTar clan distribution in ŌlappāLaiyam settlement.) When such disputes develop, the two powerful opponents each attempt to draw community support to their own side. They draw such support first from their employees and, second, from friends and relatives. Often the origins of the tension are not obvious; for the polarization process activates other dormant animosities between lesser men and causes them to side with the opposing parties. Hence, brothers and other lineal relatives often find themselves on opposite sides of local issues despite close kin ties.

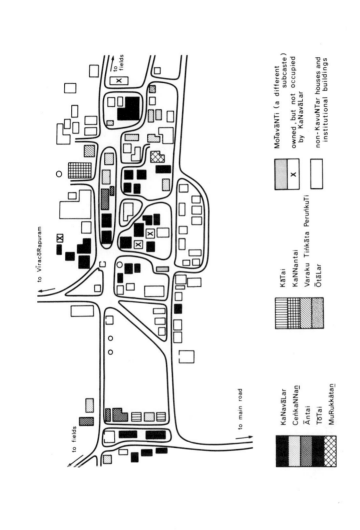

Fig. 4.20. ŌlappāLaiyam settlement site, showing buildings owned and occupied by KavuNTar clans.

The history of the current factional alignment in ŌlappāLaiyam settlement is of considerable interest as an example of this pattern and thus
worth describing in some detail:

About twenty-five years ago, the position of secular head (Kottukkārar) of the Ūr area was held by a man belonging to a KaNavāLar
family, (A). He was considered to have inherited this post in the male
line from time immemorial. The KaNavāLar claimed first place at
local ceremonies as their prerogative, as they were the first clan to
have settled at this particular site. However, also living in ŌlappāLaiyam at the time was a powerful family of ŌtāLar, (B), a clan which
preceded the KaNavāLar in the kirāmam as a whole. Their eldest
male member was also greatly respected.

One day, the ŌtāLar leader suggested that the order in which offerings to the goddess MākāLiyamman were distributed to participants
at the time of the festival be changed. He thought that the representative of the Mutaliyār community, who was a friend of his, ought to
come before that of the NāTār, the group which had traditionally
enjoyed precedence in this matter. The Kottukkārar's family objected,
and a big dispute ensued. A second argument developed over whether
the Kottukkārar himself or the ŌtāLar leader ought to be the one to
present the first animal for sacrifice. People gathered to support both
sides. Finally, government officials stepped in and locked the Mākā-
Liyamman temple. As a result of their action, no festivals were held
for several years. Then some of the wealthier KavuNTars of the village
got together and built a little thatch-roofed temple for the Ūr goddess, next to the old stone one which still remained locked. The festivals began again and for a while they proceeded along traditional
lines. By this time, the powerful ŌtāLar family concerned in the original dispute had left the vicinity.

Unfortunately, more difficulties soon arose. An old rivalry between
two brothers of a second KaNavāLar family, (C), rose to the surface
over the question of inheriting family land. One year, as the time for
the MākāLiyamman festival drew near, C_1, who was in charge of
temple funds, began to collect contributions to finance the event and
tried to prevent C_2 from making a donation. C_2, who had inherited
leadership of the dissident faction from the ŌtāLar, wanted to contribute. He tried several times to give his money to a middleman, the
barber. Each time, C_1 detected the source of the money and refused
it. On the day of the festival, all the local residents gathered to boil
their pots of poṅkal rice. When the priest came to collect a spoonful
from each pot for an offering to the deity, C_1 ordered that rice not be
taken from C_2's pot. At this C_2 became very angry and started a quarrel. Several friends supported him. Most of these friends were from
the poorer KavuNTar families of the settlement, while C_1 had several
of the wealthier families supporting him. C_2 and his friends became
more and more angry. Finally, they walked off in a huff, threatening
to build their own MākāLiyamman temple next to the two, one in
stone and one in thatch, already standing.

The friends of C_2 began collecting donations and about ten families
helped to build this third and newest temple. One man who helped in

The "Eastern" MākāLiyamman temple is shown in the center as a small thatched hut. An extension to it which leads to the right has just been built for celebration of the annual festival. The older MākāLiyamman temple, which used to be common to the hamlet as a whole but which is now locked, can just be seen to the right of the "Eastern" temple. It is a solid plaster building. The "Western" MākāLiyamman temple is not shown, but its new extension, also under construction for the coming festival, can be seen at the far left.

The image of the "Eastern" MākāLi-yamman, inside the thatched hut, dressed up ready for the festival.

The nāTTukkal stone, marking the settlement site. It is being worshipped during a local resident's wedding ceremony.

the construction was the younger son of the Kottukkārar's family (A). He associated himself with this new temple and thus broke with his elder brother who had inherited the position of Kottukkārar at the former. There are now three temples: a locked stone one, an "Eastern" thatched one and a "Western" thatched one. The residents of the village have gradually aligned themselves on one side or the other, and the two thatched temples have been rivals now for about ten years. They each have a separate temple organization, a separate temple fund, and a separate, but usually simultaneous, festival each year. (Local residents have named the two temples "Eastern" and "Western" to describe their location in terms of the compass points.)

These two rival factions now split the KavuNTar community of Ōlappā-Laiyam neatly in half. The membership of the two groups is very close to being equal. Furthermore, every single KavuNTar clan in the settlement, except the ŌtāLar, who are represented by only one household, is split— some of its households being aligned with each group. In general, the splits have occurred between fairly distant kin, but in four cases brothers belong to opposite temple groups. In every one of these cases, the brothers are members of the KaNavāLar clan; that is, they belong to the numerically and economically dominant descent group of the Ūr area. It would appear, therefore, that the intensity of conflict, as measured by its ability to divide close kin, is directly proportional to the local economic and political power of those concerned.

Although the two factions may be relatively equal in terms of numbers, in terms of power there is a decided imbalance. The Eastern temple represents the interests of the wealthier landowners of the area, and the Western temple the interests of the poor. With a few prominent exceptions, the members of the latter group are landless. All the NāTār of the area, except one unrelated newcomer, support the wealthier temple. They lend their support to the landlords who patronize it, not out of sympathy, but out of economic interest. KavuNTar members of the poorer faction do not, on the whole, own fine palmyra palms. All the other subcastes of the village—with the exception of a few ritual service groups that have remained neutral for professional reasons—tend to support the poorer temple.

The two factions differ not only in membership, but also in character. The Eastern temple, unlike the Western one, insists on preserving a certain formality in its ceremonies. Thus all members must step forward to receive the deity's blessings in a specified traditional order. To arrive at this order, the various subcastes involved are ranked, and within each subcaste the clans are ranked. Within each clan men step forward according to their age, older men generally preceding younger ones. Thus each worshipper at the Eastern temple knows which other participants he is expected to follow, and which to precede.[75] At the moment, there are no disputes over the established ranking, but the matter has frequently been a cause of disputes in the past.

The Western temple, by contrast, operates on a first-come, first-served basis. There is no *mirās,* or ritually fixed order, and members of this group assert that equality before the goddess is a good thing. Furthermore, the Eastern temple maintains the post of Kottukkārar and the tradition that NāTārs must pay for the offerings presented to the goddess during the first seven days of the festival. The Western temple has no Kottukkārar or secular headman, and equal contributions are collected from all members to finance the first seven days. Finally, there is a general air of camaraderie about the Western temple. So far it has been free from bitter disputes over leadership.

Despite the Eastern temple's considerable formality in ritual matters, however, its members are actually less interested in MākāLiyamman and her festival than are those of the poorer faction. It is the Western temple whose monthly meetings are the most regular, and best attended. Money from the temple fund is lent out at higher rates of interest at this temple than at the Eastern one. Western temple funds can be borrowed in ten-rupee lumps at an average interest rate of 9 per cent a month.[76] The wealthier Eastern faction lends its funds in twenty-rupee lumps but commands an average interest of only 6 per cent a month. Accumulated interest is used to finance the festivals. In general, Eastern temple members are not as enthusiastic about these events as Western temple members. They spend less money on festivals and also cancel them more frequently. Members of the poorer faction are proud of this contrast and enjoy their display of relative piety.

Of the nine MākāLiyamman temples in Kannapuram kirāmam, five have canceled their festivals completely in recent years as a result of severe factional difficulties. Two others, including ŌlappāLaiyam, have worked out an arrangement whereby rival groups either celebrate the festival independently, or in alternate years. Only two of the nine temples, are, for the moment, relatively untroubled by such paralyzing disputes. Moreover, in all cases the confrontation has been phrased in terms of a dispute over which family or clan should take precedence in the particular ritual to be held. Underlying the formal issue, however, are always economic and personal rivalries.

[75]What is most important is that the KavuNTars step forward first, and that the KaNavāLar clan precede others. There is less concern over secondary and tertiary positions, and age is only important where an obvious difference exists.

[76]The money is actually auctioned off, and so the rate varies. It also varies with the month of the year, tending to be highest in March and September (planting periods) and lowest in November (on the eve of the harvest). With the help of Informant no. 20, I have kept a record of these temple meetings and the amounts of money auctioned off for more than four years.

At the moment, the factional division within ŌlappāLaiyam does not have wide ramifications. The dispute does not seriously affect work teams or day-to-day activities. Members of both factions, for example, will attend the same festival when kirāmam deities rather than Ūr deities are involved. What the factionalism does seem to express is the degree of dominance of a particular local descent group, and the resultant rivalry that has developed within that group over positions of community leadership. It would appear that the main contenders for factional leadership will remain KavuNTars, and perhaps even KavuNTars of the locally dominant clan, for some time to come.

This chapter has been concerned with the Ūr as a significant social area with its own guardian deity and its own ritual boundaries. Within the Ūr it has been shown that there are clear differences in right- and left-caste organization. Particular attention has been paid, for example, to the contrasts that these two groupings exhibit in their approach to food exchange in the hamlet. Differences in their economic positions and occupational preferences have also been discussed. Finally, the dynamics of faction-formation and the special importance of the leading landowning clan in such local rivalries has been analyzed. The next chapter will consider these same factors as they make for right-left differences in the individual household.

5

THE INDIVIDUAL HOUSEHOLD: KUTUMPAM

THE KUTUMPAM: DEFINITION AND DESCRIPTION

In the preceding chapters, social organization in Koṅku as it exists at four distinct, territorially defined levels has been discussed. These spatial units have been studied in decreasing order of size: first the region as a whole, then the subregion or nāTu, next the kirāmam, and following this, the Ūr. Each of these levels of organization is significant in the eyes of the local populace. Differences between right and left subcastes have been pointed out at each step of the discussion. The whole is like a set of Chinese boxes, each unit having roughly the same shape, while fitting neatly inside the previous container. The final "box" in this series is the individual household, or *kuTumpam*. Here, too, each social unit enjoys a clear territorial dimension, and here again differences between right- and left-division organization can be found.

The kuTumpam is the basic commensal group. It is simultaneously the basic unit in all kin networks. By definition, it is built around the hearth of a married couple. Some people explicitly say, "PeN illai, kuTumpam illai," meaning "Without a woman there can be no household." This saying refers simultaneously to the role of the female as food preparer and as a sexual mate; for the two are co-terminous in the Koṅku area. A non-consanguine female who cooks for a man in his household or territory is thus, by definition, his wife.[1] A man who kept a woman without marrying her would not expect her to cook for him. In such a situation, the man and the woman would continue to eat food prepared on the hearth of their respective official marriage partners, or in the kitchen of a member of their family of origin.

Furthermore, if a man had two wives, he would have two kuTumpams. Each wife would cook for him on her own designated hearth, and he

---

[1] A man can take food from such a woman without the same implications when he is a guest in her father's or brother's house.

FIGURE 5.1(a)

EXAMPLES OF KUTUMPAM UNITS

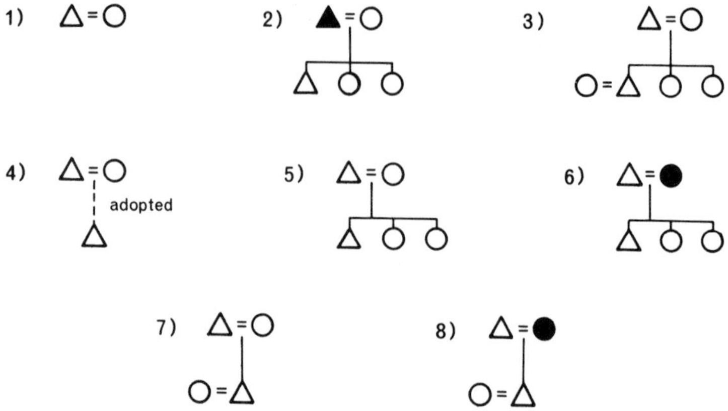

would take some of his meals from each. It is very unusual, however, for a man to have more than one wife. If three or four generations of people are clustered together, then their eating habits determine whether they are a single kuTumpam or several. If ego eats regularly with his parents' kuTumpam, he belongs to it. If he eats separately with a sexual partner and her children, then he has formed a separate household.

Implied in sharing food is the sharing of the responsibilities and hardships undertaken to get that food. My cook and her son (Informants nos. 21 and 20) sometimes spoke of me as a member of their kuTumpam, even though according to strict usage this was impossible since I was not related by blood or by marriage to its other members. This unusual situation arose because I shared food with this unit and contributed to its support.

In its broadest sense, the term *kuTumpam* can also refer to all of a man's close relatives. This provides one more example of how the definition of a term can vary according to the level of social organization to which the user intends to refer: recall the earlier examples, *nāTu* and *ūr*. The general term for close relations, however, is *pakkattāla contam*. The term *kuTumpam* is usually reserved for single commensal units.[2]

In several of the examples of kuTumpam units given in diagram form in Figure 5.1, one partner of an initial married pair is either dead or absent. The remaining partner still participates in a kuTumpam, if he or she lives with one or more children who are considered socially to be offspring of

---

[2]The meaning of the term *kuTumpam* in this account differs from Mayer's description of a similar word, *kutumb*, in central India. See Adrian C. Mayer, *Caste and Kinship in Central India* (London: Routledge and Kegan Paul, 1960), pp. 169–72.

FIGURE 5.1(b)

EXAMPLES OF NON-KUTUMPAM UNITS

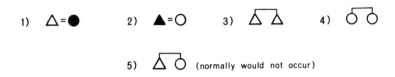

NOTE: In Figure 5.1 (a) and (b), the filled-in circles and triangles signify that the partner represented is dead.

the original union. If such a person lives alone or with a sibling of the same sex, however, his commensal unit ceases to constitute a kuTumpam. Thus, marriage itself or a parent-child tie resulting either from a previous marriage or from adoption is an essential prerequisite for forming such a unit. Questions of joint property are considered to be quite irrelevant to its definition.

In addition to the commensal and sexual implications of kuTumpam life, an important spatial definition of this social unit also exists. The easiest way to identify a kuTumpam operationally is to locate a hearth area and inquire as to who eats from it. In addition to this focal point, there is usually a living area which may be more or less well-defined, depending on the economic means of the household in question. This area has a ritual boundary, which can be marked either by a wall or by the sharp contrast between a well-swept, dung-groomed area and a neglected, dusty one.[3] Both procedures serve equally to mark off the kuTumpam living site. It is not unusual for two or more kuTumpams to share a large compound, but only under extreme economic hardship will two kuTumpams share the same demarcated sleeping area or store rooms.

Other markers of the household living site are erected on special occasions. If there should be a serious pox-type illness in the family, for example, an archway of margosa leaves will be tied across the main entrance to the affected household area. This arch is intended to warn visitors and also to prevent the intrusion of unwelcome spirits who are thought to draw

---

[3]A similar purpose can be served by a thorn fence, a trench, a row of stones, etc.

near the living site during such crises.[4] The boundary of the living site is also marked during a funeral. At such times, a chicken, or a goat, is beheaded and carried bleeding around the edge of this area, counterclockwise. It is then given to a Paraiyar for disposal. The use of blood rather than leaves is required, as the danger from evil spirits is at a peak during this period preceding the burial.[5]

Every household has a *naTu vīTu,* or central spot, generally located on a major wall facing north or east. This central spot may be unmarked, but usually there is a small indentation in the plaster or earth finish which is intended to hold a lamp. Printed pictures of various Indian divinities are often hung in the same area. Any members of the household who die are laid at right-angles to this wall, with their head on the *naTu,* or central spot. They remain there during the funeral proceedings and until they are taken for burial. Thus the area has a strong association with ancestors. Offerings are set out here during the ancestral pūjā each year in the month of ĀTi. The deceased are said to partake of the food before the family divides it in preparation for the traditional feast enjoyed on this day.

In addition to the naTu vīTu, a number of households have small shrines outside the house, generally located over the burial site of a recently deceased family member. Such shrines are referred to as *camātis,* and only members of the household of which the deceased was a member will generally worship there. These shrines can be erected by any family group; one Brahman shrine was erected just outside the temple where the deceased was a priest. In all the other cases illustrated here, however, the shrine has been built over the grave. Examples of these household shrines follow:

> *(1) Aiyar Brahman* The FF of the present Brahman priest at the Kannapuram Civā temple was famous for his knowledge of astrology and of magical chants. When he died, a small alcove which faces north, located outside the main temple compound, was dedicated to him and a stone image of a man in meditation was placed inside it. People used to pay their respects at this alcove as they came in and out of the main temple, and the descendants of this man would perform a pūjā there. Now, however, the shrine is neglected and nearly forgotten.

> *(2) Koṅku KavuNTar* The FF of one of the leading KavuNTar families of the KaNavāLar clan in ŌlappāLaiyam was famous for his knowledge of magical chants that would cure snake bites. On his death, he was buried on family land north of the village and a camāti was built on the site. His immediate descendants occasionally perform a pūjā at this shrine. However, there is now a bitter rivalry between

---

[4]Similar strings of leaves, but from a different tree, are tied around the boundary of the living site during the Tai nōmpu festival and on a newly built house before occupation.
[5]Informant no. 20.

The fine, old-style rural home of a Mutaliyār family. Notice the neatly plastered walls, the hand-carved stone pillars, and the heavy tile roof.

The one-room home of a relatively poor KavuNTar family. A second private area has been made by screening off part of the porch with woven coconut fronds. Such areas are often constructed to accommodate women during menstrual and birth pollution periods, as at these times they are not generally allowed to enter the house interior.

The one-room house of a poor NāTār family. (The woman standing in front is a Nāyakkar.) Until recently, thatch was the only material for roofing that lower castes were permitted. Note the cot to the right, with grain drying on it.

his grandsons over this piece of land, and consequently, his descendants do not worship there as a group. The shrine is in a dilapidated condition.

(3) OkaccāNTi PaNTāram The MFF of the present Māriyamman priest in ŌlappāLaiyam was known for his knowledge of magical chants. On his death his relations erected a small shrine for him in the village where he lived, ten miles to the north. People used to worship there, but the shrine has now more or less fallen into disuse.

(4) Kaikkōlar Mutaliyār The F of one of the present Mutaliyār merchants in ŌlappāLaiyam is buried on a small piece of family land north of the village. A very modest camāti has been built on the spot and members of his son's family place offerings there.

(5) VaTuka Nāyakkar A small boy belonging to this group died several years ago. He then appeared to his father in a dream and asked for a camāti. His father built a small raised platform, with a little shrine to shelter a light, over his tomb.

In all the above cases the camāti shrine has been dedicated to a man, often one with a particularly honorable reputation in the community. I know of only one case of a shrine of this sort dedicated to a woman. This small temple belongs to a distinct subcaste of Mutaliyār, the MēLakārar, who used to serve as temple drummers and dancers at the big Civā temple in Kaṇṇapuram. Since descent is in the female line for this particular community, a shrine to a female ancestor is particularly appropriate.[6]

These shrines to noteworthy deceased relatives are common to all subcastes. Normally, they receive attention for only a decade or two; then interest fades and the shrine deteriorates. In a few cases, however, it appears that these shrines become a focal point for the descent group as a whole. In such cases they may be reconstructed and enlarged. Finally, if they are important enough, periodic festivals may be initiated at the spot by clan members. By this time, the specific ancestral connection will have been forgotten, and the deity will have become more generalized. Thus, these household shrines for the deceased gradually change with time: they either fade into obscurity as the original household itself is forgotten, or they become enlarged and transformed to express the household's gradual incorporation into a larger descent unit.

Households range in size from approximately one to fifteen members. The most common time for a division is on the occasion of a son's marriage.[7] Some families remain joint, however, until the most senior male is

---

[6]Unfortunately, I did not study this group in any detail. Temple dancing has been outlawed in Madras for more than a generation now, and this community is quickly losing its distinctiveness by merging, through marriage and general behavior, with the other Mutaliyārs in the area.

[7]I speak of Koṅku KavuNTars here. I am not sure whether this would hold true for Brahmans, PiLLais, and higher-ranking left-division groups; for it seems to me that these

unable to manage the family property competently. Sometimes the original members even remain together until after this man's death. I have not recorded a single case of de facto division of family property which did not entail a division of cooking arrangements as well.[8] Indeed, the break-up usually starts by partitioning the kitchen; a separation of living quarters follows; and the division of family property comes last of all.

In classifying the various types of households which can be found in the Koṅku area according to their composition or the extent to which they are joint, the following terms have been used:

Household Types[9]

A₁ *Nuclear Household.* A commensal unit consisting of a single, married couple and their non-adult children, or of a married couple without children.[10]

A₂ *Subnuclear Household or Single Adult.* A commensal unit consisting of a single parent and his or her non-adult children, or a single adult living alone.

B₁ *Joint Household.* A commensal unit having as a core two or more married couples.

B₂ *Supplemented Nuclear Household.* A commensal unit having as a core a married couple and, in addition, at least one widowed parent, adult sibling, or adult child. Also one adult parent living with an adult child, and any other situation where a subnuclear household has been added to or supplemented by the presence of additional relatives.

---

groups tend to divide their kuTumpams later than the higher-ranking right-division communities do.

[8] Property is sometimes divided in the accountant's register for the purpose of evading land-ceiling legislation, however, without a division of the commensal unit.

[9] These definitions correspond to those previously suggested by Pauline Kolenda in her extensive work on the distribution of joint households in India. The correspondence is as follows:

Kolenda's Category	Category Used Here
1	A₁
3, 4	A₂
2, 5	B₁
6, 7, 8, 9, 10, 11	B₂

See Pauline M. Kolenda, "Region, Caste and Family Structure: A Comparative Study of the Indian 'Joint' Family," in Milton Singer and Bernard Cohn, eds., *Structure and Change in Indian Society* (Chicago: Aldine, 1968), pp. 346–47. For the purposes of this study I could not see the usefulness of the very detailed differentiation which Kolenda had made. Thus, I have lumped some of her categories together, as can be seen. The primary data are available to anyone who would like to undertake a more elaborate analysis.

[10] An adult was defined as a man over thirty years of age, or a woman over twenty-five. These ages are intended to represent the upper limit of the age-range in which people usually marry.

TABLE 5.1
JOINT HOUSEHOLD STATISTICS
(by subcaste)

Subcaste Name	(1) Percentage of Nuclear Households	(2) Percentage of Subnuclear Households	Total Percentage of (1) and (2)	(3) Percentage of Joint Households	(4) Percentage of Supplemented Nuclear Households	Total Percentage of (3) and (4)	Sample Size (Households)
Neutral Division:							
Aiyar Brahman	43.0	14.0	57.0	27.0	16.0	43.0	37
Right Division:							
Koṅku KavuNTar	49.0	21.0	70.0	15.0	15.0	30.0	187
OkaccāNTi PaNTāram	57.0	14.0	71.0	11.0	18.0	29.0	28
Koṅku UTaiyār	60.0	29.0	89.0	0.0	11.0	11.0	17
Maramēri NāTār	66.0	18.0	84.0	10.0	6.0	16.0	51
Koṅku Nāvitar	87.0	0.0	87.0	0.0	13.0	13.0	8
Koṅku Paṟaiyar	64.0	28.0	92.0	5.0	3.0	8.0	39
Total Average			76.0			24.0	330
Left Division:							
CōLi Ācāri	67.0	0.0	67.0	13.0	20.0	33.0	30
Kaikkōlar Mutaliyār	45.0	9.0	56.0	13.0	31.0	44.0	23
VaTuka Nāyakkar	63.0	15.0	78.0	11.0	11.0	22.0	27
VaTuka VaNNār	76.0	0.0	76.0	6.0	18.0	24.0	33
Teluṅku Mātāri	60.0	6.0	66.0	20.0	14.0	34.0	82
Total Average			68.0			32.0	195
Average of all subcastes, weighted by number of households			74.0			26.0	562

NOTES: Figures on right VaNNārs, left Nāvitars, neutral PiLLais, and on both divisions of CeTTiyārs have been omitted from the table because of lack of sufficient information.
Averages have been taken by weighting each subcaste in a given division equally.

Table 5.1 provides figures on the proportions of these various types of households, by subcaste, in the Kāṅkayam area. The statistics include households from other settlements in the Kāṅkayam area, in addition to a full tally for households in ŌlappāLaiyam proper. My information on other settlements was collected from kinsmen resident in ŌlappāLaiyam. The figures, therefore, represent a purposive rather than a random sample of the area.

The proportion of joint and supplemented nuclear households in the Kāṅkayam area (26 per cent of the total, according to Table 5.1) is quite low when compared to other parts of India.[11] Probably, however, it is not out of line with other parts of Madras State. There are only three sets of published figures on other Madras populations, as shown in Table 5.2,

TABLE 5.2
COMPARISON OF THE PERCENTAGE OF NUCLEAR AND
JOINT HOUSEHOLDS IN SELECTED DISTRICTS

District	Caste Name	Percentage of Nuclear Households	Percentage of Joint Households	Author
Tanjore	Brahman	58.0	42.0	Gough
N. Arcot (resident in Bangalore)	Paraiyar	76.0	24.0	Woodruff
Madurai	KaLLar	92.0	8.0	Dumont
Madras State (rough average)		75.0	25.0	

SOURCE: As summarized by Pauline M. Kolenda, "Regional Differences in Indian Family Structure," in Robert I. Crane, ed., *Regions and Regionalism in South Asian Studies: An Exploratory Study*, Duke University Program in Comparative Studies on Southern Asia, Monograph No. 5 (Durham, N.C., 1967), pp. 152–53.

and each of these is limited to one particular community. Averaging the findings of the authors listed in the table, we arrive at a general figure of 25 per cent. This proportion of joint or supplemented households agrees with the results of the present study. Kolenda's unpublished data on several communities in the Tinnevelly (Tirunelveli) District help to reinforce this general pattern.[12] Madras State is apparently an area which has a relatively low proportion of joint and supplemented households in the general population.

If we speak of the average or normal proportion of joint and supplemented households in the Koṅku population as roughly 25 per cent, we can then speak of the tendency of particular groups in the area to deviate

[11]Pauline M. Kolenda, "Regional Differences in Indian Family Structure," in Robert I. Crane, ed., *Regions and Regionalism in South Asian Studies: An Exploratory Study*, Papers presented at a symposium held at Duke University, April 7–9, 1966, Duke University Program in Comparative Studies on Southern Asia, Monograph and Occasional Papers Series, Monograph No. 5 (Durham, N.C.: Duke University, Program in Comparative Studies on Southern Asia, 1967), pp. 147–226.
[12]Personal communication.

from this norm. In analyzing the data in Table 5.1 in this way, it becomes clear that the Brahmans in the sample have a considerably higher-than-average proportion of joint families for the region. The left-division groups tend to follow their lead, all of them scoring close to the average or considerably above it. No right-division subcaste, by contrast, scores very much above the average, while most fall considerably below it.

This difference in the proportion of joint and supplemented families, by division, lies in the direction that might be predicted from other findings. The left bloc attempts to emulate the ideals of family harmony and co-operation as set down in the classical law books.[13] Those of the right tend either to play down or to defy openly such standards. The difference observed between the two divisions in this matter of joint family is also fully in keeping with the high rate of literacy among the higher-ranking left-division groups. The more a family is imbued with the teachings of India's classical literature, it seems, the stronger the emphasis it places on family harmony with close kin and on respect for elders. This highly respected tradition lays stress on the deference that a son should show to his father, a wife to her husband, and a bride to her mother-in-law. These attitudes restrain family conflict and tend to delay the break-up of joint households into individual or nuclear units.[14]

These general right-left differences in attitude toward joint living are somewhat obscured, however, by the tendency for all high-ranking communities to have a higher proportion of joint families than lower-ranking ones.[15] Thus, leading groups of both the right and the left divisions have above-average proportions of joint and supplemented families, but left groups such as the Mutaliyār and the Ācāri exceed the average by more than their counterparts on the right. Furthermore, the percentage of these types of households among the lower-ranking right-division groups drops off much more quickly than the percentage does for lower-ranking groups that belong to the left. The contrast between the two untouchable communities, the Paṟaiyar and the Mātāri, is particularly striking.[16] The pattern of right-left differences observed in terms of the nāTu, kirāmam, and

---

[13]The *Dharma Sāstras.*

[14]The later the break-up of families, on the average, the higher is the proportion of joint households that appears in a sample count.

[15]This general tendency is confirmed as an all-India pattern by Kolenda's study as well. See Kolenda, "Region, Caste and Family Structure," p. 381.

[16]Nonetheless, the Mātāri community must be admitted to be something of an exception to all of these generalizations. Its figure of 34 per cent for joint households clearly cannot be explained either by literacy or by social status. Here a certain support for the classical ideals mentioned as associated with left-division membership would seem to be bolstered by the exigencies of extreme poverty. The Mātāri, after all, are by far the most economically depressed group in the sample. One wonders if a re-analysis of Kolenda's more extensive data on joint families might yield a similar set of caste and subcaste contrasts in other areas of India.

Ūr levels, therefore, can be seen to emerge at the kuTumpam or household level as well.

THE LOGIC OF THE KINSHIP TERMINOLOGY: AN OVERVIEW

One way to develop an understanding of the kin universe as a speaker of Tamil perceives it, is to study the logic of the kinship terminology. The analysis that follows will clarify the basic categories of kinsmen, and the rules that regulate their application. After this, certain interesting differences in right- and left-division usage will be discussed.

One single conceptual opposition is of the utmost importance in the organization of the Tamil kinship terminology, but foreign to the English speaker. This is the distinction speakers of Tamil make between cross and parallel relatives. From ego's perspective, the members of his or her family of origin—father, mother, brothers, and sisters—are always classified as parallel relatives. Cross relatives, by contrast, consist of ego's siblings' spouses, his own spouse, and all parents of these marriageable persons. These distinctions are given in diagram form in Figure 5.2. From this core contrast between ego's own family and the family of his spouse and his siblings' spouses, it is possible to move outward along the kin network to more distant relations, classifying each in turn into one of these two basic categories.

Cross relatives of ego's own generation are potential marriage partners for ego and for all ego's siblings. A relationship of mutual gift-giving and reciprocity sets the standard for interaction with these persons. Parallel relatives of the same generation are like ego's own siblings. They share ego's rights of inheritance and the proper relationship between such persons is one of mutual restraint and respect. Sexual overtones in interaction between such persons are minimized and marriage, even between distant parallel relatives, is generally not allowed.

The logic of this terminological system can be stated quite easily if one simple rule is taken into account: the relatives who belong to that generation which is immediately above ego's own are classified according to the inverse of the logic used to classify relatives in ego's own generation and in the one just below it. For relatives in more distant generations no cross-parallel distinction is usually made, although some important subcastes, notably the KavuNTars, include immediate grandparents in this all-important scheme.

Whatever the specific custom of a group as to which relatives are to be included in the basic model, the logic of classification remains everywhere the same. Ego's own parents, siblings, and children are always his parallel relatives. Working outward from this basic core, he will classify the opposite-sex siblings of his two parents in the opposite category to that of the parents themselves. Since parents are always parallel relatives for ego,

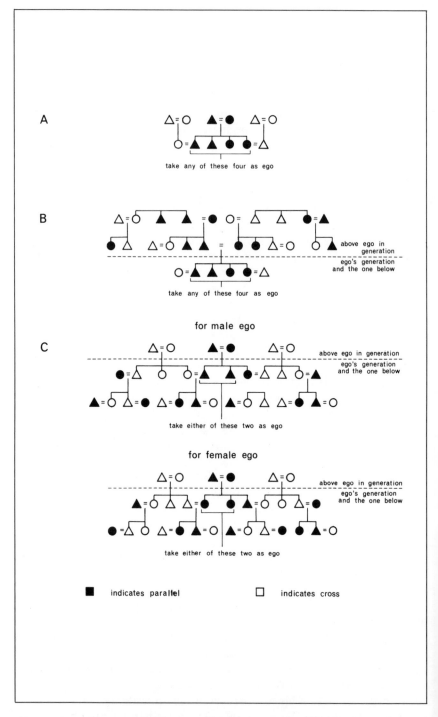

Fig. 5.2. Genealogical illustrations of cross–parallel distinctions.

then this will make his parents' opposite-sex siblings (that is, his MB and his FZ) relations in the cross category.[17] Extending this rule, one finds that in senior generations the partners to any marriage are always classified in the same category, while opposite-sex siblings are assigned to the opposite one. Furthermore, male children are placed in the same category as that of their parents, while female children belong to the opposite category to that of their parents.

This logic, it is important to note, becomes inverted in ego's own generation and the one just below. Here ego will always classify his siblings as his parallel relatives, whatever their sex, while he will always think of his spouse as a member of the opposite or cross category. Generalizing on this, any ego will classify all sibling pairs, of whatever sex or sexes, in his own generation and the one just below it as members of one group; and all marriage partners will necessarily fall into the category opposite to that of their respective spouses. Finally, ego classifies each member of his own generation and the one below as belonging to the same category as that person's parent who was or is of ego's own sex.

Hence the Tamil speakers' cross-parallel logic has an egocentric quality. Only where this terminological system is combined with a moiety organization at the clan level, as is the case for some subcastes, does such a classification of the kin universe into two halves for any one ego match the classification of that same universe for a number of related speakers of different sexes and generations. This logic, as I have come to understand it, is given here in the form of a list of rules for the sake of reference. The reader may want to compare this list with an illustration of the same logic provided by Figure 5.2.

Rules of Terminological Classification

(1) Rules for classifying relatives who are of the two generations immediately above ego (see (b) in Figure 5.2):
   (a) Marriage joins two people of the same category.
   (b) Males are classified in the same category as their fathers; females in the category opposite that of their fathers.
   (c) Opposite-sex siblings always belong to opposite categories, and same-sex siblings to the same category.

(2) Rules for classifying relatives who are of the same generation as ego, or of the first one below (see (c) in Figure 5.2):
   (a) Marriage joins two people of opposite categories.
   (b) Children are classified in the same category as that parent who bears the same sex as ego.
   (c) All children in a sibling set belong to the same category.

---

[17]As pointed out in chapter 3, n. 35, kinship terms are coded as follows: B (brother), D (daughter), F (father), H (husband), M (mother), S (son), W (wife), and Z (sister). This code is used in the diagrams discussed here, and throughout this section on Tamil kin terminology.

Each of the rules just listed requires a point of reference, as all of them are couched in terms of same or opposite only. The classification of any relative, therefore, rests on his or her relationship to another member of ego's kin network whose classification is already known. Ultimately, this will be a member of ego's family of origin. Starting from there, a person can carry the cross-parallel classification along his kin network, following these rules, until he reaches the unclassified relative in question. This person can then be categorized with reference to that particular spouse, parent, sibling, or child who serves to link him with other known relatives. Even if relatives of very senior generations (for example, FFZ and FFM) are not themselves classified as cross or parallel by the Tamil terminology, in using the logic described, links through such persons may be needed in order to calculate the categorical membership of some distant relative in ego's own generation.

This exercise in logic, which any Tamil speaker now and then performs, is not just academic. Ego must discover, upon meeting a distant kinsman, whether he belongs to the cross or the parallel category in order to ascertain how to act in his presence. Each time he meets a new member of his kin network, he must ascertain this fundamental detail in order to determine whether joking and flirtation, appropriate with cross relatives, or a reserved and respectful demeanor, appropriate with parallel relatives, will constitute the correct way to behave in his or her presence. Only with ego's grandchildren, and sometimes with his grandparents, is this cross-parallel distinction allowed to lapse. Here the generational distinction is so marked that it takes precedence over all else in defining appropriate behavior: indulgence on the part of the grandparent and affection mingled with respect on the part of the grandchild.

Once the category of a relative of a particular generation has been determined, the selection of a specific kin term to refer to him is not at all difficult. In each generation there is usually only one term for the parallel and the cross relatives of each sex.[18] For parallel relatives in senior generations, a simple modifier—*periya* ("big"), or *cinna* ("little")—is added to the basic term to indicate whether a person is older or younger relative to ego's own parent or grandparent of the same sex. Once the basic logic of the cross-parallel contrast has been grasped, the Tamil kin terminology is one of the simplest of all classificatory kin systems to employ.

It is important to clarify further the unusual position of women in this conceptual scheme. Unlike men, who are always classified in the same category as their fathers, women who are above ego in generation are classified in the category opposite to that of their fathers. Or viewed in another way, parallel women of senior generations produce parallel chil-

[18]There are some slight variations in this matter from caste to caste. Some of these are outlined later.

dren, while parallel women in ego's own generation or below produce children who belong to the cross category. This difference between women of senior and junior generations is so important that I have tried to illustrate the situation with a further figure. In the first column of Figure 5.3, I have classified women according to their generation and their sibling or marital tie to men of ego's own descent line. The terms in the first column are used for the sisters of parallel males, those in the second for wives of parallel males, those in the third for sisters of cross males, and so forth. Note that a "sister" is the equivalent of a wife of a cross male, and vice versa.

Now consider the shading in Figure 5.3. All the terms for "parallel" women have been shaded to contrast with the terms for "cross" women. Assume that the left half of the diagram constitutes one extended household containing four generations of parallel males, their sisters, and their wives. Hold this "household" composition constant and consider the three smaller diagrams in Figure 5.4. These represent the composition of the women of the household from the point of view of these several generations of males. Note that the pattern of cross-parallel contrasts always reverses between the generation into which the man viewing the system was born, and the generation into which his parents were born. The categories used by the father for women in his generation are reversed by his son. This makes very good sense when one remembers the obvious: a woman must be a "cross" relative in the eyes of her husband, but she will always be a "parallel" relative and a mother to her sons.[19]

Despite the importance of the cross and parallel categories in Tamil, these remain essentially unnamed groupings for the speakers themselves. The terms "cross" and "parallel," therefore, are not direct translations of particular Tamil words. They are simply a convenient way of characterizing this pervasive opposition for the purposes of explanation and discussion. We know that the categories exist; for they are the only reasonable way to explain the classification of a large number of relatives in ego's own and adjacent generations under a single four-fold scheme, in which the male-female and cross-parallel distinctions are combined. Extra oppositions, such as that between wife-giver and wife-taker, are introduced by some castes; but this in no way alters the basic cross-parallel contrast employed by all groups.

The best one can do for Tamil equivalents of these parallel and cross categories are the terms *paṅkāLi* and *maccāṉ* respectively. *PaṅkāLi,* from *paṅku* ("to share"), refers to the members of a single male descent group, who share ancestral property rights. It is a term with essentially legal

---

[19]Note the interesting affinity between the term *ammā* ("mother"), and the term *ammāyi* ("mother's mother"). Similarly, there appears to be a certain linguistic association between the term *attai* ("father's sister"), and the term *āttā* ("father's mother").

Generation	Parallel Males'			Cross Males'		
	Sisters	Wives	Sisters	Wives	Sisters	Wives
Father's father	Ammāyi	Āttā	Āttā	Ammāyi		Ammāyi
Father	Attai	Ammā	Ammā	Attai		Attai
Ego	Akkā Taṅkacci	Naṅkayā KoRuntiyā	Naṅkayā KoRuntiyā	Akkā Taṅkacci		Akkā Taṅkacci
Son	MakaL	Marumakal	Marumakal	MakaL		MakaL

Parallel women   Cross women

Fig. 5.3.   Female kin terms for male ego.

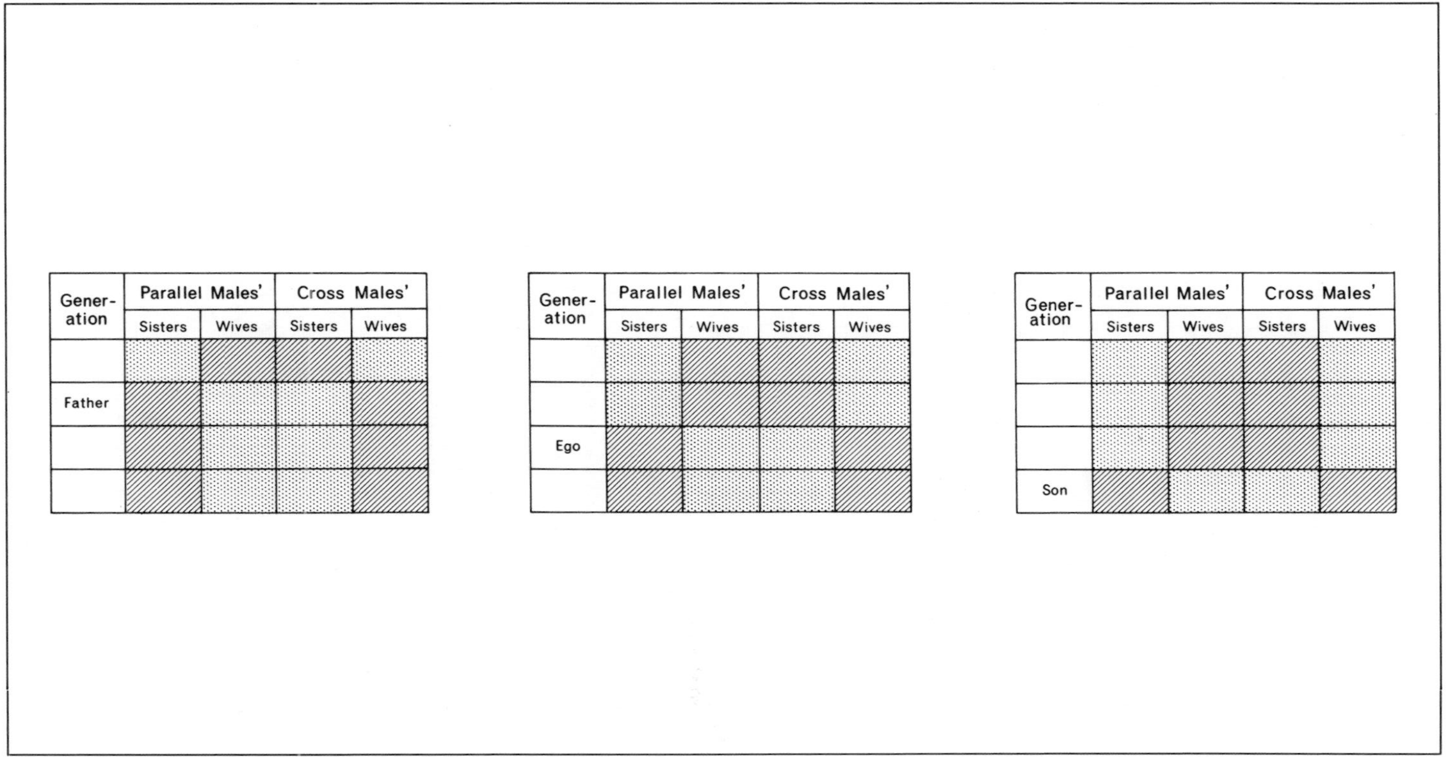

Fig. 5.4. Change in the category of kin terms used to refer to one female by three consecutive generations of males. (Parallel and cross categories are indicated in the same way as in Fig. 5.3.)

connotations. As a label for the category as a whole, its meaning is metaphorical. In the latter sense, it includes the women who "share" in family property, and all others who are not lineally related but who are incorporated following the logic of similarity, for example, as husbands of wives' "sisters."

Maccān, in contrast to *paṅkāLi*, is a word with a heavy sexual connotation. It is an unsophisticated form of *maittuṉaṉ*, and both words are probably related to the Sanskrit *maithuna*, referring to sexual intercourse.[20] Feminine forms, among others, are *maccini* and *maittuṉi*. As extended to the category described, *maccāṉ* carries the implication of sexual license, and refers to those whom ego and his parallel relatives may marry. The term for a son-in-law and for all who are potentially sons-in-law is also interesting. It is constructed out of the term *makaṉ* ("son") and the verb stem *maṟu* (" to change"). Thus a *marumakaṉ* is literally a "changed son" or a son-like person of the opposite category. The same holds true with the term for "daughter-in-law."[21]

The test of this procedure of cross-parallel classification just described arises in situations in which the genealogical connection between ego and the girl in question is not precisely known. How extensive the search for a common relative may be varies with the party concerned. Usually the inquiry is carried further on the father's side than on the mother's. Furthermore, since the place where ego's FF resided is generally known, the most important question is usually whether the girl's FF, or indeed any of her direct male ancestors, have come from the same village. If the answer is "yes," then a parallel relationship will be suspected. Any suspicion of a parallel relationship, unless contradicted by concrete evidence, will most usually rule out the prospects of a marriage contract. It may be concluded that there is evidence here of a culturally defined fear that associates overlooking such a lineal connection with the sanctioning of an incestuous relationship. Vague doubts are enough to break off most marriage negotiations. Ignorance of any connection, however, does entitle a girl to classification in the cross category.

It is impossible to obtain figures on how many people have actually married without an exact knowledge of the previous genealogical connections that may link them to their prospective spouse. Many informants simply claim that they married *tūratta contam*, or a distant relation. Others say that their wife was *contam illai*, that there was no relationship at all

---

[20]In chapter 3, I mentioned that male members of subcastes of the right division often address men of similar standing in the left bloc with the term *maccāṉ*. Between men, the term has a sense of playfulness about it, but women use it with some embarrassment, particularly if they are unmarried.

[21]This was pointed out to me by my assistant, Thomas Storm IV. Though I have known these two words for years, the obvious interpretation had never occurred to me.

prior to the marriage. Whether the parents of these people knew something more at the time the wedding was arranged is always difficult to ascertain. My general impression is that quite a large number of people do marry genealogically unrelated women, as long as both families claim membership in the same endogamous subcaste. Probably the percentage of such marriages is gradually rising, as travel becomes increasingly easy.[22]

The logic of the cross-parallel distinction is of particular importance when the issue of potential marriage partners is raised. Only women who stand in the cross relationship are potential mates, while all relatives of the opposite sex who fall into the parallel category are, in principle, to be excluded from consideration. The only castes to apply this rule consistently, however, are the Brahmans, the PiLLai, and two high-ranking groups of the left, the KōmuTTi CeTTiyār and the CōLi Ācāri. The Koṅku KavuNTar community, by contrast, deviates more radically from these terminological guidelines than any other subcaste in the region. For this dominant, landed group, it is clan membership, rather than the niceties of the cross-parallel terminology, that ultimately distinguishes marriageable from unmarriageable relations. Thus a man may marry any woman whose father was not a member of his own clan group. Such a definition includes many women (for example, the MBWBD) who are classified as parallel relatives by the terminology. Nevertheless, it would not be correct to suggest that KavuNTars seek out "terminologically wrong," or terminologically parallel, marriage partners. Their concern, rather, is with finding an economically suitable partner, generally one who is wealthy and/or able to work. If a woman is suitable for such practical reasons, and is not the daughter of a fellow clansman, then other fine points may be overlooked. The more closely a woman is related to a man's own mother, however, the stronger the economic motivation has to be in order to justify ignoring this imperfection. Marriage with a MMZDD is commonplace.[23] Marriage with a MZD is less frequent, and with an actual MZ it is very rare, although I have recorded a few.[24]

Other right-division communities are influenced by the KavuNTars' practical attitude in this matter, but are somewhat more resistant to these radical or terminologically "wrong" marriages than KavuNTars themselves. The NāTār are the second most lenient, while the ritual service

---

[22]A rough estimate of the percentage of people of all castes who currently marry women to whom no clear genealogical connection can be traced would be ten to fifteen per cent. This figure is an estimate derived from my genealogies for marriages in rural areas.

[23]Also included in the commonplace category would be marriage with such relatives as a FZSWZ, a MBWBD, or a FBWZ.

[24]I collected two examples of this latter type of marriage in the Kannapuram kirāmam area. Both were highly disapproved of by the general residents of the community, but were allowed to pass because it was understood that the match had been arranged for financial reasons. One can find similar examples of FW_2Z (father's second wife's sister) marriage.

groups of the right are somewhat more scrupulous in this matter than either of the preceding two groups. The lower-ranking left-division communities, excluding untouchables, are similar to these right-division ritual service groups; that is, they are less rigid than the vegetarian communities, which include the Brahmans, PiLLais, CeTTiyārs, and CōLi Ācāris, but less casual than KavuNTars and NāTārs. These general contrasts are recorded in Table 5.3.

The untouchable subcastes of the left division supply the third distinct approach to marriage rules. In a sense, they extend both the right and left variations shown in Table 5.3 to their logical meeting point. Among the VēTar, Kuṟavar, and the four subcastes of Mātāri where I made inquiries, male descent groups were always described as belonging to one of two over-arching exogamous groupings.[25] These moieties were never named, however. In each case, the description given by informants is similar. All the clans in the endogamous group are either "brothers" to ego's own clan, or one of a series of "brother" clans in the opposite (cross) moiety. Clans with "brother" status cannot marry among themselves. Each division must marry women from the other. Exogamy by clan groups makes the marriage rules of a group completely consistent with the categories of the kin terminology. Since each moiety contains all the relatives who are terminologically "cross" to members of the other who are of ego's own generation or below, there is little chance that a "confusing" marriage will occur.[26]

What is most interesting about the variations in the number of terminologically confusing marriages a subcaste will allow, is that permissibleness is so highly associated with the variable strength of clan groupings as discussed in chapter 2, pp. 78–108. Of the touchable castes, KavuNTars and NāTārs have the most highly developed clan organization. They are also the groups that are most permissive in this matter of terminologically incorrect marriages. Brahmans, PiLLais, and high-ranking left-division groups have the weakest clan organization and the strongest prohibitions on these unusual marriages. Other touchable groups, all of middling social rank, fall between the extremes on both counts. Of the untouchables, the right Paṟaiyar follow their own division superiors closely. The left-division untouchables, by contrast, have their own rules for marriage arrangements. These groups, like the right-division leaders, have strong clan groupings. Their moiety solution to sexual eligibility is, in a sense, the

---

[25]Some of the organizational features of these groups have already been discussed in chapter 2.

[26]With the exception of ZD marriage, of course, which is common to all castes of the Koṅku area. Sister's daughter unions confuse the generational distinctions but do not alter cross-parallel categories.

TABLE 5.3
MARRIAGES ALLOWED WITH TERMINOLOGICALLY PARALLEL RELATIVES
(by subcaste)

Subcaste Name	Marriages Allowed
Neutral Division:	
Aiyar Brahman	ZD
KaruNĩkar PiLLai	ZD
Right Division:	
Koṅku KavuNTar	ZD, MMZDD, MZD (and even MZ)
OkaccāNTi PaNTāram	ZD, MMZDD
Koṅku UTaiyār	ZD, MMZDD
Maramēri NāTār	ZD, MMZDD, MZD
Koṅku VaNNār	ZD, MMZDD
Koṅku Nāvitar	ZD, MMZDD
Koṅku Paraiyar	ZD, MMZDD
Left Division:	
Koṅku Ācāri	ZD, MMZDD
Kaikkōlar Mutaliyār	ZD, MMZDD
VaTuka Nāyakkar	ZD, MMZDD
VaTuka VaNNār	ZD, MMZDD
PāNTiya Nāvitar	ZD, MMZDD
VēTar[f]	ZD
KūTai Kuravar	ZD
Teluṅku, Āṉappu, ToTTi, Moracu Mātāri	ZD

NOTES: This table represents an approximation, as gathered from discussions with subcaste members and examples collected in my genealogies. As no caste brags about these exceptions, and as the "rules" are not formally stated, there seems to be no more exacting way to collect information on the matter. With MMZDD I include such marriages as FZSWZ and MBWBD.
[f]I include the VēTar here as I have information on this particular topic for them. They are not considered in much of the other comparative discussion, however, for lack of data.

perfect compromise with left-division attitudes. By raising the cross-parallel distinction to the level of the subcaste as a whole, it makes descent-group exogamy the primary criterion of marriageability without causing terminological confusion. With this arrangement, the terminological system is no longer relative to a particular individual; for the same marriageable and non-marriageable alignments exist for all members.

The primacy of descent-group exogamy as the factor responsible for permitting terminological inconsistencies among the touchable communities can be deduced, in part, from an examination of how such confusions are resolved when they do arise. Figure 5.5 presents a set of hypothetical genealogies illustrating the types of confusion that can occur, with a key indicating how the terminological problem is settled in each case. Note that each resolution requires a choice between conflicting terms, each of which would be equally accurate according to the "rules" provided earlier. From the choices, further "rules of priority" can be abstracted that indicate which relationships are considered primary or, from another perspective, which relationships it is most dangerous to overlook.

FIGURE 5.5

Four Examples of Specific Terminological Conflicts
and Their Resolution

Example 1:

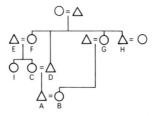

For A, F	=	MM (not FZ)	For E, D	=	WB (not DH)
G	=	MMZ (not WM)	For H, C	=	BW (not ZD)
For D, E	=	WF (not ZH)	For I, C	=	ZH (not MB)
I	=	WZ (not ZD)			

NOTE: Since E calls D *maccān*, D may reciprocate with *maccān* rather than with *māmā*. The latter term is preferred, however, as the more respectful.

Example 2:

For A, B = HFB (not ZH)   For B, A = WZ (not BSW)

Example 3:

For A, B = *FM* (not WM or MM) For F, G = Z   (not HM)
      C = WB   (not MB)   H = HF   (not ZH)
      D = *FF*   (not WF or MF)   I = ZD* (not HZ)
      E = WBS (not MBS)

*This is a parallel term for a female speaker.

FIGURE 5.5 *Continued*

Example 4:

For A, B = *FM* (not MZ or HM)   For E, F = *FM* (not MZ or WM)
     C = *FF* (not MZH or HF)   G = *FF* (not MZH or WF)
     D = MZD (not HZ)   H = MZS (not WB)

NOTE: The terms given in italics in examples 3 and 4 are "invented" by the speaker to circumvent an awkward choice. They do not designate an actual relationship.

From these examples in Figure 5.5 the following order of priorities can be extracted:

Parallel grandparental term	Other parallel term	Cross term by ego's marriage	Cross term by another marriage in ego's generation or below	Cross term by a marriage in a senior generation
0	1	2	3	4

When two or more possible kin terms may be applied to a relative, the term belonging to a category further to the left will take precedence over one belonging to a category further to the right.[27] If more than one possibility exists within any one category, then the more respectful term, the one which indicates greater age relative to ego, will be selected. This final qualification would seem to make category 1 unnecessary. I have retained it because in cases of cross-parallel conflict in the possible terms for a spouse's parents, ego will "invent" a grandparental term to circumvent the difficulty.

Grandparental terms are interesting for another reason as well. Earlier

[27]These same rules seem to be consistent with the data reported by William McCormack in his article, "Sister's Daughter Marriage in a Mysore Village," *Man in India* 38, no. 1 (1958): 34–48. Emeneau reports material that gives "an untraceable relationship through a matrilineal sib" precedence. See M. B. Emeneau, "Language and Social Forms: A Study of Toda Kinship Terms and Dual Descent," in Leslie Spier, ed., *Language, Culture and Personality* (Wisconsin: Sapir Memorial Publication Fund, 1941), pp. 158–79. This question should be investigated further, as it suggests that for some groups, a further category referring to clan or descent-group membership should be inserted between nos. 0 and 1 in the order of priorities.

commentators on the terminology have suggested that there is no cross-parallel contrast at all in the terms for grandparents, just as there is no contrast in the terms for grandchildren.[28] This is true when a person is speaking in a general manner. For most subcastes of the Koṅku area, however, there are additional terms which may be used to distinguish mother's parents (cross) from father's parents (parallel). Since three subcastes that have a very weak clan organization (the Aiyar Brahman, Karu-Nīkar PiLLai, and CōLi Ācāri subcastes) were the only ones that did not report the presence of specific MF and MM terms, it is likely that the development of this contrast is correlated with the development of clan organization more generally.[29] But it may be that the contrast is entirely absent in areas outside Koṅku. If so, the relative emphasis on the detailed classification of grandparents in Koṅku is probably associated with the general importance given to clans in this region.

Turning now to the larger implications of the rules of priority, it is clear that there is a consistent concern with avoiding the use of cross terms, implying marriageability, for anyone to whom ego can trace a parallel relationship. The first rule of priority, therefore, avoids the possibility that one could "forget" a trace of parallel descent by opting for a cross term. The second rule avoids overlooking the closer or more recent relationship for one of longer standing. When we remember that many subcastes allow marriages with terminologically parallel relatives, as long as ties of common clanship are not transgressed, a clear pattern emerges. Parallel terms are given great importance when descent-group membership is weak or absent. Parallel terms may be ignored in marriage arrangement only when a concern for avoiding a common descent-group name takes their place. These two seem to serve as complementary guarantees against the possibility of inadvertent incest.[30] In more general terms, therefore, concern with exogamy does not appear to be entirely absent in the Dravidian kinship system, as some people have previously argued.[31]

---

[28]The term for grandson in Tamil is *pēraṉ,* and for granddaughter, *pētti.* The generalized terms for grandparents are probably related: they are *pāTTaṉ* ("grandfather") and *pāTTi* ("grandmother"). Children are traditionally named after grandparents, as the term *pēraṉ* ("one who bears the name") suggests.

[29]Dumont has recorded the contrast but underemphasized it in his general analysis. Louis Dumont, *Une Sous-Caste de l'Inde du Sud* (Paris: Mouton, 1957), pp. 277–80.

[30]It is interesting to note that even in the highly cosmopolitan setting of Colombo, rules of prohibition remain prominent, while "positive rules" (as the preference for cross-cousin marriages has been described) are greatly attenuated. See Nur Yalman, *Under the Bo Tree* (Berkeley: University of California Press, 1967), p. 222. Elsewhere in the South, where *kiLai,* or female exogamous units, occur, these take a similar precedence over the terminological categories in matters of marriage. See Louis Dumont, *Hierarchy and Marriage Alliance in South Indian Kinship,* Occasional Papers of the Royal Anthropological Institute, no. 12 (London, 1957), p. 28.

[31]Yalman, *Under the Bo Tree,* p. 337.

The other important observation to be made from the examples of conflicts in the kin terminology described is the ease with which usages slip across generational lines. In the Koṅku region, a child of either sex may refer to its mother's husband as *aNNan* (elder B), *appā* (F), or even as *aiyā* (FF), according to the age difference and the degree of intimacy that exists between the child and the man concerned. As a result, one cannot establish who in a household is a man's exact genealogical father simply by listening to conversation. Although *aNNan* is now thought to be an old-fashioned way to address or refer to a father, one can still hear it used spontaneously in ŌlappāLaiyam by children of modest, unsophisticated families. Interestingly enough, there is no similar "slippage" associated with the terms for mother and sister.

A father, when addressed as "elder brother" by his children, does not reciprocate by using a term for younger B or younger Z, at least not in the Kāṅkayam area. This might be explained by the fact that it is the general rule to refer to all relatives who are younger than oneself in age by name. However, in the Pollachi area, in the western extreme of Koṅku, fathers often refer to their sons as *appan* ("father," informal) and to daughters as *ammiNi* (a diminutive of *ammā*, "mother"). Despite some variation within Koṅku, the widespread disregard for generational distinctions within the nuclear family indicates the lack of emphasis on this aspect of the terminology as a whole. Perhaps such usage occurs only in those regions of South India where cross-generational marriage is frequent and generally approved. In Koṅku the simultaneous presence of both features is at least consistent.

TABLE 5.4
CROSS-GENERATION SLIPPAGE IN KIN TERMS

Generation	Parallel-Category Terms		Cross-Category Terms	
	Male	Female	Male	Female
Father's Father	Aiyā	Āttā	[Appucci	[Ammāyi
Father	Appā	Ammā	⊢ Māman	⊢ Attai
Ego elder	ANNan	Akkā	∟ Maccān	∟ Naṅkayā
Ego younger	Tampi	Taṅkacci	[MāpiLLai	[KoRuntiyā
Son	[Makan	[MakaL	⊢ Marumakan	⊢ MarumakaL
Son's Son	∟ Pēran	∟ Pētti	∟ Pēran	∟ Pētti

NOTES:
[Indicates "slippage" in accordance with general usage.
⎰ Indicates further "slippage" necessarily resulting from certain types of cross-generation marriages.

One or two further details in terminological differences among subcastes illustrate the same pattern of right-left contrasts described earlier. These variations appear in Table 5.5.

In the terms for clan, as shown in Table 5.5, the Brahmans and PiLLais use the traditional Sanskrit *kōttiram* and three of the highest-ranking left-division subcastes follow their example.[32] The leading right-division groups counter this with a quite different term, *kulam.* Thus, as in so many other respects, one finds the higher-ranking left groups following the

TABLE 5.5
DIFFERENCES IN KIN TERMINOLOGY
(by subcaste)

Subcaste Name	Term for Clan	Presence or Absence of Equivalence Between		
		FZH-MB FZ-MBW	FZS-MBS FZD-MBD	FF-MF FM-MM
Neutral Division:				
Aiyar Brahman	kōttiram	≠	≠	=
KaruNĩkar PiLLai	kōttiram	≠	≠	=
Right Division:				
Koṅku KavuNTar	kulam	=	=	≠
OkaccāNTi PaNTāram	nāTu	=	=	≠
Koṅku UTaiyār	nāTu	=	=	≠
Maramēri NāTār	kulam*	=	=	≠
Koṅku VaNNār†	nāTu	=	=	≠
Koṅku Nāvitar	nāTu	=	=	≠
Koṅku Paraiyar	nāTu	=	=	≠
Left Division:				
CōLi Ācāri	kōttiram	=	=	=
KōmuTTi CeTTiyār	kōttiram	≠ (?)	=	≠
Koṅku Ācāri	kōttiram	=	=	≠
Kaikkōlar Mutaliyār	kūTTam	=	=	= (?)
VaTuka Nāyakkar	kūTTam	=	=	≠
VaTuka VaNNār	nāTu	=	=	≠
PāNTiya Nāvitar†	nāTu	=	=	≠
Kuravar	kūTTam	=	=	≠
ToTTi Mātāri‡	kūTTam	=	=	≠

NOTES:
=   Equivalent. The two terms are the same.
≠   Not equivalent. The two terms are not the same.
(?) Some informants showed a tendency to slide over this detail and merge with the dominant pattern. In each case, however, at least one person indicated that the difference existed.
*   In one or two cases, I recorded *kūTTam* for this subcaste. Hardgrave, however, has recorded a general usage of the term *kūTTam* among NāTārs in Tirunelvelly. Since many NāTārs claim that they have migrated north into Koṅku from this area, one might speculate that certain changes have gradually come about in their kin terminology in the latter region as a result of KavuNTar emulation. See Robert Hardgrave, *The Nadars of Tamilnad* (Berkeley: University of California Press, 1969), p. 38.
†   I do not have precise information on these groups, but presume that they follow the dominant pattern.
‡   I do not have information on these particular details for the Telugu Mātāri, the group I refer to in most of the other tables.

Brahman custom, and the higher-ranking right groups rigorously up-holding a contrasting custom. The other right-division subcastes, all service groups, use a territorial term, *nāTu,* which seems to be derived from

---

[32]Use of the term *kōttiram* (*gotra* in Sanskrit), however, does not mean that these groups follow the elaborate rules of avoidance described in the Sanskrit texts (for example, the prohibition against marrying kōttiram members with whom there is a connection within the previous seven generations, and the prohibition against marrying a woman whose MB's kōttiram is the same as that of ego's MB). All these groups employ in practice the simple reasoning about cross and parallel relatives already described.

an old-fashioned KavuNTar usage.[33] Two left-division service groups, barbers and washermen, may also follow this pattern. The rest of the left division uses a fourth term, *kūTTam*. This is a word used by Brahmans elsewhere in the South for descent groupings.[34] This finding upholds the general pattern of imitation, rather than defiance, of Brahman behavior by the communities of the left division.

Finally, Table 5.5 illustrates a few differences in the extent to which the basic kin terms are elaborated for certain relatives. All the right-division communities, for example, make a distinction between the maternal and paternal grandparents, emphasizing the fact that these two sets of kinsmen belong to different descent groups. The Brahmans and one, or perhaps two, high-ranking left-division groups, by contrast, do not make this distinction in their terminology. This practice reflects their greatly reduced emphasis on descent divisions in general. In the same way, the Brahman and PiLLai custom of distinguishing the wife-giving relatives (MB and MBS) from wife-taking relatives (FZH and FZS) corresponds to their special concern with the bride's father as a dowry-provider. The use of separate terms enables these groups to give the "takers" more respect and the "givers" less.[35] One high-ranking left-division caste appears to imitate this pattern, while all the right-division groups ignore it.

These contrasts in the details of the kinship terminology of different castes serve simply to reinforce the general pattern of right-left differences already well established on other grounds. These contrasts will be examined now as they relate to actual marriage arrangement.

PRACTICAL CONSIDERATIONS IN MARRIAGE ARRANGEMENT

Weddings are occasions of great pomp and show. They often represent the largest single expense of a lifetime. People are frequently willing to sell land or to go into debt in order to celebrate a marriage in a fashion that they consider appropriate to their station in life. Conducting all the essential ceremonies requires about twenty-four hours nowadays, but used to take up to five days in the past. Inviting and feeding a huge crowd of guests plays a significant role, and important people are always flooded with more invitations to weddings than they can possibly accept. It is not necessary to know a guest with high prestige personally. The mere fact

---

[33]KavuNTars used to be exogamous by nāTu area, according to folk tradition, and have only changed over to the present system some few hundred years ago. (See chapter 3 for details.)

[34]E. Kathleen Gough, "Brahman Kinship in a Tamil Village," *American Anthropologist* 58 (1956): 829.

[35]Informants from these communities openly say that the FZH should be given extra respect, while the MB is ever so slightly inferior. See Appendix F for a full list of kin terms for the subcastes in question. Also see my discussion of this topic in the Introduction, p. 13.

that he takes the trouble to attend and that he accepts food at the wedding feast generally enhances the status of the host.

The amount of the dowry, the number of expensive saris the bride can display, and the amount of pure gold, or even diamonds, in her ornaments, are topics of comment among the wedding guests. The very wealthy go to great lengths to entertain with well-known musicians and dancers brought from far-away places. Perhaps the scale of grand weddings has increased in recent years, but this merely measures the increased wealth of the groups which participate. The prevalence of grand weddings illustrates an old theme: marriage confirms in one event both the ritual and the economic status of the family which celebrates it.

There is no shortage of marriageable women in the Koṅku region. Most people agree that brides are readily available and that men of all castes are in a good bargaining position. The reasons underlying this perception of a disparity in the proportionate representation of the two sexes are probably complex. A very large male-female differential does not actually show up in my genealogies or census counts. It is true that a few men migrate to the towns and marry girls they meet there, but this trend is still negligible in the Kāṅkayam area. The fact that girls marry younger than men is more persuasive. They are considered to be eligible as brides at puberty, although many wait several years, perhaps until they are sixteen or seventeen. Men often do not marry until they are in their twenties.

Unmarried young women are noticed and are the subject of comment and gossip. If they wait too long their respectability and reputation are considered to be in danger. Men, however, can easily remain unmarried until their late twenties. The economic burden of marriage also falls more heavily on men and sons of poor families are reluctant to commit themselves to having more mouths to feed. Women without nursing children can more or less support themselves by agricultural labor and various other manual jobs. Nevertheless, in the long run, a man is taking on a greater financial burden by marrying, while the family of the girl he marries is lightening its burden. All these considerations lead, it seems, to a perception on the part of informants that there is an abundance of marriageable women.

The distance to which families go in their search for brides is some indication of their availability, if the various considerations determining choice already discussed are taken into account. Of a sample of 200 marriages, only 6 per cent were between residents of the same settlement. This does not imply any aversion to marrying within one's own residential area, but rather that considerations of family wealth, respectability, and the character of the girl often outweigh the convenience of immediate proximity. In most cases, there is simply not a wide enough choice of girls of suitable age and family within a man's own village.

The same consideration applies to the distances that people will go to marry. Subcastes that have large populations in any one settlement also tend to be populous in nearby hamlets. Thus, it is natural for members of small communities to have immediate marriage connections over a wider region than do members of larger groups. It is also true, however, that the subcastes that are closely tied to the land prefer to reinforce their local position by selecting brides whose families reside within walking distance. The closer to each other two families reside, the more they will be able to cooperate to maintain their local rights and privileges.

An impression of the varying distances to which members of different communities go in search of a spouse can be gained from the analysis in Table 5.6. Only subcastes for which the sample size was five or more have been included. From the figures, it is possible to make several interesting generalizations. First, the two relatively high-ranking land-tied communities of the right division tend to find their spouses within a five-mile

TABLE 5.6
MARRIAGE-DISTANCE ANALYSIS
(by subcaste)

Subcaste Name	Percentage of Intra-settlement Marriages	Average Marriage Distance (miles)	Percentage of Marriages Contracted Over 20 Miles Away	Sample Size
Neutral Division:				
Aiyar Brahman	0.0	20	40.0	5
Right Division:				
Koṅku KavuNTar	4.0	4–5	4.0	116
OkaccāNTi PaNTāram	0.0	12	55.0	7
Koṅku UTaiyār	0.0	20	60.0	10
Maramēri NāTār	18.0	5	0.0	11
Left Division:				
CōLi and Koṅku Ācāri	7.0	20	65.0	16
Kaikkōlar Mutaliyār	30.0	15	50.0	10
Koṅku Nāyakkar	7.0	12	40.0	16
Incomplete Data				
Others*	. . .	. . .	. . .	9
Average for all subcastes	6.0	10	20.0	
Total				200

NOTES: This table includes all extant unions in ŌlappāLaiyam in 1965 where at least one partner to the marriage was still living, plus the marriages of the children of these couples, regardless of where they resided. It includes separations. (No formal divorces had occurred.) No distinction between first and second marriages was necessary, since no true polygamy was discovered. In one case, where a man's first wife turned out to be feeble-minded, she was sent home and he later married her younger sister. In this situation, the latter marriage was counted as the extant union, even though the first wife was still alive. The sample defined is considerably smaller than that used in the tables that follow. This is so because my data on marriage distance and type of residence are incomplete for a more inclusive group. It is also a different sample from that described in Table 5.1. Distance is defined by measuring the shortest practicable road or path between two settlements.
*These include the KaruNīkar PiLLai, KōmuTTi CeTTiyār, Nāvitar, and VaNNār groups. Sample sizes were too small to have any individual significance.

radius of their own residence. Both these subcastes have a high local population density, and both have a strong interest in reinforcing their claims to local territory. The two main service groups of the right division, by contrast, go twelve to twenty miles, on the average, for their spouses. These subcastes have small local populations and their marriage connections extend over a much wider area.

The left-division subcastes for which there are data also show a tendency to go to a considerable distance for their brides. This pattern is consistent with their tendency to give great weight to ritual and status considerations in marriage arrangements. For the higher-ranking groups of the left division, in particular, the average distance at which a spouse is found is between fifteen and twenty miles, while for the lower-ranking Nāyakkar, or well-diggers, it is only twelve. If more data were available, we might find that there is a general tendency for the marriage distance of the left-division communities to decrease with decreasing wealth and prestige. If any generalization can be made about the right, it would be that these groups exhibit an inverse correlation between local power or status and the distance they will go in search of brides.[36] Brahmans, of course, fit the left-division pattern well even though they remain officially above the division.

The most extreme and striking example of tight intermarriage discovered in the course of the present inquiry was among a group of Ceṅkuntam Mutaliyārs who live near Bhavani, in the northeast corner of Koṅku. There are about six hundred of these Mutaliyār families, who are all close relatives and who all live in three Ūr—actually four settlements—lying in a circle with a radius of no more than ten miles.[37] These Mutaliyārs say that they have never married outside these three hamlets within the memory of the oldest living members of their group. I collected and checked genealogies covering about seventy-five marriages made over a period of four generations and found no exceptions to their claim. This is not to say that mismarriages could not have occurred, but they must be very few in number. Only in the past six years have two determined and well-educated members of this group succeeded in marrying women from elsewhere. They did this over extremely strong objections from close relatives.

This example, drawn from the Mutaliyār caste, is interesting for its combination of two factors: territorial proximity and a remarkably tight-knit marriage circle. It is appropriate that such a situation should occur

---

[36]The very wealthy would have to be exempted from this statement, as they also may be forced to search at a distance to find a partner of suitable economic status.

[37]I first learned of this from Informant no. 31. A similar situation may exist for a group of Aiyaṅkār Brahmans who live in the Pollachi area, but I have not had the opportunity to check this in detail.

in this particular community. As has been pointed out before, this is the one group that displays a high degree of ambivalence about its divisional membership. The marriage pattern described is in many ways typical; for here, as in other aspects of their behavior, the Mutaliyār have attempted to "have it both ways," or to take account of both right- and left-division concerns simultaneously.[38] For them, the right's concern with territoriality and the left's concern with a tight-knit marriage community consisting entirely of known relatives have been skillfully combined.

In addition to marriage distance, it is important to consider the type of residence pattern common among the several subcastes of each division. In the question of residence after marriage, all groups express a general preference for the couple to settle with or near the family of the groom. However, the higher-ranking communities of the right are willing to overlook this patrilocal ideology if there are definite economic gains from settling uxorilocally. Leading castes of the left division, by contrast, object strongly to uxorilocal residence. They point out that respect ought to be given by the bride and her family to the groom. When a groom resides uxorilocally, he is reversing this expected pattern by indicating his dependence on his wife's family. Lower subcastes of both divisions are less concerned about these distinctions. At the same time, they are often economically more pressed. Uxorilocal residence among them is fairly frequent.

Specific Examples of Uxorilocal Residence

(1) KavuNTar

Once A owned a little land in his father's village. However, he couldn't make ends meet and, furthermore, there was no large landowner nearby for whom he could work as a day laborer. He went into debt and was then forced to sell his land to cover it. Afterwards he moved to his wife's village. He has now established himself by trading in cattle.

(2) NāTār

B was born some three miles from his present place of residence. However, after his marriage the palmyra palm trees in his natal village began to decline in quality. The quantity of sap which they would yield grew smaller each year. After some time, he moved to his wife's village and began tapping trees there.

---

[38]Stephen Barnett, of Princeton University, has recently completed a study of a KoNTai KaTTi VēLāLar Mutaliyār group in Chingleput. His findings appear to bear out the same conclusion with regard to many other aspects of Mutaliyār behavior. Stephen A. Barnett, "The Structural Position of a South Indian Caste: Kontaikatti Vēlālars in Tamilnadu" (Ph.D. dissertation, Department of Anthropology, University of Chicago, 1970).

(3) Ācāri

C was born some twenty-seven miles from his present place of residence. Soon after his marriage, an astrologer told him that if he continued to live patrilocally his parents would die. Thus he decided to settle neolocally with his wife in the town of Karur. Years later, however, after his parents had died, he decided to move his goldsmith's business to his wife's natal village, where he lives at present.

(4) Nāvitar

D moved to his present place of residence twenty-one years ago. At that time, there was a barber there who was overburdened with work. As this man was getting old and could no longer manage alone, he began looking for a son-in-law who would help him. Finally he found D and offered him his daughter if he would come to live in his natal village and help him out. D agreed. For a while he lived in his father-in-law's house, but later he bought some government land and built his own, separate home. His father-in-law is now deceased.

From these examples, it is clear that there are many types of uxorilocal residence, depending on the point in time at which a man moves to his wife's village and on how close he lives to her home. Table 5.7 provides some information on the frequency of such occurrences, based on a very broad definition: any man who lives in his wife's natal settlement, but not necessarily in her father's house, and who intends to remain there permanently has been included in the "uxorilocal" category. The sample size is too small to draw any solid conclusions but, nonetheless, a general pattern seems to emerge which the collection of more data might support. The two high-ranking, land-tied, right-division communities exhibit a fairly steady rate of uxorilocality consistent with their interest in preserving and expanding local territorial claims. The higher-ranking left-division groups, by contrast, seem to exhibit a preference for neolocality whenever patrilocal residence is impractical. There are probably two reasons for this: first, these communities are more sensitive than their right-division counterparts to the patrilocal ideal set forth in the classical law books; second, their professional interests are often better served by moving to an area where relatives are not present and where, in consequence, there is a greater demand for their skills.

The same right-left pattern is noticeable in the rate of permanent separation of husbands and wives.[39] The high left-division communities would seem to place the most emphasis on remaining together: they have a 3 per cent separation rate. The leading right-division groups, with a 6 per cent separation rate, pay less attention to this ideal. Again there appears to be more concern with classical norms, particularly with feminine subservience

---

[39]Legal divorce is complicated by the fact that most couples never sign a marriage certificate. Such proceedings can also be very expensive. Simple separation is generally accepted and even preferred.

TABLE 5.7

UXORILOCAL AND NEOLOCAL RESIDENCE

(by subcaste)

Subcaste Name	Percentage of Uxorilocal Residence	Percentage of Neolocal Residence	Percentage of Patrilocal Residence	Sample Size
Neutral Division:				
Aiyar Brahman	0.0	0.0	100.0	5
Right Division:				
Koṅku KavuNTar	6.0	6.9	87.1	116
OkaccāNTi PaNTāram	0.0	14.3	85.7	7
Koṅku UTaiyār	0.0	0.0	100.0	10
Maramēri NāTār	27.3	0.0	72.7	11
Left Division:				
Cōli and Koṅku Ācāri	6.2	25.0	68.8	16
Kaikkōlar Mutaliyār	0.0	50.0	50.0	10
Koṅku Nāyakkar	0.0	18.7	81.3	16
Incomplete Data:				
Others	. . .	. . .	. . .	9
Average for all Subcastes	4.9	14.4	80.7	
Total				200

NOTES: The sample referred to here is exactly the same as the one defined and used in Table 5.6 on marriage distance. The term "uxorilocal" refers to intended permanent residence in the same settlement as the wife's parents, but not necessarily in the same house. Likewise, "neolocal" means intended permanent residence in a different settlement from that of either set of parents. The remaining proportion of the populations considered are patrilocal (that is, living in the same settlement as the husband's parents), but again the figures do not necessarily refer to joint residence.

and family unity, among important left-division groups. The orientation is more practical and more egalitarian among corresponding groups of the right. The low-ranking subcastes are more tolerant of separation than the higher castes of either division: they have a 9 per cent separation rate.[40] This pattern is correlated with the relative economic equality of men and women in these groups where the female has a major role as a breadwinner.

Despite the strict surveillance of women, it is difficult to prevent a young girl from having an affair. A child born under such circumstances, or, more commonly, one born to a recognized concubine, is said to belong to the caste of its father. It was often argued, for example, that a son resembles his father in looks. However, the fact that a child remains for so long in its mother's womb and that it later feeds at her breast are arguments people use to stress the connection the child has by blood, and perhaps by internal fluids generally, with the mother. The mother, it seems, therefore, is most closely associated with the ritual status of the child. Her cooking and ceremonial cleaning of the household are associated with the

[40]I refer here to low-ranking touchable groups. Unfortunately, I have no information for untouchables on this point.

purity of the family in general. The child of a widow or of mixed parentage is not really *cuttam* ("clean"), and the implication is that this soiled aspect is transmitted by the mother.

People often refer to children of such circumstances by saying "Atu cuttamāṉa KavuNTar alla," or "That is not a real, clean KavuNTar." It is taken for granted that children of mixed unions will have difficulty in marrying and are likely to make a match with others of a mixed background similar to their own. Wealth, however, can make a difference. By offering the promise of a secure income, or of a large dowry in the case of a girl, people of mixed-caste ancestry sometimes manage to arrange a "good" match with someone of a more respectable descent than their own.

In the Koṅku region, it is traditional that a girl receive a certain share in the family inheritance at the time of her marriage. This share consists of a sufficient number of household pots, clothing, and gold jewelry to allow her to set up a new household at a level similar to that to which she is accustomed. The groom offsets this expenditure on the part of the bride's family by providing a gold marriage necklace and a fixed bride-price called a *paricam*. The bride's family provides the groom's wedding clothes, and the groom's family provides a marriage sari for the bride. The expenses of the actual ceremony and the feeding of guests are more or less equally shared between the two families, at least under the traditional arrangements.

The paricam is a fixed ceremonial sum that is supposed to be a standardized payment required equally of all grooms within any given sub-caste. Most informants know what the present sum is, but in many cases the amount has recently been raised and what was "traditional" is, therefore, a matter of confusion. Current sums vary from about 10-1/4 rupees among some untouchable groups to 72-1/2 rupees for PaNTārams and 101-1/4 rupees for KavuNTars. "Traditional" sums quoted for these three groups varied, but an approximate guess might put them at 1-1/4, 31-1/4, and 51-1/4 rupees respectively.[41] A few informants suggested that the amount could be reduced if the marriage was arranged with one of the particular cross cousins over whom the groom is considered to have a special right.[42] Even this reduction, however, is not general practice.

Only two groups, the Brahmans and the CōLi Ācāri, claim to have no traditionally "fixed" paricam sum. They speak rather of an amount to be decided upon individually by the parties concerned during the wedding arrangements. If the parties agree, the sum need not be paid at all. It is most interesting, therefore, that these groups place the most stress on

---

[41]In a very general way, the amount of the paricam varies according to the general wealth and social status of the community. Odd sums are considered to be auspicious. The extra 1/4 rupee is an indication of "increase" and thus a good omen of future prosperity.

[42]This concept of a "rightful" or *urimai* girl, will be discussed in the following section.

dowry. Dowry in this sense, refers to more than the bride's jewels and household effects. It refers to an actual lump sum of money demanded by the groom from the bride's family. This sum varies in amount with the groom's earning capacity and with his general social status. Dowry, in this sense, can be subject to a great deal of bargaining during the marriage arrangements. The only word that informants knew for this was the Sanskrit term *varataTcanai.* The general household gifts that a girl accepts at her wedding are, more simply, *kuTukka vēNTiya murai,* "that which she has the right to receive."

Many wealthy families are now beginning to adopt the dowry in the sense of a lump sum of money paid by the bride's father to the groom's family. This custom is growing in prestige, although it has not yet greatly affected those who live in the rural areas. Dowry is associated with the classical literary theme of a father making a gift of his virgin daughter, and like the term *varataTcanai,* it is rather foreign to most informants.[43] The concept of dowry, and the importance attached to it by Brahmans and higher-ranking left groups, will be discussed in more detail in the following section, which is concerned with the ritual aspects of marriage.

RITUAL CONSIDERATIONS AND ALLIANCE CLAIMS IN MARRIAGE ARRANGEMENT

The two favorite topics of conversation for speculation and intrigue in Koṅku, are material wealth and marriage, two questions that are closely related. Material considerations of family property and earning power are fundamental to the arrangement of marital unions. As pointed out in the previous section, the marriage ceremony itself is usually the largest, most ostentatious affair a family will ever be called upon to finance. At the same time, however, the concern that marriage should be with close relatives of the "cross" category is persistently expressed, both by parents in arranging matches and in ritual.

For all the castes in Koṅku there is a specific *urimaippeN,* one particular girl whom "a man has a right to marry." All informants agree that this term refers only to a man's actual FZDs or MBDs. There is no conception of *urimai* ("right") in regard to more distant cross cousins or in regard to a ZD. This specific meaning of *urimaippeN* is unaltered by the fact that these others are also very desirable categories for marriage and that, statistically, women of these specifications are even more frequently chosen than

---

[43]It is interesting that it is those very families which are adopting the dowry that are at the same time beginning to refuse *muy* payments at weddings. *Muy* is a gift of a few rupees presented publicly, after the ceremonies, by a male representative of each household who was a guest at the wedding. A record of the gift is kept. The host is then expected to pay a similar or slightly larger sum at the next festival when he becomes the guest, and his previous guest, the host. These payments are an important aid to the host in financing the occasion. Refusal is part of the increased emphasis on the bride's father making the whole occasion part of a important gift for which he alone foots the bill.

the urimai girl herself. Conversely, a girl may refer to her *urimai māppiL-Lai* ("rightful groom"), a FZS or a MBS. However, people say, "āNukku urimai nereya uNTu," or "a man has a very strong right," implying that the woman's claim is less. Thus the question is usually discussed from the male point of view.[44]

The meaning of *urimai* in a ritual context is even more specific. The urimaippeN is either the MBD or the FZD, not both. The variation is by subcaste, as illustrated in Table 5.8, but the MBD right is by far the more common of the two. Furthermore, only one urimai exists for each sibling group as a whole. Once one brother has married a girl of the correct genealogical specification, then the other brothers have no further claim upon other girls in the same category. Some informants say it should be the eldest brother who makes such a marriage and the younger ones who are "free" to marry elsewhere, but no one would argue over this fine point, as long as one of several brothers will consent to take the urimai girl.[45]

Insistence on an urimai marriage is now considered old-fashioned. Few people press such claims today. Most adults, however, at least know the meaning of the term, and consider that urimai was quite important in arranging marriages in the past. The MBD preference is dominant in the Koṅku region—it is the KavuNTar practice—and informants are much clearer about details in this regard than they are about the unusual FZD claim. Nonetheless, I made a special point of inquiring into this claim as well, and there is no doubt that the FZD right is traditional in some communities.

As is the case in many other matters, no marked difference exists between the low subcastes of the right and the low subcastes of the left in the question of the urimai girl. However, there is a certain differentiation between the higher-ranking groups of the two divisions in this regard. The FZD urimai is found only among Brahmans and two higher-ranking communities of the left. Within the group of subcastes that emphasize MBD urimai, a further distinction exists between those which perform a ceremony called the *iNaiccīr* ("uniting ceremony") at their weddings, and those for which the ritual associated with the question of urimai right is

---

[44] *Urimai* can also mean "right" in the sense of an inheritance claim on property. Informants always kept this meaning of the term separate. Nonetheless, claims on a marriage partner and claims to inheritance are not entirely unconnected. See Yalman, *Under the Bo Tree*, p. 133, for emphasis on this association.

[45] In a number of my genealogies, for example, that of Informant no. 20, the eldest sibling of a set has married an immediate cross cousin or a father's sister's daughter, while younger siblings have married women of no known connection. Dumont has described a similar practice among the Pramalai Kallar (Pirāṉmalai KaLLar). He accounts for it as an expression of the emphasis placed on the transmission of an alliance relationship between male lineages through successive generations. See Dumont, *Une Sous-Caste*, pp. 188–96, and also his *Hierarchy and Marriage Alliance*, pp. 23–24.

minimal. All subcastes of the right division, save one, perform the iNaiccīr ritual, while only a single left-division group observes this custom. This group consists of the Kaikkōlar Mutaliyār, who are already familiar for their divisional ambivalence.

The iNaiccīr is a ceremony performed by the groom and his sister, not by the nuptial couple itself. It is one of a group of rituals performed at weddings that emphasize the ties of the groom with his mother and his sisters; that is, the women of his own descent group. During the iNaiccīr, the

TABLE 5.8

CROSS-COUSIN OR URIMAI MARRIAGE RIGHTS

(by subcaste)

Subcaste Name	Marriage Right
Neutral Division:	
Aiyar Brahman	FZD
Aiyaṅkār Brahman	FZD
KaruNīkar PiLLai	MBD
Right Division:	
Koṅku KavuNTar*	MBD
OkaccāNTi PaNTāram*	MBD
Koṅku UTaiyār*	MBD
Maramēri NāTār[1]	MBD
Koṅku Nāvitar*	MBD
Koṅku Paraiyar*	MBD
Left Division:	
CōLi Ācāri	MBD
KōmuTTi CeTTiyār[2]	FZD
VēTTuvar KavuNTar	FZD
Koṅku Ācāri	MBD
Kaikkōlar Mutaliyār*	MBD
VaTuka Nāyakkar	MBD
VaTuka VaNNār	MBD
VēTar	MBD
ToTTi and Moracu Mātāri	MBD

NOTES:
[1] Robert Hardgrave reports a similar NāTār preference in Tirunelvelly. Robert Hardgrave, *The Nadars of Tamilnad* (Berkeley: University of California Press, 1969), p. 36.
[2] I have no information on the KōmuTTi CeTTiyār of other areas of the South, but Thurston's descriptions seem to imply that where they are a right-division subcaste, they have a MBD urimai. See Edgar Thurston, *Castes and Tribes of Southern India*, 7 vols. (Madras: Government Press, 1909), 3:314–33, and 340.
*Subcastes which have the iNaiccīr ritual as part of their marriage ceremony.

sister is understood to make a ritual request for one of her brother's future daughters in marriage for her own son. Thus the ceremony concerns a promise by the groom to his sister about a marriage in the succeeding generation. If the groom does not consent and complete the ritual, then his own marriage cannot proceed. Thus, with each wedding, the promise of a marriage in the succeeding generation has already been given. If a man should marry a second time, however, the iNaiccīr will be omitted.

INaiccīr: A Short Description[46]

The groom is first seated in front of a huge mound of raw, husked rice. His sister comes and stands to his right. The wedding sari, with the bride's *tāli* ("wedding necklace") tied in it, is then placed in a winnowing fan with fruits and other gifts. (Later, the bride will wear this sari for the culminating marriage rituals.) The sister takes this fan and its contents, places it on her head and circles twice, clockwise, the place where the groom is sitting. The contents of the fan are then given to the groom. The sister stands with her feet on the winnowing basket and the groom gives her back the gifts of fruit, which she ties in her apron. He also hands her a few betel leaves and some areca nuts. The wedding sari is then stretched between the sister's hands and the brother's right arm. While the sari is held between them, the brother's hands are placed, cupped together with the palms up, in the center of the huge mound of rice. Several auspicious songs are sung by the barber and then the brother and sister circle the mound of rice together. It is preferred, though not essential, that the sister performing the ritual be unmarried.

This description makes clear how the iNaiccīr emphasizes the tie between a brother and sister. Proper regard for this connection is said to contribute to the prosperity and fertility of the brother's family, and many local folktales recount examples of how a pure and devoted sister can bring strength and good fortune to her brothers, especially if she is a virgin. At the same time, the sister has a claim on her brother's daughter as a wife for her own son. In the ceremony, she ritually requests a part of the fruits of his prosperity, a daughter, for the continuance of her own family through her son's marriage. Everyone I interviewed about the ceremony was explicit in saying that it symbolized such a request. The gift of betel leaves and areca nuts to the sister by her brother is considered to indicate his consent.

Before the brother can marry and turn to the concerns of his new family, the sister's claim must be met. Her well-being is essential to his own prosperity. If at any time in the future she suffers, he must support her, and feed her, if necessary. Should he not fulfill these obligations, the sister can curse him and his family and curtail their prosperity. If, when the time comes for the marriage between the brother's daughter and the sister's son, the brother refuses, then the sister can take an earthen pot full of salt and break it on the door step of her brother's house. Such a curse is considered to rest upon the household forever. It is generally agreed that a sister would not go to this extreme nowadays, but that she would certainly bar her door to her brother and break off all association with him.

Other subcastes which claim the MBD as the urimai girl, but which do not perform the iNaiccīr, have a much simpler—though in some ways

---

[46]This description is taken from my field notes.

The bride and groom of a wealthy KavuNTar family seated before a plate of husked, raw rice topped by betel leaves, areca nut, and a large lump of local palmyra-palm sugar. This plate is symbolic of family prosperity and is a major ritual element in the wedding ceremony.

Another KavuNTar family performing the iNaiccīr ("uniting ceremony"). The wedding sari is stretched between the groom and his sister. He has his hands in the plate of rice and she stands in a winnowing fan. In the ritual he promises to give one of his daughters in marriage to his sister's son.

The completion of the iNaiccīr, where the sister circles the brother, carrying both the winnowing fan and the wedding sari on her head. Also in the fan are other gifts for the bride. The sister carries a pot of sacred water in her right hand and is assisted by two female cross relatives.

similar—ceremony. These groups include all those in Table 5.8 (concerning cross-cousin rights) which have a MBD right, but which do not have an asterisk beside their names. For these subcastes, which for the most part belong to the left division, the sole ceremonial reference to a future marriage between the ZS and the BD takes place after the culminating rituals of the marriage ceremony, rather than before it. This alone may indicate that the emphasis on the urimai right in these castes is not so strong: the brother is already married and thus refusal of the sister's demand does not give her recourse to interrupt the ceremony. Usually, in the case of these groups, the ceremony takes place when the couple attempts to enter the groom's house together for the first time, soon after the major wedding rituals are completed. In this short ceremony, the sister refuses to let the couple enter her father's house until she succeeds in winning a promise from her brother that he will give his future daughter to her son. The two will jest for a moment and then the brother is supposed to consent. The sister then opens the door. For the KaruNīkar PiLLai, a second small game is played in addition to the one just described. In this game, the newly married couple swing a cradle and the sister asks for a doll in it as a bride for her son. Her brother, after some joking, is expected to agree to this request.

During the PiLLai wedding ceremony just described, the groom and his sister sing a particular song together. The text of the song is given here:[47]

> *Groom:* Who closed the door of this great beautiful house? Please open the latch. It is late. I have come.
> *Sister:* Brother, I will open the door if you promise to give your daughter to my son and thus make me happy.
> *Groom:* Sister, I will give you what ever you ask for, there is no question about that, but I will not agree to give my daughter to your son.
> *Sister:* What fault do you find with me? Tell me or I will despair of this world and become an ascetic.
> *Groom:* Your son may spend his time in the homes of prostitutes, and thus lose his land, money, and honor.
> *Sister:* You don't know the fine character of my son. He will never go on that path.
> *Groom:* Your son must be a match for my daughter. I want you to promise this and keep it in mind.
> *Sister:* The handsome man who is the perfect match for the daughter of my brother will be my son.
> *Groom:* Sister, your son is not learned. No one has said that he is a form of wealth for our family.
> *Sister:* He is an ocean of learning, a master of arithmetic, a gentleman, a hero, and a benefactor of poets.

---

[47]In the song a young sister is supposedly addressing her elder brother. The text was supplied by Informant no. 32. The language used is rather archaic, and Dr. E. Annamalai of the University of Chicago provided valuable assistance with the translation.

Groom: If it is so, I will give my dear daughter to your son. How much will you give [as a bride-price]?

Sister: There is no objection to crores of rupees and beautiful gems. These gifts will be given under the wedding canopy you construct.

Groom: I will follow your suggestion, sister, and call in a learned pandit to fix the wedding date. Be happy.

Sister: Oh, my famed brother, adorned with beautiful ornaments. I am pleased at your words and I open the door.

In all the versions of the ritual just described, it is the sister who makes the demand of her brother at his wedding. This can happen years before she herself is married and before the children in question are even born. For the subcastes which speak of the urimaippeN as the FZD, however, a ceremony takes place only when the daughter in question is about to marry another, non-urimai man. In these groups, the priest customarily inquires into the relationship between the bride and groom as part of the wedding ceremony. These questions will be posed to the parents of the couple just before the final preparations to tie the wedding necklace are made. If the groom is not the man with the urimai, the priest will ask the latter to step up to the wedding platform from the audience. The actual groom's father must then pay the urimai man 1-1/4 rupees or 2-1/4 rupees as compensation.[48] After the urimai man has accepted this money, he is honor-bound to let the ceremony proceed.[49]

In this case of the FZD urimai, it should be noted that the person who makes the demand is the BS, and not the groom's sister. Furthermore, he makes this ritual request at the time the girl over whom he had a "right" is actually being married to another man and not years earlier. The man's father, according to this tradition, has no power to curse his sister, as with a pot of salt, if the latter's daughter is married elsewhere. He may only demand a compensation payment for his son. The difference in the ceremony in the two cases suggests that a sister has special powers she can use to curse her brother and to affect adversely his prosperity. The brother has no reciprocal sanction over a perverse sister. The claim is that of his son, and it is made only at the time of the ZD's marriage elsewhere. The FZD ritual, therefore, has a legalistic rather than a supernatural character.

In terms of strict logical operations, Rodney Needham has pointed to the vitally different social consequences of a rigidly enforced rule of marriage with the MBD versus a similarly upheld rule of marriage with the FZD. In both cases the marriage partner must be assumed to be the actual

---

[48]Informants nos. 27 and 52.

[49]Note the parallel with Dumont's description of the *eTTupponpeN*, which may mean, "the girl for which the bride-price is eight gold pieces," in *Une Sous-Caste*, p. 191. See also certain similarities with Yalman, *Under the Bo Tree*, pp. 167, 170, and with E. Kathleen Gough, "Female Initiation Rites on the Malabar Coast," *Journal of the Royal Anthropological Institute* 85 (1955): 59.

cross cousin and not a more distant, terminologically equivalent person.[50] When MBD marriage is stated in this form as a strict rule, then it can be shown to entail a repetitive, one-directional movement from one clan (A) to a second (B). FZD marriage, on the other hand, entails a reversal of the direction of movement in each generation. Here women will travel from clan A to clan B in the first generation, from B to A in the second, and back from A to B in the third. The first situation will create long chains of giving and receiving clans (A→B→C→D, etc.), while the second will cause clans to pair off from others and exchange only among themselves (A⇌B, C⇌D, etc.). When the absolute requirement of marriage to a MBD or FZD is replaced by a ritual statement of preference for one of these two cousins over all other possible brides, the same contrast in exchange patterns can be expected to exist in a milder form.

The major difference between MBD and FZD urimai, therefore, is that the first type of marriage repeats an existing connection between clans or lineage groups. A woman is given in the same direction: she is transfered from one descent group to a second in generation after generation. In the case of Koṅku residents, however, this relationship between groups is always stated to be a right which exists over particular, living kinsmen. I have never heard the urimai rule expressed in terms of an exchange between lineages, nor have I heard the relationship between, say, a FZS and a MBD, described in terms of their descent-group membership.[51]

Claude Lévi-Strauss, the most prominent theorist to discuss the implications of such formal marital preferences, has attempted to predict certain basic structural differences which he argues must develop in groups that express either a strong matrilateral or a strong patrilateral cross-cousin marriage preference without necessarily having a rule which requires marriage with an actual cross cousin of the approved type.[52] Much discussion has ensued from his work, *The Elementary Structures of Kinship*, which was published in 1949 and reissued in 1969, some of it concerned with specifying more precisely the kinds of marriage preferences to which his larger theory could be considered applicable.

Debate continues as to what might constitute the best definition of a unilateral preference from the point of view of the logical demands of Lévi-Strauss' theory. Fortunately, in the Preface to the English transla-

[50]Rodney Needham, *Structure and Sentiment* (Chicago: University of Chicago Press, 1962). This work was intended to be a clarification of Claude Lévi-Strauss, *Les Structures élémentaires de la parenté* (Paris: Presses Universitaires de France, 1949), of which a discussion follows shortly. In this discussion, an English translation is used: Claude Lévi-Strauss, *The Elementary Structures of Kinship*, translated by Bell, Von Sturmer, and Needham, editor, revised ed. (Boston: Beacon Press, 1969).

[51]I am indebted to Harold Scheffler for helping me clarify this important point. For a further discussion of the issue, see Harold W. Scheffler, "*The Elementary Structures of Kinship* by Claude Lévi-Strauss: A Review Article," *American Anthropologist* 72 (1970): 251–68.

[52]Lévi-Strauss, *The Elementary Structures of Kinship*, p. xxxiii.

tion of his work, the author himself has clarified somewhat the types of situations to which he initially intended his predictions to apply. He suggests that he is concerned with the presence of express rules in a society that single out and encourage marriages of a unilateral type, and not with the statistical frequency with which such marriages actually take place in a given group.[53] Lévi-Strauss is further concerned with situations where the actual MBD or FZD is recommended, but where marriages with genealogically distant relatives who have been classified in the same terminological category are also permitted and even encouraged.[54]

The urimai rules that have been described here for the Koṅku area fit both of these specifications nicely. It is therefore appropriate to "test" Lévi-Strauss' prediction in this most interesting case, a situation in which FZD and MBD ritualized preferences occur among different subcastes that live together in the same geographic and cultural region.

Lévi-Strauss makes his theoretical predictions in terms of a polar contrast, both in values and in organization, which he suggests should be observable between societies expressing a FZD preference on the one hand, and a MBD preference on the other. He then suggests that it will be sufficient if the actual social situation observed can be said to be "bent" in the predicted direction.[55] In his predictions, Lévi-Strauss has argued that in the case of a MBD marriage rule: (1) descent and residence will be patrilineal and patrilocal respectively; (2) marriage alliances will form open-ended arcs, within which secondary cycles will tend to develop; and (3) there will be a theoretical stress on equality, but an actual tendency towards anisogamy, leading to inequalities in practice.[56] In the presence of a FZD rule, by contrast, Lévi-Strauss has predicted the following: (1) residence and descent will follow in opposite sex lines; (2) marriage alliances will form closed and very particularized cycles; and (3) the group concerned will be divided into many bits and pieces, and will exhibit only an artificial unity.[57]

Let us now see to what extent the communities that express a MBD urimai rule in the Koṅku area fulfill the predictions. On the first count Lévi-Strauss has clearly predicted correctly; for all these groups follow both patrilineal and patrilocal traditions. Furthermore, if one considers the KavuNTars to provide the strongest case, as they have both the urimai rule and the iNaiccīr, then they go well beyond Lévi-Strauss' prediction in having well-defined and functioning patrilineal clans and lineages which have some practical importance in day-to-day life. In reference to the

---

[53]Ibid.
[54]Ibid., pp. xxx–xxxiii.
[55]Ibid., p. xxxiii.
[56]Ibid., pp. 241, 266. Anisogamy is the general term Lévi-Strauss uses to cover both hypergamy and hypogamy.
[57]Ibid., pp. 352, 441, 445–48.

second point, KavuNTar marriages do tend to create open-ended alliances within which small cycles centered on upwardly mobile families often develop. For example, any Koṅku KavuNTar of wealth could attempt to arrange a marriage between one of his sons and a daughter of one of the four PaTTakkārar, or titled families in Koṅku. In fact, however, these families, as a local elite, have for the most part developed a restricted set of marriage alliances among themselves. As to the third point, finally, the KavuNTars can be said to place more value on equality than many other communities of the area.[58] For example, they allow a most unusual uniformity in life-cycle ceremonies among themselves and their right-division followers. Furthermore, they exhibit a willingness to eat cooked rice from the hands of their more important allies. In doing so, they deviate remarkably from the general hierarchical tenor of such exchanges as pictured by others. In all these ways, then, it can be said that Lévi-Strauss has accurately predicted the social correlates of a MBD marriage preference as it is found in the Koṅku area.

But are his predictions valid for the opposite group, the communities which exhibit a FZD urimai rule?[59] Here the evidence is not so positive, although some weak indications of the presence of the pattern expected by Lévi-Strauss can be found. Like the Koṅku KavuNTars, these subcastes also enjoy a patrilineal tradition with regard both to descent and to residence. Here the evidence conforms, to a certain extent, to Lévi-Strauss' prediction for the opposite condition, a MBD marriage rule. In addition, these groups which ritually favor the FZD do not adopt opposite sex lines for descent and residence rules, as he anticipated in his first prediction.

It can be said, however, that the patrilineal groups in communities with a FZD urimai are much weaker than those of the Koṅku KavuNTars, and that for these subcastes the practical significance of clan and lineage units is nil. Instead, those groups which have a FZD urimai rule are broken up into numerous small marriage communities, providing a definite contrast with the Koṅku KavuNTars, who insist that they have no marital subdivisions at all. This finding is in keeping with Lévi-Strauss' third prediction for groups having a FZD marriage rule: that they will break into small marriage circles. Moreover, there is a greater concern for the exis-

---

[58]Toward the end of this section, on pp. 255–56, the theoretical emphasis on equality in the marriage arrangements of right-division groups in general is discussed and contrasted with the left-division custom of ranking wife-givers and wife-receivers. However, this principle of equality can be brushed aside, as already suggested, in order to achieve upward economic mobility through marriage.

[59]I refer specifically to the Brahmans and the KōmuTTi CeTTiyār in this part of the discussion, as I know little about VēTTuvar KavuNTar preferences in marriage arrangement. As indicated earlier, in Table 5.8, the VēTTuvar KavuNTars have a FZD marriage preference.

tence of a previous genealogical connection between marriage partners among groups with a FZD urimai, than there is in the KavuNTar community. Even if one does not encounter a strict closure of their marriage cycles, which would fulfill Lévi-Strauss' second prediction, there is clearly a tight-knit quality about the kin groupings of those subcastes which claim a FZD marriage preference.

Taken as a whole, one may conclude that Lévi-Strauss has predicted the nature of the contrasts between these several groups rather well. One might add that his description of the bilateral pattern, with its presumed stress on inclusion and exclusion, also fits well with the values expressed by the castes preferring the FZD urimai rule.[60] Finally, there is the problem of the two Ācāri subcastes, both of which share the social characteristics just enumerated for the Brahmans and the KōmuTTi CeTTiyār, but which express a MBD preference. If we take the FZD urimai rule as deviant and unusual in the larger regional context, however, then it is not surprising that only a few very determined communities actually adhere to it, while others that might elect it in principle, are swayed by the larger cultural pattern towards the MBD rule. Despite these important modifications, the success with which Lévi-Strauss has managed to predict the general contrast between a FZD and a MBD preference in the Koṅku area is impressive.

To summarize the implications of the foregoing discussion, it should be clear that only Brahmans and two relatively high-ranking left-division subcastes, the KōmuTTi CeTTiyār and the VēTTuvar KavuNTars, have a FZD urimai tradition; the other neutral group, the KaruNīkar PiLLai, follows the dominant KavuNTar pattern in the urimai question. All the other left-division groups have a MBD urimai, but of these only the Kaikkōlar Mutaliyār subcaste practices the full iNaiccīr ritual. This is the very group, of course, that also deviates from the left-division pattern in many other respects.

By contrast, all the right-division communities except the NāTār have both a MBD urimai and the iNaiccīr. The latter pattern of repeated alliances between descent units through the continual transfer of women in one direction fits the KavuNTar concern for maintaining territorial claims. It is juxtaposed in a vivid fashion to the much weaker form of MBD urimai that exists among the lower left-division subcastes, and is even replaced by the inverse of the MBD marriage preference, the FZD urimai rule, in the case of two high-ranking left groups.

All men belonging to subcastes with MBD urimai were traditionally allowed the freedom of secretly slipping a marriage necklace on a girl standing in this relationship. If a man could succeed in this, no member

---

[60]Lévi-Strauss, *The Elementary Structures of Kinship,* p. 441.

of the family could object. The couple were then considered as married.[61]
Two examples of this occurring in the recent past were brought to my
attention.

(1) Police Sub-Inspector, Nearby Town (Subcaste Unknown). This
man, who had considerable social prestige, had his eye on his urimai
girl, his MBD. For some reason, however, his MB had been refusing
to let the wedding proceed. Therefore, the Sub-Inspector appeared
one night at the house where the girl lived. Together with a few male
friends he took the girl, whether by ruse or by force was not clear, put
her in a cart, and set off for the famous Murukan Temple at Palani.
There he slipped the wedding necklace on the girl and thus quickly
and unceremoniously married her. The story is a whispered one, however. The Sub-Inspector's relatives are a bit embarrassed about it.

(2) Maraméri NāTār, ŌlappāLaiyam. Not too long ago, there was a
NāTār girl of marriageable age in the village. Her father wanted to
marry her to someone on his side of the family, and her mother to
someone on hers. One night, therefore, without her husband's knowledge, the mother arranged for her BS to come and take the girl away
in a cart. He quickly slipped the marriage necklace on her neck and
the matter was settled. The husband, however, objected strongly to his
wife's behavior. As a result, a subcaste meeting was called. It was decided that the wife should pay 1-1/4 rupees as a fine—a formal sum—
and feast the men at the meeting. The wedding itself was accepted
without further ado.

On the whole, such manoeuvers are now considered old-fashioned.
Most people must be closely questioned before they clarify whether it is
the MBD or the FZD who is their actual urimai girl. In general conversation, people speak as if a man has "rights" over any of his immediate
cross cousins. I collected one story in ŌlappāLaiyam that illustrates this
point. It was told to me by Informant no. 29.

Once upon a time, there lived a poor KavuNTar man and his son.
However, the same KavuNTar happened to have a sister, far wealthier than himself. This sister had a lovely daughter. When the time for
her marriage came, the KavuNTar's son was overlooked because of
his poverty and another bridegroom was selected. One day, after the
date of the wedding had been fixed, the poor KavuNTar's son went to
a patch of open ground to graze some sheep. It was the rainy season
and when he saw some thick clouds coming, he took off his clothes,
leaving only his loin cloth on, and hid them in an earthen pot he had
used to carry his lunch in. He turned the pot upside down on a hillock
so that the water would not run into it. After the rain, he dried himself off and dressed again.

[61]In this one case only it was admitted that a marriage could occur without a ceremony.
No one would agree that the grandeur or expense of a wedding could be less, when pre-
arranged, simply because the girl was an urimaippeN, or any other variety of close relative.
A few informants (nos. 4, 18, 53, 54), however, said the paricam, or bride-price, could be
reduced in such a case.

Just after the rain, a wandering ascetic happened to pass through the field. His hair was matted and he was shivering in his wet clothing. He addressed the young boy, saying, "I have learned so many magical verses and yet I am wet. How is it that you, a mere boy, remain dry in the rain? Will you not teach me your magic?" The boy promised to teach him, but he asked him in return to teach him the magic that would win him his FZD in marriage. The ascetic agreed and gave the boy three stones, teaching him something to say when he threw each stone at the right moment. The boy was very pleased and he taught the ascetic the simple trick he had used to keep his clothes dry. The older man then took his leave and continued his wanderings.

A few days later, the day of the girl's wedding arrived. The father of the boy refused to attend in his anger, but the young boy told his father he would represent the family despite the affront that he was about to suffer. The young boy joined the crowd inconspicuously and sat down, holding the three stones in his hand. The bride and the pre-arranged bridegroom were seated, facing east, ready for the priest to hand the marriage necklace to them. Then the boy threw away his first stone and made a wish that none in the crowd should be able to stand up. People began to murmur when they realized they were fixed to their places. Then the boy threw a second stone, wishing that the marriage would be prevented and that he, the man with urimai, would be substituted as the groom. The assembled guests then realized the error. The prearranged bridegroom, hearing their discussion of the situation, became frightened and ran away. Then the poor KavuN-Tar's son was called up to the wedding dais instead, and was married to the girl. The boy then threw his third stone with the wish that all the guests be fed. The food prepared for the previous groom was brought out and all the crowd ate well. The poor boy, his magic having worked, was well satisfied with the events of the day.

The story makes quite clear the urimai or right a man has to marry his female cross cousin. This right should override any differences in wealth or status between the two families. UrimaippeN rights are reinforced by magical sanctions that are dangerous and can bring bad luck if they are violated. The story was told by a KavuNTar, about a KavuNTar family. Yet the girl specified is the FZD, not the MBD. When the story-teller was asked about this anomaly in his account, his answer was simple. For Ka-vuNTars, the FZD is a kind of second urimai girl. The "right" extends to her too. The story, according to the teller, could just as well have been told about the MBD. It can illustrate either urimai, as the teller pleases. That some castes make MBD the ritualized preference, some the FZD, was not a distinction of great interest to this man, nor was it to most others I talked with. At the present day, the term *urimai* tends to be used loosely. It must be remembered, therefore, that the distinctions described in these examples were obtained only by carefully questioning older informants.

In addition to the ritualized urimai preference for an immediate cross cousin, marriage with the ZD is generally warmly approved. This is, in fact, a more frequent marriage statistically than a match with an urimai girl, as shown in Figure 5.6. All subcastes in the Koṅku area appear to contract ZD marriages with equal frequency. Within a group, however, there is a marked variation, by family. At the same time that marriage with the sister's daughter is generally approved, a certain awareness exists that this marriage is not equally sanctioned elsewhere in the South. One KōmuTTi CeTTiyār woman was able to quote the saying, "Tai māmaṉukku kuTuttāl, virutti ākātu, kuTumpam mēlē varātu," which, when translated, reads, "If one gives a girl to her MB there will be no flourishing, the family will not prosper." Others in ŌlappāLaiyam recognized this warning, but no one could say why it was so. Whatever inauspiciousness may be implied by tradition, the fear is ignored in actual discussion of such marriages. There is positive enthusiasm for their arrangement.

Three excerpts from actual genealogies will serve to show how developed the interest in ZD marriage is in some families. These genealogies are presented in diagram form in Figure 5.6.

Genealogy 1 is taken from a family of Mutaliyār merchants who have been settled in ŌlappāLaiyam for at least four generations and have developed a prosperous roadside business. They are proud of the tradition of ZD marriage in their family and they already speculate on the next in the series, that of a boy of fifteen with his ZD, now about eight. They can only trace their genealogy with certainty back to ego's grandparents, but the previous history of uxorilocal residence is known and the family speculates that two previous generations of similar marriages may have occurred.

Genealogy 2 concerns the family in ŌlappāLaiyam which had the right to the position of village accountant, a powerful local office which has, until recently, been filled on the basis of hereditary criteria. An inquiry into the marriage history of this family brought out three MB unions and one MMZS union (terminologically MB) in a sibling group of four sisters. It also uncovered the unusual marriage of a man with his MBWZ (terminologically FZ). The genealogy shows the intense concern with keeping the advantages of a hereditary post within the immediate family group. The heavy lines in the diagram indicate the descent of the right to the KarNam's office in two villages through three generations. In the case of Cokkaṉūr, the family has twice resorted to adoption because of the absence of direct heirs. The office passed first to a BDS and then to a ZS.

Genealogy 3, that of a family of PaNTāram priests who have rights at the local Māriyammaṉ temple, shows an even more complex situation of tight intermarriage. Within two generations, the descendants of five siblings have, between them, made four ZD marriages. There have also been one FZD and one MBD marriage. Furthermore, there are two cases of sororate (A and B), an example of a direct exchange of sisters between brothers-in-law (C), and a case where two sisters have married two brothers (D). Finally, there is one example of a MFBD marriage, terminologically a MZ union (E). All these matches

genealogy 1 : Mutaliyār

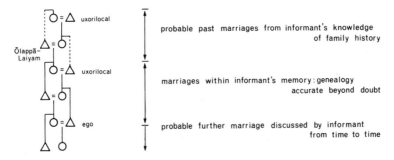

probable past marriages from informant's knowledge
of family history

marriages within informant's memory : genealogy
accurate beyond doubt

probable further marriage discussed by informant
from time to time

genealogy 2 : KaruNīkar PiLLai

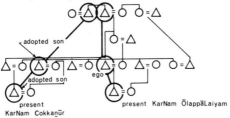

Cokkanūr KarNam (government post)   ŌlappāLaiyam KarNam (government post)

adopted son

adopted son
ego

present
KarNam Cokkanūr

present KarNam ŌlappāLaiyam

genealogy 3 : PaNTāram

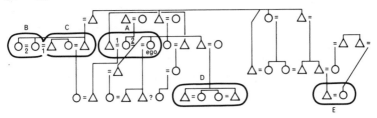

A, B   cases of sororate
C   exchange of sisters between brothers − in − law
D   marriage of two sisters to two brothers
E   MFBD marriage (terminologically : MZ)
?   Proposed marriage

Fig. 5.6.   Three genealogical examples of tight intermarriage.

were made by the descendants of one set of siblings. Here, as before, their major interest in such close intermarriage was in preserving specific economic rights. In this example, the rights concern the proceeds of pūjās or oblations performed at local temples.

In more general terms, the genealogies I collected bear out a pattern of especially tight intermarriage in households of a middling economic status, particularly among those families which have inherited special rights that they want to preserve. The possibility of a girl sharing in the economic rights of her mother's natal family and of their passing through her to her son, who will be both a BS and a ZDS, is an important consideration in arranging a ZD marriage. If the marriage is repeated in a second generation, ego's daughter will benefit, in a similar fashion, from his ZS's inheritance. Furthermore, people say that if the family is living jointly, a ZD can rule the household and enjoy seniority over her HBWs by claiming that these women are "outsiders." A ZD is in an excellent position to curry favor with her husband's parents in order to gain their support in such daughter-in-law rivalries. Several people told me stories to this effect.

The genealogies I collected indicate that both very wealthy and very poor families tend to marry outsiders more. In one case, it is a matter of cutting ties with close kin and looking for alliances with better-placed people; in the other it is a case of being ignored by close relatives and thus being forced to search for brides elsewhere. Families whose wealth ranks above that of their close relations are continually trying to sever their ties with the latter, particularly if the entire family does not hold joint rights to a particular economic privilege.[62]

At the same time, however, the disregard of poor relations is considered irresponsible and unfeeling. The ideal is a tie of mutual respect and strong feeling between brother and sister, so immutable that they can promise each other a generation in advance that their children will marry. This is the feeling behind the conception of urimai and it accounts for the extreme bitterness and ill-will which can arise between brother and sister when such an agreement is broken. It will invariably be interpreted as expressing a feeling of superiority on the part of one sibling relative to the other, and as arising from a situation that is considered not to have existed when they were children, but rather to have developed as a result of economic disparity in later life.

Despite the strong approval of close marriages in all communities, the actual statistical frequency of these unions is not high. The figures tabu-

---

[62]F. R. Hemingway has commented that "A girl who is married by virtue of her relationship to her husband is called the *urimai* girl. One chosen to enhance her husband's position or wealth, on the other hand, is called a *perumai* or 'dignity' girl." F. R. Hemingway, *Gazetteer of the Trichinopoly District* (Madras: Government Press, 1907), p. 94. I did not come across this interesting usage, however, in the Konku area.

lated from the material gathered for this account correspond, in general, with those that have been reported from elsewhere, as shown in Table 5.9. Apart from the figures given in Table 5.9 by Sivertsen, whose counts appear surprisingly high, and by Robinson, who has no record of FZD unions, the frequencies of actual cross-cousin and sister's daughter marriages recorded for Koṅku appear to fall well within the range reported for other parts of South India and even for Ceylon. If the measure used consists of the total numbers of actual MBD, FZD, and ZD unions recorded, then the range observed is something like five to twenty per cent

TABLE 5.9

STATISTICAL FREQUENCY OF CLOSE MARRIAGES IN SOUTH INDIA AND CEYLON

| Area | Author | Percentage of Marriages Contracted with: | | | Percentage Total of (1), (2), and (3) | Percentage of all marriages where ego could specify exact relation to spouse | Number |
		(1) Actual MBD	(2) Actual FZD	(3) Actual ZD			
Bangalore	McCormack*	6.5	4.8	9.8	21.1	26.2	518
Coimbatore	Beck	5.9	5.0	6.5	17.4	34.7	525
Tanjore	Gough	4.0	4.0	4.0	12.0	unspecified	not given
Tanjore	Sivertsen†	15.2	15.2	20.3	50.7	65.0	157
Kandy	Robinson	5.7	0.0	none	5.7	unspecified	87
Kandy	Yalman	7.7	5.3	none	13.0	unspecified	169

SOURCES: William McCormack, "Sister's Daughter Marriage in a Mysore Village," *Man in India* 38, no. 1 (1958): 36; E. Kathleen Gough, "Brahman Kinship in a Tamil Village," *American Anthropologist* 58 (1956): 844; Dagfinn Sivertsen, *When Caste Barriers Fall* (Oslo: Universitetsforlaget, 1963), p. 96; Marguerite Robinson, "Some Observations on the Kandyan Sinhalese Kinship System," *Man* n.s. 3, no. 3 (1968): 405; and Nur Yalman, *Under the Bo Tree* (Berkeley: University of California Press, 1967), p. 213.

NOTES: The areas are listed according to their geographical location, from north to south. The figures summarizing my own data are calculated directly from the total number of marriages in my sample (which is defined in the note to Table 5.6, p. 231), and not as an average of the percentages of such marriages in different subcastes.
*McCormack's figures on MBD, FZD, and ZD include a count of marriages with near classificatory kin of the same category and thus must be considered inflated for the purposes of this table.
†Sivertsen's figures undoubtedly derive from an addition of actual and classificatory cases similar to that of McCormack's (see note above).

of each sample studied. Of the three types of marriages considered, ZD is clearly the most popular, while MBD runs second, and FZD unions are generally the least frequent of the three.

In addition to the over-all frequency of such marriages, the question arises of variations in their frequency in different communities. Table 5.10 provides figures by subcaste. The variation observed is difficult to interpret, as much of it may be due to the small sample size available for some groups. Nonetheless, I will hazard the suggestion that certain broad patterns would be evident if more data were collected. First, high-ranking subcastes, on the whole, appear to be somewhat more closely intermarried than the lower-ranking ones. Second, the preference for MBD marriage seems to exist with equal strength in both divisions, while the FZD appears to be selected slightly more often as a marriage partner by members of

TABLE 5.10

COMMON CLOSE MARRIAGES

(by subcaste)

Subcaste Name	Percentage of Marriages Contracted With:			Total Percentage of (1), (2), and (3)	Percentage of Marriages Contracted with Relatives	Percentage of Marriages Contracted with Non-relatives	Number
	(1) Actual MBD	(2) Actual FZD	(3) Actual ZD				
Neutral Division:							
Aiyar Brahman	14.3	7.1	0.0	21.4	35.7	64.3	14
KaruNīkar PiLLai	16.7	0.0	25.0	41.7	50.0	59.0	12
Average	15.5	3.5	12.5	31.5	42.9	57.1	
Total							26
Right Division:							
Koṅku KavuNTar	7.1	5.5	6.7	19.3	31.4	68.6	255
OkaccāNTi PaNTāram	9.1	9.1	12.1	30.3	39.4	60.6	33
Koṅku UTaiyār	0.0	0.0	12.5	12.5	15.0	85.0	16
Maramēri NāTār	2.4	2.4	2.4	7.2	19.5	80.5	41
Koṅku Nāvitar	0.0	0.0	0.0	0.0	50.0	50.0	4
Koṅku Paṟaiyar	0.0	0.0	0.0	0.0	20.0	80.0	15
Average	3.1	2.8	5.6	11.5	29.2	70.8	
Total							364
Left Division:							
CōLi Ācāri	9.3	0.0	6.3	15.6	40.6	59.4	32
KōmuTTi CeTTiyār	11.1	0.0	0.0	11.1	33.3	66.7	9
Koṅku Ācāri	0.0	0.0	0.0	0.0	54.5	45.5	11
Kaikkōlar Mutaliyār	2.6	7.9	10.5	21.0	36.8	63.1	38
VaTuka Nāyakkar	0.0	9.8	0.0	9.8	35.5	64.6	31
VaTuka VaNNār	0.0	12.5	0.0	12.5	37.5	62.5	8
Moracu Mātāri	0.0	0.0	16.7	16.7	33.3	66.7	6
Average	3.3	4.3	4.8	12.4	38.8	61.2	
Total							135

NOTES: The sample included only the marriages of people living in ŌlappāLaiyam in June, 1965, and the marriages of their siblings and their children who now live outside the settlement. This is why the number for some groups is so small. Records of other close marriages were not analyzed in this table, despite their general interest, to avoid a bias in the calculation in the direction of my argument. I have also included figures on two untouchable genealogies, for balance, even though neither of the subcastes represented has members resident in ŌlappāLaiyam settlement.

It is easy to raise questions about counting procedure, particularly when genealogies become complex and there are large numbers of close marriages. In these situations several genealogical connections between ego and his wife often exist. In establishing the categories in this table, I have always given the relationship having the fewest genealogical links preference in classifying a particular union. It is possible, of course, to find a situation where a spouse is equally a FZD and a MBD. I did not encounter this problem in my data, but if I had, my procedure would have been to establish a separate category to cover such occurrences. Other details of the counting rules were as follows: 1) half-siblings and second marriages were included; 2) where a WB married a HZ (or a WZ married a HB), then one of the two marriages was counted as with someone "related," unless additional links of other kinds were found; 3) if a marriage had taken place in a senior generation and then descendants married into the family again in a succeeding generation, then only the latter marriages were considered to be with someone "related"; 4) when a claim of relationship was made, but the informant could not specify the genealogical connection, the marriage was classified as being with a non-relative. No marriages contracted outside a subcaste group were reported.

left-division groups. The association between ritual and actual preference, however, is not maintained in detail, as one of the two subcastes which have a FZD urimai and on which I have marriage data, the KōmuTTi CeTTiyār, do not, in fact, contribute any FZD marriages to the study.[63] This may be an accident associated with the smallness of the sample, but further research is definitely needed before actual marriage preferences can be safely compared to ritual ones. Both divisions show a considerable enthusiasm for ZD unions.

Dowry, as we saw in the previous section, has a literary connotation; and it is most clearly associated with Brahmans, the one community that consistently makes a FZH-MB and FZS-MBS distinction in its kin terminology, and one of the few that uphold the FZD urimai pattern. All three factors—dowry, the distinction made between wife-givers and wife-takers by using kin terms which imply inferiority and superiority respectively, and the importance attached to FZD marriage—fit together.[64] A father, or a brother, gives away a girl to a groom of higher social standing than himself. The gift of a sum of money, or dowry, with the girl is one way of emphasizing this status difference. The father, or brother, acquires "merit," it is reasoned, by giving a woman of his family to a man with more prestige and more economic security than himself. However, this status differential between a brother and his sister's husband is dangerous at the same time. It could lead to a gradual erosion of the brother-sister connection.

Thus the brother's son has an urimai or "right" to claim his FZD in marriage in order to "redress" the balance and affirm a continuing bond between the two families. Such a reversal of the direction in which women are given would be unthinkable in some areas of North India. In Koṅku, where a subtle status distinction is thought to have developed, the right to reverse it also appears. This unusual situation can perhaps be best understood as a kind of combination of the prestige of hypergamy and dowry, with a more immediate concern for the purity of a tightly knit endogamous community. In Koṅku, this combination of elements is stressed, in particular, by the Brahmans and by some high-ranking communities of the left division.

The right-division groups in Koṅku, on the other hand, do not have a tradition of dowry, nor do they lay any stress on a difference of status

---

[63]The two subcastes which have a FZD urimai and on which I have marriage data are the Aiyar Brahmans and the KōmuTTi CeTTiyār. The VēTTuvar KavuNTars, as previously noted, also have a FZD urimai, but unfortunately I do not have any genealogies for this community.

[64]Recall the description of differentiation between wife-givers and wife-takers in kin terminology given on p. 13 of the Introduction and on p. 229 of this chapter. Although the KaruNīkar PiLLai—the other neutral group—distinguish terminologically between the FZH and the MB, as we have seen they do not exhibit a FZD urimai preference; instead they favor marriage with the MBD.

between the groom's and the bride's families. By contrast, the kin terminology, the importance of the paricam, and the tradition of joint financing, all point to the wedding as creating a substantial equality between a brother and his ZH for right-division communities. This equality is borne out by the wedding ritual itself, where the new in-laws must hold hands beneath a single mound of husked rice. The emphasis here is on the sister being well cared for and well placed, but in a position equal to that of her brothers.

This essential theme of brother-sister equality is further expressed when the sister makes the demand that her brother's daughter be considered an urimaippeN ("rightful bride") for her own son. In this the sister is asking for a kind of assurance from her brother that he will continue to concern himself with her welfare, even after his own marriage. Thus, he must marry her well enough so that her son will make an appropriate groom for his own daughter. The assurance of the brother's support and protection are emphasized by his gift of fruits to her and by the wedding sari which is stretched between them during this "uniting" ritual.

In sum, the right-division communities of Koṅku have a clear ritual preference for the MBD which is dramatically expressed at the brother's wedding in the form of an iNaiccīr ceremony. The left subcastes either have a contrasting FZD preference or a much milder form of MBD obligation. The FZD preference, which results in a restricted and reversible system of exchange, is found in association with a persistent ranking of givers and takers. The MBD urimai, by contrast, provides for an extended, one-way type of exchange. It also is associated with an egalitarian treatment of givers and takers. The left-division groups can be seen to stress purity and hierarchy, two classical and heavily religious values; while members of the right division emphasize a generalized alliance pattern, which, in turn, can be linked to an intense concern with economic and political control of local territory. These ritualistic preferences are borne out only weakly in actual practice. They seem to be most commonly followed by families of middling economic status. Both the very wealthy and the very poor are prone to disregard these traditional notions of "right" in the face of more immediate economic concerns.

The main themes in marriage are shared by groups of both divisions. The bond between brother and sister and the responsibilities that they have toward one another are fundamental. A sister must be protected and married well by her brother; for this will ensure the prestige and prosperity of his own family. She has the power to bless her brother's family or, equally, to curse it if he does not do his utmost for her. Similarly, a man must be careful in the choice of a spouse. A wife's purity and her family's general status will help to ensure the position his sons will inherit. The man arranges marriages and determines a family's economic position, but the women—sisters, wives, and daughters—are vital to a household's purity and general prosperity.

Thus far, the question of marriage arrangement has been discussed from the perspective of the individual household. Marriage, however, is always intimately bound to the issue of subcaste. The problem of defining this important unit, and an attempt to identify its boundaries furnish the themes for the final pages that follow.

MARRIAGE AND THE FLEXIBILITY OF SUBCASTE BOUNDARIES

Tentatively, a subcaste may be defined as a social peer group whose members are treated as ritually equivalent for the purposes of life-cycle ceremonies, food exchange, and (in the past) other regulated items of behavior such as dress and house construction. All of these dimensions of peer group rules or norms are, of course, interwoven. Thus the notion of a subcaste as a group that shares specific dietary restrictions vis-à-vis other units, similarly defined, goes hand in hand with the notion of marriageability. The people with whom one shares, in principle, both food habits and food taboos are the same people whom it is appropriate to marry. Commensality and marriage ties, furthermore, imply a common tradition of life-cycle ceremonies, and of temple affiliation. With all this in common, members of such groups are also likely to share a single name, a label which serves to express their common social identity in relation to the outside world.

Castes are more inclusive groupings than subcastes. They can be thought of as labels for categories of subcastes which have emerged in general parlance for ease of reference. Since subcastes are local groupings that exist in great variety, there is an ever-present need to group these into larger units for the purpose of identifying strangers and of structuring interaction at large gatherings. Caste names also serve to lump together a variety of subcastes where internal differentiation is irrelevant for the purposes of interaction. Brahmans, for example, are unconcerned with internal divisions in the Mātāri community, since, for them, social movement and exchange with all untouchable groups are governed by the same basic restrictions.

Caste names generally reflect vague occupational or socio-economic criteria, while subcaste names are mainly ceremonial or territorial in nature. Since a group's occupation is generally linked to its ritual and economic status, this kind of generalization serves as a rough estimate of the types of interaction that are appropriate with people whose specific subcaste is unfamiliar. Even more general than the caste categories, of course, are the *varna* distinctions, which were described in the Introduction. As we saw there, the four terms for these distinctions, Brahman, Kshatriya,

Vaishya, and Shudra, further generalize about types of people and link the plethora of specific caste groups to a single over-arching theory of Indian society. Such terms are useful in theoretical discourse, but have little to do with everyday behavior.

Foreigners have tended to conceive of each of these levels of the Indian social order as containing within it a number of discrete and easily identified units: individual subcastes, or castes, as the case may be. Repeatedly, however, the boundaries of these units have escaped direct observation. The whole social edifice, it would seem, is built not so much on the entities themselves as on the various oppositions used in its construction. This principle of definition by opposition can be clarified when some actual examples are taken. Dumont has discussed that set of conceptual oppositions which serve to define the varna categories.[65] In essence, according to Dumont, the Brahmans in this social theory are contrasted with the members of other varnas as those who may perform sacrifices for the gods, versus those who may only pay for such ceremonies. Brahmans (priests or scholars) and Kshatriyas (kings or warriors) together, however, are further contrasted with Vaishyas (farmers and merchants) and Shudras (laborers) as those who rule men, in contrast to those who rule only animals and crops. And finally, the Brahmans, Kshatriyas, and Vaishyas together are contrasted with the Shudras, as the former three groups are twice-born and hence may study the sacred texts, whereas members of the remaining group are defined as once-born and are not allowed this privilege.

At the subcaste level, such contrasts take the form of interaction rules, rather than the form of these more generalized rights or privileges. They can be observed in the form of actions, spoken or otherwise, that specify that members of group X will share food and exchange women, while they will not marry women of Y, take curds from Z, or remove the eating leaves of Q. It is not fixed sub-units that are important in such a situation, but rather the set of oppositions between groups of people that are enforced at a given moment in a given locale. Castes are distinguished in a similar manner, except that here interaction rules are less specific and are more readily expressed in terms of inherited rights or privileges. Hence, landowning castes may follow certain rules of dining in some areas and different ones in others, but such groups are always assumed to dominate members of the service castes and hence to have some set of rules to distinguish themselves from them.

In defining a subcaste as a unit whose boundaries are demarcated by interaction rules in specific locales, I differ substantially from many previous authors who have spoken of the subcaste as a grouping that is primarily defined by endogamy. From their discussions one gets the impression that all one need do is to trace kinship connections in a wide area and

---

[65]Louis Dumont, *Homo hierarchicus* (Paris: Gallimard, 1966), p. 96.

one will eventually reach the "edge" of any given subcaste network and have to turn back.[66] Despite this constant reference to the existence of subcaste boundaries, however, almost no one has focused his research efforts on empirically locating such edges.[67] Louis Dumont is the only ethnographer I know of to have attempted this kind of research. Nevertheless, his report of his effort leaves the reader with an impression of hopeless complexity; at one point, indeed, Dumont says, "I did not follow the rainbow, which receded when I thought I was about to touch it."[68] Perhaps others have not attempted to locate boundaries because they have intuitively sensed the futility of such a task.

In order to understand the problem of subcaste groupings clearly, one must accept an undeniable difference between theory and fact. According to the principles of subcaste, as understood by Indians and Western interpreters alike, membership in such groupings is totally ascribed, and the persons belonging to each such unit can be counted easily at any point in time. Parties to any slips, such as a mismarriage or its progeny, are supposedly relegated to new subcaste groupings, in order to preserve the absolutely distinct character of previously existing ones. Table 5.11 shows how one CeTTiyār informant, for example, explained the history of several different divisions of his own caste.[69] Whether or not the assertions outlined in this table are true cannot be determined. It is important only to note that according to the theory, subcaste formation results from the accidental intermarriage of ideally "fixed" groups.

In fact, however, it would appear that only a few such deviant marriages ever become nodal points for subcaste differentiation. Where a match is economically advantageous, the background of the potential spouse is sometimes not examined in very much detail. It is only important that the potential in-laws behave "as if" they were members of the appropriate community. In many cases, no one knows who is a true member of the community and who is not. Genealogies soon become complex and may quietly be altered to suit the interests of the most influential party concerned. The most common sanction placed on a socially disapproved match is to force the deviant couple to migrate to some far-away area. There they are free to claim membership in some other plausible group and eventually to marry off their children there.

---

[66]For example, F. G. Bailey, *Caste and the Economic Frontier* (Manchester: Manchester University Press, 1957), p. 15; K. S. Mathur, *Caste and Ritual in a Malwa Village* (Bombay: Asia Publishing House, 1964), p. 5, and M. N. Srinivas, *Religion and Society Among the Coorgs of South India* (1952; reprint ed., London: Asia Publishing House, 1965), p. 24.

[67]Even Mayer, whose ethnography stresses the difference between castes (defined by local interaction), and subcastes (defined by regional kin networks), does not convincingly explore the boundaries of subcastes.

[68]Louis Dumont, "Distribution of Some Maravar Sub-castes," Bala Ratman, ed., *Anthropology on the March* (Madras: The Book Centre, 1963), p. 304.

[69]Informant no. 47.

TABLE 5.11
MISMARRIAGE AND SUBCASTE FORMATION

Subcaste of CeTTiyār	Mismarriage Which Resulted in its Formation		Approximate Number of Years in Existence
	Husband	Wife	
C_1	PāNTiya Nāvitar	Koṅku KavuNTar	more than 100
C_2	CeTTiyār	KavuNTar	About 50
C_3	CeTTiyār	Mutaliyār	Unknown
C_4	CeTTiyār	Nāyakkar	About 80
C_5	CeTTiyār	Mātāri	Unknown

NOTE: The precise names of the subcastes are not provided, as members might find such accusations about their unorthodox history offensive.
Note that in the case of C_1, neither spouse was a CeTTiyār by origin.

As in other matters, attitudes concerning this question of a potential spouse's background differ with the subcaste community in question. KavuNTars, for example, are less particular about the ancestry of their brides than any other caste group in the region.[70] Within this community, as we have seen, there is very little subcaste differentiation, despite a large local population. In Kaṇṇapuram kirāmam itself, there were a few KavuNTar families known to be of questionable descent, but these people were in no way ritually distinguished from other families.

The neutral castes and the higher-ranking groups of the left division are more particular about ancestry than the higher-ranking communities of the right. Correspondingly, they exhibit many more ritually identifiable subdivisions. This proliferation of small, theoretically endogamous groups is a sign of the greater concern of these groups with a descent-linked orthodoxy. One could argue that the tightly knit Ceṅkuntam Mutaliyār can almost be defined in terms of a body count of membership in the three villages in which they live. Even in such cases, where marriage presumably takes place within a limited circle of villages, I imagine one would find borderline cases. The "true" descendants of a particular subcaste group can always lose their impeccable ascribed status if their behavior does not measure up to the standards set by others. Even those with the most impressive genealogies can lose place on account of extreme poverty and/or because of activities that are disapproved of socially. In such cases, others will hesitate to marry into that particular family or cluster of relatives, and the deviant members will be forced to search for marriage partners elsewhere, among people with less certain ancestry. The tradition that every male has an urimaippeN, or marriage rights over a particular cross cousin, would seem to be intended, in part, to counterbalance just such a tendency. By contrast, an unorthodox parentage can always be overcome to some extent by repeated years of prosperity coupled with socially correct behavior.

[70]Srinivas' description of the Coorgs suggests a possible parallel with a similarly dominant and high-ranking caste of a neighboring area. See his *Religion and Society*, p. 37.

The term "subcaste," as used throughout this book, refers to a set of people perceived as a discrete kin grouping and defined in relation to other such groups in a specific locality and at a specific point in time. Subcastes, in this sense, do not always exist as individual mappable units with clear spatial boundaries. At the same time, subcastes are real entities when viewed in a local context, where their organizational differences exhibit a clear and repetitive pattern of competing alliances.[71]

Here, once again, the varna theory can help us understand the ideas that lie behind the everyday realities of the caste system. This theory combines a concept of logical opposition (priest versus patron, ruling man versus ruled man, etc.) with the underlying themes of exclusiveness, of inherited position, and, most important, of types of power. Indeed, we find behind this whole scheme a notion of relative importance, based on relative degrees of control. This basic idea both animates the scheme and gives it flexibility. Similarly, we may speak of this present study of caste and subcaste contrasts, undertaken at the level of social action as opposed to the level of theory, as pervaded by a certain theme. Where the study of the customs or the boundaries of any one community in isolation might have led to a variety of exceptions and to confusion, a study of the larger patterns of alliance existing among discrete status groups in a specific locality does suggest the existence of a kind of structural continuity at higher levels. I refer here to the repeated pattern of right-left differences that has been described. This framework, as opposed to the characteristics of any one subcaste taken individually, appears to have lent both a form and a resiliency to social organization in the Kònku region, and hence to have enabled it to endure long.

[71]Perhaps André Béteille has come closest to my view when he speaks of subcastes as local status groupings evidencing a highly competitive spirit. See André Béteille, *Caste, Class and Power* (Berkeley: University of California Press, 1965), especially p. 188.

6

CONCLUSION

The foregoing chapters have described the social organization of the Koṅku area by focusing consecutively on five nesting, territorially defined units: the entire geographical region, Koṅku; the nāTu, or subregion; the kirāmam, or revenue unit; the Ūr, or hamlet; and the kuTumpam, or individual household unit. These various levels or tiers of territorial organization were found to form the backbone of the residents' own conception of local social structure. No evidence was found to suggest a topical breakdown of the data similar to that which appears in most ethnographic accounts.

At each level of social organization, clear differences in the customs and traditions of various subcastes emerged. These differences form an over-all pattern that corresponds remarkably well to the right and left blocs into which these communities were organized in past centuries. Although the names and the rhetoric associated with such a partition are no longer used, the social contrasts connected with it continue to endure. A clear pattern of differences between right and left groups can still be observed today at each of the five territorial levels discussed in this study.

At the level of the region as a whole, first of all, there is a clear contrast in the economic and political rights of these two groups of subcastes. The right division has an extensive territorial organization headed by four PaTTakkārar or titled families of the area. Rights in land, and to the produce of the land, are enjoyed by this group of communities largely to the exclusion of those of the other division. The left-division subcastes, by contrast, live for the most part by their inherited skills and move about the area according to where their services are in the most demand. The right-division subcastes have traditionally relied on their PaTTakkārar for arbitration and ultimate counsel in times of dispute. The left subcastes do not share in this traditional inter-caste authority structure. Instead, they take their complaints only to respected men within their own communities.

There is also a distinct contrast in the folk histories recounted about these two blocs of local subcastes. There is a long regional epic describing the conquest of local territory by the leading subcastes of the right division and their subsequent defense of it against marauding bands. Members of this right division, furthermore, claim to have been born from a pot of fire held in the right hand of the goddess who guards local areas. In contrast, the left communities describe their history as interwoven with that of a conglomeration of persecuted minorities, accustomed to the fate of harassment and the life of refugees. Their stories associate them with a goddess who was cast out from heaven and obliged to wander on earth for lack of a single-minded devotion to her husband. Some of this mythology will be studied in greater depth in a subsequent work.

At the nāTu or subregional level, the main contrast to emerge relates to the internal political and descent-group organization of these right and left subcastes. The two leading communities of the right division still maintain formal positions of leadership which between them provide headmen for each of the major territorial divisions. Thus the leading agricultural caste, the Koṅku KavuNTars, have four PaTTakkārar at the regional level and also their own local Ūr official in each important hamlet. The Maramēri NāTār, or palmyra palm tapping, community complements the KavuNTar leadership pattern with a ceremonial leader at the kirāmam level, and a political officer or headman for each nāTu area. Koṅku KavuNTars also have officials for these intermediate levels, but their importance at the present time is greatly attenuated. The higher-ranking left-division subcastes have few community headmen that correspond to these territorial units; instead, they tend to have a system of gurus or religious leaders whose organization stretches throughout the South and is focused on distant pilgrimage sites.

The descent-group organization of the leading members of these two divisions is equally different. The communities associated with the right have an extensive clan and lineage organization, closely tied to nāTu and kirāmam territorial claims. The leading subcastes of the left, however, have no descent-based organization at all. The only trace of such groupings is a set of Sanskrit names having great prestige. These are the gotras, vague descent lines that have little practical importance.

At the kirāmam level, the contrast in the rights and privileges of the two social blocs is again clear. The right-division subcastes have important duties to perform at the local goddess' festival each year; the left-division groups have none. In the past, women belonging to the left groups may have even been excluded from the ritual area where these annual ceremonies were performed. The leading communities of the right have an extensive mythology and long genealogies supporting their claims to local land. They are the participants in squabbles over the question of ritual precedence when festivals are performed.

The leading communities of the right division exhibit only a mild interest in education and in new, urban-oriented occupations. High-ranking left-division groups, by contrast, have responded eagerly to increased opportunities for schooling and are correspondingly the ones to seek out the more modern and innovative jobs. This difference in attitude toward education and the professions appears to be consistent with the differences between the prestige structures of the two divisions. For the right, territorial control is the major criterion for prestige, and this factor could explain the apparent reluctance of leading members of this division to encourage advanced education for their children, which would very likely result in attracting their sons into occupations not related to land. Excluded for the most part from territorial control and the prestige associated with it, the high-ranking members of the left have developed a rival structure of their own. In their definition of prestige they have emphasized material wealth, ritual purity, and adherence to an all-South Indian literary and philosophical tradition. Their model has thus incorporated the traditional Brahman ideal of scholarship. Among these groups, an interest in education is traditional, and enthusiasm for it is to be expected. Moreover, the non-polluting white-collar occupations that are defined by members of the left as more prestigious than agricultural work are made available to them through educational achievement.

At the level of the individual Ūr or hamlet areas, further right-left contrasts can be observed. Of particular interest here are the different strategies the two groupings use in the competition for local status. The right-division leaders have sought to establish a "ritual alliance" similar to that which Adrian Mayer has already described for Malwa in Central India.[1] This alliance acknowledges the leadership of the KavuNTar agricultural community. Several high-ranking left-division groups, however, attempt to withdraw from many of the situations involving interaction where ranking or status evaluation can occur. Instead they take their cue from the Brahmans' claim that exclusiveness and non-interaction are superior criteria in the assignment of prestige. The same contrast appears when local factional alignments are considered. Disputes over leadership are always linked to local, territorial rights and are the prerogative of right-division leaders. These rivalries fade where cooperation in terms of wider territorial alliances is required, but when they do occur, left-division members are rarely involved at all.

Finally, we come to the differences between subcastes of the two divisions that become apparent at the kuTumpam or individual household level. These include a contrast in marriage preferences, in kinship terminology, and in questions of residence and dowry payment. The right-

[1]Adrian C. Mayer, *Caste and Kinship in Central India* (London: Routledge and Kegan Paul, 1960), pp. 37–38, 44–47, 81, 88, 131.

division communities, and particularly their KavuNTar leaders, stress the importance of wealth and of local political power in making marriage arrangements. They specify a ritual preference for the matrilateral cross cousin, which is consonant with their interest in strengthening a network of local alliances. The tone of these contracts is egalitarian, and both parties contribute equally to the wedding costs; entirely consistent with this concept of equality is the absence of a distinction in these communities between bride-givers and bride-takers, either in practice or in the kin terminology used. Uxorilocal residence is readily agreed to, particularly if it will increase the claims of a man on his wife's father's property.

The leading left-division communities stress the purity and orthodoxy of the marriage tie more than their right-division counterparts do. Thus these groups strictly adhere to the rules of the kin terminology, bring their brides from a greater distance, and strongly disapprove of uxorilocal residence. The rates of joint family living are higher among these communities than among corresponding subcastes of the right; and where residence with the groom's family is impractical, a neolocal arrangement is preferred. There is some evidence of a patrilateral cross-cousin preference among higher-ranking left-division groups. Similarly, dowry is emphasized in these communities and the inferiority of the wife-giving household is affirmed. All of these differences serve to create small, tight-knit circles of kinsmen for the higher-ranking groups of the left division, as opposed to the expansive alliance-style ties among leading communities of the right. Similarly, subcaste multiplication is endemic among left-division groups, but appears to be attenuated, or almost absent, among the land-tied members of the right.

This summary of contrasting features has been carefully and repeatedly qualified by the terms "leading" and "higher-ranking," which indicate that the description refers to the groups with the most prestige in each division.[2] This is so because the opposition tends to fade, and in a few instances even to be reversed, among the members of lower-status groups in each bloc. These less powerful and more heavily dependent communities are not in a position to make the clear choices which confront their superiors. Instead, the low-ranking subcastes are often forced to follow the lead of more powerful and higher-ranking groups, because of their economic dependence on them. Therefore they tend to compromise and to combine what they can from the many examples before them. In general, however, the influence of the right-division pattern is predominant over the lower ranks of the social order, as the less powerful members of both divisions are heavily dependent on the patronage of land-owning KavuNTars for a livelihood.

[2]As pointed out in the Introduction, throughout this work status or rank has been defined by subcaste seating order at a Brahman feast.

Finally, there is the Mutaliyār community, a relatively high-status group which is caught squarely in the middle of these right-left division differences. Their ancestry is martial, and although members of this caste officially belong to the left, they have come to identify with the right in many respects. Thus the Mutaliyār can be seen to vacillate between the two poles of social organization outlined in this work. In a sense they may be seen as striving for a neutral position like that of the Brahmans and the PiL-Lai, both of whom are generally agreed to stand above this extensive bifurcate structure.

Some of the larger implications of this over-arching partition of the Koṅku social order must now be considered. Essentially, I view the situation as derived from two concomitant, pre-existent conditions. First, a pervasive disjunction has existed for many centuries in India between those groups which held direct rights in land or claimed them indirectly through services provided for landowners, and which were thus immobile, and those groups such as weavers, together with many artisan and merchant communities, whose professions accorded monetary wealth, mobility, and a certain independence. Not all agricultural groups need have been allied, nor all professional groups joined in opposition, for a right-left alignment to have arisen. Rather a single dominant agricultural community could have formed the node around which dependent groups clustered to form one division, while a few relatively wealthy and independent professional communities developed as leaders of an opposition bloc. Given an over-all scheme of polarization along these lines, smaller groups could always align themselves with one bloc or the other on other grounds. The VēT-Tuvar KavuNTars are one example: they are thought of as left because they are a small group of landowners who rival the Koṅku KavuNTars without seriously challenging the latter's regional dominance. Another example is provided by the Koṅku UTaiyār who, as potters, are artisans who serve both blocs. Yet in practice this group has become ritually allied with the Koṅku KavuNTars as a result of economic dependence on them.

The second condition is that in Koṅku the top position in the local commensal hierarchy has long been occupied by a group of Brahmans who do not own any significant amount of land, and hence who qualify for social precedence by virtue of their ritual status alone. Given such a situation, the landed dominant community would have a choice. It could either attempt to combine territorial control with a Brahman-like concern for ritual purity, or it could concentrate on the economic and political dominance of a local population and territory and give little weight to considerations of purity and ritual abstinence. In the former case, this landed group would very likely fail to interact sufficiently with the community at large to exercise true control over local economic activities, and its position of dominance would be open to challenge by shrewd entrepreneurs. In the second case, the dominant group could agree to attend local non-Brahman feasts, to use the plow, and in general to enter fully into local activities in order to control them. However, by doing so it would leave itself open to challenge from any relatively established but landless professional group that claimed to enjoy a higher social standing in terms of complementary criteria, material wealth and ritual purity. (As we saw in the Introduction, the classical texts do not make clear the relative rank of such combinations of different types of power.) In neither case is the position of the Brahman at the top of the local ceremonial hierarchy severely questioned. But in the former case, groups ranking below the Brahmans are likely to align themselves in a single hierarchy, while in the second type of social order they are likely to bifurcate into competing blocs, each group claiming rank according to the criterion for prestige used by the leaders of the particular division to which it belongs.

In Koṅku only one group, the KaruNīkar PiLLai, has managed to refuse the food of all other non-Brahmans at village feasts, while simultaneously controlling land and maintaining a measure of local power. In the region where this study was conducted, these PiLLais constitute a very small subcaste whose members lack sufficient power to influence substantially the existing social structure which surrounds them. However, in areas to the East and South where this group and others like it are larger than they are in Koṅku, the over-all organization of local society is likely to be considerably different from that of the latter region. It would seem that only where landed, political power and ritual purity—the two major routes to status in Hindu India—remain largely separate, can a right-left division such as the one described in this work be expected to develop fully. In the classical Indian world-view, material wealth by itself is inadequate as a third, parallel route to prestige. Unless it is combined with one or both of the other status criteria, it cannot contribute to social superiority over more than the lowest-ranking groups. Thus people who possess material wealth but who have been traditionally excluded from land ownership tend to develop an interest in ritual purity in order to offset the inferior power of their riches. Kinglike territorial dominance implies an indirect control of men, animals, and goods, but it in turn is outranked by attaining personal purity, which signifies to the Hindu control over the cosmic forces themselves. It is in the mixture of power criteria just described that the means of challenging the status of those with only a single claim, their local political hegemony, can be found.

A test of the interpretation given here is possible for future researchers; that is, to conduct a similar study in another area of India that resembles Koṅku. This area would feature a pre-eminent, relatively landless group of Brahmans whose status rests on the single criterion of ritual purity and a politically dominant, non-Brahman community that displays a relative nonchalance toward these matters. Members of the latter type of group would be landowners who enjoyed exclusive control of local territory, who agreed to eat meat and to dine with other non-Brahmans, and who used the plow. From my interpretation, one would predict that such a region would exhibit a similar pattern of social differences between groups with landed political power and groups which, traditionally denied access to land ownership, are for the most part dependent on professional skills. Furthermore, such differences that are found should be gradually fading now, under the dual impact of property purchases by groups previously excluded from owning land, and of the increasing prestige of an industrial, urban economy as opposed to a rural, agricultural one.

In order to encourage comparative research of some rigor, a few details which have been critical to this study are provided here on ownership of land in the Koṅku area. In my view, the ability to control agricultural production is the key factor in understanding KavuNTar dominance, and their exclusive power position is the key to the development of the extensive social oppositions observed. If the KavuNTars did not control the land, their textually unorthodox ritual traditions, and their non-vegetarian diet would result in a much lower social status than that which they actually enjoy. The proportion of local land owned by a single subcaste is not in itself, however, a sufficient measure of a group's dominance. Equally critical is the number of households which own land. Each household directing agricultural activities provides more people, of that subcaste, who are either directing other people's work or who are self-employed and hence free of control by others.

In the Kāṅkayam area of Koṅku all the land is technically "dry."[3] In this area I would estimate that five to ten acres of good land is a minimal subsistence holding for a small household. About twenty, or roughly fifty per cent of all land-owning households, have holdings that fall below this minimum and hence are dependent on supplementary income from other sources. ŌlappāLaiyam is a "typical" settlement, as far as land-holding patterns are concerned, for this area. The actual breakdown, by subcaste, of households in ŌlappāLaiyam that own more than five acres is shown in Table 6.1.

It is clear that out of the twenty households in this particular settlement which own enough land either to subsist independently, or to employ others extensively, a full seventeen or nearly ninety per cent belong to the KavuNTar community. In addition, four KavuNTar families are tenants.[4]

---

[3]This is by land-revenue definition.

[4]One NāTār family also held a position as a tenant. Both Brahman and PiLLai landowners rent out their holdings to tenants; for, as explained in the Introduction, religious scruples prevent them from working on the land themselves. This further reduces their opportunities to dominate others.

TABLE 6.1
SIZE OF SIGNIFICANT LAND HOLDINGS IN ŌLAPPĀLAIYAM SETTLEMENT
(by subcaste)

Subcaste Name	Number of Households		
	"Subsistence" (5.1 to 10.0 acres)	"Requires Extrafamilial Labor" (10.1 to 40.0 acres)	"Requires Tenancy" (40.1 acres and over)
Koṅku KavuNTar	7	9	1
Aiyar Brahman	0	2	0
KaruNĭkar PiLLai	0	1	0

Tenancy is a respected position that gives one a fair amount of control over production activities. By obtaining medium-size holdings, therefore, a group achieves the maximum possibilities for local dominance. Holdings that are too large can actually endanger a household's local position, as it then becomes impossible to retain full personal control over them. Once a landowner rents to tenants, he cedes a fair amount of his control over day-to-day production activities to others, while absentee ownership yields even more power to persons in an intermediate position. Tenants interact with owners only at critical points in the agricultural cycle, such as at planting and harvesting times, while absentee owners generally see their local representative once a year.[5]

The real issue in dominance is the degree of control the members of a particular group have over those of other communities. In a traditional agricultural economy, control of land is simply one convenient way of measuring the degree of a group's control over other men. In Koṅku, the extensive control of land by the KavuNTars places this group in a clearly dominant position in rural areas. How much land some other group might need to hold in order to challenge KavuNTar dominance is a question that can be answered only by additional research. Moreover, the amount of mechanization in agriculture, the types of crop specialization, and the amount of importance given to external governmental or private business controls, could also affect the parameters necessary for local hegemony.

For these reasons, my theory explaining the development of a bifurcate social organization can best be stated in terms that specify the mechanisms at work, rather than the precise quantities of specific social arrangements required. Probably both upper and lower limits exist on the size of land holdings that can play a significant role in a local dominance syndrome, but the precise specifications of these parameters must be defined with reference to particular settings.

---

[5]For this reason the four PaTTakkārar families of Koṅku, for example, have always resided on or near the lands that they own. They continue to manage large tracts themselves and only lease to tenants acreage that is in excess of what they and their own close relatives can oversee.

In conclusion, the right-left opposition can be considered a social corollary that combines the principle of limited access to primary resources with the specific Hindu view of power and rank. As such it is a significant and interesting human institution. However, the conditions that are responsible for its development are not yet fully understood. Comparative research on similar settings elsewhere in India is urgent, before the pressure of a modern industrial economy and the accompanying principle of random access to resources combine to make this traditional pattern of social organization obsolete.

Appendix A
THE CONDITIONS OF FIELDWORK

This study is based on eighteen months of fieldwork in the Koṅku region. Most of the information was collected during my stay in one settlement near the center of this area, from January 1965 through August 1966. This core of material, however, has been heavily supplemented by my frequent trips to different parts of the Koṅku region. It also owes much to work carried out by my research assistant, K. Cuntaram, since my departure. In addition to these months in Koṅku itself, I spent another sixteen weeks just before and just after this period traveling in Madras State and in India as a whole.

The decision to conduct a study somewhere in the Koṅku region was made long before I reached India. My resolve stemmed from a suggestion made to me by Professor Louis Dumont in Paris as early as May, 1964. His reasons were twofold: first, Koṅku was an unstudied area known to have some traditional and distinctive characteristics; and second, he had met immigrants from the Koṅku area in his own fieldwork near Madurai, whose descriptions of the area he found of great interest. The actual selection of a location for intensive fieldwork, however, involved a long series of further specifications and judgments upon my arrival in India. These refinements of my initial decision are described, in sequence, below.

When I first arrived in Coimbatore city, on December 1st, 1964, I began to question local people about their knowledge of the Koṅku region. After a few weeks of initial adjustment and inquiry, it became clear that the area around the town of Kāṅkayam was considered to be one of the important centers of the region's traditional culture. Kāṅkayam was characterized as socially conservative, and it was also conveniently near the geographic center of the region as a whole. If I were to concentrate on a study of traditional and rural life in Koṅku, it seemed to me that a settlement linked to a central market-town might be a good place to start out. Thus I began to collect the names of various people living in Kāṅkayam and to prepare to move there from Coimbatore city. For this initial trip to a rural area I arranged to have a female companion, a friend with a background in social work.

In Kāṅkayam I was lucky to find a doctor who was a distant relative of this woman, and who was familiar with the villages of the area because of his many rural patients. He generously described a number of settlements and drove us about the countryside in his car. In this way we were able to visit about fifteen locales that could have made a possible base for my work. When it came to a final selection of a place to begin research, I tried to bring to bear several pre-established criteria. Only settlements which approximated most of these specifications were considered. The points I held uppermost in my mind were the following:

(1) That the settlement be at least five or six miles from a town and preferably off a main road.

(2) That it not be obviously and exclusively dominated by one landlord.

(3) That it have people from all or almost all the major castes of the area settled either within its boundaries or nearby.

(4) That the settlement be reasonably large, but not so large as to make it impossible to know everyone. (I considered a settlement of roughly one-hundred families to be of suitable size.)

(5) That it be an old one with an interesting array of temples.

(6) That my introduction to the settlement be through a local person who was both congenial and apparently respected, but who was neither a large landowner nor a man of low caste:

The availability of a house to live in, and the possibility of employing a respected older woman as a cook were further considerations, but ones that I was determined to leave aside until after an initial selection of location had been made.

On the basis of these criteria I originally selected a place some miles from Kāṅkayam. My introduction there was through a government health employee, and it was agreed that I would initially live with her and continue to explore the area further on foot, accompanying her on her daily round of the nearby settlements. The details about where I would eventually settle and who would cook for me were left open. After a few days in that locale, however, it became apparent that the particular woman I had contacted was a poor choice for entrance into village life. I soon learned that her sexual liaisons were much discussed by local residents, and that she was associated with an unpopular political faction which was about to lose a local Panchayat election. I was without an interpreter at this point, but was able to sense the inappropriateness of the setting by tones of voice, by the general aloofness towards me exhibited by local residents, and by the recognition of several unfavorable words that were already in my limited Tamil vocabulary.

After spending a few days, by invitation, with a leading family of the opposite political faction, I finally decided that the initial acquaintances I had made in this village did not augur well for intensive fieldwork. I feared that, as the weeks progressed, I might become even further imprisoned in an elaborate mesh of political and social jealousies. Thus, after about ten days in this area I finally decided to extricate myself and to move back to Kāṅkayam. There I was rejoined by my friend from Coimbatore, and together we re-opened the search for a suitable settlement. On the second attempt, we came upon one about six miles east of the town, where we had had an initial introduction to a roadside cloth merchant. His name had been given to us by a social worker from Coimbatore who had once lived in the area.

This settlement, ŌlappāLaiyam, met all the criteria previously noted, except that it was quite close to a main road. Waiving this one disadvantage, I finally decided to settle there, after my third exploratory visit. The roadside merchant and one of his friends, a government agent for agricultural development, helped me find a house and a congenial local female companion. My friend from Coimbatore stayed with me until I had actually moved into the house and left only when I had settled in with my new friend, PāppammāL.

This time I sensed my good luck. People were friendly and were putting themselves out to help me in small ways. Furthermore, my reservations about the settlement being close to a main road, and therefore considerably influenced by contact with townsmen, gradually diminished. They were overcome entirely when I discovered an important compensatory feature, that the roadside shops might serve as an important nerve center where I could learn about events and people in neighboring settlements. Furthermore, my general research interest moved gradually away from the study of an isolated, rural settlement towards the investigation of regional and subregional levels of social organization. Living in a settlement where I could catch a bus by only a few minutes' walk and where I could meet travelers and hear news quickly turned out to be a great advantage. It meant that I could expand my scope of operations easily and thus enabled me to generalize about a larger area with increased facility.

My greatest stroke of luck, however, was in finding a devoted companion in PāppammāL, my housekeeper and cook. PāppammāL belonged to a non-Brahman caste of priests and cooks called PaNTāram. Members of this group take care to follow the dominant agricultural community of the area in all ritual particulars; yet they are considered somewhat beneath them both in wealth and in general prestige. Thus she felt at home in her position as employee; at the same time, though, she was respected by the leading families of the village and was very familiar with their customs. Furthermore, she was strong and nimble and soon proved to be highly intelligent.

After a time, PāppammāL began to address me as "daughter" (she had only sons herself); her youngest son, Cuntaram, who was about my age, came to address me as "elder sister." This son came to see us frequently and he too proved to be unusually intelligent and conscientious. In a few months I decided to employ him formally as my assistant. Thus we became both a family and a work unit in which I was equally "daughter," "sister," and "head of household."

Neither PāppammāL nor Cuntaram was formally educated. She was totally illiterate, while he had the advantage of four years of local schooling plus many more of self-education. As a result of his motivation for study, I found Cuntaram to be far in advance of his official level of competence. Gradually, he became an indispensable part of the research effort, taking responsibility for recording all my Tamil texts, for drawing maps, and for many other kinds of work as well.

Unquestionably, Cuntaram and PāppammāL were my two most important sources of information throughout my stay. However, more than sixty other people, both in ŌlappāLaiyam and scattered through the region, were responsible for specific contributions on certain topics. Most of these informants have been listed in Appendix B, where their subcaste and place of residence are given; in the text, information obtained from them has been carefully noted by a code ("Informant no. 1, 2," etc.).

I also had the good fortune to find a comfortable place to live. My moderately sized rural home, which was built in the traditional style, was rented from a member of the dominant land-owning subcaste. It was near the center of the settlement, but it had previously been vacant for a number of years because a series of unfortunate deaths had occurred within it. The memory of these deaths had receded far enough into the past that people were no longer very concerned about the matter. The fact that the main entrance to the house faced west, however, never ceased to trouble PāppammāL, who always blamed her colds and stomach aches on this inauspicious architectural feature.

During the first few months of my stay in ŌlappāLaiyam, I was quite circumspect in my behavior, and in so far as I knew how, I scrupulously attempted to follow local custom. In a matter of days I learned the rules of bathing, of eating, and of menstrual avoidance, and I tried to observe them all. Moreover, I always wore a sari. I also tried to maintain a relatively shy and modest demeanor. At first I never ventured outside the house without a companion. This initial restraint served to win the confidence of local residents with relative speed. Of course, the beginning of my stay was also the period when I was most hampered by my meagre, though gradually expanding, knowledge of Tamil.

Later in my stay, when I could speak more fluently and after people had become accustomed to my presence, I began to behave more boldly and independently. I now walked through the streets alone and interviewed acquaintances of all ages, my one constraint being that I always tried to converse with men in a place where I could be seen by passers-by. After a while, I became accustomed to riding my bicycle alone to other settlements when following up inquiries at a distance. As far as I know, none of the liberties I took with local custom near the end of my stay were resented. It would seem that the confidence I won initially and the friendships gained then served to give me more freedom in the end than I might otherwise have enjoyed. In addition, I found that in general my status as a woman was a great advantage. I was less open to suspicion about being a spy or an agent of some sort than a man might have been. I found it easier to request assistance, and I was able to converse more freely with men than a man could have succeeded in doing with women.

Despite my friendship with residents in ŌlappāLaiyam and my good luck there, people were understandably puzzled during the initial weeks of my stay about why I had come. When asked about this, I would explain that the government of my country sent food to India (some of which the local residents had seen), and that it also sent students to learn about the people and the customs of this distant land which received its aid. I told them that I had been requested to return to North America after my two-year stay, to teach people there about Indian social customs. This answer was generally accepted as reasonable by my questioners. I hope that local residents and friends will view this work as a partial realization of my purpose as expressed in response to these early inquiries.

Appendix B

LIST OF MAJOR INFORMANTS CITED IN THE TEXT

Number Used in Text	Name	Place of Residence	Caste Affiliation
1.	PaRaniyappan	Kannapuram hamlet, Kannapuram kirāmam	Koṅku Paraiyar
2.	KirusNā (KiTTäNTi)	ŌlappāLaiyam settlement, Kannapuram kirāmam	OkaccāNTi PaNTāram
3.	Ellammāl	ŌlappāLaiyam settlement, Kannapuram kirāmam	VaTuka VaNNār
4.	Raṅkacāmi	ŌlappāLaiyam settlement, Kannapuram kirāmam	CōLi Ācāri
5.	Rāmacāmi	ŌlappāLaiyam settlement, Kannapuram kirāmam	VaTuka Nāyakkar
6.	Nācciyappan	VīracōRapuram hamlet, Pāppini kirāmam	Moracu Mātāri
7.	PaRaniccāmi Pulavar	Tirupur town	Pulavar (Mutaliyār)
8.	KirusNacāmi Pulavar	Muttūr town	Pulavar (Mutaliyār)
9.	Kāṅkappa Pulavar	VīracōRapuram hamlet, Pāppini kirāmam	Pulavar (Mutaliyār)
10.	Mārimuttu	MaTaviLakam hamlet, Pāppini kirāmam	OkaccāNTi PaNTāram
11.	ĀNTa CivacuppiramaNiya PaNTitar	Karumāpuram, via TiruccaṅkōTu	KurukkaL (Brahman) or NāTār (?)
12.	Rāmacāmi	ŌlappāLaiyam settlement, Kannapuram kirāmam	Maramēri NāTār
13.	Muttukkarupan	ŌlappāLaiyam settlement, Kannapuram kirāmam	Maramēri NāTār
14.	PaRaniyappan	VīracōRapuram hamlet, Pāppini kirāmam	Maramēri NāTār
15.	Citamparam Sri Kamalamūrtti	Chidambaram town, Tanjore	KurukkaL (Ācāri)
16.	Mārimuttu	CūTāmaNi, via Cinna Dharapuram	VēTar
17.	Rāman	ReTTipāLaiyam, via Karur	ToTTi Mātāri
18.	Māran	PWD Bungalow, Kodumudi town	ToTTi Mātāri
19.	Nācci	KāṅkayampāLaiyam hamlet, Kannapuram kirāmam	ToTTi Mātāri
20.	Cuntaram	ŌlappāLaiyam settlement, Kannapuram kirāmam	OkaccāNTi PaNTāram

Number Used in Text	Name	Place of Residence	Caste Affiliation
21.	PāppammāL	ŌlappāLaiyam settlement, Kannapuram kirāmam	OkaccāNTi PaNTāram
22.	KaNapati	VeLLakōvil town	OkaccāNTi PaNTāram
23.	Nācci	RaTTivalacu hamlet, Kannapuram kirāmam	KūTai Kuravar
24.	Mārimuttu	KoLuntakavuNTanūr, via Karur	Anappu Mātāri
25.	KiTTān	Karur town	Moracu Mātāri
26.	Cantānam	Karur town	Moracu Mātāri
27.	Cuppulaksmi	ŌlappāLaiyam settlement, Kannapuram kirāmam	Aiyar Brahman
28.	NāmakiriyammāL	ŌlappāLaiyam settlement, Kannapuram kirāmam	CōLi Ācāri
29.	CeṅkōTaiyan	ŌlappāLaiyam settlement, Kannapuram kirāmam	Koṅku KavuNTar
30.	Muttucāmi	PaRaiyakōTTai kirāmam	OkaccāNTi PaNTāram
31.	Aṅkappan	KĪRvāni, via Bhavani	Ceṅkuntam Mutaliyār
32.	Avanāci Liṅkam	ŌlappāLaiyam settlement, Kannapuram kirāmam	KaruNĪkar PiLLai
33.	PaRaniyappan	ŌlappāLaiyam settlement, Kannapuram kirāmam	Koṅku Nāvitar
34.	Cuntaramūrtti	ŌlappāLaiyam settlement, Kannapuram kirāmam	Aiyar Brahman
35.	VeṅkaTācalam	KāTaiyur, via Kāṅkayam	KōmanāNTi PaNTāram
36.	Kuppucāmi	RaTTivalacu hamlet, Kannapuram kirāmam	Koṅku KavuNTar
37.	Muttucāmi	MurukkaṅkāTu hamlet, Kannapuram kirāmam	Koṅku KavuNTar
38.	PaRanicāmi	Kannapuram settlement, Kannapuram kirāmam	Koṅku KavuNTar
39.	Muttucāmi	ŌlappāLaiyam settlement, Kannapuram kirāmam	OkaccāNTi PaNTāram
40.	Rāman	Kodaikanal town	VaTuka Mātāri
41.	KiTTān	CaṅkaṅkāTu, Kannapuram hamlet, Kannapuram kirāmam	ToTTi Mātāri
42.	Periyacāmi	Kannapuram settlement, Kannapuram kirāmam	Koṅku KavuNTar
43.	Cēmalaiyappan	ŌlappāLaiyam settlement, Kannapuram kirāmam	Koṅku KavuNTar
44.	Cinnucāmi	ŌlappāLaiyam settlement, Kannapuram kirāmam	Koṅku KavuNTar
45.	KiTTucāmi	ŌlappāLaiyam settlement, Kannapuram kirāmam	Koṅku KavuNTar
46.	KaruppaNacāmi	ŌlappāLaiyam settlement, Kannapuram kirāmam	Koṅku KavuNTar

Number Used in Text	Name	Place of Residence	Caste Affiliation
47.	PaRaniyappan	ŌlappāLaiyam hamlet, Kannapuram kirāmam	Nakaram CeTTiyār
48.	Periyacāmi	ŌlappāLaiyam settlement, Kannapuram kirāmam	Konku UTaiyār
49.	?	VaLLiyeraccal kirāmam	MēLakārar Mutaliyār
50.	Ārumukam	IlliumpaTTi, via Lakkamanayakkan-paTTi	Konku Ācāri
51.	Cinnucāmi	TaNNīrpantalvalacu hamlet, Kannapuram kirāmam	Konku KavuNTar
52.	Cakuntalā	ŌlappāLaiyam settlement, Kannapuram kirāmam	KōmuTTi CeTTiyār
53.	Nāccimuttu	Muttūr Town	MēLakārar Mutaliyār
54.	VaLLiyammāL	ŌlappāLaiyam settlement, Kannapuram kirāmam	VaTuka Nāyakkar
55.	CaravaNan	ŌlappāLaiyam settlement, Kannapuram kirāmam	KaruNīkar PiLLai
56.	Tankavēlu	ŌlappāLaiyam settlement, Kannapuram kirāmam	CōLi Ācāri
57.	Māriyappan	ŌlappāLaiyam settlement, Kannapuram kirāmam	Kaikkōlar Mutaliyār
58.	Tiyākarājan	ŌlappāLaiyam settlement, Kannapuram kirāmam	KōmuTTi CeTTiyār
59.	Kōvīntan	ŌlappāLaiyam settlement, Kannapuram kirāmam	VaTuka Nāyakkar
60.	PaRani	Pūcārivalacu settlement, Kannapuram kirāmam	Moracu Mātāri

Appendix C
NOTE ON THE TRANSLITERATION
OF TAMIL WORDS

All proper names and Tamil terms are given in their current English spelling without diacritical marks when they are well known and there is a standard form for them in use. However, for the names of small towns and geographical features rarely mentioned in English-language sources, I have used a transliteration scheme geared directly to the accepted Tamil spelling. In the spelling of the names of deities, I have used this transliteration scheme in every case. Personal names are similarly treated; nevertheless, where the name of an author of a Tamil work has an English spelling established in print, this is used. I have transliterated all caste names from the Tamil, with the exception of the name "Brahman," which is already well known to the reader. All other Tamil words have been transliterated. The scheme I have used for transliterating Tamil into English is given in Figure C.1.

In this transliteration scheme, common English letters are used as equivalents for Tamil ones wherever possible. The exceptions are the capital letters *R, L, N,* and *T,* which represent retroflex sounds. These generally occur only in the middle of a word. The *n* and $\underline{n}$ distinguish two Tamil letters, both pronounced like the English *n.* The *r* and $\underline{r},$ similarly, represent two Tamil letters, both pronounced like a slightly rolled English *r.* Long vowels, finally, have been distinguished from short ones by adding a macron. Thus *o* should be read as very short, and *ō* as very long.

In a number of cases, particularly that of subcaste names, I have ignored rules of word combination for the sake of clarity. Hence I have written "NāTTu KavuNTar" instead of NāTTukkavuNTar," and "Kaikkōlar Mutaliyār" rather than "Kaikkōlamutaliyār," even though the latter spellings would be technically more correct. With the exception of the Brahmans and the KavuNTars, I have given the names of castes and clans in the singular when a group is referred to as a whole. I have simply added *s* to these and to other proper names in places where I want to refer only to some members of a group, even though this does not correctly transliterate the Tamil plural form.

A guide to accurate pronunciation necessitates a long list of rules. For a detailed discussion of this matter, the reader is referred to J. R. Firth, "A Short Outline of Tamil Pronunciation," appearing as an appendix in A. H. Arden, *Arden's Grammar of Common Tamil,* Fourth Edition,

short vowels: a , e , i , o , u

long vowels: ā , ē , ī , ō , ū

consonants:

1)	க	k	8)	ங	ṅ	14)	ய	y
2)	ச	c	9)	ந	n	15)	ர	r
3)	ட	T	10)	ண	N	16)	ல	l
4)	த	t	11)	ன	n̲	17)	வ	v
5)	ற	r̲	12)	ம	m	18)	ள	L
6)	ப	p	13)	ஸ	s	19)	ழ	R
7)	ஜ	j						

Fig. C.1.   Scheme used for transliterating Tamil words.

Christian Literature Society of India (Madras: Diocesan Press, 1934). The most recent edition, which appeared in 1942 and was reprinted in 1952 and 1962, unfortunately no longer contains this description. The new edition of this grammar, however, does contain some useful notes on pronunciation in the first chapter.

An approximate pronunciation of common words appearing in the text has been provided in the Glossary.

Appendix D
AUSPICIOUS AND INAUSPICIOUS TIMES

In Koṅku, each day of the week and each month of the year is classified as auspicious or inauspicious. Moreover, people are continually referring to the time when something happened either as a *nalla nēram* ("auspicious moment or period of time") or as a *keTTa nēram* ("inauspicious moment or period of time").

For knowledge about individual moments of the day, as well as for periods of several years together which are under the influence of one planet or another, a specialist is usually consulted. The most important of these specialists are the Brahman priests, who refer to printed astrological handbooks *(pañcāṅkam)* providing detailed information on auspicious and inauspicious times, and non-Brahman astrologers who make a business from the writing and examination of personal horoscopes *(jātakam)*. The time for major events such as weddings or the building of a new house is fixed after consultation with an expert. Similarly, an astrologer will be asked to determine whether or not the moment a birth or a death occurred was inauspicious. If so, certain supplementary ceremonies must be performed.

A general knowledge on the part of the public about such matters, coupled with the information provided by professionals, makes for a very flexible system of explanation. The outline is enough to guide the individual in decisions about everyday activities, while the complication in detail is always sufficient to provide some excuse for misfortune. Table D.1 in this Appendix provides a layman's general outline of auspicious and inauspicious times.

People also take a general interest in local forms of divination. Certain everyday events can be taken as omens in these matters: if one sees a single Brahman or a single Ācāri approaching him, for example, it is a bad sign; but an encounter with two persons belonging to either of these groups is considered auspicious. If a bad omen has been noticed, nothing important must be undertaken until a better omen has appeared.

TABLE D.1
AUSPICIOUS AND INAUSPICIOUS TIMES

Days of the Week

*Monday:** A good day to start anything. An excellent day for the birth of a boy. It is said to be Civā's birthday. Monday is also a good day for temple pūjās, or ceremonial oblations.

Tuesday: An average to rather poor day. Not a good day to set out on a trip.

*Wednesday:** A good day for any undertaking, although not quite as good as Monday. Wednesday is a good day to be born on and a good day for starting a trip. It is also a good day for temple pūjās.

Thursday: An average to poor day. One should not begin anything new, especially a trip.

*Friday:** A good day for most things. It is an excellent day for the birth of a girl, but inauspicious for the birth of a boy. People say it is Pārvati's birthday. It is an excellent day for temple pūjās, but not a good day to travel.

Saturday: An inauspicious day. One should avoid travel and, in general, beginning anything new.

Sunday: An average day, neither very good nor very bad. It is best to avoid travel and any new undertakings.

Months of the Year

Cittirai: (April–May) An inauspicious month. Most castes will not hold weddings at this time, and it is not a good month for travel or for starting new things. It is not a good month to be born in.

*Vaikāci:** (May–June) An auspicious month for weddings, births, and the start of anything new.

*Āni:** (June–July) An auspicious month for weddings, births, and the start of anything new.

ĀTi: (July–August) In general an inauspicious month. However, an excellent time for making offerings to the deceased and for exorcising malign spirits. These two activities are best done while the moon is waxing. This is the one month when no caste will celebrate a wedding, but a number of temple festivals are held. Births that occur during this month are considered particularly inauspicious.

*ĀvaNi:** (August–September) An auspicious month for weddings, births, and the start of anything new.

PuraTTāci: (September–October) For the majority of castes, this is an inauspicious month for weddings, and for childbirth. However, it is a good month for temple pūjās. Special offerings are also made to the deceased on the dark moon day.

*Aippaci:** (October–November) An auspicious month for weddings, births, and the start of anything new.

*Kārttikai:** (November–December) An auspicious month for weddings, births, and the start of anything new.

MārkaRi: (December–January) For the majority of castes, this is an inauspicious month for weddings, and for childbirth. During this month many preparatory pūjās and fasts are made for the festival which begins on the first day of Tai.

*Tai:** (January–February) An auspicious time for weddings and for childbirth. There is a big poṅkal festival held on the first three days. This is a general festival month for all deities.

*Māci:** (February–March) An auspicious month for weddings and for childbirth. Special pūjās for the deceased are performed on Civanrāttiri.

*Paṅkuni:** (March–April) An auspicious month for weddings and for childbirth. Also a festival month for the gods.

SOURCE: Information for this table was provided by Informant no. 20.
NOTES: This table includes only details that are common knowledge to all adults.
*Time which is generally considered auspicious, and during which all castes will hold weddings.

Appendix E
WEIGHTS, MEASURES, WAGES, AND PRICES IN RURAL KOŇKU, 1966

Standard Measures

The standard measure used in purchasing grain and other dry foodstuffs is the *paTi*. One paTi equals about two heaped cupfulls (standard cooking measure) or about 1.2 pounds in weight. Larger quantities of agricultural produce are measured as follows:

$$4 \text{ paTi} = 1 \text{ vaLLam}$$
$$16 \text{ vaLLam} = 1 \text{ moTā}$$
$$24 \text{ vaLLam} = 1 \text{ mūTTai}[1]$$
$$6 \text{ moTā} = 1 \text{ poti}$$
$$4 \text{ mūTTai} = 1 \text{ poti}$$
$$1 \text{ maNaṅku} = 25 \text{ pounds of produce (approx.)}$$

Average Consumption Rate

At a rough estimate, a hard-working man will eat the following quantities of grain:

$$1 \text{ paTi a day}$$
$$1/2 \text{ moTā a month}$$
$$1 \text{ poti a year}$$

(Since a man also needs vegetables, spices, cooking oil, salt, cloth, and other commodities, he needs to earn at least 1 moTā of grain a month (or its equivalent in cash) in order to support himself.)

Agricultural Wages

In 1966, the standard wage for full-time field labor by a man of touchable caste was 20 vaLLam of grain (cōLam, raki, or kampu) a month. The wage for untouchable field labor was 16 vaLLam a month or Rs. 15 to Rs. 35 a month plus a daily meal at noon. Average daily wages for field labor were Rs. 1-1/2 for men and Rs. 3/4 for women; a man could make a maximum of Rs. 2, while the most a woman could earn was Rs. 1. Untouchable laborers could also be paid by the year, and in this case a worker

---

[1]Sometimes 22-1/2 vaLLam = 1 mūTTai.

was entitled to one-sixteenth to one-eighth of the grain reaped at the time of the harvest by his employer.

Nonagricultural Wages

In 1966, weavers earned from Rs. 40 to Rs. 60 a month. Other skilled laborers such as masons and carpenters were earning from Rs. 60 to Rs. 90 a month (or Rs. 100 in some cases). Small roadside merchants, at an estimate, made an income of Rs. 100, or thereabouts, a month.

Average Yield per Acre

One acre of good land fertilized with 100 cartloads of manure will produce in a good year one of the following crops:

> 3 poti of cōLam
> 4 poti of kampu
> 5 poti of raki
> 6 poti of paddy (if land is very well irrigated).

One acre of good land without fertilizer will produce in a good year one of the following crops:

> 2 poti of cōLam
> 3 poti of kampu
> 4 poti of raki
> 4-1/2 poti of paddy (if land is well irrigated).

One acre of poor land without fertilizer will produce in a good year one of the following crops:

> 1 poti of cōLam
> 1-1/2 poti of kampu
> 2 poti of raki
> 2-1/2 poti of paddy (if land is irrigated).

Land prices are given in Table E.1.

Market Price of Grain

In July, 1966, grains were selling in the Kāṅkayam weekly market at approximately the prices given below:

> 1 mūTTai of raki–Rs. 50
> 1 mūTTai of kampu–Rs. 56
> 1 mūTTai of cōLam–Rs. 67
> 1 mūTTai of paddy–Rs. 120 (high-quality paddy)

These prices were calculated at 22-1/2 vaLLam to the mūTTai.

TABLE E.1
ESTIMATED LAND PRICES IN ŌLAPPĀLAIYAM, 1966

Quality of Land	Description	Maximum Price Per Acre (rupees)
Good:	"Dry" by revenue assessment standards, but watered by good and reliable wells.	10,000
Moderate:	Soil less good, but still watered by reliable wells.	7,000
Poor:	Poor soil and moderate wells.	5,000
Worst:	Poor, rocky soil and shallow or unreliable wells.	4,000

NOTES: As land did not come onto the market very frequently, the prices listed here are highly speculative. Land prices have been rising rapidly. Informants claimed that they had doubled between 1956 and 1966.

Livestock Prices

1 bull	–Rs. 400 to 600	1 male buffalo	–Rs. 200 to 250
1 cow	–Rs. 200 to 300	1 female buffalo	–Rs. 200 to 250
1 pregnant cow	–Rs. 300 to 400	1 pregnant buffalo	–Rs. 300 to 400
1 calf (of cow)	–Rs. 50 to 150	1 buffalo calf	–Rs. 30 to 100

1 chicken–Rs. 4 to 6
1 chick   –Rs. 3/4 to 1-1/2

Cart Prices

A single-yoke cart–Rs. 250 to 350
A twin-yoke cart –Rs. 400 to 500

Building Prices

In 1966 a small, solid house cost about Rs. 1,000 to build, but thatched huts or minute dwellings could be constructed for less. A good, spacious home, such as landed KavuNTar families are accustomed to, would have cost at least Rs. 5,000 to build.

Appendix F
TAMIL KIN TERMINOLOGIES AND
TERMS OF ADDRESS

Tamil Kin Terminologies

TABLE F.1
KIN TERMS USED BY THE KOṄKU KAVUNTARS

	Kin Term	Relation to Speaker
1	Appāru	FF, FFB, MMB, FMZH, MBWF, MZHF, BWMF, ZHMF, WMF, WFMB, WMFB
2	Appicci	MF, FMB, MFB, FFZH, MMZH, FBWF, FZHF, BWFF, ZHFF, WFF, WFFB, WMMB
3	Āttā (Appattā)	FM, FMZ, MFZ, FFBW, MMBW, MBWM, MZHM, BWMM, ZHMM, WMM, WFFZ, WMMZ
4	Ammāyi (Ammicci)	MM, MMZ, FFZ, FMBW, MFBW, FBWM, FZHM, BWFM, ZHFM, WFM, WFMZ, WMFZ
5	PāTTaṉ	FFF, FMF, MMF, MFF, FFFB, FFFF, FFMF, FFMB, FMFB, FMMF, FMMB, MFFF, MFFB, MFMF, MFMB, MMFF, MMFB, MMMF, MMMB, WFFF, WMFF, WMMF, WFMF
6	PāTTi	MMM, MFM, FFM, FMM, MMMZ, MMMM, MMFM, MMFZ, MFMZ, MFFM, MFFZ, FMMM, FMMZ, FMFM, FMFZ, FFMM, FFMZ, FFFM, FFFZ, WMMM, WFMM, WFFM, WMFM
7	Appā (Ayyā)	F, FB, MZH, FFBS, FMZS, MFZS, MMBS, MBWB, MZHB, BWMB, ZHMB, SWMF, DHMF, WMB, WFZH, WBWF, WZHF
8	Ammā	M, MZ, FBW, FFZD, FMBD, FZHZ, FBWZ, MFBD, MMZD, BWFZ, ZHFZ, SWMM, DHMM, WFZ, WMBW, WBWM, WZHM
9	Māmā (Māmaṉ)	MB, FZH, BWF, ZHF, FFZS, FMBS, FBWB, FZHB, MFBS, MMZS, BWFB, ZHFB, DHFF, SWFF, WFB, WMZH

287

TABLE F.1 (continued)

	Kin Term	Relation to Speaker
10	Attai	FZ, MBW, BWM, ZHM, FFBD, FMZD, MFZD, MMBD, MBWZ, MZHZ, BWMZ, ZHMZ, SWFM, DHFM, WM, WMZ, WFBW
11	ANNan* Tampiṭ	B, FBS, MZS, FZDH, MBDH, BWZH, ZHZH, ZSWF, ZDHF, SWMB, DHMB, WZH, WFZS, WMBS, WBWB, WZHB
12	Akkā* Taṅkacciṭ	Z, FBD, MZD, FZSW, MBSW, BWBW, ZHBW, SWMZ, DHMZ, WBW, WFZD, WMBD, WBWZ, WZHZ
13	Cammaṇti	SWM, SWF, DHM, DHF, BDHF, BDHM, BSWF, BSWM
14	Marumakaṇ (MāppiḻḻLai)	ZS, DH, BDH, SWB, DHB, FZSS, FBDS, MBSS, MZDS, BWBS, BSWB, BDHB, ZHBS, SSWF, SDHF, WZDH, WBS
15	MarumakaL	SW, SWZ, DHZ, BSW, BWBD, BDHZ, BSWZ, DDHM, DSWM, WBD, WZSW
16	Akkā MakaL	ZD, MBSD, MZDD, FBDD, FZSD
17	Maccāṇ (Maittuṇar)	ZH, BWB, FZS, MBS, ZHB, FBDH, MZDH, SWFB, DHFB, WB, WFBS, WMZS
18	MaccānTār* KoRuntaṇārṭ	HB
19	Naṅkayā* KoRuntiyāṭ	BW, FZD, MBD, BWZ, ZHZ, FBSW, MZSW, ZSWM, ZDHM, SWFZ, DHFZ, WZ, WFBD, WMZD
20	KaNavaṇ (Purucaṇ, VīᴛTukkārar)	H
21	Maṇaivi (PoNTāTTi, PeNcāti)	W
22	Makaṇ	S, BS, ZDH, FBSS, FZDS, MBDS, MZSS, BWZS, ZHZS, ZSWB, SWZH, DHZH, DDHF, WZS, WBDH
23	MakaL	D, BD, ZSW, FBSD, FZDD, MBDD, MZSD, BWZD, ZHZD, ZSWZ, SWBW, DHBW, SSWM, WZD, WBSW
24	Pēraṇ	SS, DS, BSS, BDS, ZSS, ZDS, SSS, SDS, SDH, DSS, DDS, DDH, BSSS, BSDS, BSDH, BDSS, BDDS, BDDH, ZSSS, ZSDS, ZSDH, ZDSS, ZDDS, ZDDH, SWBS, SWZS, SSWB, SSSS, SSDS, SSDH, SDSS, SDDS, SDDH, SDHB, DSSS, DSDS, DSDH, DDSS, DDDS, DDDH, DSWB, DHBS, DHZS, DDHB, WBSS, WZSS, WBDS, WZDS

TABLE F.1 (concluded)

	Kin Term	Relation to Speaker
25	Pētti	SD, DD, BSD, BDD, ZSD, ZDD, SSD, SDD, SSW, DSD, DDD, DSW, BSSD, BSDD, BSSW, BDSD, BDDD, BDSW, ZSSD, ZSDD, ZSSW, ZDSD, ZDDD, ZDSW, SWBD, SWZD, SSWZ, SSSD, SSDD, SSSW, SDSD, SDDD, SDSW, SDHZ, DSSD, DSDD, DSSW, DDSD, DDDD, DDSW, DSWZ, DHBD, DHZD, DDHZ, WBSD, WZSD, WBDD, WZDD

SOURCES: Informant no. 29, with assistance from Informant no. 20.
NOTES: This listing of terms was initially made with the help of Informant no. 29. It was later expanded with the assistance of Thomas Storm IV and K. Cuntaram (Informant no. 20). I am grateful to both these men for their considerable effort in enlarging this table and this Appendix as a whole.
  This table lists in full the kin terms used by the Koṅku KavuNTars. In all cases it is the term of reference that is given. All terms listed are used by both male and female speakers, unless the relationship itself (in the case of a husband or wife referring to his or her spouse) indicates the sex of the speaker. To the best of my knowledge, the following groups all use the Koṅku KavuNTar terminology in detail: Koṅku CeTTiyār, Kaikkōlar Mutaliyār, ŌkaccāNTi PaNTāram, Koṅku UTaiyār, Maramēri NāTār, Koṅku Nāvitar, Koṅku VaNNār, and Koṅku Paraiyar. (Most of these are groups that serve the Koṅku KavuN-Tar community.) Sometimes *ANNi* serves as a prestigious alternate form for *Naṅkayā* for members of these groups. Kin terms that are used by other subcastes and which differ from those listed in this table are given in Table F.2.
*These terms are used only for relatives who are elder than ego.
†These terms are used only for relatives who are younger than ego.

TABLE F.2

VARIATIONS ON KOṄKU KAVUNTAR USAGE IN THE KIN TERMINOLOGY OF OTHER CASTES

Number of Term in Table F.1	Kin Term	Relation to Speaker
(a) Aiyar Brahman:		
1 & 2	Tāttā	FF, MF
3 & 4	PāTTi	FM, MM
9	Ammān	MB
	Māmā	FZH
17	Ammānci	MBS
	Attān	FZS
19	AmmaṅkāL	MBD
	AttaṅkāL	FZD
(b) CōLi Ācāri:		
1 & 2	Tāttā	FF, MF
3 & 4	PāTTi	FM, MM
17	Attān*	MBS, FZS
19	ANNi*	MBD, FZD
(c) Kaikkōlar Mutaliyār:		
1 & 2	Tāttā	FF, MF
3 & 4	PāTTi	FM, MM
(d) KōmuTTi CeTTiyār (mother tongue—Telugu):		
1	Ayyā (Jēyāyyā, Appārayyā)	FF
2	Tāttā	MF
3	Ammayyā (Appattā)	FM
4	Avvā (PāTTi)	MM
9	Māmayyā (Māmā)	FZH
	Māmā	MB
10	Attammā (Attai)	MBW
	Attai	FZ

TABLE F.2 (concluded)

Number of Term in Table F.1	Kin Term	Relation to Speaker
(d) KōmuTTi CeTTiyār (continued)		
14	AlluTu	DH, ZS [male speaker], BS [female speaker]
15	KōTalu	SW, BD [female speaker]
17	Pāvā (Maccān)*	MBS, FZS
19	Otunai (ANNi)*	MBD, FZD
(e) VaTuka Nāyakkar (mother tongue—Telugu):		
1	PēTTayyā (Appārayyā)	FF
2	Tātta (Appucci)	MF
3	PēTTiyammā (Appattā)	FM
4	Tāttammā (Ammāyi)	MM
17	Pāvā*	MBS, FZS
19	Vatanā (Naṅkai)*	MBD, FZD
(f) Moracu Mātāri (mother tongue—Kannada):		
2	PāTTan	MF
3	Appattā (ToTTavi, PāTTi)	FM
4	PāTTi (PāTTivi)	MM
10	Akkā	FZ, MBW
17	Māmā*	MBS, FZS [also used for MB and FZH]
19	Connavi (Cinnammā)*	MBD, FZD
(g) KūTai Kuravar:		
2	PāTTā (Appicci)	MF
10	Akkā (Attai)	MBW, FZ

SOURCES: (a) Informant no. 34, (b) Informant no. 56, (c) Informant no. 57, (d) Informant no. 58, (e) Informant no. 59, (f) Informant no. 60, (g) Informant no. 23.
NOTES: Informant no. 55 gave the same usage for the KaruNīkar PiLLai as that given by Informant no. 34 for the Brahmans, with one exception: he said that the former group prefer *Ammān* for both MB and FZH. Thus it would seem that the distinction between these two relatives may not be made as clearly by this group as it is by the Brahmans.
*These terms are used only for relatives who are elder than ego.

Terms of Address

A full discussion of the modifications of the terminology given in Tables F.1 and F.2 in actual address would require a separate publication. However, a few general comments can be made. It is uncommon, for example, for anyone to address a person of a younger generation except by their name.

For people of ego's own generation important simplifications of the reference terminology take place. All cross males younger than a male ego will be addressed as *MāppiLLai* and those of roughly equal or slightly greater age as *maccān*. (Much older males in ego's generation, particularly if they are in the position of having taken a woman from ego's descent group, may be addressed as *māmā* to show greater respect.) Hence, in address, the distinctions between different types of cross males used in reference are dropped in favor of a general classification in terms of degree of respect.

TABLE F.3
TERMS OF ADDRESS
(right-division subcastes)

Generation	Male Speaker					Female Speaker			
	Parallel Males	Cross Males	Parallel Females	Cross Females		Parallel Males	Cross Males	Parallel Females	Cross Females
				Married	Unmarried				
+1 Elder*	ANNan̲	Māmā	Akkā	Naṅkayā	Naṅkayā	ANNan̲	Māmā	Akkā	Naṅkayā
Same Age* as ego	Name	Maccān̲	Name	Name	No term of Address	Name	Maccān̲	Name	Name
Younger*	Name	MāppiLLai (or name)	Name	Name	Name	Name	MāppiLLai (or name)	Name	Name
−1	Name					Name			

Address Term = Reference Term

NOTES:
+1 Generation directly above that of ego.
−1 Generation directly below that of ego.
*Same generation as that of ego.

The terms for unmarried cross females of roughly ego's age are not used at all by males. Instead, the general practice is to use no term or name at all. Females, however, will address all elder cross males of their own generation as *māmā* and those who are somewhat younger as *maccāṉ*. Very young cross males of their own generation can either be called *māppiLLai* or be addressed by name. The principle of classification by degree of respect due is thus the same as that employed by male speakers for the same relatives. Women address other cross women who are older than themselves as *naṅkayā,* the appropriate term of reference, while males limit this usage to married women in this category. Both sexes address all cross relatives of the same sex who are younger than they are by name. Terms for spouse are not used in address by either sex.

In generations senior to ego the terms of reference are also the terms of address. There are no complications here except for the fact that a very old person in ego's parents' generation is sometimes addressed by the appropriate term for a grandparent. For parallel relatives who are younger than ego, however, the first name is substituted for the correct kin term. *Cammaṇti* is never used in address, the appropriate parallel term for a nuclear family relative being employed instead.

The general pattern of usage for address is given in Table F.3.

There is also a series of general address terms that are used in a manner rather like "Boy," "Mister," and "Sir," in English. These terms, which form a clear hierarchical set, are listed in Table F.4.

TABLE F.4
TAMIL GENERAL TERMS OF ADDRESS

	For Males	For Females
1.	ṅka (verb ending)	ṅka (verb ending)
2.	appā	ammā
3.	pā	mā
4.	Tā, Tē	Tī, lē

The first three terms in Table F.4 can be used for addressing strangers, and the individual makes his choice among them according to the degree of respect he wishes to indicate. The first, which implies respect by a verb ending, avoids the problem of direct address. It is used when one wishes to express great respect. *Appā* or *ammā* is used for addressing people of roughly equal status, and the shortened forms of these terms, *pā* and *mā,* are used for addressing those of lower rank. The third and fourth terms in the male list can alternately be used to address male children, as expressions of endearment. In the female list, however, only the third can be used to address a female child. The fourth terms in this list have an insulting and heavily sexual overtone. They are used only in private, as expressions of endearment for girl friends or wives.

Appendix G
INHERITANCE CLAIMS

The rules of inheritance among the right-division castes serve to stress the unity and also the equality of all clan males. For propriety's sake, it is better to wait to divide the property until after the father's death, but many families do so earlier. Among these castes uxorilocal residence is generally accepted. If there is any difference in the inheritance tradition among left-division castes, it lies in the direction of a strong disapproval of uxorilocal residence and the subsequent passing of property to a grandson via females, a technique of circumventing traditional law. This attitude is in keeping with the greater stress the left-division castes place on the prestigious Mitāksarā legal tradition as set down in the classical Sanskrit law books.[1]

The most important single fact in understanding these inheritance rules is that a man holds all his own inherited property in common with his sons.[2] The basic terms used in connection with this joint holding are *paṅku*, meaning "share," and *paṅkāLi*, meaning "those who share." A man and his sons can divide the whole into equal shares at any time, although it is considered better to manage it jointly until the former's death. In theory, a father cannot sell any part of his inherited property without consulting his sons, as he would be selling something in which they have a right by birth. However, in practice, a boy is not considered adult until he reaches sixteen. Fathers often manage all the property without consulting their sons before they reach this age.

From the joint property of a father and his sons stems a joint obligation to support the wife-mother and, later, any daughters-in-law. Adequate dowry must also be supplied to each of the father's daughters and they should be married to men whose financial position at least equals that of their own brothers. Only after the father has died and these other obligations have been met is it seemly to divide the remainder of the inheritance equally among the male siblings. Usually a girl's dowry is taken from the family's liquid assets, while any land and animals are inherited strictly in the male line. Jewelry, female clothing, and household utensils, on the

---

[1]Two people, both belonging to left-division groups (the VēTTuvar KavuNTars and the VēTar), were the only ones to tell me that such practices are explicitly forbidden and that property must pass, in the absence of a biological son, to a man's own brothers.

[2]Property that a man has earned or acquired on his own is distinct from inherited property, and he may dispose of it as he pleases. Nonetheless, such assets are usually not treated separately from what a man has formally inherited, and what remains of them after his death becomes inherited property for the next generation.

other hand, are passed down in the female line. Thus anything a woman received at her own marriage that remains intact and that she can spare will be divided in turn among her daughters at their marriages. After marriage, however, a girl cannot expect any further share in her parents' property. If any of a woman's property remains after all her daughters have been married, it will be passed on at the time of her death to her sons. There is an important difference here between men and women. A girl receives her entire share in the inheritance at the time of her marriage. Brothers, on the other hand, are expected to retain their joint holding until their father's death, and do not necessarily receive individual shares until then.

If a man should die without sons, after provision has been made for his wife and daughters, his property should be divided among his surviving brothers (and brothers' sons). A clever man can avoid this eventuality, however, by adopting a boy. The only stipulation is that the child must be fathered by a man of the same clan, and preferably by a BS or FBS. Adoption is referred to as *tattu eTuttal* ("to jump or leap over") in Tamil, and an adopted son is a *tattu makan* ("a son who has leaped over"). The adopted son acquires full rights to his father's property, just as a real son would have done. There is a small ceremony for adoption; this is as follows:

> At an adoption, a tumbler full of water mixed with turmeric powder is prepared. The adopting mother must drink the first half of the contents and the son to be adopted the second half. The adopting parents must then provide a feast for relations.

An adopted son is expected to perform the funeral rites for his adopted parents and to continue to perform oblations for them after their deaths, should they request it in a dream. He is also obliged to support the widow of his adopted father and to provide dowry for any of the latter's unmarried daughters, just as actual sons would have done. In other words, an adopted son acquires all the social rights and responsibilities of a male heir actually born into the family.

There is also a second possibility open to a man without sons. He may invite his daughter's husband to reside uxorilocally and let his property pass through this daughter to her sons. Both the adoption of a son and the uxorilocal residence of a son-in-law are ways of circumventing the strict letter of the classical inheritance law. Both solutions are common in the KavuNTar community. However, these techniques frequently create an uproar of objection among a man's more distant pankāLi, who stand to lose what would otherwise be their share. Many traditional KavuNTar stories turn on this theme.

According to current law used in the state courts, widows can inherit from their husbands, and on the parents' demise, daughters inherit equally with sons. Personal wills are recognized as superceding both claims. People point out that these laws give new teeth to the old techniques of circumvention just described. Everyone has heard rumors that both daughters and adopted children can now take their claims to court, although few have actually tried it. My informants still thought of these laws as just a new way 'to get around' the old tradition. The following is a detailed example of a recent legal adoption and its operation against the backdrop of traditional inheritance claims. It concerns the division of rights to proceeds from the yearly Māriyamman temple festival in Kannapuram by a group of PaNTāram priests. This PaNTāram subcaste is closely associated with the KavuNTar community.

There are three distinct groups of OkaccāNTi PaNTāram who currently have rights at the Kannapuram Māriyamman temple. The third group are recent immigrants to the area. They trace the history of their temple rights back to their FF, CēmalaiyāNTi. About 1900, the KavuNTar family in RaTTivalacu invited him to settle there, and it had assured him that he would receive a full third of the temple income. The first two groups were to receive the festival proceeds for two successive years. CēmalaiyāNTi was to receive the full proceeds once every three years.

CēmalaiyāNTi had five sons (see Fig. G.1). Some time ago, the division of rights was complicated by the decision that the first time (*a*) the festival fell to them, his sons Rāmacāmi, KirusNā, and Cinnucāmi would take one-fifth, two-fifths, and two-fifths of the proceeds respectively. The next time (*b*) the festival fell to them, Rāmacāmi would again take one-fifth, while the other brothers, PaRanicami and Mārimuttu, would each take two-fifths. Thus Rāmacāmi was to get one-fifth every three years and the other four brothers two-fifths every six years. Each brother was then left to divide his share into equal portions with his own sons.

One of the five brothers, Rāmacāmi, had no sons. On his death, his widow Cellammā tried to prevent the loss of the temple rights to her husband's brothers' descendants by arranging for the share to descend via her daughter's husband to her grandson. At this suggestion, however, the paṅkāLi raised loud objections. Finally she abandoned this idea and adopted her HBS (who was also her own ZS) as an heir. The paṅkāLi were not pleased but let it pass. The adopted son does not yet feel altogether secure in his right to this share. While normally it is not necessary for all the claimants to be present at any one festival to receive their portions of the proceeds, the adopted son has made it a point to take on temple responsibilities and to be present at any discussions about temple management. While, in the long run, an individual must do his share of the festival work in order to receive his part of the proceeds, the other paṅkāLi will swap their work around informally. The position of the adopted son is somewhat envied by his male cousins and could still be a cause for dispute in the future.

At about the same time that this man was adopted by Rāmacāmi's widow, he had decided to sell the share in the proceeds which he had inherited from his own father, to his brother's son. This share came to

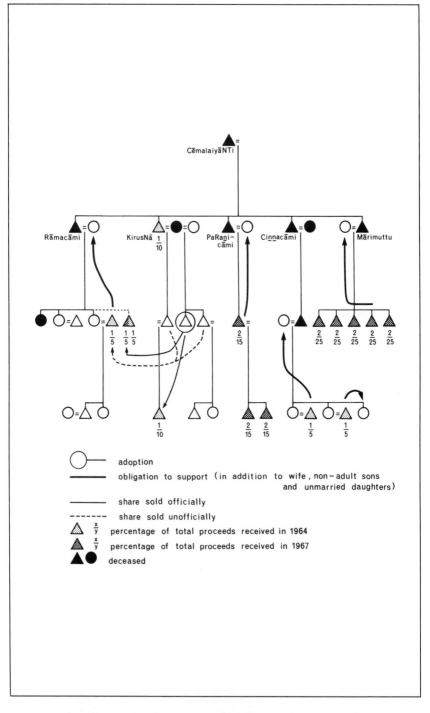

Fig. G.1. An example of the division of inheritance claims.

(2/5) × (1/4) or one-tenth of the proceeds every six years. In order to sell it, he had to obtain permission from his father and both his brothers, as they held the right to the initial two-fifths jointly. They agreed, and he sold it for 200 rupees several years ago.

The adopted son's two brothers have both mortgaged their share of the inheritance to their FBDH for 200 rupees. This type of sale is unofficial but common. It means that the two brothers have the opportunity to spend in the present, but that when the festival time comes around they must turn over their proceeds to the relative from whom they obtained the loan. This is an informal agreement, and not necessarily a permanent arrangement. Thus it does not require the assent of the other brothers or of the father, as in the previous case. Figure G.1 illustrates how the proceeds were actually divided in 1964 and in 1967.

When a man has had sons outside the formal bond of marriage, the question of inheritance is a very delicate one.[3] Sons born under these circumstances can never press formal claims, but it is said that their demands can easily move a man sentimentally. Physiological paternity has a claim on a man's affection, and no one would like to ignore such a son entirely. In these cases, a man usually gives presents to his offspring during his own lifetime, often gifts of cash or of moveable goods, such as he would give to a daughter in dowry. The claims of illegitimate sons on their fathers, however, are strongest, of course, when they are accepted by the community at large. A son born of a passing affair with a low-caste woman suffers a much higher risk of being disclaimed or ignored than that faced by the son of an established concubine drawn from a man's own community.

---

[3]Note, for example, in Figure G.1, that the sons of both KirusNā's wives inherited equally.

A Glossary of Tamil Terms

NOTE: The approximate English pronunciation of each word, where not evident from the transliteration, appears in brackets.

Ācāri (Asari)

A caste whose traditional occupation is considered to be that of a craftsman who works with gold, brass, iron, stone, and wood. The two subcastes described in this account are the CōLi and the Koṅku Ācāri. Both are considered to be members of the left division.

Aippaci (Aippasi)

The Tamil month of October–November.

Āṇi

The Tamil month of June–July.

AṅkāLamman (Angalamman)

A goddess particularly linked to childbirth and strongly associated with left-division groups.

aNNan

The term for "elder brother."

appāru

The term for "grandfather," particularly father's father.

Arumaikkārar

A ritual specialist (male or female) of a particular subcaste who performs certain important ceremonies at the life-cycle celebrations of that particular group. Literally, "a very auspicious person."

ĀTi (Adi)

The seventh month of the traditional Tamil year (July–August). It is considered an inauspicious month and is associated with offerings to the gods, to the deceased, and to malign spirits.

ĀvaNi

The Tamil month of August–September.

Brahman

A caste whose traditional occupation is considered to be scholarship and the priesthood. The members of this group enjoy an elevated ritual status in the Koṅku region. Except where otherwise specified, the persons described in this account are members of the Aiyar subcaste. They are considered to be above the right-left division.

cakti (sakti)

A form of divine power, usually associated with women.

camāti (samadi)

A shrine constructed to the memory of a recently deceased family member.

cankarānti

Time when the sun passes from one sign of the zodiac to another, particularly in January at the time of the Tai nōmpu or ponkal festival.

canyāci

A person who has vowed to renounce his worldly ties and become a wandering ascetic in search of release from ordinary social life and who seeks contact with the divine.

cēri (cheri)

An untouchable settlement or living area.

CeTTiyār (chettiar)

A caste whose traditional occupation is considered to be business. Except where otherwise specified, the persons described in this account are members of the KōmuTTi subcaste. They are considered to be members of the left division.

cinna (sinna)

A term meaning "small," which can also refer to a lack of importance or prestige. Usually contrasted with *periya,* meaning "large."

Cittirai (Sittirai)

The month of April–May. At present the month that begins the Tamil year. (Traditionally the Tamil year began in Tai, corresponding to our January–February.)

Civā (Siva)

One of the great Hindu male gods, married to the goddess Pārvati. His name is commonly spelled as "Siva" or "Shiva."

Civanrāttiri (Sivanrattiri)

Civā's night. An important festival honoring the deceased which takes place in the month of Māci (February–March).

cōLam (cholam)

Holcus sorgum. Similar to field corn in appearance and in taste.

cuttam (suttam)

An adjective used to describe a state of ritual purity.

eL

Sesamum seed.

ēRu civālayankaL (erusivalayangal)

A blanket term for the seven temples dedicated to the god Civā in Konku which are specifically associated with the region as a whole.

iNaiccīr (inaisir)

A special ceremony emphasizing the tie between a brother and a sister which is performed just before the former's marriage ritual is completed by the tying of the wedding necklace.

IruLappan

A minor male deity whose name suggests an association with darkness. He is similar in character to the better-known KaruppaNacāmi.

iTankai (idangai)

Term used to refer to the left division. Literally, it means, "of the left side."

Jāti

A caste. A socially recognized grouping of persons that is formed on the basis of general economic, occupational, and ritual criteria.

jāti

A subcaste. A specific grouping of alleged kinsmen identified within a larger caste category on the basis of their particular ritual, territorial, and/or occupational identity.

jāti piLLai

A group whose members are characterized as the "children" of some particular subcaste. The term usually indicates a ritual tie between the group and the subcaste in question, but it can have a derogatory significance pointing to miscegenation.

KāLi (also KāLiyamman)

The great goddess KāLi, said to be the terrifying form of Civā's consort Pārvati.

kampu (kambu)

Penicellaria spicata. A small, greenish millet.

Kannimār

The seven sisters or young goddesses who are worshipped at local lineage festivals.

KarNam

A village accountant appointed by the government to keep the official land records up-to-date.

kārru kālam

The windy season, July and August.

Kārttikai

The Tamil month of November–December.

KaruppaNacāmi

A male deity who serves as a guardian of prominent goddesses. He is also the guardian of local territory and of the fields.

kaTai vīti (kadai vidi)

A row of shops strung out along a main road.

kāTu (kadu)

Non-irrigated land, for which cultivation depends on rainfall alone.

KavuNTar (Goundar)

A caste whose traditional occupation is considered to be farming. This group controls most of the cultivable land in Konku today. Except where otherwise stated, the persons described in this account are members of the Konku (or VēLāLar) subcaste. They are considered to be leaders of the right division.

kirāma cānti (girama sandi)

A special ceremony said to bring calm and coolness to the kirāmam area.

kirāma teyvam

Goddess associated with the kirāmam or revenue-village area.

kirāmam

A division of a nāTu, referred to as a revenue village by British administrators and traditionally used as the base unit in land-tax collection. Kirāmam areas are generally associated with a local goddess who is their guardian and for whom an annual festival is celebrated.

KirusNā

A major Hindu deity and form of the god VisNu, Civā's brother-in-law.

koL

Phaseolus trilobus. Wild horse grain.

Koṅku (Kongu)

A large cultural and historical region, comprising most of the northwest corner of the present Tamilnadu (Madras) State.

kōttiram (gotra)

A Sanskrit term for clanlike descent units used mostly by Brahmans and certain high-ranking left-division groups.

Kottukkārar

Leader of an Ūr or hamlet area.

kula teyvam

General term for a clan deity.

kulam

A term for clan units, used mostly by KavuNTars and their close associates.

Kuṟavar

A caste that is classified as "untouchable" and whose traditional occupation is considered to be basketmaking. The subcaste discussed in this account is known as KūTai. Its members are said to belong to the left division.

kūTTam

A term for clan units, used mostly by left-division groups.

kuTumpam (kudumbam)

A household unit or group of kinsmen who share a common residence and eat food from the same cooking hearth.

maccāṉ (machan)

The term for potential husband or brother-in-law. A cross relative.

Māci (Masi)

The Tamil month of February–March. It is of special ritual importance to Brahmans and the higher-ranking castes of the left division.

Mahabarata

One of the great Indian classical epics, along with its counterpart, the *Ramayana*.

malai

A mountain or prominent hill.

māman

The term for "mother's brother." A cross relative.

māman/maccān

A term used to characterize cross relatives in general. It is a combination of the terms for "mother's brother" and for a potential husband or brother-in-law.

maNaṅku (manangu)

A traditional measure of sugar. (See Appendix E for further details.)

maNiyārar

A village munsif who is appointed by the government and given the responsibility for land-tax collection in a particular revenue village or kirāmam area.

maRai kālam

The rainy season, September through November.

Māriyamman

Goddess of the kirāmam or revenue-village area. She has a particularly important association with smallpox and blindness, and is also thought to control the rains.

MārkaRi (Margali)

The Tamil month of December–January

Mātāri (Madari)

A caste that is classified as "untouchable" and whose traditional occupation is considered to be leatherworking. The caste is known elsewhere as Cakkiliyan. Several subcastes are discussed in this account. They are all said to belong to the left division.

mā viLakku

Small lamps of paste made with rice flour and water, which hold a little oil and a cotton wick. They are presented as offerings to the local goddess Māriyamman during her annual festival.

muni

A terrifying giant who demands blood sacrifices in return for service as a guardian.

muppāTTan

The term for "grandfather's grandfather," or ancestors in general.

muppāTTukkārar

The title of a subcaste leader at the kirāmam level.

Murukan (Murugan)

The most important and beloved of all South Indian gods. He is considered to be Civā's second son and is known in the Sanskrit literature by the name of Skanda.

Mutaliyār (Mudaliar)

A caste whose traditional occupation is considered to be weaving, military service, and business. Except where otherwise stated, the persons described in this account are members of the Kaikkōlar subcaste. They are considered to be members of the left division, but their position appears to be ambivalent as, in practice, they exhibit some characteristics that are typical of the left and others that are typical of the right.

muyal vēTTai

A hare hunt, an event which occurs annually in many revenue villages (kirāmam) of the Koṅku area.

nākakkal (nagakal)

Stone images carved to suggest the shape of a cobra.

NāTār (Nadar)

A caste whose traditional occupation is considered to be that of palmyra-palm climbers (toddy-tappers). Except where otherwise specified, the persons described in this account are members of the Maramēri subcaste. They are considered to be members of the right division.

nāTTāmaikkārar

The title of a subcaste leader at the nāTu level.

nāTTār

The title of a subcaste leader at the nāTu level.

nāTTu KavuNTar (nattu Goundar)

Title of a KavuNTar community leader at the nāTu level.

nāTTukkal

A stone marking the site of a deity who protects a specific residential neighborhood.

NāTu (Nadu)

A region or large area that is thought to be culturally and historically distinct.

nāTu (nadu)

A subdivision of a region that forms an administratively and ritually distinct area. The same word is used as a term for clan units by some of the service castes.

naTu vīti (Nadu vidi)

The central street.

naTu vīTu (Nadu vidu)

An indentation in the central wall of the house, intended to hold a lamp lighted in memory of the ancestors.

Nāvitar (Navidar)

A caste whose traditional occupation is considered to be that of barber. The two subcastes discussed in this account are the Koṅku and the PāNTiya. The first are considered to be members of the right division, and the second members of the left.

Nāyakkar

A caste whose traditional occupation is considered to be well-digging, stone excavation, and road-building. Except where otherwise specified, the persons described in this account are members of the VaTuka subcaste. They are considered to be members of the left division.

nōmpu (nombu)

An important festival day. There are two big nōmpus in the Tamil ceremonial calendar, one on the first three days of Tai (January–February) and the other on the dark moon day of ĀTi (July–August).

pakkattāla contam (condam)

A term used for characterizing close relatives as a group.

panchayat

The basic unit of local, present-day government, roughly corresponding in size and function to the traditional kirāmam area.

paṇi kālam

The "cold" season, starting in December and lasting through the first half of February.

paṅkāLi (pangali)

Men of the same lineage, who can trace their descent, through males alone, to a common male ancestor. The term literally means "those who share." It is the Tamil term most often used to characterize the relationship appropriate to so-called parallel relatives. The term derives from the verb *paṅku,* meaning "to share."

Paṅkuṇi (Panguni)

The Tamil month of March–April.

pantam (pandam)

A traditional torch used as a light on festive occasions.

PaNTāram (Pandaram)

A caste whose traditional occupations are considered to be those of festival cook, local priest, flower-tier, and eating-leaf provider. Except where otherwise stated, the persons described in this account are members of the OkaccāNTi subcaste. They are considered to be members of the right division.

Paṟaiyar

A caste that is classified as "untouchable" and whose traditional occupation is considered to be drumming. The subcaste discussed in this account is known as Koṅku. Its members are said to belong to the right division.

Paramakāmuni

A huge and frightening deity who takes blood sacrifices. The name suggests an association with the natural, rocky protuberances found in the Kāṅkayam nāTu area.

paricam (parisam)

A ritual sum paid by the groom to the bride's family in some communities at or just before the wedding ceremony.

Pārvati

Civā's wife, and an important goddess in her own right.

PaTTakkārar

A man who bears a title, called a *paTTam,* conferred by a king.

paTTam

A local title, granted by kings, which is passed from father to eldest son in the male line and accords certain families in the Koṅku region great prestige.

pāTTan̲

The term used for grandfather's father.

PattirakāLi (Badrakali)

Local form of the great goddess KāLi.

periya

A term meaning "large," "prestigious," or "very important." Usually contrasted with *cin̲n̲a,* meaning "small."

Periyatan̲akkārar

A subcaste leader of a nāTu area.

PiLLai

A caste whose traditional occupation in the Koṅku area is considered to be accountancy. Except where otherwise specified, the persons described in this account are members of the KaruNīkar subcaste. They are considered to be above the right-left division.

piracātam (prasatam)

Offerings of food that have been blessed by a deity and are intended for distribution to devotees.

poṅkal (pongal)

A very important festival held on the first three days of the traditional Tamil new year.

pūjā

A ceremonial oblation made to a god.

pulavar

A local poet and genealogist.

PuraTTāci (Purattasi)

The Tamil month of September–October. It is of particular ritual importance to Brahmans and the higher-ranking castes of the left division.

rājā
>A king or military overlord of a large region.

rāki (ragi)
>*Eleusine coracana.* A small, dark brown, very nourishing millet.

Tai
>The first month of the traditional Tamil year (January–February). Also a word for "mother."

tampi (tambi)
>The term for "younger brother."

TaṅkāttaL
>The younger sister of the two brothers of the famous *Story of the Brothers.* She has become a deity in her own right.

Tēṉ vīti (vidi)
>The southern street.

tōraNam
>A leaf-decorated archway used to mark a ritual boundary on ceremonial occasions.

tōTTam
>Well-irrigated land, suited to growing such crops as cotton, tobacco, vegetables, and pulses.

Ūr
>A hamlet area which enjoys both a ritual and an economic unity. Such a hamlet may include several ūr, or residential sites.

ūr
>A residential site, a permanent cluster of homes, surrounded by countryside.

Ūr KavuNTar (Ur Goundar)
>KavuNTar leader of an Ūr, or hamlet area.

Urimai
>A traditional right, obtained by virtue of birth.

UrimaippeN
>The girl a man has a "right" to marry. Either his matrilateral or patrilateral cross cousin, depending on the subcaste in question.

UTaiyār (Udaiyar)
>A caste whose traditional occupation is considered to be that of potter and house-builder. Except where otherwise specified, the persons described in this account are members of the Koṅku subcaste. They are considered to be members of the right division.

Vaikāci (Vaigasi)
>The Tamil month of May–June.

valaṅkai (valangai)
>Term used to refer to the right division; literally it means, "of the right side."

vaLLam

A traditional measure of grain. See Appendix E for further details.

VaNNār

A caste whose traditional occupation is considered to be that of washerman. The two subcastes discussed in this account are the Koṅku and the VaTuka. The first are considered to be members of the right and the second members of the left division.

varataTcaṉai

A Sanskrit term for dowry, used in Koṅku by those castes who make such wedding payments.

varna

One of the four classes or orders of Indian society, according to traditional Hindu social theory as found in early texts.

vaTakku vīti (Vadaku vidi)

The northern street.

vayal

Well-watered and highly fertile land, mostly found along the banks of canals and rivers.

vēsTi

A man's lower cloth, wrapped something like a long skirt in the Koṅku area.

veyyil kālam

The hot or "sunny" season, lasting from the second half of February until the end of June.

Vināyakar (Vinayagar)

The beloved great god of India famous for his elephant-trunked face. He is thought to be the first son of Civā and Murukaṉ is said to be his younger brother.

VisNu

One of the great Hindu male gods, married to the goddess Laksmi.

Bibliography

Aberle, E. Kathleen (formerly E. Kathleen Gough). "Brahmin Kinship in a Tamil Village." *American Anthropologist* 58 (1956): 826–53.

——. "Caste in a Tanjore Village." In *Aspects of Caste in South India, Ceylon and North-West Pakistan,* edited by E. R. Leach, pp. 11–60. Cambridge: Cambridge University Press, 1960.

——. "A Comparison of Incest Prohibitions and the Rules of Exogamy in Three Matrilineal Groups of the Malabar Coast." *International Archives of Ethnography* 46, part 1 (1952): 82–105.

——. "Criteria of Caste Ranking in South India." *Man in India* 39, no. 2 (1959): 115–26.

——. "Female Initiation Rites on the Malabar Coast." *Journal of the Royal Anthropological Institute* 85 (1955): 45–78.

——. "The Social Structure of a Tanjore Village." In *India's Villages,* edited by M. N. Srinivas, pp. 90–102. 2nd ed., rev. Bombay: Asia Publishing House, 1960.

——. "The Social Structure of a Tanjore Village." In *Village India,* edited by McKim Marriott, pp. 36–52. Chicago: University of Chicago Press, 1955.

Adiceam, E. *La Géographie de l'irrigation dans le Tamilnad.* Paris: École française d'Extrême Orient, 1966.

Aiyappan, A. "Cross-cousin and Uncle-niece Marriages in South India." *Congrès International des Sciences Anthropologiques et Ethnologiques,* Compte-rendu de la première session, pp. 281–82. Londres, Institut royal d'anthropologie, 1934.

——. *Social Revolution in a Kerala Village.* Bombay: Asia Publishing House, 1965.

Ananthakrishna Iyer, L. K. *The Cochin Tribes and Castes.* 2 vols. Madras: Higginbotham, 1909–12.

——. *The Mysore Tribes and Castes.* 4 vols. Mysore: Mysore University, 1928–36.

——. *Travencore Tribes and Castes.* Madras: Higginbotham, 1939.

Andreen, A. *Annual Report for the T.E.L.C. Pioneer Board.* Polachi: Lutheran Church, 1954–55.

Arokiaswami, M. "The Cult of Mariamman or the Goddess of Rain." *Tamil Culture* 2, no. 2 (1953): 153–57.

——— . *The Early History of the Vellar Basin: A Study in Vellala Origin and Early History*. Madras: Madras University, 1954.

——— . *The Kongu Country*. Madras: Madras University Press, 1956.

AruNācala KavuNTar, K. *PaRaiyakōTTai PaTTakkārar NāTTu PāTalum Pūrva PaTTayamum* [History of the titled family of PaRaiyakōTTai]. Tirunelveli: S. R. CūppiramaNiya PiLLai, 1965.

Babb, Lawrence A. "Marriage and Malevolence: The Uses of Sexual Opposition in a Hindu Pantheon." *Ethnology* 9, no. 2 (1970): 137–48.

Baden-Powell, B. H. *The Indian Village Community*. 1892. Reprint. New Haven: Human Relations Area File Press, 1957.

Bailey, F. G. *Caste and the Economic Frontier*. Manchester: Manchester University Press, 1957.

——— . *Tribe, Caste and Nation*. Manchester: Manchester University Press, 1960.

Bannerjee, Mrs. Bhavani. *Marriage and Kinship of the Gangadikara Vokkaligas of Mysore*. Deccan College Dissertation Series, no. 27. Poona: Deccan College Postgraduate and Research Institute, 1966.

Barnett, Stephen A. "The Structural Position of a South Indian Caste: Kontaikatti Vēlālars in Tamilnadu." Ph.D. dissertation, University of Chicago, 1970.

Barth, Fredrick. "Segmentary Opposition and the Theory of Games: A Study of Pathan Organization." *Journal of the Royal Anthropological Institute* 89 (1959): 5–21.

——— . "The System of Social Stratification in Swat." In *Aspects of Caste in South India, Ceylon and North-West Pakistan*, edited by E. R. Leach, pp. 113–46. Cambridge: Cambridge University Press, 1960.

Beals, Alan R. "Conflict and Interlocal Festivals in a South Indian Region." *The Journal of Asian Studies* 23 (1964): 99–114.

——— . *Gopalpur: A South Indian Village*. New York: Holt, Rinehart and Winston, 1962.

Bechu, Rev. L. *Short History of the Coimbatore Mission*. Coimbatore: Victoria Press, 1927.

——— . *Story of the Coimbatore Mission*. Bangalore: Paris Foreign Mission Society, 1948.

Beck, Brenda E. F. "Colour and Heat in South Indian Ritual." *Man*, n.s. 4, no. 4 (1969): 553–72.

———. "The Examination of Marriage Ritual Among Selected Groups in South India." B. Litt. thesis, Oxford University, 1964.

———. "The Right-Left Division of South Indian Society." *The Journal of Asian Studies* 29, no. 4 (1970): 779–98.

———. "Social and Conceptual Order in Koṅku: A Region of South India." D.Phil. dissertation, Oxford University, 1968.

Beidelman, Thomas O. *A Comparative Analysis of the Jajmani System.* Locust Valley, New York: Association for Asian Studies, 1959.

Béteille, André. *Caste, Class and Power.* Berkeley: University of California Press, 1965.

———. "Elites, Status Groups and Caste in Modern India." In *India and Ceylon: Unity and Diversity,* edited by Philip Mason, pp. 83–120. Institute of Race Relations. London: Oxford University Press, 1967.

———. "Social Organization of Temples in a Tanjore Village." *History of Religions* 5, no. 1 (1965): 74–92.

———. "Sripuram: A Village in Tanjore District." *Economic Weekly* 14 (1962): 141–46.

Blunt, E. A. H. *The Caste System of Northern India with Special Reference to the United Provinces of Agra and Oudh.* London: Oxford University Press, 1931.

Bouglé, Célestin. *Essais sur le régime des castes.* 1908. Reprint. Paris: Alcan, 1927.

Boulnois, J. *La Caducée et la symbolique dravidienne indo-méditerranéenne, de l'arbre, de la pierre, du serpent et de la déesse-mère.* Paris: Librairie d'Amérique et d'Orient, 1939.

Buchanan, Francis Hamilton. *A Journey from Madras Through the Countries of Mysore, Canara, and Malabar.* Vol. 1. London: T. Cadell and W. Davies, 1807.

Burrow, T., and Emeneau, M. B. *A Dravidian Etymological Dictionary.* Oxford: Clarendon Press, 1961.

Ciṉṉucāmi KavuNTar, S. A. R. *Koṅku VēLāLar* [The VēLāLars of Koṅku]. Erode: TamiRaṉ Accakam, 1963.

Clothey, Frederick. "The Murukaṉ Festival Cycle." Paper delivered at a workshop on South Indian Festivals, sponsored by the Association for Asian Studies, June 4–6, 1971, at Haverford College.

Codrington, K. de B. "Caste or Nation? A Mala Salavadi's Badge of Office." *Man* 31, article 208 (1931).

Cohn, Bernard S. "Political Systems of Eighteenth Century India." *Journal of the American Oriental Society* 82 (1962): 312–20.

Coomaraswamy, A. K. *Spiritual Authority and Temporal Power in the Indian Theory of Government.* New Haven: American Oriental Society, 1942.

Crane, Robert I., ed. *Regions and Regionalism in South Asian Studies: An Exploratory Study.* Papers Presented at a Symposium held at Duke University, April 7–9, 1966. Duke University Program in Comparative Studies on Southern Asia, Monograph and Occasional Papers Series, Monograph no. 5. Durham, N.C.: Duke University Program in Comparative Studies on Southern Asia, 1967.

Cuppaiyā, CivakaLai M. *Koṅku NāTTu KōyilkaL* [The temples of Koṅku NāTu]. Madras: Pāri Accakam, 1967.

Dasan, C. J. *Tamil Lexicon.* 7 vols. Madras: Madras University Press, 1936.

Day, Winefred. "Relative Permanence of Former Boundaries in India." *Scottish Geographical Journal* 65, no. 3 (1949): 113–22.

Den Ouden, J. H. B. "The Komutti Chettiyar: Position and Change of a Merchant Caste in a South-Indian Village." *Tropical Man* 2 (1969): 45–59.

A Dictionary Tamil and English; based on Johann Philip Fabricus's Malabar-English Dictionary. 2nd ed. Tranquebar: Evangelical Lutheran Mission, 1933.

Diehl, Carl Gustav. *Church and Shrine.* Upsaliensis Historia Religionum. No. 2. Uppsala: Acta Universitatis, 1965.

D'Souza, Victor S. "Caste and Endogamy: A Reappraisal of the Concept of Caste." *Journal of the Anthropological Society of India* 11, no. 1 (1959): 11–42.

―――. "Caste Structure in India in the Light of Set Theory." *Current Anthropology* 13, no. 1 (1972): 5–14.

Dube, S. C. *Indian Village.* Ithaca: Cornell University Press, 1955.

―――. "Ranking of Castes in Telangana Villages." *The Eastern Anthropologist* 8, nos. 3 and 4 (1955): 182–90.

―――. "Shirmirpet: The Social Structure of an Indian Village." *Man in India* 32 (1952): 17–22.

Dubois, J. A. *Hindu Manners, Customs and Ceremonies.* Oxford: Clarendon Press, 1906.

Dumont, Louis. "Descent, Filiation and Affinity." *Man* 61, article 11 (1961).

――――. "Distribution of Some Maravar Sub-castes." In *Anthropology on the March,* edited by L. K. Bala Ratnam, pp. 297–305. Madras: The Book Centre, 1963.

――――. "The Dravidian Kinship Terminology as an Expression of Marriage." *Man* 54, article 224 (1953).

――――. "The Functional Equivalents of the Individual in Caste Society." *Contributions to Indian Sociology* 8 (1965): 85–99.

――――. *Hierarchy and Marriage Alliance in South Indian Kinship.* Occasional Papers of the Royal Anthropological Institute, no. 12. London, 1957.

――――. *Homo hierarchicus.* Paris: Gallimard, 1966.

――――. "Kinship and Alliance Among the Pramalai Kallar." *The Eastern Anthropologist* 4, no. 1 (1950): 3–26.

――――. "Les Mariages Nayar comme faits indiens." *L'Homme* 1 (1961): 11–36.

――――. "Marriage in India: The Present State of the Question. I. Marriage Alliance in South-East India and Ceylon." *Contributions to Indian Sociology* 5 (1961): 75–95.

――――. "Marriage in India: The Present State of the Question. Postscript to Part One and II. Nayar and Newar." *Contributions to Indian Sociology* 7 (1964): 77–98.

――――. "Marriage in India: The Present State of the Question. III. North India in Relation to South India." *Contributions to Indian Sociology* 9 (1966): 90–114.

――――. "A Note on Locality in Relation to Descent." *Contributions to Indian Sociology* 7 (1964): 71–76.

――――. "A Structural Definition of a Folk Deity of Tamil Nad: Aiyanar the Lord." *Contributions to Indian Sociology* 3 (1959): 75–87.

――――. "Structural Theory and Descent Group Theory in South India." *Man* 60, article 125 (1960).

――――. *Une Sous-caste de l'Inde du Sud.* Paris: Mouton, 1957.

Dumont, Louis. "World Renunciation in Indian Religions." *Contributions to Indian Sociology* 4 (1960): 33–62.

Dumont, Louis and Pocock, David. "Pure and Impure." *Contributions to Indian Sociology* 3 (1959): 9–39.

———. "Village Studies." *Contributions to Indian Sociology* 1 (1957): 23–41.

Dupuis, Jacques. *Madras et le nord du Coramandel: étude des conditions de la vie indienne dans un cadre géographique.* Paris: Librairie d'Amérique et d'Orient, Adrien-Maisonneuve, 1960.

Elmore, Wilbur Theodore. *Dravidian Gods in Modern Hinduism.* Lincoln: University of Nebraska Press, 1915.

Emeneau, M. B. "Kinship and Marriage Among the Coorgs." *Journal of the Royal Asiatic Society of Bengal* 4 (1938): 123–47.

———. "Language and Social Forms: A Study of Toda Kinship Terms and Dual Descent." In *Language, Culture and Personality,* edited by Leslie Spier, pp. 158–79. Wisconsin: Sapir Memorial Publication Fund, 1942.

———. "Toda Marriage Regulations and Taboos." *American Anthropologist* 39 (1937): 103–12.

Emeneau, M. B., and Burrow, T. *Dravidian Borrowings from Indo-Aryan.* Berkeley: University of California Press, 1962.

Epstein, T. Scarlett. *Economic Development and Social Change in South India.* Manchester: University of Manchester Press, 1962.

———. "A Note on Regional Development and Social Change." *Journal of Asian and African Studies* 1, no. 1 (1966): 63–66.

———. "Productive Efficiency and Customary Systems of Rewards in Rural South India." In *Themes in Economic Anthropology,* edited by Raymond Firth, pp. 229–52. London: Tavistock, 1967.

Estborn, S. *The Church Among Tamils and Telugus.* Lucknow: Lucknow Publishing House, 1961.

Fawcett, Fred. "On Basavis: Women who, through dedication to a deity assume masculine privileges." *Journal of the Anthropological Society of Bombay* 2 (1889): 322–53.

Firth, J. R. "A Short Outline of Tamil Pronunciation." In A. H. Arden, *Arden's Grammar of Common Tamil.* 4th ed. Madras: Christian Literature Society, 1934.

The fifth edition appeared in 1942 and was reprinted in 1954 and 1962, but it does not contain the outline of pronunciation by Firth.

Fox, Richard G. "Avatars of Indian Research." *Comparative Studies in Society and History* 12, no. 1 (1970): 59-72.

———. "Resiliency and Change in the Indian Caste System: The Umar of U. P." *The Journal of Asian Studies* 26, no. 4 (1967): 575-87.

Freed, Stanley. "An Objective Method for Determining the Collective Caste Hierarchy of an Indian Village." *American Anthropologist* 65 (1963): 879-91.

Frykenberg, Robert Eric. *Guntur District 1788-1848*. Oxford: Clarendon Press, 1965.

Frykenberg, Robert Eric, ed. *Land Control and Social Structure in Indian History*. Madison: University of Wisconsin Press, 1969.

Gardner, Peter M. "Dominance in India: A Reappraisal." *Contributions to Indian Sociology*, n.s. 2 (1968): 82-97.

Ghurye, G. S. *Caste and Race in India*. London: Kegan Paul, 1932.

Gough, E. Kathleen. *See* Aberle, E. Kathleen.

Gould, H. A. "The Hindu Jajmani System: A Case of Economic Particularism." *Southwestern Journal of Anthropology* 14 (1958): 428-37.

———. "Priest and Contrapriest: A Structural Analysis of Jajmani Relationships in the Hindu Plains and the Nilgiri Hills." *Contributions to Indian Sociology*, n.s. 1 (1967): 26-55.

Guttman, Louis. "The Basis for Scalogram Analysis." In Stouffer, Samuel A.; Guttman, Louis; Suchman, Edward A.; Lazarsfeld, Paul F.; Star, Shirley A.; and Clausen, John A., *Measurement and Prediction*, pp. 60-90. Studies in Social Psychology in World War II, vol. 4. 1949-50. Reprint. New York: John Wiley and Sons, Inc., 1966.

Hardgrave, Robert. *The Nadars of Tamilnad*. Berkeley: University of California Press, 1969.

———. "The New Mythology of a Caste in Change." *Journal of Tamil Studies* 1, no. 1 (1969): 61-87.

Harper, Edward B. "Fear and the Status of Women." *Southwestern Journal of Anthropology* 25, no. 1 (1969): 81-95.

———. "A Hindu Village Pantheon." *Southwestern Journal of Anthropology* 15, no. 3 (1959): 227-34.

Harper, Edward B. "Ritual Pollution as an Integrator of Caste and Religion." In his *Religion in South India,* pp. 151–96. Seattle: University of Washington Press, 1964.

―――. "Shamanism in South India." *Southwestern Journal of Anthropology* 13, no. 3 (1957): 267–87.

―――. "Social Consequences of an 'Unsuccessful' Low Caste Movement." In *Social Mobility in the Caste System in India,* edited by James Silverberg, pp. 35–65. Comparative Studies in Society and History, Supplement 3. The Hague: Mouton, 1968.

Hazlehurst, Leighton. "Multiple Status Hierarchies in India." *Contributions to Indian Sociology,* n.s., 2 (1968): 38–57.

Hemingway, F. R. *Gazetteer of the Trichinopoly District.* Madras: Government Press, 1907.

Hiebert, P. G. *Konduru: Structure and Integration in a South Indian Village.* Minneapolis: University of Minnesota Press, 1971.

Hocart, A. M. *Caste: A Comparative Study.* London: Methuen, 1950.

―――. "Duplication of Office in the Indian State." Section G, Archaeology and Ethnology. *Ceylon Journal of Science* 1, part 4 (1928): 205–210.

Hutton, J. H. *Caste in India, Its Nature, Function, and Origins.* Cambridge: Cambridge University Press, 1946.

India, Dominion of. *Census of India, 1901.* Vol. XII. *Madras.* Part I. *Report.* Madras: Government Press, 1901.

―――. *Census of India, 1911.* Vol. XII. *Madras.* Part I. *Report.* Madras: Government Press, 1912.

―――. *Census of India, 1911.* Vol. XII. *Madras.* Part II. *Imperial and Provincial Tables.* Madras: Government Press, 1912.

―――. *Census of India, 1911.* Vol. XXI. *Mysore.* Part I. *Report.* Madras: Government Press, 1912.

―――. *Census of India, 1921.* Vol. XIII. *Madras.* Part II. *Imperial and Provincial Tables.* Madras: Government Press, 1922.

India, Dominion of; Madras Presidency. *Madras District Manuals: Coimbatore.* Vol. 2. Madras: Government Press, 1898.

―――. *Manual of Administration of the Madras Presidency.* Vols. 1–3. Madras: Government Press, 1893.

India, Dominion of; Madras Presidency, Department of Agriculture. *Madras Agricultural Calendars 1911–17.* Coimbatore: Agricultural College and Research Institute, 1918.

India, Republic of. *All India Rural Household Survey.* Vol. II. *Income and Spending.* Prepared by the National Council of Applied Economic Research. New Delhi: Government Press, 1963.

————. *Census of India, 1961.* Vol. IX. *Madras.* Part II-A. *General Population Tables.* Madras: Government Press, 1963.

————. *Census of India, 1961.* Vol. IX. *Madras.* Part VI. *Village Survey Monographs.* No. 3. Arkasanahalli, p. 10. Madras: Government Press, 1964.

————. *Census of India, 1961.* Vol. IX. *Madras.* Part VI. *Village Survey Monographs.* No. 6. Kanakagiri. Madras: Government Press, 1964.

————. *Census of India, 1961.* Vol. IX. *Madras.* Part IX. *Atlas of the Madras State.* Madras: Government Press, 1964.

————. *Census of India, 1961.* Vol. IX. *Madras.* Part X-i. *District Census Handbook, Coimbatore.* 2 vols. Madras: Government Press, 1964.

————. *Census of India, 1961.* Vol. IX. *Madras.* Part VI. *Village Survey Monographs.* No. 18. Alatipatti. Madras: Government Press, 1965.

————. *Census of India, 1961.* Vol. IX. *Madras.* Part VI. *Village Survey Monographs.* No. 17. Iswaramoorthipalayam. Madras: Government Press, 1965.

————. *Census of India, 1961.* Vol. IX. *Madras.* Part XI-D. *Temples of Madras State, iii. Coimbatore and Salem.* Madras: Government Press, 1968.

Indian Council of Agricultural Research. *Farmers of India.* New Delhi: Government Press, 1961.

Irshick, Eugene. *Politics and Social Conflict in South India.* Berkeley: University of California Press, 1969.

Ishwaran, Karigaudar. "Goldsmith in a Mysore Village." *Journal of Asian and African Studies* 1, no. 1 (1966): 50–62.

————. *Tradition and Economy in Village India.* London: Routledge and Kegan Paul, 1966.

Jakannātan, K. V. *Nalla Cēnāpati* (The present-day PaTTakkārar of Pa-RaiyakōTTai). Madras: Amuta Nilaiyam, 1963.

Kanakasabhai, V. *The Tamils Eighteen Hundred Years Ago.* 2nd ed. Madras: South India Saiva Siddhanta Works, 1956.

Kane, Pandurang Vamana. *History of Dharmaśāstra*. Poona: Bhandarkar Oriental Research Institute, 1930.

Karve, Irawati. *Kinship Organization in India*. 2nd rev. ed. Bombay: Asia Publishing House, 1965.

Kolenda, Pauline M. (formerly Pauline M. Mahar). "A Multiple Scaling Technique for Caste Ranking." *Man in India* 39, no. 2 (1959): 127–47.

————. "Region, Caste and Family Structure: A Comparative Study of the Indian 'Joint' Family." In *Structure and Change in Indian Society*, edited by Milton Singer and Bernard Cohn, pp. 339–96. Chicago: Aldine, 1968.

————. "Regional Differences in Indian Family Structure." In *Regions and Regionalism in South Asian Studies: An Exploratory Study*, edited by Robert I. Crane, pp. 147–226. Papers Presented at a Symposium held at Duke University, April 7–9, 1966. Duke University Program in Comparative Studies on Southern Asia, Monograph and Occasional Papers Series, Monograph no. 5. Durham, N.C.: Duke University Program in Comparative Studies on Southern Asia, 1967.

————. "Toward a Model of the Hindu Jajmani System." *Human Organization* 22, no. 1 (1963): 11–31.

KōtaNTarāman, K. K. *KoṅkunāTum CamaNamum* [Tidbits on Koṅku NāTu]. Coimbatore: Kōvai Nilaiya Patippakam, 1953.

Krishnamoorthy, Sengottu Velan, and Narayanan. *Kongu Nadu*. Second International Conference-Seminar of Tamil Studies. Coimbatore: Coimbatore District Reception Committee, n.d.

Kumar, Dharma. *Land and Caste in South India*. Cambridge: Cambridge University Press, 1965.

Kuppusvāmi. *Everyday Life in South India or the Story of Coopooswamy: An Autobiography*. London: Religious Tract Society, 1885.

Leach, E. R. *Aspects of Caste in South India, Ceylon and North-West Pakistan*. Cambridge: Cambridge University Press, 1962.

————. *Pul Eliya, a Village in Ceylon: A Study of Land Tenure and Kinship*. Cambridge: Cambridge University Press, 1961.

Lévi-Strauss, Claude. *The Elementary Structures of Kinship*. Rev. ed. Translated by James Harle Bell, John Richard von Sturmer, and Rodney Needham. Edited by Rodney Needham. Boston: Beacon Press, 1969.

The original was *Les Structures élémentaires de la parenté*. Paris: Presses Universitaires de France, 1949.

Love, H. D. *Vestiges of Old Madras.* 3 vols. London: John Murray, 1913.

Maclachlan, Morgan, and Beals, Alan. "The Internal and External Relationships of a Mysore Chiefdom." *Journal of Asian and African Studies* 1, no. 2 (1966): 87–99.

Madras, Government of. *Madras District Gazetteers, Coimbatore,* by B. S. Baliga. Madras: Government Press, 1966.

Madras. Madras University Library. Manuscript D, no. 2751 (also Manuscript R, no. 1572). MacKenzie Manuscript Collection.

Mahalingam, T. V. *Administration and Social Life Under Vijayanagar.* Madras: Madras University Historical Series, 1940.

——— . *South Indian Polity.* Madras: Madras University Historical Series, 1955.

Mahar, Pauline M. *See* Kolenda, Pauline M.

Marriott, McKim. *Caste Ranking and Community Structure in Five Regions of India and Pakistan.* Poona: Deccan College Postgraduate Research Institute, 1965.

——— . "Caste Ranking and Food Transactions: A Matrix Analysis." In *Structure and Change in Indian Society,* edited by Milton Singer and Bernard Cohn, pp. 133–71. Chicago: Aldine, 1968.

——— . "Interactional and Attributional Theories of Caste Ranking." *Man in India* 39, no. 2 (1959): 92–107.

——— . "Multiple Reference in Indian Caste Systems." In *Social Mobility in the Caste System in India,* edited by James Silverberg, pp. 103–114. Comparative Studies in Society and History, Supplement 3. The Hague: Mouton, 1968.

Mathur, K. S. *Caste and Ritual in a Malwa Village.* Bombay: Asia Publishing House, 1964.

Mauss, Marcel. *The Gift.* Translated by I. Cunnison. London: Cohen and West, 1954.

Mayer, Adrian C. *Caste and Kinship in Central India.* London: Routledge and Kegan Paul, 1960.

——— . "Change in a Malwa Village." *Economic Weekly* 7 (1955): 1147–49.

——— . "The Dominant Caste in a Region of Central India." *Southwestern Journal of Anthropology* 14, no. 4 (1958): 407–27.

Mayer, Adrian C. *Land and Society in Malabar.* Bombay: Oxford University Press, 1952.

———. "Some Hierarchical Aspects of Caste." *Southwestern Journal of Anthropology* 12, no. 2 (1956): 117–44.

Mayfield, R. C. *The Spatial Structure of a Selected Interpersonal Contact: A Regional Comparison of Marriage Distances in India.* Technical Report no. 6. Spatial Diffusion Study. Evanston: Northwestern University Press, 1967.

McCormack, William. "Sister's Daughter Marriage in a Mysore Village." *Man in India* 38, no. 1 (1958): 34–48.

Mencher, Joan P. "Changing Familial Roles Among South Malabar Nayars." *Southwestern Journal of Anthropology* 18, no. 3 (1962): 230–45.

———. "Growing Up in South Malabar." *Human Organization* 22, no. 1 (1963): 54–65.

———. "Kerala and Madras: A Comparative Study of Ecology and Social Structure." *Ethnology* 5, no. 2 (1966): 135–71.

———. "Namboodiri Brahmins: An Analysis of a Traditional Elite in Kerala." *Journal of Asian and African Studies* 1, no. 3 (1966): 183–96.

Mencher, Joan P., and Goldberg, Helen. "Kinship and Marriage Regulations Among the Namboodiri Brahmans of Kerala." *Man,* n.s. 2, no. 1 (1967): 87–106.

Metcalf, Thomas R. *The Aftermath of Revolt.* Princeton: Princeton University Press, 1965.

Miller, Eric J. "Caste and Territory in Malabar." *American Anthropologist* 56 (1954): 410–20.

———. "Village Structure in North Kerala." In *India's Villages,* edited by M. N. Srinivas, pp. 42–55. 2nd ed., rev. Bombay: Asia Publishing House, 1960.

Mukherjee, Nilmani. *The Ryotwari System in Madras 1792–1827.* Calcutta: K. L. Mukhopadhyay, 1962.

Nagaswamy, R. "Architecture in Tamilnad." *Journal of Tamil Studies* 1, no. 1 (1969): 139–53.

Nair, Kusum. *Blossoms in the Dust.* London: Gerald Duckworth & Co., 1962.

Nakara VaRi KāTTi [The city signpost]. Kāṅkayam, 1969.

Neale, Walter C. "Land is to Rule." In *Land Control and Social Structure in Indian History*, edited by Robert Eric Frykenberg, pp. 3–16. Madison: University of Wisconsin Press, 1969.

Needham, Rodney. *Structure and Sentiment*. Chicago: University of Chicago Press, 1962.

Nelson, J. H. *The Madura Country: A Manual*. Madras: William Thomas, 1968.

Newnham, T. O. *South Indian Village*. London: Longmans, 1967.

Nicholson, F. A. *Manual of the Coimbatore District*. Madras: Government Press, 1887.

———. *Manual of the Coimbatore District*. Vol. 2. Edited by H. A. Stuart. Madras: Government Press, 1898.

Nilakanta Sastri, K. A. *A History of South India*. 3rd ed. Madras: Oxford University Press, 1966.

Obeyesekere, Gananath. *Land Tenure in Village Ceylon*. Cambridge: Cambridge University Press, 1967.

Oliver, Georges. *Anthropologie des Tamouls du sud de l'Inde*. Paris: École française d'Extrême Orient, 1961.

O'Malley, L. S. S. *Popular Hinduism*. Cambridge: Cambridge University Press, 1935.

Oppert, Gustav. *On the Original Inhabitants of Bharatavarsa or India*. Westminster: A. Constable and Co., 1893.

Orans, Martin. "Maximizing in Jajmani Land: A Model of Caste Relations." *American Anthropologist* 70 (1968): 875–97.

PaRaṇiccāmi Pulavar, K. *Koṅku Celvi* [The goddesses of Koṅku]. Coimbatore: Pudumalar Press, 1948.

PaRaṇiccāmi Pulavar, K., ed. *Ōtālar Kuṟavaṇci eṉum Alakumalai Kuṟavaṇci* [The Ōtālar clan story or the drama of Alaku Mountain]. Coimbatore: Kāntitācaṉ Accakam, 1969.

Pocock, David F. " 'Difference' in East Africa: A Study of Caste and Religion in Modern Indian Society." *Southwestern Journal of Anthropology* 13, no. 4 (1957): 289–300.

———. "The Hypergamy of the Patidars." In *Professor Ghurye Felicitation Volume*, edited by K. M. Kapadia, pp. 195–204. Bombay: Popular Book Depot, 1954.

Pocock, David F. "Inclusion and Exclusion: A Process in the Caste System of Gujarat." *Southwestern Journal of Anthropology* 13, no. 1 (1957): 19–31.

————. "The Movement of Castes." *Man* 55, article 79 (1955).

————. "Notes on Jajmani Relationships." *Contributions to Indian Sociology* 6 (1962): 78–95.

PonnaRakarennum KaLLaRakar Ammānai [The story of Ponnar, the KaLLar]. Madras: R. G. Pati Co., 1965.

Pradhan, M. C. *The Political System of the Jats of Northern India.* Bombay: Oxford University Press, 1966.

H. R. H. Prince Peter of Greece and Denmark. "The Mother Sibs of the Todas of the Nilgiris." *The Eastern Anthropologist* 5, nos. 2, 3 (1952): 65–73.

Pulavar KuRantai. *Koṅku NāTu* [Koṅku country]. Erode: Vēlā Patippakam, 1968.

Radcliffe-Brown, A. R. "Dravidian Kinship Terminology." *Man* 53, article 169 (1953).

Rajamanikam, S. "Factors in the Growth of the Christian Movement in the Ex-Methodist Area of the Tiruchirappalli Diocese and Their Relation to Present-Day Problems." B.D. thesis, United Theological College, Bangalore, 1950–51.

Ramachandra Chettiar, C. M. "A Chapter in the History of Kongu Nadu." *The Quarterly Journal of the Mythic Society* 21, no. 1 (1930): 39–49.

————. "Geographical Distribution of Religious Places in Tamilnad." *Indian Geographical Journal* 16 (1942): 42–50.

————. "The Geographical Limits of Kongu Nadu at Various Epochs." *Indian Geographical Journal* 5, nos. 2, 3 (1930): 59–69.

————. "Growth of Modern Coimbatore." *The Journal of the Madras Geographical Association* 14, no. 2 (1939): 101–16.

————. "Jainism in Kongu Nadu." *The Quarterly Journal of the Mythic Society* 25, nos. 1, 2, 3 (1934–35): 87–94.

————. *Koṅku NāTTu Varalāru* [The story of Koṅku NāTu]. Annamalai: Annamalai University Press, 1954.

————. "Place-Names in Tamil Nad." *The Journal of the Madras Geographical Association* 13 (1938): 32–57.

Ramachandran, Ranganathan. "Spatial Diffusion of Innovation in Rural India: A Case Study of the Spread of Irrigation Pumps in the Coimbatore Plateau." Ph.D. dissertation, Clark University, 1969.

Raman, K. V. *The Early History of the Madras Region.* Madras: Amudha Nilayam Ltd., 1959.

Ramanujan, A. K. "The Structure of Variation: A Study in Caste Dialects." In *Structure and Change in Indian Society,* edited by Milton Singer and Bernard Cohn, pp. 461–74. Chicago: Aldine, 1968.

Rangaswami Aiyangar, K. V., ed. *Professor K. V. Rangaswami Aiyangar Commemoration Volume.* Madras: G. S. Press, 1940.

Rao, M. S. A. "Occupational Diversification and Joint Household Organization." *Contributions to Indian Sociology,* n.s. 2 (1968): 98–111.

Reddy, N. S. *See* Subha Reddi, N.

Rice, Benjamin Lewis. *Mysore Gazetteer.* Vol. 1. London: Westminster, 1897.

Richards, F. J. "The Village Deities of Vellore Taluk, North Arcot District." *The Quarterly Journal of the Mythic Society* 10, no. 2 (1920): 109–20.

Riviere, P. G. "A Note on Marriage with the Sister's Daughter." *Man,* n.s. 1, no. 4 (1966): 550.

Robinson, Marguerite. "Some Observations on the Kandyan Sinhalese Kinship System." *Man,* n.s. 3, no. 3 (1968): 402–23.

Scheffler, Harold W. *"The Elementary Structures of Kinship,* by Claude Lévi-Strauss: A Review Article." *American Anthropologist* 72 (1970): 251–68.

Sebring, James M. "Caste Indicators and Caste Identification of Strangers." *Human Organization* 28, no. 3 (1969): 199–207.

Senart, Émile. *Les Castes dans l'Inde: les faits et le système.* Paris: E. Leroux, 1894.

Silverberg, James. "Caste-Ascribed 'Status' versus Caste-Irrelevant Roles." *Man in India* 39, no. 2 (1959): 148–162.

Silverberg, James, ed. *Social Mobility in the Caste System in India.* Comparative Studies in Society and History, Supplement 3. The Hague: Mouton, 1968.

Singaravelu, S. *Social Life of the Tamils: The Classical Period.* Kuala Lumpur: Marican, 1966.

Singer, Milton. "The Great Tradition in a Metropolitan Center: Madras." In his *Traditional India,* pp. 141–82. Philadelphia: American Folklore Society, 1959.

―――. "The Indian Joint Family in Modern Industry." In *Structure and Change in Indian Society,* edited by Milton Singer and Bernard Cohn, pp. 423–52. Chicago: Aldine, 1968.

Singer, Milton, and Cohn, Bernard., eds. *Structure and Change in Indian Society.* Chicago: Aldine, 1968.

Singh, Kashi N. "The Territorial Basis of Medieval Town and Village Settlement in Eastern Uttar Pradesh, India." *Annals of the Association of American Geographers* 58, no. 2 (1968): 203–20.

Sivertsen, Dagfinn. *When Caste Barriers Fall: A Study of Social and Economic Change in a South Indian Village.* Oslo: Universitetsforlaget, 1963.

Spate, O. *India and Pakistan: A General and Regional Geography.* London: Methuen, 1954.

Srinivas, M. N. "A Caste Dispute Among the Washermen [Madivāla Shetti or Agasa] of Mysore." *The Eastern Anthropologist* 7, nos. 3 and 4 (1954): 148–68.

―――. *Caste in Modern India and Other Essays.* Bombay: Asia Publishing House, 1962.

―――. "The Dominant Caste in Rampura." *American Anthropologist* 61 (1959): 1–16.

―――. "A Joint Family Dispute in a Mysore Village." *Journal of the M. S. University of Baroda* 1 (1952): 7–31.

―――. *Marriage and Family in Mysore.* Bombay: New Book Co., 1942.

―――. *Religion and Society Among the Coorgs of South India.* 1952. Reprint. London: Asia Publishing House, 1965.

―――. "The Social Structure of a Mysore Village." *Economic Weekly* 3 (1951): 1051–56.

―――. "The Social System of a Mysore Village." In *Village India,* edited by McKim Marriott, pp. 1–35. Chicago: University of Chicago Press, 1955.

Srinivas, M. N., ed. *India's Villages.* 2nd ed., rev. Bombay: Asia Publishing House, 1960.

Srinivasa Iyengar, P. T. "Geographical Control of Early Kongu History." *Indian Geographical Journal* 5, nos. 2 and 3 (1930): 54–58.

Srinivasa Iyengar, P. T. *History of the Tamils from the Earliest Times to 600 A.D.* Madras: Madras University Press, 1929.

Srinivasa Raghavaiyangar, S. *Memorandum on the Progress of the Madras Presidency During the Last Forty Years of British Administration.* Madras: Government Press, 1893.

Srinivasachari, C. S. "The Origin of the Right and Left Hand Caste Division." *Journal of the Andhra Historical Research Society* 4 (1929): 77–85.

————. "Right and Left Hand Caste Disputes in Madras in the Early Part of the 18th Century." *Indian Historical Records Commission Proceedings of Meetings* 12 (1930): 68–76.

Staal, J. F. "Notes on Some Brahmin Communities of South India." *Arts and Letters* 32, no. 1 (1958): 1–7.

————. "Sanskrit and Sanskritization." *The Journal of Asian Studies* 22, no. 3 (1963): 261–75.

Stein, Burton. "Brahman and Peasant in Early South Indian History." *The Adyar Library Bulletin.* Vols. 31–32. Dr. Raghavan Felicitation Volume (1967–68): 229–69.

————. "Coromandel Trade in Medieval India." In *Merchants and Scholars,* edited by John Parker, pp. 45–62. Minneapolis: University of Minnesota Press, 1965.

————. "The Economic History of India: A Bibliographic Essay." *The Journal of Economic History* 21 (1961): 179–207.

————. "Historical Ecotypes in South India." Mimeographed. Paper read at the 2nd International Conference-Seminar of Tamil Studies, January, 1967, at Madras, pp. 1–10.

————. "Integration of the Agrarian System of South India." In *Land Control and Social Structure in Indian History,* edited by Robert Eric Frykenberg, pp. 175–216. Madison: University of Wisconsin Press, 1969.

————. "Social Mobility and Medieval South Indian Hindu Sects." In *Social Mobility in the Caste System in India,* edited by James Silverberg, pp. 78–94. Comparative Studies in Society and History, Supplement 3. The Hague: Mouton, 1968.

————. "The State, the Temple, and Agricultural Development: A Study in Medieval South India." *The Economic Weekly Annual* (February 4, 1961): 179–88.

Stevenson, Henry. "Status Evaluation in the Hindu Caste System." *Journal of the Royal Anthropological Institute* 84 (1954): 45–65.

Stokes, C. S. H. "The Custom of Kareiyid or Periodical Redistribution of Land in Tanjore." *The Indian Antiquary* 3 (1874): 65–69.

Subha Reddi, N. "Community Conflict Among the Depressed Castes of Andhra." *Man in India* 30, no. 4 (1950): 1–12.

———. "Spatial Variance of Custom in Andhra Pradesh." In *Anthropology on the March,* edited by L. K. Bala Ratnam, pp. 283–96. Madras: The Book Centre, 1963.

Subhashini Subramanyam, Y. "A Note on Cross-Cousin Marriage Among Andhra Brahmans." *Journal of Asian and African Studies* 2 (1967): 266–72.

Subramanian, N. *Sangam Polity: The Administration and Social Life of the Sangam Tamils.* New York: Asia Publishing House, 1968.

Swedish Lutheran Mission. *Tranquebar Almanac.* Tranquebar: Tranquebar Publishing House, 1964.

Tambiah, S. J. "Kinship Fact and Fiction in Relation to the Kandyan Sinhalese." *Journal of the Royal Anthropological Institute* 95, part 2 (1965): 131–73.

Thapar, Romila. "The Elite and Social Mobility in Early India." Paper read, April, 1968, at the University of Chicago.

Thirunaranan, B. M. "The Traditional Limits and Subdivisions of the Tamil Region." In *Professor K. V. Rangaswami Aiyangar Commemoration Volume,* edited by K. V. Rangaswami Aiyangar, pp. 159–69. Madras: G. S. Press, 1940.

Thurston, Edgar. *Castes and Tribes of Southern India.* 7 vols. Madras: Government Press, 1909.

TiruvāNan. *Maṅkalyam Tanta Makarāci* [The queen who gave away her wedding necklace]. Madras: Vānati Patippakam, 1960.

Torgerson, Warren. "Deterministic Models for Categorical Data." In his *Theory and Methods of Scaling,* pp. 298–359. New York: John Wiley and Sons, 1965.

Tyler, Stephen A. "Parallel/Cross: An Evaluation of Definitions." *Southwestern Journal of Anthropology* 22, no. 4 (1966): 416–32.

VeLLiyaṅkiri KavuNTar, V. C. *EṅKaL NāTTuppuram* [The story of our region]. Coimbatore: Kōvai Nilaiya Patippakam, 1951.

Viennot, Odette. *Le Culte de l'arbre dans l'Inde ancienne.* Paris: Presses Universitaires de France, 1954.

Viswanatha, S. V. "The Gangas of Talakkād and Their Kongu Origin." *The Quarterly Journal of the Mythic Society* 26, nos. 1, 2 (1935): 247–54.

Weber, Max. *The Religion of India.* Glenco: Free Press, 1958.

Whitehead, H. *Village Gods of South India.* London: Oxford University Press, 1916.

Wiser, W. H. *The Hindu Jajmani System.* Lucknow: Lucknow Publishing House, 1936.

Witney, Rev. T. C. *A Hundred Years of Salem Mission History.* Nagercoil: London Mission Press, 1936.

Yalman, Nur. "Dual Organization in Central Ceylon." In *Anthropological Studies in Theravada Buddhism,* edited by Manning Nash, pp. 197–223. Yale University Southeast Asia Studies, Cultural Report Series no. 13. Detroit: The Cellar Book Shop, 1966.

————. "The Flexibility of Caste Principles in a Kandyan Community." In *Aspects of Caste in South India, Ceylon and North-West Pakistan,* edited by E. R. Leach, pp. 78–112. Cambridge: Cambridge University Press, 1960.

————. "On the Purity of Women in the Castes of Ceylon and Malabar." *Journal of the Royal Anthropological Institute* 93, part 1 (1963): 25–58.

————. "Sinhalese-Tamil Intermarriage on the East Coast of Ceylon." *Sociologus* 12 (1962): 36–54.

————. "The Structure of the Sinhalese Kindred: A Re-examination of the Dravidian Terminology." *American Anthropologist* 64 (1962): 548–75.

————. *Under the Bo Tree.* Berkeley: University of California Press, 1967.

Zelliot, Eleanor Mae. "Dr. Ambedkar and the Mahar Movement." Ph.D. dissertation, University of Pennsylvania, 1969.

General Index

NOTE: Page numbers for plates are in italics.

Caste and Subcaste Index